THE WORKS OF CHARLES STUART
CALVERLEY

GEORGE BELL & SONS

LONDON : YORK STREET, COVENT GARDEN
NEW YORK : 66, FIFTH AVENUE, AND
BOMBAY : 53, ESPLANADE ROAD
CAMBRIDGE : DEIGHTON, BELL & CO.

Yours ever
C.J. Halverstey

THE COMPLETE WORKS

OF

C. S. CALVERLEY

WITH A BIOGRAPHICAL NOTICE

BY

SIR WALTER J. SENDALL, G.C.M.G.

GOVERNOR OF BRITISH GUIANA

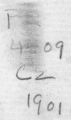

LONDON

GEORGE BELL AND SONS

1901

CHISWICK PRESS: CHARLES WHITTINGHAM AND CO.
TOOKS COURT, CHANCERY LANE, LONDON.

CONTENTS

MISCELLANEOUS POEMS

CONTENTS

TRANSLATIONS INTO ENGLISH

b

THEOCRITUS. Translated into English Verse

CONTENTS

TRANSLATIONS INTO LATIN

TRANSLATION INTO GREEK

PROSE ARTICLES

BIBLIOGRAPHICAL NOTE

VERSES AND TRANSLATIONS. Fcap. 8vo.

First published, 1861; reprinted, 1862, 1865, 1871, 1874, 1877, 1880, 1884 (Feb. and June), 1885, 1886, 1888, 1890, 1894.
Cheap edition published Oct. 1900; reprinted, Jan., 1901.

FLY LEAVES. Fcap. 8vo.

First published, March, 1872; reprinted, July, 1872, 1873, 1876, 1877, 1880, 1882, 1883, 1884, 1885, 1886, 1887, (Jan. and Nov.), 1889, 1890, 1891, 1895, 1899.

VERSES AND FLY LEAVES. Crown 8vo.

First published in one volume, 1885; reprinted, 1887, 1890, 1894, 1897, 1898.

TRANSLATIONS. Crown 8vo.

First published, 1866; second edition, revised, 1885; reprinted, 1897.

THEOCRITUS. Crown 8vo.

First published, 1869; second edition, revised, 1883; reprinted, 1891.

LITERARY REMAINS. Crown 8vo.

First published, Oct., 1885; reprinted, Dec., 1885, 1891.

*** A uniform edition in four vols. was published in Oct., 1896. (Vol. I, Literary Remains; Vol. II. Verses and Fly Leaves; Vol. III. Translations; Vol IV. Theocritus.)

BIOGRAPHICAL NOTICE [1]

I.

SCARCELY had the grave closed over the head of Charles Stuart Calverley, when there began to be expressed, amongst those who had known him, a very general desire that some brief account of his character and career should be given to the world. It was thought, we may suppose, that the memory of one whose natural powers had made so extraordinary an impression upon his contemporaries, and whose published writings had given evidence of so very distinct and striking an individuality, should not be suffered to pass into oblivion, without some more enduring record than a paragraph in the newspapers, or an article in a magazine.

It is in the belief that this was a well-grounded sentiment, and that those who have hitherto known " C. S. C." only as a writer of polished and epigrammatic verse, would be glad, now that he is gone, to learn something of the personality which lay behind those familiar letters, that the present task has been undertaken ; and it may be permitted here to express a wish that the work, though truly in this case a labour of love, of delineating a character so unique, might have been entrusted to hands more practised than those of one whom circumstances have long since consigned to the pursuit of avocations quite other than literary.

It must be added that the uneventful record of Calverley's life contains no materials for a full and lengthened biography ; all that can be attempted is to place before the reader's mind some slight sketch of the man, as he appeared in the eyes of his familiar friends.

[1] This Notice is based on an article which appeared in " The Fortnightly Review," June, 1884, and on the Memoir published with the " Literary Remains of Charles Stuart Calverley " (1885).

A bright, sunny boyhood, fearless and careless ; a youth full of brilliant promise, and studded with intellectual triumphs ; a manhood marked by no stirring incidents, no ambitious struggles, no alternations of failure and success—darkened, alas ! in later years, and brought to an untimely close by the ravages of a fatal and insidious malady—such are in brief the outlines of a career which in itself would seem to present little that is worthy of record, and to possess but scanty claims upon the attention of the general observer. But if the incidents and events of his life were thus trite even to commonplace, yet his own bearing amongst them, and the physical and intellectual personality which marked each successive stage, would be found, if accurately and adequately portrayed, to present a striking and an interesting picture. From childhood upwards there never was a time when he failed to impress in some enduring manner those amongst whom he moved. His boyhood was distinguished by feats of physical activity and daring, which almost eclipsed even his marvellous precocity of mind, and have already passed in school traditions, like the deeds of ancient heroes, into the region of myth and legend.

At a later period, though he was still remarkable for bodily strength and agility, it was the exceptional quality of his intellect which fascinated and enchained his associates. And as to this there can be but one verdict amongst all who were even slightly acquainted with him. As an intellectual organism of the rarest and subtlest fibre, he stood altogether apart from amongst his contemporaries. And this not by virtue of any predominant excellence in one or other of the acknowledged lines in which men of talent or genius show themselves above their fellows. Brilliant and incisive in speech sparkling with epigrams, he was still neither a great talker nor a professed wit ; capable of reasoning closely, he neither sought nor achieved reputation in debate ; nor could he at any time have claimed precedence upon the score of acquired knowledge. Yet those who consorted with him derived from his conversation an impression which the most accomplished and encyclopædic of talkers might fail to produce. I do not know how better to express this phenomenon than by describing it as due to the spontaneous action of pure intellect. Without conscious effort, without the semblance of a desire for display, his mind appeared to *act* upon the matter in hand, like a solvent upon a substance. The effect of this was often as the revelation of an unknown force. A few words casually spoken became, as it were, a *fiat lux*, an act of creation. Let those who knew him at his best endeavour to account to themselves for the sense of power with which his conversation affected them, and they will, I think, be compelled to admit, that though his talk was often witty, always scholarly, and not seldom wise, yet what they marvelled at in him was neither the wit nor the wisdom nor the scholarship, but the exhibition of sheer native mind.

And herein, I think, to those who really knew him, will be found the all-sufficient explanation of that nameless excellence which all agree to discover in his writings, and which constitutes the key-stone of his reputation. About his most trifling, as about his most serious work, there is an inimitable and indescribable something, which is neither gracefulness only, nor is it merely finish or polish or refinement, while at the same time it is each and all of these, and still defies analysis as securely as the scent and hue of a flower.

But whatever theory be accepted as true respecting the intellectual side of Calverley's character, this view of him alone will not sufficiently account for his personal ascendancy, nor for the unique place which he occupied in the estimation and in the affections of his friends. For he was fully as much and as deservedly loved as he was admired ; and if he owed the one distinction to his natural gifts of reason unalloyed, he was indebted for the other, in no less degree, to that singleness and sincerity which were his most conspicuous characteristics upon the ethical side.

That he was absolutely free from all taint of littleness or doublemindedness was manifest, it may be assumed, to the most careless observer ; that he was an ardent lover of and seeker after truth for its own sake, that the windows of his soul were open to all the airs of heaven, and his heart waxen to the impress of whatsoever things are true, lovely, and of good report, was discernible by whosoever had eyes to see behind the very ill-fitting mask of seeming recklessness and indifference with which it sometimes pleased him to disguise himself for the mystification of the overwise ; but there was yet more in him than this, and to the few who penetrated into the inmost recesses of his nature there was revealed a depth of tenderness, humility, and trust, the existence of which even those who had a right to think they knew him well might be pardoned if they never had suspected.

And it is doubtless here, in these central well-springs of his being, that the true secret of his influence is to be sought. Under whatever crust of indifference or reserve, behind whatever veil of inconsistencies, wilful or unintended—the beautiful real nature of the man shone or glimmered irrepressibly, winning all hearts by the power of sympathy and truth.

Endued, however, as he was, with infinite capacities of faith, in the matter of beliefs he was an incarnation of the principle of private judgment, and to mere dogmatic teaching always and for ever impervious. "Unsanctified intellect" was, I believe, the term applied to him by a certain school at the University; unsophisticated intellect would, I think, more fitly have expressed the fact, if it wanted to be expressed by an epithet.

An extraordinary carefulness and consideration for others was always a conspicuous characteristic in Calverley; and he endeared himself, particularly amongst his poorer friends and neighbours, by a hundred acts of unaffected kindness. In the Somersetshire village in which, previous to his marriage, his home life was chiefly spent, many stories are current, illustrating his active and sympathetic good-nature ; and when the news of his untimely death passed like an electric shock through the circle of his acquaintance, nowhere was there awakened a feeling of sorrow more deep and true than amongst the cottages of his old home.

Let it not be for a moment supposed that by these imperfect touches I am picturing to myself, or attempting to convey to the reader, the outlines of a faultless character. Calverley had important shortcomings, of which no one was more sensible than himself; and amongst these was an infirmity of will. It is true that he was never subjected to the bracing stimulus of poverty, and that he was without those promptings of personal ambition which might have supplied its place ; still some natural deficiency must be recognized here, and it must be confessed that, had he been endowed with a strength of purpose at all commensurate with his intellectual gifts, he would certainly have achieved work more truly worthy of his genius.

In his undergraduate days, though capable at times of the intensest application, he was somewhat prone to self-indulgence, and was a grievous sinner in the matter of lying late in bed. During the months when he was (or ought to have been) reading for his degree, it was the daily task of one or two faithful friends to effect his dislodgment from his couch before the precious morning hours should be wholly lost. Upon these occasions his chamber became the scene of a conflict which reduced it to a condition resembling that of a ship's cabin at sea in a hurricane. He, with his sturdy frame and resolute countenance, clinging, like "Barbary's nimble son,"—

"By the teeth, or tail, or eyelid,"

to each successive covering, as one by one they were ruthlessly torn from him, amid a storm of good-humoured objurgation, charged with expletives of every shape and size, ancient and modern, of which he had a perfect arsenal on hand—so the battle raged until, having conscientiously removed every portable article of bed-clothing, his assailants retired victorious, only to return in half an hour and find him peacefully sleeping between the mattresses.

II.

"C. S. C." came of a good old English stock. He was born at Martley, in Worcestershire, on the 22nd December, 1831; his father, then known as the Rev. Henry Blayds, removing afterwards to the Vicarage of South Stoke, near Bath. The family, who had borne the name of Blayds from the beginning of the century, in 1852 resumed their proper name of Calverley, under which they had flourished from before the Norman Conquest in their native county of York—having indeed a collateral connection with that Walter Calverley, the story of whose ferocious deeds, and still more ferocious punishment, is preserved in the pages of "A Yorkshire Tragedy," one of the many spurious plays attributed in an uncritical age to Shakespeare, and included in some of the earliest editions of his works. It was as Blayds that Charles Stuart won his reputation at Harrow and Oxford; at Cambridge he was known as Calverley.

Upon his mother's side, Calverley belonged to a branch of the ancient and honourable family of Meade; Thomas Meade, Esq., of Chatley, in Somersetshire, having been his maternal grandfather; and to those who are interested in such speculations, a further examination of his ancestry, on both sides, would probably yield ample and satisfactory proofs of hereditary capacity.

Having passed through the hands of more than one private tutor, and after a brief sojourn (of no more than three months' duration) at Marlborough School, Calverley entered Harrow in the autumn of 1846, and from that time forward never ceased to be an object of interest and attention to a widening circle of friends and acquaintances. He is described as a curly-haired, bright-eyed boy, with a sunny smile and a frank, open countenance; a general favourite for his manliness and inexhaustible good-nature, though already, it is said, distinguished for a certain self-sufficing independence of character which remained with him through life, keeping him always somewhat apart from his fellows, and inducing him, even at this early age, to stand aloof from the little cliques and coteries into which the world of school divides itself as readily and naturally as the world at large. He is exhibited in a unique degree, just that mixture of *insouciance*, reckless daring and brilliancy, which never fails to win the unbounded applause and admiration of every genuine schoolboy.

The place is still pointed out where he once leaped down the entire flight of what are known as the school steps, being a clear spring of seventeen feet with a drop of nearly nine, on to hard gravel; and having been unsuccessful in this attempt to break his leg or his neck, he on another occasion sprang over the wall separating the school yard from the " milling ground," an ugly fall of some nine or ten feet, accomplishing this latter exploit with his hands in his pockets, and alighting (so the story goes) squarely on to the top of his head; a result with which he was so little satisfied that he at once returned and repeated the jump, reaching ground this time, normally, upon his feet.

These and other similar anecdotes, illustrative of his physical daring, have already been given to the public in various forms; the following, which bears witness to his extraordinary readiness and aptitude in classical composition, is, I think, new, and rests upon unimpeachable authority. He was out walking with a lad who had upon his mind, as a school exercise, a certain passage from "The Prophecy of Capys," to be done into longs and shorts, and who propounded to his companion the following couplet, asking him how *he* would do it into Latin :

> "Raging beast and raging flood,
> Alike have spared their prey."

Calverley appeared to take no notice, and continued for several minutes talking upon indifferent subjects, when all at once he stopped, and said, "How would *this* do?"

> "Sospes uterque manet, talem quia laedere praedam
> Nil furor aequoreus nil valet ira ferae."

It may be admitted that many a ripe and practised scholar has spent hours in turning out less satisfactory work than this, the impromptu of a sixth-form boy.

Calverley's career at Oxford, though a failure for academic purposes, was distinguished by a series of *tours de force*, intellectual and physical, sufficient to have furnished forth a dozen ordinary reputations. He won the Balliol scholarship by a marvellous copy of Latin verses, written off with such rapidity as to be almost an improvisation. His exploits in the way of daring and impossible jumps were long talked of and pointed out, and their memory may perhaps still linger amongst the traditions of the place. Having, in common with the other students, to prepare a Latin theme, to be submitted on a given day at a *vivâ voce* lecture, Calverley appeared in the lecture-room provided like the rest with a neat manuscript book, the pages of which were entirely blank. He had trusted to luck, and hoped that he might escape being "put on." Luck failed him, and in due course the examiner called upon "Mr. Blayds." Whereupon he stood up and, to the amazement of those who knew the real state of the case, proceeded without the least hesitation, and in calm, fluent tones, to read from his book the exercise which he had not written, and of which not a word had up to that moment been composed.

Among the academic functions established at Balliol, and possibly also at other Oxford colleges, was a ceremony known as "Collections," for which Cambridge experience furnishes no equivalent. It appears to have consisted in a kind of intellectual and moral stock-taking, at which the assembled students were put through an examination upon a variety of subjects, sacred and profane, receiving praise or reprobation in accordance with their deserts. The following episode occurred during one of Calverley's appearances at "Collections," the Master (Dr. Jenkyns) officiating. *Question:* "And with what feelings, Mr. Blayds, ought we to regard the decalogue?" History relates that Calverley, who had no very clear idea of what was meant by the decalogue—his studies not having lain much in that direction—but who had a due sense of the importance both of the occasion and of the question, made the following reply: "Master, with feelings of devotion, mingled with awe!" "Quite right, young man, a very proper answer," exclaimed the master.

It must indeed have been felt that a youth imbued with these just and admirable sentiments would guide his words with discretion, and might even be trusted never to "speak disrespectfully of the Equator."

The good opinion which he thus obtained by subtlety did not, however, avail him long, and during his second year of residence his connection with Balliol and with Oxford was brought to an abrupt termination. His biographer, while chronicling this fact, must at the same time not fail to insist that the offences against discipline for which he justly suffered were due to an exuberance of animal spirits rather than to any graver form of delinquency. That at this period of his career he vexed the souls of dons, and maintained a perpetual warfare with constituted authority, is to be admitted and regretted. Into most of his escapades, however, there entered an element of humour which, while it does not redeem them from censure, invests them with an interest in relation to his special cast of mind. Calverley's coolness, wariness, and consummate dexterity of speech, rendered him at all times a dangerous opponent in an encounter of wits; he had, moreover, when provoked, a knack of employing words, in themselves most artless and innocent, in such a way as to affect the other side with an uncomfortable sensation of being quizzed.

Of the numerous stories current respecting his Oxford days,

some of which went the round of the newspapers at the time of
his death, it will be sufficient to notice one or two, the authen-
ticity of which can be vouched for.

The following incident is related rather on account of the
punning verses to which it gave rise, than for its own intrinsic
interest. The election to scholarships at Balliol took place
upon St. Catharine's Day (November 25), and on the evening
of the same day the newly-elected scholars received formal
admission, in the college chapel, at the hands of the Master
and Fellows. When Calverley's turn came to be presented to
the Master for the purpose of taking the customary oath upon
admission to the privileges of a scholar, the fact that he had
quite recently been indulging in a pipe forced itself upon the
attention of Dr. Jenkyns, who had the strongest dislike to
tobacco. On withdrawing from the chapel, the Master turned
to the Fellows who accompanied him, and said, "Why, the
young man is *redolent of the weed*, even now!" It was no
doubt this remark of the famous old Master of Balliol which
afterwards suggested to their unknown author the following
lines, which, like the "Sic vos non vobis" of Virgil, received
their first publication in the form of a mural inscription :

> "O freshman, running fast to seed,
> O scholar, redolent of weed,
> This motto in thy meerschaum put,
> The sharpest *Blades* will soonest cut."

To which Calverley at once replied :

> "Your wit is tolerable, but
> The case you understand ill ;
> The Dons would like their *Blayds* to cut,
> But cannot find a handle."

Dr. Jenkyns was the most conspicuous figure in the University of his day, and there was something in his somewhat
pompous (though in truth most kindly) nature, which invariably
struck sparks when brought into collision with this audacious
and keen-witted undergraduate.

The keeping of dogs in college was, it is needless to say,
strictly prohibited at Balliol, and was especially reprobated by
the Master; it is almost equally needless to add that the pro-
hibition was systematically evaded ; and one of the most in-

corrigible offenders in this respect was Calverley. Meeting him one day on the way to his rooms, with a tawny nondescript treasure trotting at his heels, the Master exclaimed, "What! another dog, Mr. Blayds!" "Master," was the wily response, "they do tell me that some people think it is a squirrel." This reply, while it committed the speaker to nothing, was really calculated to mystify the Master—not, it may be guessed, himself a very close observer of specific distinctions—for the creature in question, though undoubtedly a dog, did to an inattentive eye bear no slight external resemblance to the other-named animal.

He advanced at Oxford the reputation he had brought with him from Harrow, of being one of the best writers of Latin verse of his time; the Hexameters, with which he obtained the Chancellor's prize in 1851,[1] still remain one of the most beautiful of his many beautiful compositions.

It is customary for these prize poems to be printed and published, with the author's name and that of his college attached. When Calverley's manuscript was sent to the press, it bore, in anticipation of his impending doom, the following signature:

CAROLUS STUART BLAYDS
e COLL BALLIOL.
prope ejectus.

It was actually so printed, and it was only through the opportune interference of one of the college tutors that it was not so given to the world. When called upon for an explanation, Calverley is said to have declared that "those tiresome printers would do *anything*."

III.

Calverley quitted Oxford in the beginning of 1852, and in the following October was admitted as a freshman at Christ's College, Cambridge. It was here that the present writer first became acquainted with him. He was then at the zenith of his powers, both mental and bodily. Short of stature, with a powerful head of the Greek type, covered thickly with crisp, curling masses of dark brown hair, and closely set upon a frame whose supple joints and well-built proportions betokened

[1] Subject, *Parthenonis ruinæ.*

both speed and endurance—he presented a picture of health, strength, and activity. In disposition he was unselfish, and generous to a fault; without a trace of vanity or self-esteem; somewhat reserved amongst strangers, though bearing himself at all times with a charming simplicity and frankness of demeanour; slow to form friendships, but most loyal and constant to them when formed; a faithful, affectionate, wholehearted, thoroughly lovable human soul; with an intellect as keen, swift, and subtle as any that ever tenanted a human body.

It is not at all easy, indeed, it is hardly possible, to convey by description an adequate idea of the singular charm of his conversation. It must always be understood that though he said many good things, he was by no means an inventor and utterer of *bons mots*. Instead of expending itself in a succession of flashes, his wit was, as it were, a luminous glow, pervading and informing his entire speech, investing the thing spoken of with a novel and peculiar interest, and not seldom placing it in a vivid light, at once wholly unexpected and wholly appropriate. There was also in him a great quickness both of sympathy and of apprehension, enabling him to seize upon your point of view with rapidity and precision; and when to this is added a perfect honesty of intellect, free from any warpings of prejudice, egotism, or other pregnant source of self-mystification, the result is a set of conditions for rational intercourse of a rare and very special kind, the pervading feature of which is a wholesome atmosphere of security, an almost physical sense of comfort and *bien-être*—like the feeling of warmth and good cheer—which those who have experienced it will acknowledge to be as attractive as it is uncommon.

Cambridge discipline is, or is said to be, of a more liberal and less coercive character than that which obtains at the sister University, and Calverley, who moreover had gathered wisdom from experience, fell readily enough into the ways of conformity and obedience to rules. Though not, perhaps, exactly a favourite with the older and severer type of Don, who never quite knew how to take him, he was cordially appreciated by the authorities of his own college, themselves mostly men of a younger generation than the academic petrifactions of an earlier school. At no time, indeed, during the whole of his Cambridge course, did Calverley evince the slightest inclination to embroil himself with the ruling powers ; and it is altogether a mistake to suppose that, careless as he may have been of conventionalities, he had in his nature anything of the real Bohemian. Nor was he, either then or at any other period, a mere unprofitable idler ; and if not what is usually termed a reading man—that, namely, and nothing else—he was emphatically a man of reading ; a genuine lover of literature, and with a considerable knowledge of books.

Composition in Latin and Greek was his favourite intellectual exercise, or, it might rather be said, recreation ; the famous " Carmen Sæculare," the translation of Milton's " Lycidas " into Latin hexameters, a beautiful version of " John Anderson " in Greek Anacreontics, and several other of his most successful efforts, dating from this period. At this time, too, he was developing that incomparable vein of humour, that inimitable compound of serious irony and pure fun, blended with subtle and delicate banter, by which afterwards, in " Verses and Trans-lations," and still more decisively in " Fly-leaves," he " took the town by storm," and affected the reading world with the enjoy-ment of a new sensation. The Byronian stanzas in which he celebrates the praises and the works of Allsopp and of Bass, were in manuscript before he had taken his degree ; and it is curiously characteristic of his many-sided genius to note that at the very time when, with keen appreciative insight, he was penetrating the secret of Milton's majestic verse, and was re-producing those mournful, tender, or triumphant strains, in diction not less stately, and in numbers not less harmonious than the master's own, he could also let his sportive fancy play in airy raillery around the same pathetic theme, depicting, in a few telling strokes of mirthful mockery—

> " How Lycidas was dead, and how concerned
> The Nymphs were when they saw his lifeless clay,
> And how rock told to rock the dreadful story
> That poor young Lycidas was gone to glory."

Amongst his humorous compositions of this date, the " Pick-wick Examination Paper " has obtained a notoriety which entitles it to a passing mention.

Probably no one amongst the Cambridge men of that day

(excepting, perhaps, the late James Lempriere Hammond) equalled Calverley in close and comprehensive familiarity with the writings of Dickens. The notion (conceived at first as a pure joke) of making a great living author the subject of a competitive examination, would suggest itself naturally enough to one who had all his life been winning prizes for proficiency in the lore of ancient bards and sages, some of whom, perchance, held a far lower place in his affections than did the creator of the immortal Weller. The ingenious syllabus of questions which has attracted so much attention is not, however, interesting only as a measure of Calverley's curiously minute acquaintance with the masterpiece of Dickens; it deserves also to be noticed on account of the winners of the two prizes which were offered to the successful candidates. The first prize in the competition, which was open to all members of Christ's College, was taken by Mr. (now Sir) Walter Besant, the second by Mr. (now Professor) Skeat.

Calverley's appetite for humour, and his faculty of extracting it even from the most unpromising material, are oddly illustrated by the following "Notes," taken after he became a fellow of his college, and accidentally preserved amongst his papers :

"NOTES TAKEN AT COLLEGE MEETINGS.

At Meeting, February 28th, $11\frac{1}{2}$—2.

Remarked by the Master.—That no people give you so much trouble, if you try to extract money from them, as solicitors.

By the Jun. Dean.—Except, perhaps, parsons.

By the Senior Dean.—The latter possibly because they have not got the money.

By Mr. A.—That a ton weight is a great deal of books.

By Mr. B.—That it is just one o'clock.

By Mr. C.—That that is likely, and that in an hour it will be just two."

This record of the proceedings of a learned deliberative body is worthy of a place beside Mr. Punch's "Essence of Parliament."

To the above specimen of Calverley's humour may be added the following *jeu d'esprit* which appeared in the columns of the

"Pall Mall Gazette" in 1865, when middle-class examinations were in their infancy : [1]

"Berries from the Tree of Knowledge.

" ' By all means let classics be retained : *as the handmaids of more useful branches of study.* Valueless themselves, they may be made a vehicle to convey what is invaluable.' Thoroughly satisfied of the truth of this principle, an Oxford M.A. of eminence—he took (he mentions) high botanical honours, though ' comparatively weak ' in Latin and Greek—determined to test it at a recent middle-class examination. The result was a paper in Latin prose translation, of which he admits the candidates 'could make nothing,' but which he still 'cannot but consider a move in the right direction.' We subjoin it, adding also the interpretation, as sent—which, we may add, the words seem to us to bear, ' vix aut ne vix quidem ' in some places—for the benefit of the mere classic.

"Translate :

" ' Morum te nigram juraveris : morum vero albam fecisti. Solvi, vixdum rubum cæsium, vaccinium tuum myrtillum : teste virgine berberin circumvolitante, et baccâ sambuci patre tuo. Dederas et cheirographum : sed atramentum oxycoccus palustris. Equidem non pendo unius fragarii ribes taxi baccæ simile : permittam tamen omnibus chiococcum, te rubum Idæum prorsus exstitisse : vaccinium autem, senior, dic.'

" ' You may swear yourself black, Berry ; but you have made a mull, Berry. I paid your bill, Berry, as soon as due, Berry ; as the young woman in the bar, Berry, and your father, the elder Berry, know. I don't care a straw, Berry, for a goose, Berry, like you, Berry ; but I'll let folks know, Berry, that you've made yourself a regular ass, Berry ; and whort'll Berry senior say ? '

"The style of the Latin is more or less that of Cicero's letters ; though we think we would certainly have expressed some of the ideas—towards the end especially—in different language. We are not altogether satisfied of the rectitude of

---

[1] For this quotation I am indebted to a notice of Calverley which was published in the same journal a few days after his death—"Pall Mall Gazette," 29 February, 1884.

the 'move.' Surely it is pushing the Oxford theory a little too far. We commend the English version (fragments of which seem unaccountably familiar to us) as a useful *memoria technica* to the notice of mothers and governesses."

No account of Calverley's undergraduate life at Cambridge would be complete without some allusion to his musical talents. He had a remarkable ear, and possessed a voice of great purity and sweetness. The musical gatherings which from time to time took place in his rooms, are amongst the pleasantest of the many pleasant memories which cluster round those cheerful and hospitable quarters. When in the mood, he would take his seat at the piano and rattle off a series of extravaganzas, made up for the nonce out of the popular airs and operas of the day, interspersed not unfrequently with songs of his own composing; he also possessed the rare accomplishment of being able to whistle a perfect accompaniment to the instrument.

A general election which took place during Calverley's residence, and was the occasion of a memorable outbreak amongst the younger members of the University, deserves mention, although he himself took no active part in it, on account of a stirring episode, of which his college became the scene, and which has never, so far as the present writer is aware, been chronicled in prose or verse. It would require the pen of a Thackeray and the pencil of a Leech—*plena leporis Hirudo*—to do justice to it, and it happened on this wise.

The contest for the representation of the University was keenly watched and debated in undergraduate circles, by reason chiefly of the extraordinary popularity enjoyed by the Liberal candidate, Mr. (afterwards Mr. Justice) Denman. So great was the excitement, and so noisy were the demonstrations with which, in those days of open voting, the supporters of either party were greeted from the thronging galleries, that the Vice-Chancellor (Dr. Whewell) deemed it prudent to order the exclusion of all undergraduates from the Senate House during the hours of polling. This invasion of their ancient privileges was indignantly and violently resented by the youthful champions of Liberalism. A bonfire was made of the hustings in front of the schools. The intrepid and despotic Vice-Chancellor was himself threatened, and had to be escorted to his residence in Trinity by a strong bodyguard composed of Masters of Arts. On the morning following these events a decree was issued, directing that in every college the gates should be closed at an early hour, all persons *in statu pupillari* being required to keep themselves within. The effect of this sweeping and somewhat ill-advised measure was, that when the appointed hour arrived almost the entire undergraduate population was found to be in the streets. Forming themselves into a compact body, four or five abreast, they marched from college to college, demanding that the gates should be thrown open. In not a few instances the demand, through the undisguised sympathy of the garrison with the cause of the besiegers, was at once complied with. Service was proceeding within the college chapel when the wave of rebellion reached the massive oaken gates of Christ's, and thundered for admission. The sudden appearance of the college porter, pale and trembling, apprised the congregation, consisting of the fellows and a few scholars, of what was taking place. The Master stopped the service, and, putting himself at the head of his forces, marched in an imposing procession of some ten or twelve surpliced figures to the scene of action. Arrived at the inner side of the barred and bolted gate, the Master, having obtained a brief silence, proceeded to remonstrate with the insurgents, desiring, in tones of authority, to be informed whether they knew "who he was!" This display of vigour elicited a storm of uncomplimentary replies, for, to speak truth, the late Dr. Cartmell, though in every way a most admirable Master of his college, was not so generally popular in the University as he no doubt deserved to be. Meanwhile, an unexpected diversion was being effected by the enemy. Flanking one side of the college buildings was Christ's Lane, a private road belonging to the Society, opening into which is a side door from the college kitchens. Once in the year this road is closed to the public by means of a strong oaken bar, which at other times is hinged back and padlocked to a post. Whilst the main body were parleying at the gates, a strong force, guided by members of the college, hastened round to the lane, unshipped the bar, and employed it as a battering-ram against the kitchen door. News of this second attack was speedily conveyed to the Master. Taken thus in the rear, Dr. Cartmell wheeled gallantly round, passed rapidly across the quadrangle, and, traversing the kitchens between grinning rows of scouts and cooks, arrived at the precise moment when, its panels battered in, the door flew violently open, the victorious mob rushed by, bearing back Master, fellows, scholars, and cooks in one indistinguishable mass, swept irresistibly through the court, and, overwhelming the bewildered porter, opened the gates, and vanished from the citadel almost before its discomfited defenders had time to realize what had happened.

This incident brought hostilities to a close. Owing chiefly to the good sense and forbearance of the several college authorities, the ebullition everywhere subsided as quickly as it had arisen; the door in Christ's Lane was rebuilt more strongly, and the University resumed the even tenor of its way.

Of these great events Calverley, as has already been said, was a spectator only; a sufficient proof, if proof were needed, that the freaks of insubordination of the Oxford days indicated a purely transitory and evanescent aspect of his character. Meanwhile his list of University honours was not unworthy of his reputation and abilities. He gained the Craven Scholarship, which is the blue ribbon of undergraduate distinctions, in his second year; the Camden medal for Latin hexameters fell to him twice, the Greek Ode (Browne's medals) once, and he also took the Members' Prize for Latin prose. He finally came out second in the first class of the Classical Tripos of 1856, and within two years afterwards was elected fellow of his college.

He continued for a year or two after this to reside at Cambridge, taking private pupils and sharing in the work of the college; and in 1862 he made his first appearance in public with "Verses and Translations." Three years afterwards he was admitted to the bar as a member of the Inner Temple, and joined the Northern Circuit; having in the meantime vacated his fellowship by his marriage with his first cousin, Ellen Calverley, of Oulton, in Yorkshire. He now took up his abode permanently in London, and applied himself to the work of his profession, attending circuit regularly until his active career was interrupted by an accident which, though little was thought of it at the time, was destined to have far-reaching consequences.

Of this period of Calverley's life the writer of these pages, being then and for some years afterwards resident abroad, can give no account drawn from personal recollections. There is reason to believe that, brief as was the duration of his active connection with the bar, it was long enough to create an impression highly favourable to his prospects of future distinction. As sometimes happens with men endued with a powerful imagination, he found the study of law in itself sufficiently attractive to render comparatively easy the acquisition of legal knowledge, which his wit, resourcefulness, and acute reasoning faculty would have enabled him to turn to good account, had time and opportunity offered. But this was not to be.

The accident of which mention has just been made occurred in the winter of 1866-7, about a year and a half after his call to the bar. Calverley was skating at Oulton Hall, near Leeds (the residence of his father-in-law), when he tripped and was pitched heavily on his head, inflicting a severe blow over the right eye. Although the injury was sufficiently serious to need surgical treatment, no other attention was paid to it, and no permanent mischief was perceived or anticipated. When, however, he was induced, by symptoms which some time afterwards supervened, to consult an eminent London physician, he was declared to have sustained a concussion of the brain, the effects of which, though they might have been alleviated, and possibly altogether counteracted, by a short period of absolute rest taken at the time of the accident, were then such as to render it necessary for him to forego the strain of body and mind inseparable from the work of his profession.

From this time it may be said that for all the active business of life Calverley was practically laid upon the shelf. He had indeed still before him many years of tranquil happiness and enjoyment, in the society of wife, children, and friends, nor was he debarred from the pursuit of his favourite studies; still he chafed under the restriction from active work laid upon him by his physical condition, and, as has already been hinted, he was without the all-mastering strength of will through which a sterner or a more ambitious nature, if gifted with equal intellectual endowments, might have found in a forced period of leisure and retirement the path to solid and enduring fame. Thus it has happened that, although the work which he has left behind him is indeed exquisite of its kind, it is, as to much of it, unpurposed and fragmentary; reaching nowhere to the full height of his genius, and leaving almost wholly unevidenced his deeper qualities of mind and heart.

IV.

What will be Calverley's permanent position in literature, is a question which must be settled by the critics. The present writer has no pretensions to determine it, and must decline to attempt the task. Satisfied as those who knew him may be, that the full depth and extent of his powers are very imperfectly manifested in his writings, it is nevertheless by these that he will be chiefly judged ; and this at least is certain, that the world will never consent to form an estimate of his merits more lowly than was his own, who was at all times as little prone to see any excellence in himself, as he was prompt and eager upon all occasions to recognize it in others.

Assuming that all competent judges are agreed as to the superlative goodness of his classical compositions and translations, I will only observe in this place that in all such work his professed aim and object were faithfully to represent not the sense merely of his author but also the form and expression. It is not sufficient, in his view, that the thoughts and ideas of the original should be reproduced, in language of itself however appropriate and idiomatic, by the copy ; this is indeed indispensable, but this is not enough ; there must, in addition to a wholly faithful *sense*-rendering, be also to some extent a *word*-rendering, and even if possible a *form*-rendering. Wherever this path is ventured upon by an unskilful or incompetent workman, it is apt to lead him down a perilous incline of merely verbal resemblance, into a bathos of doggerel and sheer nonsense ; just as, on the other hand, a given version may correctly enough represent the bare meaning of the original, and yet be in itself a mere tasteless paraphrase, of the Tate and Brady order of merit. There is also this danger—of which I am reminded by a friend and former pupil of Calverley's, himself an acute scholar and an admirable translator—that in working upon the method indicated above, the ingenuity of the operator may be made too apparent, and the work show too plainly the mark of the tool. Still, I think, one sees that Calverley's method is in itself the right one ; it certainly increases, almost indefinitely, the translator's difficulties; and proportionately enhances the merit of success.

It must be understood that in speaking of *form*-rendering as one of the objects aimed at in Calverley's translations, I am as far as possible from referring to any kind of metrical imitation. Calverley totally disbelieved in all attempts to force modern language (or at all events modern English) into the mould of a classical metre; and even where this appears to have been successfully accomplished, he denied that the result was to reproduce the rhythm (*i.e.*, in the truest sense, the *form*) of ancient poetry. His views upon this subject are expressed at some length and with characteristic humour, in a paper which he contributed to the "London Student" (October, 1868). The whole article, which will be found at the end of this volume, is extremely interesting, as an example of critical analysis; and a perusal of it will, I think, be sufficient to satisfy the reader that in Calverley's opinion the business of a translator of classical poetry is to preserve as much as possible of the rhythm of his author's verses, and that this cannot be achieved by any endeavour, however successfully carried out, to imitate their scansion.[1]

Calverley's own measure of success in translating upon his own method is, I venture to think, almost if not quite unrivalled, and constitutes the distinctive mark of his performances in this department. The better to illustrate my meaning, I will cite two short specimens of his translation, one from Latin into English, and one from English into Latin. A very few lines will suffice, and our first example shall be the following stanza from an ode of Horace:

"Audivere, Lyce, di mea vota, di
Audivere, Lyce. Fis anus, et tamen
    Vis formosa videri,
    Ludisque et bibis impudens; &c."

---

[1] Upon the contents of this paper the late Professor Conington wrote to Calverley as follows:

"I read with great delight your paper on English Hexameters and Alcaics in the 'London Student,' agreeing thoroughly with what was said, and enjoying greatly the manner of saying it."

which Calverley thus translates :

> " Lyce, the gods have listened to my prayer :
> The gods have listened, Lyce.   Thou art gray,
> . And still wouldst thou seem fair ;
> Still unshamed drink, and play, &c."

Upon this translation it is to be observed, in the first place, that it is pitched in the precise key of the original—neither higher, nor lower, nor other ; and that besides adhering closely to the meaning of the Latin, it also indicates with fidelity the swing and rhythm, not merely of the particular metre, but of the particular passage ; reproducing with wonderful exactness a certain effect of intensity and compressed denunciatory force— partly the result of a skilful arrangement of words—which is not more apparent in Horace's Latin than in Calverley's English.   There is indeed in the latter nothing at all of the en- deavour (ambitiously aimed at by some translators) conjecturally to represent the manner or the phrase in which Horace, had he been an Englishman writing in English, might have been ex- pected to satirize the modern " Lyce ; " but it is a conscientious and supremely intelligent attempt to recast in English both the sense and the form of Horace's Latin words.

For our other example we will select a single couplet from the " Lycidas : "

> " For we were nursed upon the self-same hill,
> Fed the same flock by fountain, shade, and rill."

There is before the world more than one Latin version of these lines, by scholars of acknowledged reputation ; that of Calverley is as follows :

> " Uno namque jugo duo nutribamur, eosdem
> Pavit uterque greges ad fontem et rivulum et umbram."

Without claiming for the latter any special superiority upon the ground of its perfect fidelity to the meaning, I would venture to assert that no other version that can be quoted approaches it in the exquisite precision with which it follows the cadence and movement of Milton's stately measures.

The truth is that for work of this kind Calverley was magnificently equipped, both by nature and (so to speak) by

art. He was saturated with Virgil before he had left school ;
he had a most retentive memory, an inexhaustible command
of language, and a faultless ear ; and holding kinship, as he
did, with all forms of genius, his imagination readily took fire
at its touch, and burned with a corresponding flame.

The qualifications needed in a translator who should follow
the high and uncompromising standard of excellence by which
Calverley worked, would seem, at first sight, to be somewhat
inconsistent with those of a successful parodist, who may be
regarded as a kind of pseudo-translator, in so far as what he
aims at is a deliberately partial and one-sided representation of
his original ; and if, as common consent appears already to have
decided, Calverley is to be reckoned the first of English
parodists, the reason spontaneously suggested by the view
taken of him in this notice would be, that his natural powers
were greater than those of any other modern writer who has
cultivated this peculiar talent.

And accordingly we find, I think, that the element which
chiefly distinguishes his work of this class is the element of
mastery and strength. "Lovers, and a Reflection," inimitable
and unutterable nonsense though it be, is an extremely powerful piece of writing ; while of "The Cock and the Bull" I
venture to say that it will stand for all time a monument of
vigorous, effective, and most justifiable satire.

The first-named of these two celebrated burlesques is, indeed,
little else beside pure fun. It is too absurd to be satire, too
ridiculous even to be ridicule. If it is to be taken in the light
of an admonition, it is truly a loving correction, so empty of
censure, and so replete with kindly mirth, that the accomplished
authoress herself, who is its object, may (and, indeed, does)
enjoy it and laugh at it as heartily as all the rest of the world.
What moved Calverley to the perpetration of it I do not know,
but it was probably written without much premeditation. He
has been reading (we may conjecture) a well-known and
deservedly popular volume of poems ; his sense of humour is
tickled by certain seeming incoherencies of thought and expression, observable in the first poem of the series, called
"Divided ;" he "spots" here and there, with the eye of experience, sharpened by long practice on his own account, a too
palpable sacrifice of sense to the exigencies of sound ; and while

he is musing upon these things, a gentle *afflatus* steals upon him, and the thing is done; he thoughtfully takes up his pen, and in a moment—

" In moss-prankt dells which the sunbeams flatter,"

and all the rest of the inspired nonsense, is rattled off without an outward symptom of emotion stronger than a pensive chuckle.

It is pleasant to be able to record that the cordial intercourse already subsisting between poetess and poet was in no way disturbed by the appearance of "Lovers, and a Reflection;" and that, to the last, the brilliant scholar and man of letters possessed a valued and appreciative friend in this variously gifted lady, with the creations of whose graceful and womanly fancy such liberties had been taken by his audacious muse.

Of Calverley's parodies of Browning and the so-called mystical school, a somewhat different account must, I think, be given. He here strikes in earnest, and with a purpose. The present writer, who is himself a humble and sincere, though often a sorely puzzled, admirer of Browning, feeling at the first a little scandalized by the uncompromising directness of Calverley's attack upon "The Ring and the Book," once ventured to suggest remonstrance, and, with a view of convincing him of the error of his way, repeated to him those noble lines, beginning—"O lyric Love, half angel and half bird"— which form the conclusion to the opening chapter of the story. Calverley said little, but his face flushed, and his eye lit up, and it was easy to see that no want of appreciation of the strength and beauty of Browning's verse had prompted his assault upon those mannerisms and obscurities of style, which he looked upon as a grave literary offence. His own clearness and, so to speak, point-blank directness of mental vision rendered him especially impatient of all the crooked and nebulous antics and vagaries of thought or speech in which writers of the modern transcendental school are pleased to indulge; and his parodies of this class must be regarded as a genuine and out-spoken expression of resentment that so much genius should seem to take so much pains to be unintelligible. I am aware that to speak of this school of writers otherwise than in terms of respectful panegyric will savour of profanity in the eyes of those amongst their admirers who are not so much critics as votaries. To such it may not be amiss to suggest that in matters of literary taste, as well as in graver matters, *securus judicat terrarum orbis*; and that if the common sense of mankind had not long ago delivered judgment upon the affectations and extravagances of style against which Calverley's satire is directed, the word mannerism would either not have been invented or would have acquired a different connotation.

V.

As the reader already knows, Calverley was taken from us in the very prime of his manhood. At what period were sown the seeds of that cruel and treacherous malady[1] which ultimately caused his death, can now only be matter of conjecture. All that can be stated with certainty is, that long before the end came—how long it is impossible to say—he had been suffering from its unknown and unsuspected presence.

For some years his health had been gradually declining; and though his mental powers remained almost to the last intrinsically bright and clear, and the charm of his society never ceased to delight the few of us who had opportunities of enjoying it, such opportunities grew year by year rarer and rarer, giving place to intervals of physical uneasiness and mental depression, which slowly led to his more and more complete withdrawal from work and from the world. When at length the hopeless and incurable character of his disorder became fully apparent, his affectionate nature busied itself almost exclusively with thoughts of those whom he was leaving behind. A few short days before his death, in a conversation with myself about the future of his boys, his mind suddenly recurring to those fields of classic lore from which it was never long absent, he exclaimed, in tones rendered more pathetic by an increasing difficulty of utterance,—

ὦ παῖ, γένοιο πατρὸς εὐτυχέστερος.[2]

In their name we may accept, and reverently repeat the

---

[1] He died of Bright's disease.   [2] Sophocles, Ajax, 550.

aspiration embodied in this line, but we may surely also complete the prayer, by adding τὰ δ' ἄλλ' ὅμοιος ![1]

To pass through life, if so it may be, untouched by the shadow of that melancholy destiny which clouded his days and brought his years to an end as a tale that is told; not hoping, for that may hardly be, to rival him in powers of mind and intellect; but in other respects—in manliness and native worth, in truthfulness, uprightness, and simplicity of character —to be even such as he was!

He died on Sunday, the 17th of February, 1884, and was buried in the cemetery at Folkestone, by the side of his infant daughter, laid there sixteen years before. He had always liked the place, with its breezy heights, and sunny slopes, and exhilarating air; and on the morning of the Saturday following his death we took him there. And there we left him.

> "And in our ears, till hearing dies,
>   One set slow bell will seem to toll
>   The passing of the sweetest soul
> That ever looked with human eyes."
>   TENNYSON : *In Memoriam.*

----

[1] Sophocles, Ajax, 551.

FEBRUARY 17TH, 1884.

" *It was not, to restore thy flickering breath,*
Or hold thee back, just nearing towards the Light,
But—whilst that Sun of Life, whom we name Death,
Rose on thy closing, or thy opening sight—
To catch some whisper of thy new delight,
Some earnest of thy fainting soul's surprise,
And see the radiance quickening through the veil
Of palsied speech and leaden-lidded eyes,—
That we, bright Spirit! who stood and watched thee fail
And sink, and pass through gloom and utter night,
One instant, and no more, would fain have stayed thy flight!"

W. J. S.

VERSES

VISIONS

"She was a phantom," &c.

IN lone Glenartney's thickets lies couched the lordly stag,
  The dreaming terrier's tail forgets its customary wag;
And plodding ploughmen's weary steps insensibly grow quicker,
As broadening casements light them on toward home, or home-
      brewed liquor.

It is in brief the evening—that pure and pleasant time,
When stars break into splendour, and poets into rhyme;
When in the glass of Memory the forms of loved ones shine—
And when, of course, Miss Goodchild's is prominent in mine.

Miss Goodchild!—Julia Goodchild!—how graciously you
      smiled
Upon my childish passion once, yourself a fair-haired child:
When I was (no doubt) profiting by Dr. Crabb's instruction,
And sent those streaky lollipops home for your fairy suction!

"She wore" her natural "roses, the night when first we met"—
Her golden hair was gleaming 'neath the coercive net:
"Her brow was like the snawdrift," her step was like Queen
      Mab's,
And gone was instantly the heart of every boy at Crabb's.

B

The parlour boarder chasséed tow'rds her on graceful limb ;
The onyx deck'd his bosom—but her smiles were not for him :
With *me* she danced—till drowsily her eyes " began to blink,"
And *I* brought raisin wine, and said, " Drink, pretty creature,
   drink ! "

And evermore, when winter comes in his garb of snows,
And the returning schoolboy is told how fast he grows ;
Shall I—with that soft hand in mine—enact ideal Lancers,
And dream I hear demure remarks, and make impassioned
   answers :—

I know that never, never may her love for me return—
At night I muse upon the fact with undisguised concern—
But ever shall I bless that day : I don't bless, as a rule,
The days I spent at " Dr. Crabb's Preparatory School."

And yet we two *may* meet again—(Be still, my throbbing heart !)
Now rolling years have weaned us from jam and raspberry-tart.
One night I saw a vision—'Twas when musk-roses bloom,
I stood—*we* stood—upon a rug, in a sumptuous dining-room :

One hand clasped hers—one easily reposed upon my hip—
And "Bless ye ! " burst abruptly from Mr. Goodchild's lip :
I raised my brimming eye, and saw in hers an answering gleam—
My heart beat wildly—and I woke, and lo ! it was a dream.

GEMINI AND VIRGO

SOME vast amount of years ago,
   Ere all my youth had vanish'd from me,
A boy it was my lot to know,
   Whom his familiar friends called Tommy.

I love to gaze upon a child ;
   A young bud bursting into blossom ;
Artless, as Eve yet unbeguiled,
   And agile as a young opossum :

And such was he. A calm-brow'd lad,
   Yet mad, at moments, as a hatter :
Why hatters as a race are mad
   I never knew, nor does it matter.

He was what nurses call a " limb " ;
   One of those small misguided creatures,
Who, tho' their intellects are dim,
   Are one too many for their teachers :

And, if you asked of him to say
   What twice 10 was, or 3 times 7,
He'd glance (in quite a placid way)
   From heaven to earth, from earth to heaven ;

And smile, and look politely round,
   To catch a casual suggestion ;
But make no effort to propound
   Any solution of the question.

And so not much esteemed was he
   Of the authorities : and therefore
He fraternized by chance with me,
   Needing a somebody to care for :

And three fair summers did we twain
   Live (as they say) and love together ;
And bore by turns the wholesome cane
   Till our young skins became as leather :

And carved our names on every desk,
    And tore our clothes, and inked our collars ;
And looked unique and picturesque,
    But not, it may be, model scholars.

We did much as we chose to do ;
    We'd never heard of Mrs. Grundy ;
All the theology we knew
    Was that we mightn't play on Sunday ;

And all the general truths, that cakes
    Were to be bought at four a penny,
And that excruciating aches
    Resulted if we ate too many.

And seeing ignorance is bliss,
    And wisdom consequently folly,
The obvious result is this—
    That our two lives were very jolly.

At last the separation came.
    Real love, at that time, was the fashion ;
And by a horrid chance, the same
    Young thing was, to us both, a passion.

Old POSER snorted like a horse :
    His feet were large, his hands were pimply,
His manner, when excited, coarse :—
    But Miss P. was an angel simply.

She was a blushing, gushing thing ;
    All—more than all—my fancy painted ;
Once—when she helped me to a wing
    Of goose—I thought I should have fainted.

The people said that she was blue :
   But I was green, and loved her dearly.
She was approaching thirty-two ;
   And I was then eleven, nearly.

I did not love as others do ;
   (None ever did that I've heard tell of ;)
My passion was a byword through
   The town she was, of course, the belle of.

Oh sweet—as to the toilworn man
   The far-off sound of rippling river ;
As to cadets in Hindostan
   The fleeting remnant of their liver—

To me was ANNA ; dear as gold
   That fills the miser's sunless coffers ;
As to the spinster, growing old,
   The thought—the dream—that she had offers.

I'd sent her little gifts of fruit ;
   I'd written lines to her as Venus ;
I'd sworn unflinchingly to shoot
   The man who dared to come between us :

And it was you, my Thomas, you,
   The friend in whom my soul confided,
Who dared to gaze on her—to do,
   I may say, much the same as I did.

One night, I *saw* him squeeze her hand ;
   There was no doubt about the matter ;
I said he must resign, or stand
   My vengeance—and he chose the latter.

We met, we "planted" blows on blows :
   We fought as long as we were able :
My rival had a bottle-nose,
   And both my speaking eyes were sable,

When the school-bell cut short our strife.
   Miss P. gave both of us a plaister ;
And in a week became the wife
   Of Horace Nibbs, the writing-master.

    *   *   *   *   *

I loved her then—I'd love her still,
   Only one must not love Another's :
But thou and I, my Tommy, will,
   When we again meet, meet as brothers.

It may be that in age one seeks
   Peace only : that the blood is brisker
In boys' veins, than in theirs whose cheeks
   Are partially obscured by whisker ;

Or that the growing ages steal
   The memories of past wrongs from us.
But this is certain—that I feel
   Most friendly unto thee, oh Thomas !

And whereso'er we meet again,
   On this or that side the equator,
If I've not turned teetotaller then,
   And have wherewith to pay the waiter,

To thee I'll drain the modest cup,
   Ignite with thee the mild Havannah ;
And we will waft, while liquoring up,
   Forgiveness to the heartless ANNA.

> " There stands a city."
>
> INGOLDSBY.

YEAR by year do Beauty's daughters,
  In the sweetest gloves and shawls,
Troop to taste the Chattenham waters,
  And adorn the Chattenham balls.

" *Nulla non donanda lauru,*"
  Is that city : you could not,
Placing England's map before you,
  Light on a more favour'd spot.

If no clear translucent river
  Winds 'neath willow-shaded paths,
" Children and adults " may shiver
  All day in " Chalybeate baths " :

And on every side the painter
  Looks on wooded vale and plain
And on fair hills, faint and fainter
  Outlined as they near the main.

There I met with him, my chosen
  Friend—the " long " but not " stern swell," [1]
Faultless in his hats and hosen,
  Whom the Johnian lawns know well :—

Oh my comrade, ever valued !
  Still I see your festive face ;

---

[1] " The kites know well the long stern swell
  That bids the Romans close."—MACAULAY.

Hear you humming of "the gal you'd
    Left behind" in massive bass :

See you sit with that composure
    On the eeliest of hacks,
That the novice would suppose your
    Manly limbs encased in wax :

Or anon, when evening lent her
    Tranquil light to hill and vale,
Urge, towards the table's centre,
    With unerring hand, the squail.

Ah delectablest of summers !
    How my heart—that "muffled drum"
Which ignores the aid of drummers—
    Beats, as back thy memories come !

O among the dancers peerless,
    Fleet of foot, and soft of eye !
Need I say to you that cheerless
    Must my days be till I die ?

At my side she mashed the fragrant
    Strawberry ; lashes soft as silk
Drooped o'er saddened eyes, when vagrant
    Gnats sought watery graves in milk :

Then we danced, we walked together ;
    Talked—no doubt on trivial topics ;
Such as Blondin, or the weather,
    Which "recalled us to the tropics."

But—O in the deuxtemps peerless,
    Fleet of foot, and soft of eye !—
Once more I repeat, that cheerless
    Shall my days be till I die.

And the lean and hungry raven,
    As he picks my bones, will start
To observe " M. N." engraven
    Neatly on my blighted heart.

STRIKING

IT was a railway passenger,
    And he lept out jauntilie.
" Now up and bear, thou stout portèr,
    My two chattèls to me.

" Bring hither, bring hither my bag so red,
    And portmanteau so brown :
(They lie in the van, for a trusty man
    He labelled them London town :)

" And fetch me eke a cabman bold,
    That I may be his fare, his fare ;
And he shall have a good shilling,
If by two of the clock he do me bring
    To the Terminus, Euston Square."

" Now,—so to thee the saints alway,
    Good gentleman, give luck,—
As never a cab may I find this day,
    For the cabman wights have struck :

And now, I wis, at the Red Post Inn,
　　Or else at the Dog and Duck,
Or at Unicorn Blue, or at Green Griffin,
The nut-brown ale and the fine old gin
　　Right pleasantly they do suck."

"Now rede me aright, thou stout portèr,
　　What were it best that I should do:
For woe is me, an' I reach not there
　　Or ever the clock strike two."

"I have a son, a lytel son;
　　Fleet is his foot as the wild roebuck's:
Give him a shilling, and eke a brown,
And he shall carry thy fardels down
To Euston, or half over London town,
　　On one of the station trucks."

Then forth in a hurry did they twain fare,
The gent, and the son of the stout portèr,
Who fled like an arrow, nor turned a hair,
　　Through all the mire and muck:
"A ticket, a ticket, sir clerk, I pray:
For by two of the clock must I needs away."
"That may hardly be," the clerk did say,
　　"For indeed—the clocks have struck."

A B C

A is an Angel of blushing eighteen :
B is the Ball where the Angel was seen :
C is her Chaperon, who cheated at cards :
D is the Deuxtemps, with Frank of the Guards :
E is her Eye, killing slowly but surely :
F is the Fan, whence it peeped so demurely :
G is the Glove of superlative kid :
H is the Hand which it spitefully hid :
I is the Ice which the fair one demanded :
J is the Juvenile, that dainty who handed :
K is the Kerchief, a rare work of art :
L is the Lace which composed the chief part :
M is the old Maid who watch'd the chits dance :
N is the Nose she turned up at each glance :
O is the Olga (just then in its prime) :
P is the Partner who wouldn't keep time :
Q 's a Quadrille, put instead of the Lancers :
R is the Remonstrances made by the dancers :
S is the Supper, where all went in pairs :
T is the Twaddle they talked on the stairs :
U is the Uncle who "thought we'd be goin' :"
V is the Voice which his niece replied " No " in :
W is the Waiter, who sat up till eight :
X is his Exit, not rigidly straight :
Y is a Yawning fit caused by the Ball :
Z stands for Zero, or nothing at all.

VOICES OF THE NIGHT

"The tender Grace of a day that is dead."

THE dew is on the roses,
    The owl hath spread her wing;
And vocal are the noses
    Of peasant and of king:
"Nature" in short "reposes";
    But I do no such thing.

Pent in my lonesome study
    Here I must sit and muse;
Sit till the morn grows ruddy,
    Till, rising with the dews,
"Jeameses" remove the muddy
    Spots from their masters' shoes.

Yet are sweet faces flinging
    Their witchery o'er me here:
I hear sweet voices singing
    A song as soft, as clear,
As (previously to stinging)
    A gnat sings round one's ear.

Does Grace draw young Apollos
    In blue mustachios still?
Does Emma tell the swallows
    How she will pipe and trill,
When, some fine day, she follows
    Those birds to the window-sill?

And oh! has Albert faded
  From Grace's memory yet?
Albert, whose "brow was shaded
  By locks of glossiest jet,"
Whom almost any lady'd
  Have given her eyes to get?

Does not her conscience smite her
  For one who hourly pines,
Thinking her bright eyes brighter
  Than any star that shines—
I mean of course the writer
  Of these pathetic lines?

Who knows? As quoth Sir Walter,
  "Time rolls his ceaseless course:
"The Grace of yore" may alter—
  And then, I've one resource:
I'll invest in a bran-new halter,
  And I'll perish without remorse.

LINES SUGGESTED BY THE FOURTEENTH
OF FEBRUARY

ERE the morn the East has crimsoned,
    When the stars are twinkling there,
(As they did in Watts's Hymns, and
  Made him wonder what they were :)
When the forest-nymphs are beading
  Fern and flower with silvery dew—
My infallible proceeding
  Is to wake, and think of you.

When the hunter's ringing bugle
   Sounds farewell to field and copse,
And I sit before my frugal
   Meal of gravy-soup and chops:
When (as Gray remarks) "the moping
   Owl doth to the moon complain,"
And the hour suggests eloping—
   Fly my thoughts to you again.

May my dreams be granted never?
   Must I aye endure affliction
Rarely realized, if ever,
   In our wildest works of fiction?
Madly Romeo loved his Juliet;
   Copperfield began to pine
When he hadn't been to school yet—
   But their loves were cold to mine.

Give me hope, the least, the dimmest,
   Ere I drain the poisoned cup:
Tell me I may tell the chymist
   Not to make that arsenic up!
Else the heart must cease to throb in
   This my breast; and when, in tones
Hushed, men ask, "Who killed Cock Robin?"
   They'll be told, "Miss Clara J———s."

TO MRS. GOODCHILD

THE night-wind's shriek is pitiless and hollow,
   The boding bat flits by on sullen wing,
And I sit desolate, like that "one swallow"
   Who found (with horror) that he'd not brought spring:

Lonely as he who erst with venturous thumb
Drew from its pie-y lair the solitary plum.

And to my gaze the phantoms of the Past,
    The cherished fictions of my boyhood, rise :
I see Red Ridinghood observe, aghast,
    The fixed expression of her grandam's eyes ;
I hear the fiendish chattering and chuckling
Which those misguided fowls raised at the Ugly Duckling.

The House that Jack built—and the Malt that lay
    Within the House—the Rat that ate the Malt—
The Cat, that in that sanguinary way
    Punished the poor thing for its venial fault—
The Worrier-Dog—the Cow with crumpled horn—
And then—ah yes ! and then—the Maiden all forlorn !

O Mrs. Gurton—(may I call thee Gammer ?)
    Thou more than mother to my infant mind !
I loved thee better than I loved my grammar—
    I used to wonder why the Mice were blind,
And who was gardener to Mistress Mary,
And what—I don't know still—was meant by " quite contrary."

" Tota contraria," an " *Arundo Cami* "
    Has phrased it—which is possibly explicit,
Ingenious certainly—but all the same I
    Still ask, when coming on the word, " What is it ? "
There were more things in Mrs. Gurton's eye,
Mayhap, than are dreamed of in our philosophy.

No doubt the Editor of " Notes and Queries "
    Or " Things not generally known " could tell

The word's real force—my only lurking fear is
    That the great Gammer "didna ken hersel":
(I've precedent, yet feel I owe apology
For passing in this way to Scottish phraseology).

Also, dear Madam, I must ask your pardon
    For making this unwarranted digression,
Starting (I think) from Mistress Mary's garden:—
    And beg to send, with every expression
Of personal esteem, a Book of Rhymes,
For Master G. to read at miscellaneous times.

There is a youth, who keeps a "crumpled Horn,"
    (Living next me, upon the selfsame story,)
And ever, 'twixt the midnight and the morn,
    He solaces his soul with Annie Laurie.
The tune is good; the habit p'raps romantic;
But tending, if pursued, to drive one's neighbours frantic.

And now,—at this unprecedented hour,
    When the young Dawn is "trampling out the stars,"—
I hear that youth—with more than usual power
    And pathos—struggling with the first few bars.
And I do think the amateur cornopean
Should be put down by law—but that's perhaps Utopian.

Who knows what "things unknown" I might have "bodied
    Forth," if not checked by that absurd Too-too?
But don't I know that when my friend has plodded
    Through the first verse, the second will ensue?
Considering which, dear Madam, I will merely
Send the beforenamed book—and am yours most sincerely.

ODE—"ON A DISTANT PROSPECT" OF MAKING A FORTUNE

NOW the "rosy morn appearing"
　　Floods with light the dazzled heaven ;
And the schoolboy groans on hearing
　　That eternal clock strike seven :—
Now the waggoner is driving
　　Tow'rds the fields his clattering wain ;
Now the blue-bottle, reviving,
　　Buzzes down his native pane.

But to me the morn is hateful :
　　Wearily I stretch my legs,
Dress, and settle to my plateful
　　Of (perhaps inferior) eggs.
Yesterday Miss Crump, by message,
　　Mentioned "rent," which "p'raps I'd pay ; "
And I have a dismal presage
　　That she'll call, herself, to-day.

Once, I breakfasted off rosewood,
　　Smoked through silver-mounted pipes—
Then how my patrician nose would
　　Turn up at the thought of "swipes " !
Ale,—occasionally claret,—
　　Graced my luncheon then ;—and now
I drink porter in a garret,
　　To be paid for heaven knows how.

When the evening shades are deepened,
　　And I doff my hat and gloves,

C

No sweet bird is there to "cheep and
    Twitter twenty million loves;"
No dark-ringleted canaries
    Sing to me of "hungry foam;"
No imaginary "Marys"
    Call fictitious "cattle home."

Araminta, sweetest, fairest!
    Solace once of every ill!
How I wonder if thou bearest
    Mivins in remembrance still!
If that Friday night is banished
    From a once retentive mind,
When the others somehow vanished,
    And we two were left behind :—

When in accents low, yet thrilling,
    I did all my love declare;
Mentioned that I'd not a shilling—
    Hinted that we need not care;
And complacently you listened
    To my somewhat long address,
And I thought the tear that glistened
    In the downdrop eye said Yes.

Once, a happy child, I carolled
    O'er green lawns the whole day through,
Not unpleasingly apparelled
    In a tightish suit of blue :—
What a change has now passed o'er me!
    Now with what dismay I see
Every rising morn before me!
    Goodness gracious patience me!

And I'll prowl, a moodier Lara,
  Thro' the world, as prowls the bat,
And habitually wear a
  Cypress wreath around my hat :
And when Death snuffs out the taper
  Of my Life (as soon he must),
I'll send up to every paper,
  " Died, T. Mivins ; of disgust."

ISABEL

NOW o'er the landscape crowd the deepening shades,
    And the shut lily cradles not the bee ;
The red deer couches in the forest glades,
  And faint the echoes of the slumberous sea :
  And ere I rest, one prayer I'll breathe for thee,
The sweet Egeria of my lonely dreams :
  Lady, forgive, that ever upon me
  Thoughts of thee linger, as the soft starbeams
Linger on Merlin's rock, or dark Sabrina's streams.

On gray Pilatus once we loved to stray,
  And watch far off the glimmering roselight break
O'er the dim mountain-peaks, ere yet one ray
  Pierced the deep bosom of the mist-clad lake.
  Oh ! who felt not new life within him wake,
And his pulse quicken, and his spirit burn—
  (Save one we wot of, whom the cold *did* make
Feel " shooting pains in every joint in turn,")
When first he saw the sun gild thy green shores, Lucerne ?

And years have past, and I have gazed once more
  On blue lakes glistening amid mountains blue ;
And all seemed sadder, lovelier than before—
  For all awakened memories of you.
  Oh ! had I had you by my side, in lieu
Of that red matron, whom the flies would worry,
  (Flies in those parts unfortunately do,)
Who walked so slowly, talked in such a hurry,
And with such wild contempt for stops and Lindley Murray !

  O Isabel, the brightest, heavenliest theme
  That e'er drew dreamer on to poësy,
Since " Peggy's locks " made Burns neglect his team,
  And Stella's smile lured Johnson from his tea—
  I may not tell thee what thou art to me !
But ever dwells the soft voice in my ear,
  Whispering of what Time is, what Man might be,
  Would he but " do the duty that lies near,"
And cut clubs, cards, champagne, balls, billiard-rooms, and beer.

LINES SUGGESTED BY THE FOURTEENTH OF FEBRUARY

D ARKNESS succeeds to twilight :
    Through lattice and through skylight,
The stars no doubt, if one looked out,
    Might be observed to shine :
    And sitting by the embers
    I elevate my members
On a stray chair, and then and there
    Commence a Valentine.

Yea! by St. Valentinus,
  Emma shall not be minus
What all young ladies, whate'er their grade is,
    Expect to-day no doubt :
  Emma the fair, the stately—
  Whom I beheld so lately,
Smiling beneath the snow-white wreath
    Which told that she was " out."

  Wherefore fly to her, swallow,
  And mention that I'd "follow,"
And "pipe and trill," et cetera, till
    I died, had I but wings :
  Say the North's " true and tender,"
  The South an old offender ;
And hint in fact, with your well-known tact,
    All kinds of pretty things.

  Say I grow hourly thinner,
  Simply abhor my dinner—
Tho' I do try and absorb some viand
    Each day, for form's sake merely :
  And ask her, when all 's ended,
  And I am found extended,
With vest blood-spotted and cut carotid,
    To think on Hers sincerely.

"HIC *VIR*, HIC EST"

OFTEN, when o'er tree and turret,
    Eve a dying radiance flings,
By that ancient pile I linger
  Known familiarly as " King's."

And the ghosts of days departed
    Rise, and in my burning breast
All the undergraduate wakens,
    And my spirit is at rest.

What, but a revolting fiction,
    Seems the actual result
Of the Census's enquiries
    Made upon the 15th ult. ?
Still my soul is in its boyhood ;
    Nor of year or changes recks,
Though my scalp is almost hairless,
    And my figure grows convex.

Backward moves the kindly dial ;
    And I'm numbered once again
With those noblest of their species
    Called emphatically " Men : "
Loaf, as I have loafed aforetime,
    Through the streets, with tranquil mind,
And a long-backed fancy-mongrel
    Trailing casually behind :

Past the Senate-house I saunter,
    Whistling with an easy grace ;
Past the cabbage-stalks that carpet
    Still the beefy market-place ;
Poising evermore the eye-glass
    In the light sarcastic eye,
Lest, by chance, some breezy nursemaid
    Pass, without a tribute, by.

Once, an unassuming Freshman,
    Thro' these wilds I wandered on,

Seeing in each house a College,
   Under every cap a Don :
Each perambulating infant
   Had a magic in its squall,
For my eager eye detected
   Senior Wranglers in them all.

By degrees my education
   Grew, and I became as others ;
Learned to blunt my moral feelings
   By the aid of Bacon Brothers ;
Bought me tiny boots of Mortlock,
   And colossal prints of Roe ;
And ignored the proposition
   That both time and money go.

Learned to work the wary dogcart
   Artfully thro' King's Parade ;
Dress, and steer a boat, and sport with
   Amaryllis in the shade :
Struck, at Brown's, the dashing hazard ;
   Or (more curious sport than that)
Dropped, at Callaby's, the terrier
   Down upon the prisoned rat.

I have stood serene on Fenner's
   Ground, indifferent to blisters,
While the Buttress of the period
   Bowled me his peculiar twisters :
Sung "We won't go home till morning ;"
   Striven to part my backhair straight ;
Drunk (not lavishly) of Miller's
   Old dry wines at 78/ :—

When within my veins the blood ran,
  And the curls were on my brow,
I did, oh ye undergraduates,
  Much as ye are doing now.
Wherefore bless ye, O beloved ones :—
  Now unto mine inn must I,
Your "poor moralist,"[1] betake me,
  In my " solitary fly."

BEER

IN those old days which poets say were golden—
  (Perhaps they laid the gilding on themselves :
And, if they did, I'm all the more beholden
  To those brown dwellers in my dusty shelves,
Who talk to me "in language quaint and olden"
  Of gods and demigods and fauns and elves,
Pan with his pipes, and Bacchus with his leopards,
And staid young goddesses who flirt with shepherds :)

In those old days, the Nymph called Etiquette
  (Appalling thought to dwell on) was not born.
They had their May, but no Mayfair as yet,
  No fashions varying as the hues of morn.
Just as they pleased they dressed and drank and ate,
  Sang hymns to Ceres (their John Barleycorn)
And danced unchaperoned, and laughed unchecked,
  And were no doubt extremely incorrect.

---

[1] " Poor moralist, and what art thou ?
       A solitary fly."   GRAY.

Yet do I think their theory was pleasant:
   And oft, I own, my " wayward fancy roams "
Back to those times, so different from the present;
   When no one smoked cigars, nor gave At-homes,
Nor smote a billiard-ball, nor winged a pheasant,
   Nor "did" her hair by means of long-tailed combs,
Nor migrated to Brighton once a year,
Nor—most astonishing of all—drank Beer.

No, they did not drink Beer, "which brings me to "
   (As Gilpin said) "the middle of my song."
Not that "the middle " is precisely true,
   Or else I should not tax your patience long:
If I had said "beginning," it might do;
   But I have a dislike to quoting wrong:
I was unlucky—sinned against, not sinning—
When Cowper wrote down "middle " for "beginning."

So to proceed.   That abstinence from Malt
   Has always struck me as extremely curious.
The Greek mind must have had some vital fault,
   That they should stick to liquors so injurious—
(Wine, water, tempered p'raps with Attic salt)—
   And not at once invent that mild, luxurious,
And artful beverage, Beer.   How the digestion
Got on without it, is a startling question.

Had they digestions? and an actual body
   Such as dyspepsia might make attacks on?
Were they abstract ideas—(like Tom Noddy
   And Mr. Briggs)—or men, like Jones and Jackson?
Then nectar—was that beer, or whisky-toddy?
   Some say the Gaelic mixture, *I* the Saxon:

I think a strict adherence to the latter
Might make some Scots less pigheaded, and fatter.

Besides, Bon Gaultier definitely shows
    That the real beverage for feasting gods on
Is a soft compound, grateful to the nose
    And also to the palate, known as " Hodgson."
I know a man—a tailor's son—who rose
    To be a peer : and this I would lay odds on,
(Though in his Memoirs it may not appear,)
That that man owed his rise to copious Beer.

O Beer ! O Hodgson, Guinness, Allsopp, Bass !
    Names that should be on every infant's tongue !
Shall days and months and years and centuries pass,
    And still your merits be unrecked, unsung ?
Oh ! I have gazed into my foaming glass,
    And wished that lyre could yet again be strung
Which once rang prophet-like through Greece, and taught her
Misguided sons that the best drink was water.

How would he now recant that wild opinion,
    And sing—as would that I could sing—of you !
I was not born (alas !) the " Muses' minion,"
    I'm not poetical, not even blue :
And he, we know, but strives with waxen pinion,
    Whoe'er he is that entertains the view
Of emulating Pindar, and will be
Sponsor at last to some now nameless sea.

Oh ! when the green slopes of Arcadia burned
    With all the lustre of the dying day,
And on Cithæron's brow the reaper turned,
    (Humming, of course, in his delightful way,

How Lycidas was dead, and how concerned
   The Nymphs were when they saw his lifeless clay;
And how rock told to rock the dreadful story
That poor young Lycidas was gone to glory :)

What would that lone and labouring soul have given,
   At that soft moment for a pewter pot!
How had the mists that dimmed his eye been riven,
   And Lycidas and sorrow all forgot!
If his own grandmother had died unshriven,
   In two short seconds he'd have recked it not;
Such power hath Beer. The heart which Grief hath canker'd
Hath one unfailing remedy—the Tankard.

Coffee is good, and so no doubt is cocoa;
   Tea did for Johnson and the Chinamen:
When " Dulce est desipere in loco "
   Was written, real Falernian winged the pen.
When a rapt audience has encored " Fra Poco "
   Or " Casta Diva," I have heard that then
The Prima Donna, smiling herself out,
Recruits her flagging powers with bottled stout.

But what is coffee, but a noxious berry,
   Born to keep used-up Londoners awake?
What is Falernian, what is Port or Sherry,
   But vile concoctions to make dull heads ache?
Nay stout itself—(though good with oysters, very)—
   Is not a thing your reading man should take.
He that would shine, and petrify his tutor,
Should drink draught Allsopp in its " native pewter."

But hark! a sound is stealing on my ear—
   A soft and silvery sound—I know it well.

Its tinkling tells me that a time is near
    Precious to me—it is the Dinner Bell.
O blessed Bell ! Thou bringest beef and beer,
    Thou bringest good things more than tongue may tell:
Seared is, of course, my heart—but unsubdued
Is, and shall be, my appetite for food.

I go. Untaught and feeble is my pen:
    But on one statement I may safely venture:
That few of our most highly gifted men
    Have more appreciation of the trencher.
I go. One pound of British beef, and then
    What Mr. Swiveller called a "modest quencher";
That home-returning, I may "soothly say,"
" Fate cannot touch me : I have dined to-day."

ODE TO TOBACCO

THOU who, when fears attack,
    Bidst them avaunt, and Black
Care, at the horseman's back
    Perching, unseatest;
Sweet, when the morn is gray;
Sweet, when they've cleared away
Lunch; and at close of day
    Possibly sweetest:

I have a liking old
For thee, though manifold
Stories, I know, are told,
    Not to thy credit;

How one (or two at most)
Drops make a cat a ghost—
Useless, except to roast—
    Doctors have said it:

How they who use fusees
All grow by slow degrees
Brainless as chimpanzees,
    Meagre as lizards:
Go mad, and beat their wives;
Plunge (after shocking lives)
Razors and carving knives
    Into their gizzards.

Confound such knavish tricks!
Yet know I five or six
Smokers who freely mix
    Still with their neighbours;
Jones—(who, I'm glad to say,
Asked leave of Mrs. J.)—
Daily absorbs a clay
    After his labours.

Cats may have had their goose
Cooked by tobacco-juice;
Still why deny its use
    Thoughtfully taken?
We're not as tabbies are:
Smith, take a fresh cigar!
Jones, the tobacco-jar!
    Here 's to thee, Bacon!

DOVER TO MUNICH

FAREWELL, farewell! Before our prow
 Leaps in white foam the noisy channel;
A tourist's cap is on my brow,
 My legs are cased in tourist's flannel:

Around me gasp the invalids—
 The quantity to-night is fearful—
I take a brace or so of weeds,
 And feel (as yet) extremely cheerful.

The night wears on :—my thirst I quench
 With one imperial pint of porter;
Then drop upon a casual bench—
 (The bench is short, but I am shorter)—

Place 'neath my head the *havre-sac*
 Which I have stowed my little all in,
And sleep, though moist about the back,
 Serenely in an old tarpaulin.

—————

Bed at Ostend at 5 A.M.
 Breakfast at 6, and train 6·30,
Tickets to Königswinter (mem.
 The seats unutterably dirty).

And onward thro' those dreary flats
 We move, and scanty space to sit on,
Flanked by stout girls with steeple hats,
 And waists that paralyse a Briton ;—

By many a tidy little town,
   Where tidy little Fraus sit knitting;
(The men's pursuits are, lying down,
   Smoking perennial pipes, and spitting;)

And doze, and execrate the heat,
   And wonder how far off Cologne is,
And if we shall get aught to eat,
   Till we get there, save raw polonies:

Until at last the "gray old pile"
   Is seen, is past, and three hours later
We're ordering steaks, and talking vile
   Mock-German to an Austrian waiter.

Königswinter, hateful Königswinter!
   Burying-place of all I loved so well!
Never did the most extensive printer
   Print a tale so dark as thou could'st tell!

In the sapphire West the eve yet lingered,
   Bathed in kindly light those hill-tops cold;
Fringed each cloud, and, stooping rosy-fingered,
   Changed Rhine's waters into molten gold;—

While still nearer did his light waves splinter
   Into silvery shafts the streaming light;
And I said I loved thee, Königswinter,
   For the glory that was thine that night.

And we gazed, till slowly disappearing,
   Like a day-dream, passed the pageant by,
And I saw but those lone hills, uprearing
   Dull dark shapes against a hueless sky.

Then I turned, and on those bright hopes pondered
    Whereof yon gay fancies were the type;
And my hand mechanically wandered
    Towards my left-hand pocket for a pipe.

Ah! why starts each eyeball from its socket,
    As, in Hamlet, start the guilty Queen's?
There, deep-hid in its accustomed pocket,
    Lay my sole pipe, smashed to smithereens!

————

    On, on the vessel steals;
    Round go the paddle-wheels,
    And now the tourist feels
        As he should;
    For king-like rolls the Rhine,
    And the scenery's divine,
    And the victuals and the wine
        Rather good.

    From every crag we pass'll
    Rise up some hoar old castle;
    The hanging fir-groves tassel
        Every slope;
    And the vine her lithe arm stretches
    Over peasants singing catches—
    And you'll make no end of sketches,
        I should hope.

    We've a nun here (called Thérèse),
    Two couriers out of place,
    One Yankee with a face
        Like a ferret's:

And three youths in scarlet caps
Drinking chocolate and schnapps—
A diet which perhaps
    Has its merits.

And day again declines :
In shadow sleep the vines,
And the last ray thro' the pines
    Feebly glows,
Then sinks behind yon ridge ;
And the usual evening midge
Is settling on the bridge
    Of my nose.

And keen 's the air and cold,
And the sheep are in the fold,
And Night walks sable-stoled
    Thro' the trees ;
And on the silent river
The floating starbeams quiver ;—
And now, the saints deliver
    Us from fleas.

Avenues of broad white houses,
  Basking in the noontide glare ;—
Streets, which foot of traveller shrinks from,
  As on hot plates shrinks the bear ;—

Elsewhere lawns, and vista'd gardens,
  Statues white, and cool arcades,
Where at eve the German warrior
  Winks upon the German maids ;—

Such is Munich :—broad and stately,
    Rich of hue, and fair of form ;
But, towards the end of August,
    Unequivocally *warm*.

There, the long dim galleries threading,
    May the artist's eye behold
Breathing from the "deathless canvas"
    Records of the years of old :

Pallas there, and Jove, and Juno,
    "Take" once more their "walks abroad,"
Under Titian's fiery woodlands
    And the saffron skies of Claude :

There the Amazons of Rubens
    Lift the failing arm to strike,
And the pale light falls in masses
    On the horsemen of Vandyke ;

And in Berghem's pools reflected
    Hang the cattle's graceful shapes,
And Murillo's soft boy-faces
    Laugh amid the Seville grapes ;

And all purest, loveliest fancies
    That in poets' souls may dwell
Started into shape and substance
    At the touch of Raphael.

Lo ! her wan arms folded meekly,
    And the glory of her hair
Falling as a robe around her,
    Kneels the Magdalen in prayer ;

And the white-robed Virgin-mother
   Smiles, as centuries back she smiled,
Half in gladness, half in wonder,
   On the calm face of her Child :—

And that mighty Judgment-vision
   Tells how man essayed to climb
Up the ladder of the ages,
   Past the frontier-walls of Time ;

Heard the trumpet-echoes rolling
   Thro' the phantom-peopled sky,
And the still voice bid this mortal
   Put on immortality.

     *   *   *   *

Thence we turned, what time the blackbird
   Pipes to vespers from his perch,
And from out the clattering city
   Pass'd into the silent church ;

Mark'd the shower of sunlight breaking
   Thro' the crimson panes o'erhead,
And on pictured wall and window
   Read the histories of the dead :

Till the kneelers round us, rising,
   Crossed their foreheads and were gone ;
And o'er aisle and arch and cornice,
   Layer on layer, the night came on.

CHARADES

I

S HE stood at Greenwich, motionless amid
    The ever-shifting crowd of passengers.
I mark'd a big tear quivering on the lid
    Of her deep-lustrous eye, and knew that hers
Were days of bitterness. But, "Oh! what stirs,"
I said, "such storm within so fair a breast?"
    Even as I spoke, two apoplectic curs
Came feebly up: with one wild cry she prest
Each singly to her heart, and faltered, "Heaven be blest!"

Yet once again I saw her, from the deck
    Of a black ship that steamed towards Blackwall.
She walked upon *my first*. Her stately neck
    Bent o'er an object shrouded in her shawl:
I could not see the tears—the glad tears—fall,
Yet knew they fell. And "Ah," I said, "not puppies,
    Seen unexpectedly, could lift the pall
From hearts who *know* what tasting misery's cup is
As Niobe's, or mine, or blighted William Guppy's."

Spake John Grogblossom the coachman to Eliza Spinks the cook:
"Mrs. Spinks," says he, "I've founder'd: 'Liza dear, I'm over-
    took.
Druv into a corner reglar, puzzled as a babe unborn;
Speak the word, my blessed 'Liza; speak, and John the
    coachman's yourn."

Then Eliza Spinks made answer, blushing, to the coachman
      John :
" John, I'm born and bred a spinster : I've begun and I'll go on.
Endless cares and endless worrits, well I knows it, has a wife :
Cooking for a genteel family, John, it's a goluptious life !

"I gets £20 per annum—tea and things o'course not reckoned,—
There's a cat that eats the butter, takes the coals, and breaks
      my second :
There's soci'ty—James the footman ;—(not that I look after
      him ;
But he's aff'ble in his manners, with amazing length of limb ;)—

" Never durst the missis enter here until I've said ' Come in ' :
If I saw the master peeping, I'd catch up the rolling-pin.
Christmas-boxes, that's a something ; perkisites, that's some-
      thing too ;
And I think, take all together, John, I won't be on with you."

John the coachman took his hat up, for he thought he'd had
      enough ;
Rubb'd an elongated forehead with a meditative cuff ;
Paused before the stable doorway ; said, when there, in accents
      mild,
" She's a fine young 'oman, cook is ; but that's where it is,
      she's spiled."

    I have read in some not marvellous tale,
      (Or if I have not, I've dreamed)
    Of one who filled up the convivial cup
      Till the company round him seemed

To be vanished and gone, tho' the lamps upon
  Their face as aforetime gleamed :
And his head sunk down, and a Lethe crept
O'er his powerful brain, and the young man slept.

Then they laid him with care in his moonlit bed :
  But first—having thoughtfully fetched some tar—
Adorn'd him with feathers, aware that the weather's
  Uncertainty brings on at nights catarrh.

They staid in his room till the sun was high :
  But still did the feathered one give no sign
Of opening a peeper—he might be a sleeper
  Such as rests on the Northern or Midland line.

At last he woke, and with profound
  Bewilderment he gazed around ;
Dropped one, then both feet to the ground,
  But never spake a word :

Then to *my whole* he made his way ;
Took one long lingering survey ;
And softly, as he stole away,
  Remarked, " By Jove, a bird ! "

II

IF you've seen a short man swagger tow'rds the footlights at
    Shoreditch,
Sing out " Heave aho ! my hearties," and perpetually hitch
Up, by an ingenious movement, trousers innocent of brace,
Briskly flourishing a cudgel in his pleased companion's face ;

If he preluded with hornpipes each successive thing he did,
From a sun-browned cheek extracting still an ostentatious quid ;
And expectorated freely, and occasionally cursed :—
Then have you beheld, depicted by a master's hand, *my first.*

O my countryman ! if ever from thy arm the bolster sped,
In thy school-days, with precision at a young companion's head ;
If 'twas thine to lodge the marble in the centre of the ring,
Or with well-directed pebble make the sitting hen take wing :

Then do thou—each fair May morning, when the blue lake is
    as glass,
And the gossamers are twinkling star-like in the beaded grass ;
When the mountain-bee is sipping fragrance from the bluebell's
    lip,
And the bathing-woman tells you, " Now's your time to take a
    dip " :

When along the misty valleys fieldward winds the lowing herd,
And the early worm is being dropped on by the early bird ;
And Aurora hangs her jewels from the bending rose's cup,
And the myriad voice of Nature calls thee to *my second* up :—

Hie thee to the breezy common, where the melancholy goose
Stalks, and the astonished donkey finds that he is really loose ;
There amid green fern and furze-bush shalt thou soon *my whole*
    behold,
Rising " bull-eyed and majestic "—as Olympus' queen of old :

Kneel,—at a respectful distance,—as they kneeled to her, and try
With judicious hand to put a ball into that ball-less eye :
Till a stiffness seize thy elbows, and the general public wake—
Then return, and, clear of conscience, walk into thy well-earned
    steak.

III

ERE yet "knowledge for the million"
    Came out "neatly bound in boards";
When like Care upon a pillion
    Matrons rode behind their lords:
Rarely, save to hear the Rector,
    Forth did younger ladies roam;
Making pies, and brewing nectar
    From the gooseberry-trees at home.

They'd not dreamed of Pau or Vevay;
    Ne'er should into blossom burst
At the ball or at the levée;
    Never come, in fact, *my first:*
Nor illumine cards by dozens
    With some labyrinthine text,
Nor work smoking-caps for cousins
    Who were pounding at *my next.*

Now have skirts, and minds, grown ampler;
    Now not all they seek to do
Is create upon a sampler
    Beasts which Buffon never knew:
But their venturous muslins rustle
    O'er the cragstone and the snow,
Or at home their biceps muscle
    Grows by practising the bow.

Worthy they those dames who, fable
    Says, rode "palfreys" to the war
With some giant Thane, whose "sable
    Destrier caracoled" before;

Smiled, as—springing from the war-horse
    As men spring in modern "cirques"—
He plunged, ponderous as a four-horse
    Coach, among the vanished Turks :—

In the good times when the jester
    Asked the monarch how he was,
And the landlady addrest her
    Guests as "gossip" or as "coz";
When the Templar said, "Gramercy,"
    Or, "'Twas shrewdly thrust, i' fegs,"
To Sir Halbert or Sir Percy
    As they knocked him off his legs:

And, by way of mild reminders
    That he needed coin, the Knight
Day by day extracted grinders
    From the howling Israelite:
And *my whole* in merry Sherwood
    Sent, with preterhuman luck,
Missiles—not of steel but firwood—
    Thro' the two-mile-distant buck.

IV

EVENING threw soberer hue
    Over the blue sky, and the few
Poplars that grew just in the view
Of the Hall of Sir Hugo de Wynkle:
    "Answer me true," pleaded Sir Hugh,

(Striving some hardhearted maiden to woo,)
"What shall I do, Lady, for you?
'Twill be done, ere your eye may twinkle.
Shall I borrow the wand of a Moorish enchanter,
And bid a decanter contain the Levant, or
The brass from the face of a Mormonite ranter?
Shall I go for the mule of the Spanish Infantar—
(That *r*, for the sake of the line, we must grant her,)—
And race with the foul fiend, and beat in a canter,
Like that first of equestrians Tam o' Shanter?
I talk not mere banter—say not that I can't, or
By this *my first*—(a Virginia planter
Sold it me to kill rats)—I will die instanter."

The Lady bended her ivory neck, and
Whispered mournfully, "Go for—*my second*."
She said, and the red from Sir Hugh's cheek fled,
And "Nay," did he say, as he stalked away
    The fiercest of injured men :
"Twice have I humbled my haughty soul,
And on bended knee have I pressed *my whole*—
    But I never will press it again!"

V

ON pinnacled St. Mary's
    Lingers the setting sun;
Into the streets the blackguards
    Are skulking one by one :
Butcher and Boots and Bargeman
    Lay pipe and pewter down;
And with wild shout come tumbling out
    To join the Town and Gown.

And now the undergraduates
　　Come forth by twos and threes,
From the broad tower of Trinity,
　　From the green gate of Caius:
The wily bargeman marks them,
　　And swears to do his worst;
To turn to impotence their strength,
　　And their beauty to *my first*.

But before Corpus gateway
　　My second first arose,
When Barnacles the Freshman
　　Was pinned upon the nose:
Pinned on the nose by Boxer,
　　Who brought a hobnailed herd
From Barnwell, where he kept a van,
Being indeed a dogsmeat man,
Vendor of terriers, blue or tan,
　　And dealer in *my third*.

'Twere long to tell how Boxer
　　Was "countered" on the cheek,
And knocked into the middle
　　Of the ensuing week:
How Barnacles the Freshman
　　Was asked his name and college;
And how he did the fatal facts
　　Reluctantly acknowledge.

He called upon the Proctor
　　Next day at half-past ten;
Men whispered that the Freshman cut
　　A different figure then:—

That the brass forsook his forehead,
    The iron fled his soul,
As with blanched lip and visage wan
Before the stony-hearted Don
    He kneeled upon *my whole*.

VI

SIKES, housebreaker, of Houndsditch,
    Habitually swore;
But so surpassingly profane
    He never was before,
As on a night in winter,
    When—softly as he stole
In the dim light from stair to stair,
Noiseless as boys who in her lair
Seek to surprise a fat old hare—
He barked his shinbone, unaware
    Encountering *my whole*.

As pours the Anio plainward,
    When rains have swollen the dykes,
So, with such noise, poured down *my first*
    Stirred by the shins of Sikes.
The Butler Bibulus heard it;
    And straightway ceased to snore,
And sat up, like an egg on end,
    While men might count a score:
Then spake he to Tigerius,
    A Buttons bold was he:

" Buttons, I think there 's thieves about ;
Just strike a light and tumble out ;
If you can't find one go without,
    And see what you may see."

But now was all the household,
    Almost, upon its legs,
Each treading carefully about
    As if they trod on eggs.
With robe far-streaming issued
    Paterfamilias forth ;
And close behind him,—stout and true
    And tender as the North,—
Came Mrs. P., supporting
    On her broad arm her fourth.

Betsy the nurse, who never
    From largest beetle ran,
And—conscious p'raps of pleasing caps—
    The housemaids, formed the van :
And Bibulus the butler,
    His calm brows slightly arched ;
(No mortal wight had ere that night
    Seen him with shirt unstarched ;)
And Bob the shockhaired knifeboy,
    Wielding two Sheffield blades,
And James Plush of the sinewy legs,
    The love of lady's maids :
And charwoman and chaplain
    Stood mingled in a mass,
And " Things," thought he of Houndsditch,
    " Is come to a pretty pass."

Beyond all things a baby
  Is to the schoolgirl dear ;
Next to herself the nursemaid loves
  Her dashing grenadier ;
Only with life the sailor
  Parts from the British flag ;
While one hope lingers, the cracksman's fingers
  Drop not his hard-earned swag.

But, as hares do *my second*
  Thro' green Calabria's copses,
As females vanish at the sight
  Of short-horns and of wopses ;
So, dropping forks and teaspoons,
  The pride of Houndsditch fled,
Dumbfoundered by the hue and cry
  He'd raised up overhead.

　　*　　*　　*　　*　　*

They gave him—did the judges—
  As much as was his due.
And, Saxon, shouldst thou e'er be led
  To deem this tale untrue ;
Then—any night in winter,
  When the cold north wind blows,
And bairns are told to keep out cold
  By tallowing the nose :
When round the fire the elders
  Are gathered in a bunch,
And the girls are doing crochet,
  And the boys are reading Punch :—
Go thou and look in Leech's book ;
  There haply shalt thou spy

A stout man on a staircase stand,
With aspect anything but bland,
And rub his right shin with his hand,
        To witness if I lie.

PROVERBIAL PHILOSOPHY

Introductory

ART thou beautiful, O my daughter, as the budding rose of
        April ?
Are all thy motions music, and is poetry throned in thine eye ?
Then hearken unto me ; and I will make the bud a fair flower,
I will plant it upon the bank of Elegance, and water it with the
        water of Cologne ;
And in the season it shall " come out," yea bloom, the pride of
        the parterre ;
Ladies shall marvel at its beauty, and a Lord shall pluck it at the last.

Of Propriety

Study first Propriety : for she is indeed the Polestar
Which shall guide the artless maiden through the mazes of
        Vanity Fair ;
Nay, she is the golden chain which holdeth together Society ;
The lamp by whose light young Psyche shall approach un-
        blamed her Eros.
Verily Truth is as Eve, which was ashamed being naked ;
Wherefore doth Propriety dress her with the fair foliage of
        artifice :
And when she is drest, behold ! she knoweth not herself again.—
I walked in the Forest ; and above me stood the Yew,
Stood like a slumbering giant, shrouded in impenetrable shade ;

Then I pass'd into the citizen's garden, and marked a tree clipt
    into shape,

(The giant's locks had been shorn by the Dalilah-shears of
    Decorum ;)

And I said, " Surely Nature is goodly ; but how much goodlier
    is Art ! "

I heard the wild notes of the lark floating far over the blue sky,

And my foolish heart went after him, and, lo ! I blessed him as
    he rose ;

Foolish ! for far better is the trained boudoir bullfinch,

Which pipeth the semblance of a tune, and mechanically draw-
    eth up water :

And the reinless steed of the desert, though his neck be clothed
    with thunder,

Must yield to him that danceth and "moveth in the circles" at
    Astley's.

For verily, O my daughter, the world is a masquerade,

And God made thee one thing, that thou mightest make thy-
    self another :

A maiden's heart is as champagne, ever aspiring and struggling
    upwards,

And it needed that its motions be checked by the silvered cork
    of Propriety :

He that can afford the price, his be the precious treasure,

Let him drink deeply of its sweetness, nor grumble if it tasteth
    of the cork.

Of Friendship

Choose judiciously thy friends ; for to discard them is un-
    desirable,

Yet it is better to drop thy friends, O my daughter, than to
    drop thy H's.

Dost thou know a wise woman ? yea, wiser than the children of
    light ?

Hath she a position ? and a title ? and are her parties in the
    Morning Post ?

If thou dost, cleave unto her, and give up unto her thy body
    and mind ;

Think with her ideas, and distribute thy smiles at her bidding :

So shalt thou become like unto her ; and thy manners shall be
    " formed,"

And thy name shall be a Sesame, at which the doors of the
    great shall fly open :

Thou shalt know every Peer, his arms, and the date of his
    creation,

His pedigree and their intermarriages, and cousins to the sixth
    remove :

Thou shalt kiss the hand of Royalty, and lo ! in next morning's
    papers,

Side by side with rumours of wars, and stories of shipwrecks
    and sieges,

Shall appear thy name, and the minutiæ of thy head-dress and
    petticoat,

For an enraptured public to muse upon over their matutinal
    muffin.

Of Reading

Read not Milton, for he is dry ; nor Shakespeare, for he wrote
    of common life :

Nor Scott, for his romances, though fascinating, are yet in-
    telligible :

Nor Thackeray, for he is a Hogarth, a photographer who
    flattereth not :

E

Nor Kingsley, for he shall teach thee that thou shouldest not
    dream, but do.
Read incessantly thy Burke; that Burke who, nobler than he
    of old,
Treateth of the Peer and Peeress, the truly Sublime and
    Beautiful:
Likewise study the "creations" of "the Prince of modern
    Romance;"
Sigh over Leonard the Martyr, and smile on Pelham the
    puppy:
Learn how "love is the dram-drinking of existence;"
And how we "invoke, in the Gadara of our still closets,
The beautiful ghost of the Ideal, with the simple wand of the
    pen."
Listen how Maltravers and the orphan "forgot all but love,"
And how Devereux's family chaplain "made and unmade
    kings:"
How Eugene Aram, though a thief, a liar, and a murderer,
Yet, being intellectual, was amongst the noblest of mankind.
So shalt thou live in a world peopled with heroes and master-
    spirits;
And if thou canst not realize the Ideal, thou shalt at least
    idealize the Real.

CARMEN SÆCULARE

MDCCCLIII

"Quicquid agunt homines, nostri est farrago libelli."

ACRIS hyems jam venit: hyems genus omne perosa
    Fœmineum, et senibus glacies non æqua rotundis:
Apparent rari stantes in tramite glauco;
Radit iter, cogitque nives, sua tela, juventus

Trux matrona ruit, multos dominata per annos,
Digna indigna minans, glomeratque volumina crurum ;
Parte senex alia, præ.repto forte galero,
Per plateas bacchatur ; eum chorus omnis agrestum
Ridet anhelantem frustra, et jam jamque tenentem
Quod petit ; illud agunt venti prensumque resorbent.
Post, ubi compositus tandem votique potitus
Sedit humi ; flet crura tuens nive candida lenta,
Et vestem laceram, et venturas conjugis iras :
Itque domum tendens duplices ad sidera palmas,
Corda miser, desiderio perfixa galeri.

At juvenis (sed cruda viro viridisque juventus)
Quærit bacciferas, tunica pendente,[1] tabernas :
Pervigil ecce Baco furva depromit ab arca
Splendidius quiddam solito, plenumque saporem
Laudat, et antiqua jurat de stirpe Jamaicæ.
O fumose puer, nimium ne crede Baconi :
Manillas vocat ; hoc prætexit nomine caules.

Te vero, cui forte dedit maturior ætas
Scire potestates herbarum, te quoque quanti
Circumstent casus, paucis (adverte) docebo.
Præcipue, seu raptat amor te simplicis herbæ,[2]
Seu potius tenui Musam meditaris avena,
Procuratorem fugito, nam ferreus idem est.
Vita semiboves catulos, redimicula vita
Candida : de cœlo descendit σῶζε σεαυτόν.
Nube vaporis item conspergere præter euntes

---

[1] *tunica pendente :* h.e. "suspensa e brachio." Quod procuratoribus illis valde, ut ferunt, displicebat. Dicunt vero morem a barbaris tractum, urbem Bosporiam in fl. Iside habitantibus. *Bacciferas tabernas :* id. q. nostri vocant "tobacco-shops."

[2] *herbæ—avena.* Duo quasi genera artis poeta videtur distinguere. "Weed," "pipe," recte Scaliger.

Jura vetant, notumque furens quid femina possit :
Odit enim dulces succos anus, odit odorem ;
Odit Lethæi diffusa volumina fumi.

    Mille modis reliqui fugiuntque feruntque laborem.
Hic vir ad Eleos, pedibus talaria gestans,
Fervidus it latices, et nil acquirit eundo : [1]
Ille petit virides (sed non e gramine) mensas,
Pollicitus meliora patri, tormentaque [2] flexus
Per labyrintheos plus quam mortalia tentat,
Acre tuens, loculisque pilas immittit et aufert.

    Sunt alii, quos frigus aquæ, tenuisque phaselus
Captat, et æquali surgentes ordine remi.
His edura cutis, nec ligno rasile tergum ;
Par saxi sinus : esca boves cum robore Bassi.
Tollunt in numerum fera brachia, vique feruntur
Per fluctus : sonuere viæ clamore secundo:
At picea de puppe fremens immane bubulcus
Invocat exitium cunctis, et verbera rapto
Stipite defessis onerat graviora caballis.

    Nil humoris egent alii.   Labor arva vagari.
Flectere ludus equos, et amantem devia [3] currum.
Nosco purpureas vestes, clangentia nosco
Signa tubæ, et caudas inter virgulta caninas.
Stat venator equus, tactoque ferocior armo
Surgit in arrectum, vix auditurus habenam ;
Et jam prata fuga superat, jam flumina saltu.

---

[1] *nil acquirit eundo.* Aqua enim aspera, et radentibus parum habilis.
Immersum hic aliquem et vix aut ne vix quidem extractum refert schol.

[2] *tormenta p. q. mortalia.* Eleganter, ut solet, Peile, "unearthly
cannons." (Cf. Ainsw. D. *s. v.*) Perrecondita autem est quæstio de
lusubus illorum temporum, neque in Smithii Dict. Class. satis elucidata.
Consule omnino Kentf. de Bill. *Loculis,* bene vertas "pockets."

[3] *amantem devia.* Quorsum hoc, quærunt Interpretes. Suspicor equidem
respiciendos vv. 19—23, de procuratoribus.

Aspicias alios ab iniqua sepe rotari
In caput, ut scrobibus quæ sint fastigia quærant;
Eque rubis aut amne pigro trahere humida crura,
Et fœdam faciem, defloccatumque galerum.

Sanctius his animal, cui quadravisse rotundum[1]
Musæ suadet amor, Camique ardentis imago,
Inspicat calamos contracta fronte malignos,
Perque Mathematicum pelagus, loca turbida, anhelat.
Circum dirus " Hymers," nec pondus inutile, " Lignum,"
" Salmoque," et pueris tu detestate, " Colenso,"
Horribiles visu formæ; livente notatæ
Ungue omnes, omnes insignes aure canina.[2]
Fervet opus; tacitum pertentant gaudia pectus
Tutorum; "pulchrumque mori," dixere, "legendo."

Nec vero juvenes facere omnes omnia possunt.
Atque unum memini ipse, deus qui dictus amicis,
Et multum referens de rixatore[3] secundo,
Nocte terens ulnas ac scrinia, solus in alto
Degebat tripode; arcta viro vilisque supellex;
Et sic torva tuens, pedibus per mutua nexis,
Sedit, lacte mero mentem mulcente tenellam.
Et fors ad summos tandem venisset honores;
Sed rapidi juvenes, queis gratior usus equorum,
Subveniunt, siccoque vetant inolescere libro.
Improbus hos Lector pueros, mentumque virili
Lævius, et duræ gravat inclementia Mortis:[4]

---

[1] *quadr. rot^m.—Cami ard. im°.* Quadrando enim rotundum (Ang. "squaring the circle ") Camum accendere, juvenes ingenui semper nite-bantur. Fecisse vero quemquam non liquet.

[2] *aure canina.* Iterum audi Peile, "dog's-eared."

[3] *rixatore.* Non male Heins. cum Aldina, "wrangler."

[4] *Mortis.* Verbum generali fere sensu dictum inveni. Suspicor autem poetam virum quendam innuisse, qui currus, caballos, id genus omne, mercede non minima locaret.

Suetos (agmen iners), aliena vivere quadra,[1]
Et lituo vexare viros, calcare caballos.
Tales mane novo sæpe admiramur euntes
Torquibus in rigidis et pelle Libystidis ursæ ;
Admiramur opus[2] tunicæ, vestemque[3] sororem
Iridis, et crurum non enarrabile tegmen.
Hos inter comites implebat pocula sorbis
Infelix puer, et sese recreabat ad ignem,
"EVOE, BASSE,"[4] fremens : dum velox præterit ætas ;
Venit summa dies ; et Junior Optimus exit.

Saucius at juvenis nota intra tecta refugit,
Horrendum ridens, lucemque miserrimus odit :
Informem famulus laqueum pendentiaque ossa
Mane videt, refugitque feri meminisse magistri.

Di nobis meliora ! Modum re servat in omni
Qui sapit : haud illum semper recubare sub umbra,
Haud semper madidis juvat impallescere chartis.
Nos numerus sumus, et libros consumere nati ;
Sed requies sit rebus ; amant alterna Camenæ.
Nocte dieque legas, cum tertius advenit annus :
Tum libros cape ; claude fores, et prandia defer.
Quartus venit : ini,[5] rebus jam rite paratis,

---

[1] *aliena quadra.* Sunt qui de pileis Academicis accipiunt. Rapidiores enim suas fere amittebant. Sed judicet sibi lector.

[2] *opus tunicæ,* "shirt-work." Alii *opes.* Perperam.

[3] *vestem.* Nota proprietatem verbi. "Vest," enim apud politos id. q. vulgo "waistcoat" appellatur. Quod et feminæ usurpabant, ut hodiernæ, fibula revinctum, teste Virgilio :
"crines nodantur in aurum,
Aurea purpuream subnectit fibula vestem."

[4] *Basse.* cft. Interpretes illud Horatianum, "Bassum Threicia vincat amystide." Non perspexere viri docti alterum hic alludi, Anglicanæ originis, neque illum, ut perhibent, a potu aversum.

[5] *ini.* Sic nostri, "Go in and win." *rebus,* "subjects."

Exultans, et coge gradum conferre magistros.

His animadversis, fugies immane Barathrum.

His, operose puer, si qua fata aspera rumpas,

Tu rixator eris.   Saltem non crebra revises

Ad stabulum,[1] et tota mœrens carpere juventa ;

Classe nec amisso nil profectura dolentem

Tradet ludibriis te plena leporis Hirudo.[2]

---

[1] *crebra r. a. stabulum.*   " Turn up year after year at the old diggings, (*i.e.*, the Senate House,) and be plucked," etc., Peile.   Quo quid jejunius ?

[2] *Classe—Hirudo.*   Obscurior allusio ad picturam quandam (in collectione viri, vel plusquam viri, Punchii repositam,) in qua juvenis custodem stationis mœrens alloquitur.

FLY LEAVES

MORNING

'TIS the hour when white-horsed Day
    Chases Night her mares away ;
When the Gates of Dawn (they say)
      Phœbus opes :
And I gather that the Queen
May be uniformly seen,
Should the weather be serene,
      On the slopes.

When the ploughman, as he goes
Leathern-gaitered o'er the snows,
From his hat and from his nose
      Knocks the ice ;
And the panes are frosted o'er
And the lawn is crisp and hoar,
As has been observed before
      Once or twice.

When arrayed in breastplate red
Sings the robin, for his bread,
On the elmtree that hath shed
      Every leaf ;

While, within, the frost benumbs
The still sleepy schoolboy's thumbs,
And in consequence his sums
    Come to grief.

But when breakfast-time hath come,
And he's crunching crust and crumb,
He'll no longer look a glum
    Little dunce;
But be brisk as bees that settle
On a summer rose's petal :
Wherefore, Polly, put the kettle
    On at once.

EVENING

KATE ! if e'er thy light foot lingers
    On the lawn, when up the fells
Steals the Dark, and fairy fingers
    Close unseen the pimpernels :
When, his thighs with sweetness laden,
    From the meadow comes the bee,
And the lover and the maiden
    Stand beneath the trysting tree :—

Lingers on, till stars unnumber'd
    Tremble in the breeze-swept tarn,
And the bat that all day slumber'd
    Flits about the lonely barn ;
And the shapes that shrink from garish
    Noon are peopling cairn and lea ;

And thy sire is almost bearish
    If kept waiting for his tea :—

And the screech-owl scares the peasant
    As he skirts some churchyard drear ;
And the goblins whisper pleasant
    Tales in Miss Rossetti's ear ;
Importuning her in strangest,
    Sweetest tones to buy their fruits :—
O be careful that thou changest,
    On returning home, thy boots.

SHELTER

BY the wide lake's margin I mark'd her lie—
    The wide, weird lake where the alders sigh—
A young fair thing, with a shy, soft eye ;
    And I deem'd that her thoughts had flown
To her home, and her brethren, and sisters dear,
As she lay there watching the dark, deep mere,
    All motionless, all alone.

Then I heard a noise, as of men and boys,
    And a boisterous troop drew nigh.
Whither now will retreat those fairy feet ?
    Where hide till the storm pass by ?
One glance—the wild glance of a hunted thing—
She cast behind her ; she gave one spring ;
And there follow'd a splash and a broadening ring
    On the lake where the alders sigh.

She had gone from the ken of ungentle men !
    Yet scarce did I mourn for that ;
For I knew she was safe in her own home then,
And, the danger past, would appear again,
    For she was a water-rat.

IN THE GLOAMING

IN the Gloaming to be roaming, where the crested waves are
    foaming,
    And the shy mermaidens combing locks that ripple to their
      feet ;
When the Gloaming is, I never made the ghost of an endeavour
    To discover—but whatever were the hour, it would be sweet.

" To their feet," I say, for Leech's sketch indisputably teaches
    That the mermaids of our beaches do not end in ugly tails,
Nor have homes among the corals ; but are shod with neat
    balmorals,
    An arrangement no one quarrels with, as many might with
      scales.

Sweet to roam beneath a shady cliff, of course with some young
    lady,
    Lalage, Neæra, Haidee, or Elaine, or Mary Ann :
Love, you dear delusive dream, you ! Very sweet your victims
    deem you,
    When, heard only by the seamew, they talk all the stuff one can.

Sweet to haste, a licensed lover, to Miss Pinkerton the glover,
    Having managed to discover what is dear Neæra's "size " :
P'raps to touch that wrist so slender, as your tiny gift you tender,
    And to read you're no offender, in those laughing hazel eyes.

Then to hear her call you "Harry," when she makes you fetch
    and carry—
  O young men about to marry, what a blessed thing it is !
To be photograph'd—together—cased in pretty Russia leather—
  Hear her gravely doubting whether they have spoilt your
    honest phiz !

Then to bring your plighted fair one first a ring—a rich and
    rare one—
  Next a bracelet, if she'll wear one, and a heap of things beside ;
And serenely bending o'er her, to inquire if it would bore her
  To say when her own adorer may aspire to call her bride !

Then, the days of courtship over, with your WIFE to start for
    Dover
  Or Dieppe—and live in clover evermore, whate'er befalls :
For I've read in many a novel that, unless they've souls that
    grovel,
  Folks *prefer* in fact a hovel to your dreary marble halls :

To sit, happy married lovers ; Phillis trifling with a plover's
  Egg, while Corydon uncovers with a grace the Sally Lunn,
Or dissects the lucky pheasant—that, I think, were passing
    pleasant ;
  As I sit alone at present, dreaming darkly of a Dun.

THE PALACE

THEY come, they come, with fife and drum,
　　And gleaming pikes and glancing banners :
Though the eyes flash, the lips are dumb ;
　　To talk in rank would not be manners.
Onward they stride, as Britons can ;
The ladies following in the Van.

Who, who be these that tramp in threes
　　Through sumptuous Piccadilly, through
The roaring Strand, and stand at ease
　　At last 'neath shadowy Waterloo ?
Some gallant Guild, I ween, are they ;
Taking their annual holiday.

To catch the destin'd train—to pay
　　Their willing fares, and plunge within it—
Is, as in old Romaunt they say,
　　With them the work of half-a-minute.
Then off they're whirl'd, with songs and shouting,
To cedared Sydenham for their outing.

I mark'd them light, with faces bright
　　As pansies or a new coin'd florin,
And up the sunless stair take flight,
　　Close-pack'd as rabbits in a warren.
Honour the Brave, who in that stress
Still trod not upon Beauty's dress !

Kerchief in hand I saw them stand ;
　　In every kerchief lurk'd a lunch ;

When they unfurl'd them, it was grand
   To watch bronzed men and maidens crunch
The sounding celery-stick, or ram
The knife into the blushing ham.

Dash'd the bold fork through pies of pork ;
   O'er hard-boil'd eggs the saltspoon shook ;
Leapt from its lair the playful cork :
   Yet some there were, to whom the brook
Seem'd sweetest beverage, and for meat
They chose the red root of the beet.

Then many a song, some rather long,
   Came quivering up from girlish throats ;
And one young man he came out strong,
   And gave "The Wolf" without his notes.
While they who knew not song or ballad
Still munch'd, approvingly, their salad.

But ah ! what bard could sing how hard,
   The artless banquet o'er, they ran
Down the soft slope with daisies starr'd
   And kingcups ! onward, maid with man,
They flew, to scale the breezy swing,
Or court frank kisses in the ring.

Such are the sylvan scenes that thrill
   This heart ! The lawns, the happy shade,
Where matrons, whom the sunbeams grill,
   Stir with slow spoon their lemonade ;
And maidens flirt (no extra charge)
In comfort at the fountain's marge !

Others may praise the "grand displays"
   Where "fiery arch," "cascade," and "comet,"

Set the whole garden in a "blaze"!
   Far, at such times, may I be from it;
Though then the public may be "lost
In wonder" at a trifling cost.

Fann'd by the breeze, to puff at ease
   My faithful pipe is all I crave:
And if folks rave about the "trees
   Lit up by fireworks," let them rave.
Your monster fêtes, I like not these;
Though they bring grist to the lessees.

PEACE

A STUDY

HE stood, a worn-out City clerk—
   Who'd toil'd, and seen no holiday,
For forty years from dawn to dark—
   Alone beside Caermarthen Bay.

He felt the salt spray on his lips;
   Heard children's voices on the sands;
Up the sun's path he saw the ships
   Sail on and on to other lands;

And laugh'd aloud.   Each sight and sound
   To him was joy too deep for tears;
He sat him on the beach, and bound
   A blue bandana round his ears,

And thought how, posted near his door,
   His own green door on Camden Hill,

Two bands at least, most likely more,
    Were mingling at their own sweet will

Verdi with Vance. And at the thought
    He laugh'd again, and softly drew
That Morning Herald that he'd bought
    Forth from his breast, and read it through.

THE ARAB

ON, on, my brown Arab, away, away!
    Thou hast trotted o'er many a mile to-day,
And I trow right meagre hath been thy fare
Since they roused thee at dawn from thy straw-piled lair,
To tread with those echoless unshod feet
Yon weltering flats in the noontide heat,
Where no palmtree proffers a kindly shade
And the eye never rests on a cool grass blade;
And lank is thy flank, and thy frequent cough
Oh! it goes to my heart—but away, friend, off!

And yet, ah! what sculptor who saw thee stand,
As thou standest now, on thy Native Strand,
With the wild wind ruffling thine uncomb'd hair,
And thy nostril upturn'd to the od'rous air,
Would not woo thee to pause till his skill might trace
At leisure the lines of that eager face;
The collarless neck and the coal-black paws
And the bit grasp'd tight in the massive jaws;
The delicate curve of the legs, that seem
Too slight for their burden—and, O, the gleam

Of that eye, so sombre and yet so gay!
Still away, my lithe Arab, once more away!

Nay, tempt me not, Arab, again to stay;
Since I crave neither Echo nor Fun to-day.
For thy *hand* is not Echoless—there they are—
Fun, Glowworm, and Echo, and Evening Star:
And thou hintest withal that thou fain would'st shine,
As I con them, these bulgy old boots of mine.
But I shrink from thee, Arab! Thou eat'st eel-pie,
Thou evermore hast at least one black eye;
There is brass on thy brow, and thy swarthy hues
Are due not to nature but handling shoes;
And the bit in thy mouth, I regret to see,
Is a bit of tobacco-pipe—Flee, child, flee!

LINES ON HEARING THE ORGAN

GRINDER, who serenely grindest
    At my door the Hundredth Psalm,
Till thou ultimately findest
    Pence in thy unwashen palm:

Grinder, jocund-hearted Grinder,
    Near whom Barbary's nimble son,
Poised with skill upon his hinder
    Paws, accepts the proffered bun:

Dearly do I love thy grinding;
    Joy to meet thee on thy road
Where thou prowlest through the blinding
    Dust with that stupendous load,

F

'Neath the baleful star of Sirius,
   When the postmen slowlier jog,
And the ox becomes delirious,
   And the muzzle decks the dog.

Tell me by what art thou bindest
   On thy feet those ancient shoon :
Tell me, Grinder, if thou grindest
   Always, always out of tune.

Tell me if, as thou art buckling
   On thy straps with eager claws,
Thou forecastest, inly chuckling,
   All the rage that thou wilt cause.

Tell me if at all thou mindest
   When folks flee, as if on wings,
From thee as at ease thou grindest :
   Tell me fifty thousand things.

Grinder, gentle-hearted Grinder !
   Ruffians who lead evil lives,
Soothed by thy sweet strains, are kinder
   To their bullocks and their wives :

Children, when they see thy supple
   Form approach, are out like shots ;
Half-a-bar sets several couple
   Waltzing in convenient spots ;

Not with clumsy Jacks or Georges :
   Unprofaned by grasp of man

Maidens speed those simple orgies,
　　Betsey Jane with Betsey Ann.

As they love thee in St. Giles's
　　Thou art loved in Grosvenor Square:
None of those engaging smiles is
　　Unreciprocated there.

Often, ere yet thou hast hammer'd
　　Through thy four delicious airs,
Coins are flung thee by enamour'd
　　Housemaids upon area stairs:

E'en the ambrosial-whisker'd flunkey
　　Eyes thy boots and thine unkempt
Beard and melancholy monkey
　　More in pity than contempt.

Far from England, in the sunny
　　South, where Anio leaps in foam,
Thou wast rear'd, till lack of money
　　Drew thee from thy vineclad home:

And thy mate, the sinewy Jocko,
　　From Brazil or Afric came,
Land of simoom and sirocco—
　　And he seems extremely tame.

There he quaff'd the undefilèd
　　Spring, or hung with apelike glee,
By his teeth or tail or eyelid,
　　To the slippery mango-tree:

There he woo'd and won a dusky
   Bride, of instincts like his own ;
Talk'd of love till he was husky
   In a tongue to us unknown :

Side by side 'twas theirs to ravage
   The potato ground, or cut
Down the unsuspecting savage
   With the well-aim'd cocoa-nut :—

Till the miscreant Stranger tore him
   Screaming from his blue-faced fair ;
And they flung strange raiment o'er him,
   Raiment which he could not bear :

Sever'd from the pure embraces
   Of his children and his spouse,
He must ride fantastic races
   Mounted on reluctant sows :

But the heart of wistful Jocko
   Still was with his ancient flame
In the nutgroves of Morocco ;
   Or if not it 's all the same.

Grinder, winsome grinsome Grinder !
   They who see thee and whose soul
Melts not at thy charms, are blinder
   Than a trebly-bandaged mole :

They to whom thy curt (yet clever)
   Talk, thy music and thine ape,

Seem not to be joys for ever,
   Are but brutes in human shape.

'Tis not that thy mien is stately,
   'Tis not that thy tones are soft;
'Tis not that I care so greatly
   For the same thing play'd so oft:

But I've heard mankind abuse thee;
   And perhaps it's rather strange,
But I thought that I would choose thee
   For encomium, as a change.

CHANGED

I KNOW not why my soul is rack'd:
   Why I ne'er smile as was my wont:
I only know that, as a fact,
   I don't.
I used to roam o'er glen and glade
   Buoyant and blithe as other folk:
And not unfrequently I made
   A joke.

A minstrel's fire within me burn'd.
   I'd sing, as one whose heart must break,
Lay upon lay: I nearly learn'd
   To shake.
All day I sang; of love, of fame,
   Of fights our fathers fought of yore,
Until the thing almost became
   A bore.

I cannot sing the old songs now !
　It is not that I deem them low ;
'Tis that I can't remember how
　　　They go.
I could not range the hills till high
　Above me stood the summer moon :
And as to dancing, I could fly
　　　As soon.

The sports, to which with boyish glee
　I sprang erewhile, attract no more ;
Although I am but sixty-three
　　　Or four.
Nay, worse than that, I've seem'd of late
　To shrink from happy boyhood—boys
Have grown so noisy, and I hate
　　　A noise.

They fright me, when the beech is green,
　By swarming up its stem for eggs :
They drive their horrid hoops between
　　　My legs :—
It 's idle to repine, I know ;
　I'll tell you what I'll do instead :
I'll drink my arrowroot, and go
　　　To bed.

FIRST LOVE

O MY earliest love, who, ere I number'd
　Ten sweet summers, made my bosom thrill !
Will a swallow—or a swift, or some bird—
　Fly to her and say, I love her still ?

Say my life's a desert drear and arid,
　　To its one green spot I aye recur :
Never, never—although three times married—
　　Have I cared a jot for aught but her.

No, mine own ! though early forced to leave you,
　　Still my heart was there where first we met ;
In those " Lodgings with an ample sea-view,"
　　Which were, forty years ago, "To Let."

There I saw her first, our landlord's oldest
　　Little daughter.　On a thing so fair
Thou, O Sun,—who (so they say) beholdest
　　Everything,—hast gazed, I tell thee, ne'er.

There she sat—so near me, yet remoter
　　Than a star—a blue-eyed bashful imp :
On her lap she held a happy bloater,
　　'Twixt her lips a yet more happy shrimp.

And I loved her, and our troth we plighted
　　On the morrow by the shingly shore :
In a fortnight to be disunited
　　By a bitter fate for evermore.

O my own, my beautiful, my blue-eyed !
　　To be young once more, and bite my thumb
At the world and all its cares with you, I'd
　　Give no inconsiderable sum.

Hand in hand we tramp'd the golden seaweed,
　　Soon as o'er the gray cliff peep'd the dawn :

Side by side, when came the hour for tea, we'd
  Crunch the mottled shrimp and hairy prawn :—

Has she wedded some gigantic shrimper,
  That sweet mite with whom I loved to play?
Is she girt with babes that whine and whimper,
  That bright being who was always gay?

Yes—she has at least a dozen wee things !
  Yes—I see her darning corduroys,
Scouring floors, and setting out the tea-things,
  For a howling herd of hungry boys,

In a home that reeks of tar and sperm-oil !
  But at intervals she thinks, I know,
Of those days which we, afar from turmoil,
  Spent together forty years ago.

O my earliest love, still unforgotten,
  With your downcast eyes of dreamy blue !
Never, somehow, could I seem to cotton
  To another as I did to you !

WANDERERS

AS o'er the hill we roam'd at will,
    My dog and I together,
We mark'd a chaise, by two bright bays
  Slow-moved along the heather :

Two bays arch neck'd, with tails erect
  And gold upon their blinkers ;

And by their side an ass I spied;
    It was a travelling tinker's.

The chaise went by, nor aught cared I;
    Such things are not in my way;
I turn'd me to the tinker, who
    Was loafing down a by-way:

I ask'd him where he lived—a stare
    Was all I got in answer,
As on he trudged : I rightly judged
    The stare said, "Where I can, sir."

I ask'd him if he'd take a whiff
    Of 'bacco; he acceded;
He grew communicative too,
    (A pipe was all he needed,)
Till of the tinker's life, I think,
    I knew as much as he did.

"I loiter down by thorp and town,
    For any job I'm willing;
Take here and three a dusty brown,
    And here and there a shilling.

"I deal in every ware in turn,
    I've rings for buddin' Sally
That sparkle like those eyes of her'n;
    I've liquor for the valet.

"I steal from th' parson's strawberry-plots,
    I hide by th' squire's covers;
I teach the sweet young housemaids what's
    The art of trapping lovers.

"The things I've done 'neath moon and stars
    Have got me into messes :

I've seen the sky through prison bars,
   I've torn up prison dresses:

" I've sat, I've sigh'd, I've gloom'd, I've glanced
   With envy at the swallows
That through the window slid, and danced
   (Quite happy) round the gallows;

" But out again I come, and show
   My face nor care a stiver
For trades are brisk and trades are slow,
   But mine goes on for ever."

Thus on he prattled like a babbling brook.
Then I, " The sun hath slipt behind the hill,
And my aunt Vivian dines at half-past six."
So in all love we parted; I to the Hall,
They to the village.   It was noised next noon
That chickens had been miss'd at Syllabub Farm.

SAD MEMORIES

THEY tell me I am beautiful: they praise my silken
     hair,
My little feet that silently slip on from stair to stair:
They praise my pretty trustful face and innocent gray eye;
Fond hands caress me oftentimes, yet would that I might die!

Why was I born to be abhorr'd of man and bird and beast?
The bullfinch marks me stealing by, and straight his song hath
     ceased;
The shrewmouse eyes me shudderingly, then flees; and, worse
     than that,
The housedog he flees after me—why was I born a cat?

Men prize the heartless hound who quits dried-eyed his native
land ;
Who wags a mercenary tail and licks a tyrant hand.
The leal true cat they prize not, that if e'er compell'd to roam
Still flies, when let out of the bag, precipitately home.

They call me cruel. Do I know if mouse or song-bird feels ?
I only know they make me light and salutary meals :
And if, as 'tis my nature to, ere I devour I tease 'em,
Why should a low-bred gardener's boy pursue me with a besom ?

Should china fall or chandeliers, or anything but stocks—
Nay stocks, when they're in flowerpots—the cat expects hard
knocks :
Should ever anything be missed—milk, coals, umbrellas,
brandy—
The cat's pitched into with a boot or any thing that's handy.

"I remember, I remember," how one night I "fleeted by,"
And gain'd the blessed tiles and gazed into the cold clear sky.
"I remember, I remember, how my little lovers came ; "
And there, beneath the crescent moon, play'd many a little game.

They fought—by good St. Catharine, 'twas a fearsome sight to see
The coal-black crest, the glowering orbs, of one gigantic He.
Like bow by some tall bowman bent at Hastings or Poictiers,
His huge back curved, till none observed a vestige of his ears :

He stood, an ebon crescent, flouting that ivory moon ;
Then raised the pibroch of his race, the Song without a Tune ;
Gleam'd his white teeth, his mammoth tail waved darkly to and
fro,
As with one complex yell he burst, all claws, upon the foe.

It thrills me now, that final Miaow—that wierd unearthly din :
Lone maidens heard it far away, and leap'd out of their skin.
A potboy from his den o'erhead peep'd with a scared wan face;
Then sent a random brickbat down, which knock'd me into space.

Nine days I fell, or thereabouts : and, had we not nine lives,
I wis I ne'er had seen again thy sausage-shop, St. Ives !
Had I, as some cats have, nine tails, how gladly I would lick
The hand, and person generally, of him who heaved that brick !

For me they fill the milkbowl up, and cull the choice sardine :
But ah ! I nevermore shall be the cat I once have been !
The memories of that fatal night they haunt me even now :
In dreams I see that rampant He, and tremble at that Miaow.

COMPANIONS

A TALE OF A GRANDFATHER
By the Author of "Dewy Memories," &c.

I KNOW not of what we ponder'd
    Or made pretty pretence to talk,
As, her hand within mine, we wander'd
    Tow'rd the pool by the limetree walk,
While the dew fell in showers from the passion flowers
    And the blush-rose bent on her stalk.

I cannot recall her figure :
    Was it regal as Juno's own ?
Or only a trifle bigger
    Than the elves who surround the throne
Of the Faëry Queen, and are seen, I ween,
    By mortals in dreams alone ?

What her eyes were like, I know not :
    Perhaps they were blurr'd with tears ;
And perhaps in your skies there glow not
    (On the contrary) clearer spheres.
No ! as to her eyes I am just as wise
    As you or the cat, my dears.

Her teeth, I presume, were "pearly" :
    But which was she, brunette or blonde ?
Her hair, was it quaintly curly,
    Or as straight as a beadle's wand ?
That I fail'd to remark ;—it was rather dark
    And shadowy round the pond.

Then the hand that reposed so snugly
    In mine—was it plump or spare ?
Was the countenance fair or ugly ?
    Nay, children, you have me there !
My eyes were p'raps blurr'd ; and besides I'd heard
    That it's horribly rude to stare.

And I—was I brusque and surly ?
    Or oppressively bland and fond ?
Was I partial to rising early ?
    Or why did we twain abscond,
All breakfastless too, from the public view
    To prowl by a misty pond ?

What pass'd, what was felt or spoken—
    Whether anything pass'd at all—
And whether the heart was broken
    That beat under that shelt'ring shawl—
(If shawl she had on, which I doubt)—has gone,
    Yes, gone from me past recall.

Was I haply the lady's suitor?
  Or her uncle? I can't make out—
Ask your governess, dears, or tutor.
  For myself, I'm in hopeless doubt
As to why we were there, who on earth we were,
  And what this is all about.

BALLAD

THE auld wife sat at her ivied door,
  (*Butter and eggs and a pound of cheese*)
A thing she had frequently done before;
  And her spectacles lay on her apron'd knees.

The piper he piped on the hill-top high,
  (*Butter and eggs and a pound of cheese*)
Till the cow said "I die," and the goose ask'd "Why?"
  And the dog said nothing, but search'd for fleas.

The farmer he strode through the square farmyard;
  (*Butter and eggs and a pound of cheese*)
His last brew of ale was a trifle hard—
  The connexion of which with the plot one sees.

The farmer's daughter hath frank blue eyes;
  (*Butter and eggs and a pound of cheese*)
She hears the rooks caw in the windy skies,
  As she sits at her lattice and shells her peas.

The farmer's daughter hath ripe red lips;
  (*Butter and eggs and a pound of cheese*)
If you try to approach her, away she skips
  Over tables and chairs with apparent ease.

The farmer's daughter hath soft brown hair
  (*Butter and eggs and a pound of cheese*)
And I met with a ballad, I can't say where,
  Which wholly consisted of lines like these.

Part II

She sat with her hands 'neath her dimpled cheeks,
  (*Butter and eggs and a pound of cheese*)
And spake not a word.   While a lady speaks
  There is hope, but she didn't even sneeze.

She sat, with her hands 'neath her crimson cheeks;
  (*Butter and eggs and a pound of cheese*)
She gave up mending her father's breeks,
  And let the cat roll in her new chemise.

She sat, with her hands 'neath her burning cheeks,
  (*Butter and eggs and a pound of cheese*)
And gazed at the piper for thirteen weeks;
  Then she follow'd him out o'er the misty leas.

Her sheep follow'd her, as their tails did them.
  (*Butter and eggs and a pound of cheese*)
And this song is consider'd a perfect gem,
  And as to the meaning, it's what you please.

PRECIOUS STONES

AN INCIDENT IN MODERN HISTORY

MY Cherrystones! I prize them,
    No tongue can tell how much!
Each lady caller eyes them,
    And madly longs to touch!
At eve I lift them down, I look
    Upon them, and I cry;
Recalling how my Prince "partook"
    (Sweet word!) of cherry-pie!

To me it was an Era
    In life, that Dejeuner!
They ate, they sipp'd Madeira
    Much in the usual way.
Many a soft item there would be,
    No doubt, upon the carte:
But one made life a heaven to me:
    It was the cherry-tart.

Lightly the spoonfuls enter'd
    That mouth on which the gaze
Of ten fair girls was centred
    In rapturous amaze.
Soon that august assemblage clear'd
    The dish; and—as they ate—
The stones, all coyly, re-appear'd
    On each illustrious plate.

And when His Royal Highness
    Withdrew to take the air,

Waiving our natural shyness,
   We swoop'd upon his chair.
Policemen at our garments clutch'd :
   We mock'd those feeble powers ;
And soon the treasures that had touch'd
   Exalted lips were ours !

One large one—at the moment
   It seem'd almost divine—
Was got by that Miss Beaumont :
   And three, O three, are mine !
Yes ! the three stones that rest beneath
   Glass, on that plain deal shelf,
Stranger, once dallied with the teeth
   Of Royalty itself.

Let Parliament abolish
   Churches and States and Thrones :
With reverent hand I'll polish
   Still, still my Cherrystones !
A clod—a piece of orange-peel—
   An end of a cigar—
Once trod on by a Princely heel,
   How beautiful they are !

Years since, I climb'd Saint Michael
   His Mount :—you'll all go there
Of course, and those who like'll
   Sit in Saint Michael's Chair :
For there I saw, within a frame,
   The pen—O heavens ! the pen—
With which a Duke had signed his name,
   And other gentlemen.

G

" Great among geese," I faltered,
  " Is she who grew that quill ! "
And, Deathless Bird, unalter'd
  Is mine opinion still.
Yet sometimes, as I view my three
  Stones with a thoughtful brow,
I think there possibly might be
  E'en greater geese than thou.

DISASTER

'TWAS ever thus from childhood's hour !
  My fondest hopes would not decay :
I never loved a tree or flower
  Which was the first to fade away !
The garden, where I used to delve
  Short-frock'd, still yields me pinks in plenty :
The peartree that I climb'd at twelve
  I see still blossoming, at twenty.

I never nursed a dear gazelle ;
  But I was given a parroquet—
(How I did nurse him if unwell !)
  He 's imbecile, but lingers yet.
He 's green, with an enchanting tuft ;
  He melts me with his small black eye :
He'd look inimitable stuff'd,
  And knows it—but he will not die !

I had a kitten—I was rich
  In pets—but all too soon my kitten
Became a full-sized cat, by which
  I 've more than once been scratch'd and bitten.

And when for sleep her limbs she curl'd
  One day beside her untouch'd plateful,
And glided calmly from the world,
  I freely own that I was grateful.

And then I bought a dog—a queen!
  Ah Tiny, dear departing pug!
She lives, but she is past sixteen
  And scarce can crawl across the rug.
I loved her beautiful and kind;
  Delighted in her pert Bow-wow:
But now she snaps if you don't mind;
  'Twere lunacy to love her now.

I used to think, should e'er mishap
  Betide my crumple-visaged Ti,
In shape of prowling thief, or trap,
  Or coarse bull-terrier—I should die.
But ah! disasters have their use;
  And life might e'en be too sunshiny:
Nor would I make myself a goose,
  If some big dog should swallow Tiny.

CONTENTMENT

AFTER THE MANNER OF HORACE

FRIEND, there be they on whom mishap
  Or never or so rarely comes,
That, when they think thereof, they snap
  Derisive thumbs:

And there be they who lightly lose
   Their all, yet feel no aching void;
Should aught annoy them, they refuse
   To be annoy'd :

And fain would I be e'en as these !
   Life is with such all beer and skittles ;
They are not difficult to please
   About their victuals :

The trout, the grouse, the early pea,
   By such, if there, are freely taken ;
If not, they munch with equal glee
   Their bit of bacon :

And when they wax a little gay
   And chaff the public after luncheon,
If they're confronted with a stray
   Policeman's truncheon,

They gaze thereat with outstretch'd necks,
   And laughter which no threats can smother,
And tell the horror-stricken X
   That he's another.

In snowtime if they cross a spot
   Where unsuspected boys have slid,
They fall not down—though they would not
   Mind if they did :

When the spring rosebud which they wear
   Breaks short and tumbles from its stem,
No thought of being angry e'er
   Dawns upon them ;

Though 'twas Jemima's hand that placed,
    (As well you ween) at evening's hour,
In the loved button-hole that chaste
    And cherish'd flower.

And when they travel, if they find
    That they have left their pocket-compass
Or Murray or thick boots behind,
    They raise no rumpus,

But plod serenely on without:
    Knowing it's better to endure
The evil which beyond all doubt
    You cannot cure.

When for that early train they're late,
    They do not make their woes the text
Of sermons in the Times, but wait
    On for the next;

And jump inside, and only grin
    Should it appear that that dry wag,
The guard, omitted to put in
    Their carpet-bag.

THE SCHOOLMASTER

ABROAD WITH HIS SON

O WHAT harper could worthily harp it,
    Mine Edward! this wide-stretching wold
(Look out *wold*) with its wonderful carpet
    Of emerald, purple, and gold!

Look well at it—also look sharp, it
    Is getting so cold.

The purple is heather (*erica*) ;
    The yellow, gorse—call'd sometimes "whin."
Cruel boys on its prickles might spike a
    Green beetle as if on a pin.
You may roll in it, if you would like a
    Few holes in your skin.

You wouldn't ? Then think of how kind you
    Should be to the insects who crave
Your compassion—and then, look behind you
    At yon barley-ears ! Don't they look brave
As they undulate (*undulate*, mind you,
    From *unda, a wave*).

The noise of those sheep-bells, how faint it
    Sounds here—(on account of our height) !
And this hillock itself—who could paint it,
    With its changes of shadow and light ?
Is it not—(never, Eddy, say "ain't it")—
    A marvellous sight ?

Then yon desolate eerie morasses,
    The haunts of the snipe and the hern—
(I shall question the two upper classes
    On *aquatiles*, when we return)—
Why, I see on them absolute masses
    Of *filix* or fern.

How it interests e'en a beginner
    (Or *tiro*) like dear little Ned !

Is he listening?   As I am a sinner
  He's asleep—he is wagging his head.
Wake up! I'll go home to my dinner,
    And you to your bed.

The boundless ineffable prairie;
  The splendour of mountain and lake
With their hues that seem ever to vary;
  The mighty pine-forests which shake
In the wind, and in which the unwary
    May tread on a snake;

And this wold with its heathery garment
  Are themes undeniably great.
But—although there is not any harm in't—
  It's perhaps little good to dilate
On their charms to a dull little varmint
    Of seven or eight.

ARCADES AMBO

WHY are ye wandering aye 'twixt porch and porch,
  Thou and thy fellow—when the pale stars fade
At dawn, and when the glowworm lights her torch,
  O Beadle of the Burlington Arcade?
  —Who asketh why the Beautiful was made?
A wan cloud drifting o'er the waste of blue,
  The thistledown that floats above the glade,
The lilac-blooms of April—fair to view,
And naught but fair are these; and such, I ween, are you.

Yes, ye are beautiful.   The young street boys
   Joy in your beauty.   Are ye there to bar
Their pathway to that paradise of toys,
   Ribbons and rings?   Who'll blame ye if ye are?
   Surely no shrill and clattering crowd should mar
The dim aisle's stillness, where in noon's midglow
   Trip fair-hair'd girls to boot-shop or bazaar;
Where, at soft eve, serenely to and fro
The sweet boy-graduates walk, nor deem the pastime slow.

And O ! forgive me, Beadles, if I paid
   Scant tribute to your worth, when first ye stood
Before me robed in broadcloth and brocade
   And all the nameless grace of Beadlehood !
   I would not smile at ye—if smile I could
Now as erewhile, ere I had learn'd to sigh:
   Ah, no ! I know ye beautiful and good,
And evermore will pause as I pass by,
And gaze, and gazing think, how base a thing am I.

WAITING.

" O COME, O come," the mother pray'd
   And hush'd her babe: "let me behold
Once more thy stately form array'd
   Like autumn woods in green and gold !

"I see thy brethren come and go ;
   Thy peers in stature, and in hue
Thy rivals.   Some like monarchs glow
   With richest purple : some are blue

As skies that tempt the swallow back ;
　Or red as, seen o'er wintry seas,
The star of storm ; or barr'd with black
　And yellow, like the April bees.

" Come they and go ! I heed not, I.
　Yet others hail their advent, cling
All trustful to their side, and fly
　Safe in their gentle piloting

" To happy homes on heath or hill,
　By park or river.　Still I wait
And peer into the darkness : still
　Thou com'st not—I am desolate.

" Hush ! hark ! I see a towering form !
　From the dim distance slowly roll'd
It rocks like lilies in a storm,
　And O, its hues are green and gold :

" It comes, it comes !　Ah rest is sweet,
　And there is rest, my babe, for us ! "
She ceased, as at her very feet
　Stopp'd the St. John's Wood omnibus.

PLAY

PLAY, play, while as yet it is day :
　While the sweet sunlight is warm on the brae !
Hark to the lark singing lay upon lay,
While the brown squirrel eats nuts on the spray,

And in the apple-leaves chatters the jay !
Play, play, even as they !
What though the cowslips ye pluck will decay,
What though the grass will be presently hay ?
What though the noise that ye make should dismay
Old Mrs. Clutterbuck over the way ?
Play, play, for your locks will grow gray ;
Even the marbles ye sport with are clay.

Play, ay in the crowded highway :
Was it not made for you ?   Yea, my lad, yea.
True that the babes you were bid to convey
Home may fall out or be stolen or stray ;
True that the tip-cat you toss about may
Strike an old gentleman, cause him to sway,
Stumble, and p'raps be run o'er by a dray :
Still why delay ?   Play, my son, play !
Barclay and Perkins, not you, have to pay.

Play, play, your sonatas in A,
Heedless of what your next neighbour may say !
Dance and be gay as a faun or a fay,
Sing like the lad in the boat on the bay ;
Sing, play—if your neighbours inveigh
Feebly against you, they're lunatics, eh ?
Bang, twang, clatter and clang,
Strum, thrum, upon fiddle and drum ;
Neigh, bray, simply obey
All your sweet impulses, stop not or stay !
Rattle the " bones," hit a tinbottom'd tray
Hard with the fireshovel, hammer away !
Is not your neighbour your natural prey ?
Should he confound you, it 's only in play.

LOVE

CANST thou love me, lady?
  I've not learn'd to woo :
Thou art on the shady
  Side of sixty too.
Still I love thee dearly !
  Thou hast lands and pelf :
But I love thee merely
  Merely for thyself.

Wilt thou love me, fairest?
  Though thou art not fair ;
And I think thou wearest
  Someone-else's hair.
Thou could'st love, though, dearly :
  And, as I am told,
Thou art very nearly
  Worth thy weight, in gold.

Dost thou love me, sweet one?
  Tell me that thou dost !
Women fairly beat one,
  But I think thou must.
Thou art loved so dearly :
  I am plain, but then
Thou (to speak sincerely)
  Art as plain again.

Love me, bashful fairy !
  I've an empty purse :

And I've " moods," which vary ;
  Mostly for the worst.
Still, I love thee dearly :
  Though I make (I feel)
Love a little queerly,
  I'm as true as steel.

Love me, swear to love me
  (As, you know, they do)
By yon heaven above me
  And its changeless blue.
Love me, lady, dearly,
  If you'll be so good ;
Though I don't see clearly
  On what ground you should.

Love me—ah ! or love me
  Not, but be my bride !
Do not simply shove me
  (So to speak) aside !
P'raps it would be dearly
  Purchased at the price ;
But a hundred yearly
  Would be very nice.

THOUGHTS AT A RAILWAY STATION

'TIS but a box, of modest deal ;
  Directed to no matter where :
Yet down my cheek the teardrops steal—
Yes, I am blubbering like a seal ;
For on it is this mute appeal,
  " *With care.*"

I am a stern cold man, and range
   Apart: but those vague words *"With care"*
Wake yearnings in me sweet as strange:
Drawn from my moral Moated Grange,
I feel I rather like the change
      Of air.

Hast thou ne'er seen rough pointsmen spy
   Some simple English phrase—*"With care"*
Or *"This side uppermost"*—and cry
Like children? No? No more have I.
Yet deem not him whose eyes are dry
      A bear.

But ah! what treasure hides beneath
   That lid so much the worse for wear?
A ring perhaps—a rosy wreath—
A photograph by Vernon Heath—
Some matron's temporary teeth
      Or hair!

Perhaps some seaman, in Peru
   Or Ind, hath stow'd herein a rare
Cargo of birds' eggs for his Sue;
With many a vow that he'll be true,
And many a hint that she is too,
      Too fair.

Perhaps—but wherefore vainly pry
   Into the page that's folded there?
I shall be better by and by:
The porters, as I sit and sigh,
Pass and repass—I wonder why
      They stare!

ON THE BRINK

I WATCH'D her as she stoop'd to pluck
  A wildflower in her hair to twine ;
And wish'd that it had been my luck
  To call her mine.

Anon I heard her rate with mad
  Mad words her babe within its cot ;
And felt particularly glad
  That it had not.

I knew (such subtle brains have men)
  That she was uttering what she shouldn't ;
And thought that I would chide, and then
  I thought I wouldn't :

Who could have gazed upon that face,
  Those pouting coral lips, and chided ?
A Rhadamanthus, in my place,
  Had done as I did :

For ire wherewith our bosoms glow
  Is chain'd there oft by Beauty's spell ;
And, more than that, I did not know
  The widow well.

So the harsh phrase pass'd unreproved.
  Still mute—(O brothers, was it sin ?)—
I drank, unutterably moved,
  Her beauty in :

And to myself I murmur'd low,
    As on her upturn'd face and dress
The moonlight fell, "Would she say No,
      By chance, or Yes?"

She stood so calm, so like a ghost
    Betwixt me and that magic moon,
That I already was almost
      A finish'd coon.

But when she caught adroitly up
    And soothed with smiles her little daughter;
And gave it, if I'm right, a sup
      Of barley-water;

And, crooning still the strange sweet lore
    Which only mothers' tongues can utter,
Snow'd with deft hand the sugar o'er
      Its bread-and-butter;

And kiss'd it clingingly—(Ah, why
    Don't women do these things in private?)—
I felt that if I lost her, I
      Should not survive it:

And from my mouth the words nigh flew—
    The past, the future, I forgat 'em:
"Oh! if you'd kiss me as you do
      That thankless atom!"

But this thought came ere yet I spake,
    And froze the sentence on my lips:
"They err, who marry wives that make
      Those little slips."

It came like some familiar rhyme,
  Some copy to my boyhood set ;
And that 's perhaps the reason I'm
    Unmarried yet.

Would she have own'd how pleased she was,
  And told her love with widow's pride?
I never found out that, because
    I never tried.

Be kind to babes and beasts and birds :
  Hearts may be hard, though lips are coral ;
And angry words are angry words :
    And that 's the moral.

"FOREVER"

FOREVER ; 'tis a single word !
    Our rude forefathers deem'd it two :
Can you imagine so absurd
    A view?

Forever !   What abysms of woe
  The word reveals, what frenzy, what
Despair !   For ever (printed so)
    Did not.

It looks, ah me ! how trite and tame !
  It fails to sadden or appal
Or solace—it is not the same
    At all.

O thou to whom it first occurr'd
  To solder the disjoin'd, and dower
Thy native language with a word
    Of power:

We bless thee! Whether far or near
  Thy dwelling, whether dark or fair
Thy kingly brow, is neither here
    Nor there.

But in men's hearts shall be thy throne,
  While the great pulse of England beats:
Thou coiner of a word unknown
    To Keats!

And nevermore must printer do
  As men did longago; but run
"For" into "ever," bidding two
    Be one.

Forever! passion-fraught, it throws
  O'er the dim page a gloom, a glamour:
It's sweet, it's strange; and I suppose
    It's grammar.

Forever! 'Tis a single word!
  And yet our fathers deem'd it two:
Nor am I confident they err'd;
    Are you?

UNDER THE TREES

" UNDER the trees ! " Who but agrees
  That there is magic in words such as these ?
Promptly one sees shake in the breeze
Stately lime-avenues haunted of bees :
Where, looking far over buttercupp'd leas,
Lads and " fair shes " (that is Byron, and he 's
An authority) lie very much at their ease ;
Taking their teas, or their duck and green peas,
Or, if they prefer it, their plain bread and cheese :
Not objecting at all though it 's rather a squeeze
And the glass is, I daresay, at 80 degrees.
Some get up glees, and are mad about Ries
And Sainton, and Tamberlik's thrilling high Cs ;
Or if painters, hold forth upon Hunt and Maclise,
And the tone and the breadth of that landscape of Lee's ;
Or if learned, on nodes and the moon's apogees,
Or, if serious, on something of A.K.H.B.'s,
Or the latest attempt to convert the Chaldees ;
Or in short about all things, from earthquakes to fleas.
Some sit in twos or (less frequently) threes,
With their innocent lambswool or book on their knees,
And talk, and enact, any nonsense you please,
As they gaze into eyes that are blue as the seas ;
And you hear an occasional " Harry, don't tease "
From the sweetest of lips in the softest of keys,
And other remarks, which to me are Chinese.
And fast the time flees ; till a ladylike sneeze,
Or a portly papa's more elaborate wheeze,
Makes Miss Tabitha seize on her brown muffatees,
And announce as a fact that it 's going to freeze,

And that young people ought to attend to their Ps
And their Qs, and not court every form of disease.
Then Tommy eats up the three last ratafias,
And pretty Louise wraps her *robe de cerise*
Round a bosom as tender as Widow Machree's,
And (in spite of the pleas of her lorn vis-à-vis)
Goes to wrap up her uncle—a patient of Skey's,
Who is prone to catch chills, like all old Bengalese :—
But at bedtime I trust he'll remember to grease
The bridge of his nose, and preserve his rupees
From the premature clutch of his fond legatees ;
Or at least have no fees to pay any M. D.s
For the cold his niece caught, sitting under the Trees.

MOTHERHOOD

SHE laid it where the sunbeams fall
    Unscann'd upon the broken wall.
Without a tear, without a groan,
She laid it near a mighty stone,
Which some rude swain had haply cast
Thither in sport, long ages past,
And Time with mosses had o'erlaid,
And fenced with many a tall grassblade,
And all about bid roses bloom
And violets shed their soft perfume.
There, in its cool and quiet bed,
She set her burden down and fled :
Nor flung, all eager to escape,
One glance upon the perfect shape
That lay, still warm and fresh and fair,
But motionless and soundless there.

No human eye had mark'd her pass
Across the linden-shadow'd grass
Ere yet the minster clock chimed seven :
Only the innocent birds of heaven—
The magpie, and the rook whose nest
Swings as the elmtree waves his crest—
And the lithe cricket, and the hoar
And huge-limb'd hound that guards the door,
Look'd on when, as a summer wind
That, passing, leaves no trace behind,
All unapparell'd, barefoot all,
She ran to that old ruin'd wall,
To leave upon the chill dank earth
(For ah ! she never knew its worth)
'Mid hemlock rank, and fern, and ling,
And dews of night, that precious thing !

And there it might have lain forlorn
From morn till eve, from eve to morn :
But that, by some wild impulse led,
The mother, ere she turn'd and fled,
One moment stood erect and high ;
Then pour'd into the silent sky
A cry so jubilant, so strange,
That Alice—as she strove to range
Her rebel ringlets at her glass—
Sprang up and gazed across the grass ;
Shook back those curls so fair to see,
Clapp'd her soft hands in childish glee ;
And shriek'd—her sweet face all aglow,
     Her very limbs with rapture shaking—
" My hen has laid an egg, I know ;
     And only hear the noise she 's making ! "

MYSTERY

I KNOW not if in others' eyes
    She seem'd almost divine ;
But far beyond a doubt it lies
    That she did not in mine.

Each common stone on which she trod
    I did not deem a pearl :
Nay it is not a little odd
    How I abhorr'd that girl.

We met at balls and picnics oft,
    Or on a drawingroom stair ;
My aunt invariably cough'd
    To warn me she was there :

At croquet I was bid remark
    How queenly was her pose,
As with stern glee she drew the dark
    Blue ball beneath her toes,

And made the Red fly many a foot :
    Then calmly she would stoop,
Smiling an angel smile, to put
    A partner through his hoop.

At archery I was made observe
    That others aim'd more near,
But none so tenderly could curve
    The elbow round the ear :

Or if we rode, perhaps she *did*
    Pull sharply at the curb ;

But then the way in which she slid
   From horseback was superb !

She'd throw off odes, again, whose flow
   And fire were more than Sapphic ;
Her voice was sweet, and very low ;
   Her singing quite seraphic :

She *was* a seraph, lacking wings,
   That much I freely own.
But, it is one of those queer things
   Whose cause is all unknown—

(Such are the wasp, the household fly,
   The shapes that crawl and curl
By men called centipedes)—that I
   Simply abhorr'd that girl.

     *   *   *   *

No doubt some mystery underlies
   All things which are and which are not :
And 'tis the function of the Wise
   Not to expound to us what is what,

But let his consciousness play round
   The matter, and at ease evolve
The problem, shallow or profound,
   Which our poor wits have fail'd to solve,

Then tell us blandly we are fools;
   Whereof we were aware before :
That truth they taught us at the schools,
   And p'raps (who knows ?) a little more.

—But why did we two disagree?
  Our tastes, it may be, did not dovetail;
All I know is, we ne'er shall be
  Hero and heroine of a love-tale.

FLIGHT

O MEMORY! that which I gave thee
    To guard in thy garner yestreen—
Little deeming thou e'er could'st behave thee
    Thus basely—hath gone from thee clean!
Gone, fled, as ere autumn is ended
    The yellow leaves flee from the oak—
I have lost it for ever, my splendid
              Original joke.

What was it? I know I was brushing
    My hair when the notion occurred:
I know that I felt myself blushing
    As I thought, " How supremely absurd!
How they'll hammer on floor and on table
    As its drollery dawns on them—how
They will quote it "—I wish I were able
              To quote it just now.

I had thought to lead up conversation
    To the subject—it 's easily done—
Then let off, as an airy creation
    Of the moment, that masterly pun.
Let it off, with a flash like a rocket's;
    In the midst of a dazzled conclave,
Where I sat, with my hands in my pockets,
              The only one grave.

I had fancied young Titterton's chuckles,
    And old Bottleby's hearty guffaws
As he drove at my ribs with his knuckles,
    His mode of expressing applause :
While Jean Bottleby—queenly Miss Janet—
    Drew her handkerchief hastily out,
In fits at my slyness—what can it
            Have all been about ?

I know 'twas the happiest, quaintest
    Combination of pathos and fun :
But I've got no idea—the faintest—
    Of what was the actual pun.
I think it was somehow connected
    With something I'd recently read—
Or heard—or perhaps recollected
            On going to bed.

What *had* I been reading ?   The *Standard* :
    " Double Bigamy ; " " Speech of the Mayor."
And later—eh ? yes ! I meandered
    Through some chapters of Vanity Fair.
How it fuses the grave with the festive !
    Yet e'en there, there is nothing so fine—
So playfully, subtly suggestive—
            As that joke of mine.

Did it hinge upon " parting asunder ? "
    No, I don't part my hair with my brush.
Was the point of it " hair " ?   Now I wonder !
    Stop a bit—I shall think of it—hush !
There 's *hare*, a wild animal—Stuff !
    It was something a deal more recondite :

Of that I am certain enough ;
        And of nothing beyond it.

Hair—*locks !* There are probably many
  Good things to be said about those.
Give me time—that's the best guess of any—
  "Lock" has several meanings, one knows.
Iron locks—*iron-gray locks*—a "deadlock"—
  That would set up an everyday wit :
Then of course there's the obvious "wedlock ;"
        But that wasn't it.

No ! mine was a joke for the ages ;
  Full of intricate meaning and pith ;
A feast for your scholars and sages—
  How it would have rejoiced Sidney Smith !
'Tis such thoughts that ennoble a mortal ;
  And, singling him out from the herd,
Fling wide immortality's portal—
        But what was the word ?

Ah me ! 'tis a bootless endeavour.
  As the flight of a bird of the air
Is the flight of a joke—you will never
  See the same one again, you may swear.
'Twas my firstborn, and O how I prized it !
  My darling, my treasure, my own !
This brain and none other devised it—
        And now it has flown.

ON THE BEACH

WHEN the young Augustus Edward
　　Has reluctantly gone bedward
(He's the urchin I am privileged to teach),
　　From my left-hand waistcoat pocket
　　I extract a batter'd locket
And I commune with it, walking on the beach.

　　I had often yearn'd for something
　　That would love me, e'en a dumb thing;
But such happiness seem'd always out of reach:
　　Little boys are off like arrows
　　With their little spades and barrows,
When they see me bearing down upon the beach;

　　And although I'm rather handsome,
　　Tiny babes, when I would dance 'em
On my arm, set up so horrible a screech
　　That I pitch them to their nurses
　　With (I fear me) mutter'd curses,
And resume my lucubrations on the beach.

　　And the rabbits won't come nigh me,
　　And the gulls observe and fly me,
And I doubt, upon my honour, if a leech
　　Would stick on me as on others,
　　And I know if I had brothers
They would cut me when we met upon the beach.

　　So at last I bought this trinket;
　　For (although I love to think it)

'Twasn't *given* me, with a pretty little speech :
   No! I bought it of a pedlar,
   Brown and wizen'd as a medlar,
Who was hawking odds and ends about the beach.

   But I've managed, very nearly,
   To believe that I was dearly
Loved by Somebody, who (blushing like a peach)
   Flung it o'er me saying, "Wear it
   For my sake"—and I declare, it
Seldom strikes me that I bought it on the beach.

   I can see myself revealing
   Unsuspected depths of feeling,
As, in tones that half upbraid and half beseech,
   I aver with what delight I
   Would give anything—my right eye—
For a souvenir of our stroll upon the beach.

   O! that eye that never glisten'd
   And that voice to which I've listen'd
But in fancy, how I dote upon them each!
   How regardless what o'clock it
   Is, I pore upon that locket
Which does not contain her portrait, on the beach!

   As if something were inside it
   I laboriously hide it,
And a rather pretty sermon you might preach
   Upon Fantasy, selecting
   For your "instance" the affecting
Tale of me and my proceedings on the beach.

I depict her, ah, how charming!
I portray myself alarming
Her by swearing I would "mount the deadly breach,"
　　Or engage in any scrimmage
　　For a glimpse of her sweet image,
Or her shadow, or her footprint on the beach.

　　And I'm ever ever seeing
　　My imaginary Being,
And I'd rather that my marrowbones should bleach
　　In the winds, than that a cruel
　　Fate should snatch from me the jewel
Which I bought for one and sixpence on the beach.

LOVERS, AND A REFLECTION

IN moss-prankt dells which the sunbeams flatter
　　(And heaven it knoweth what that may mean;
Meaning, however, is no great matter)
　　Where woods are a-tremble, with rifts atween;

Thro' God's own heather we wonn'd together,
　　I and my Willie (O love my love):
I need hardly remark it was glorious weather,
　　And flitterbats waver'd alow, above:

Boats were curtseying, rising, bowing,
　　(Boats in that climate are so polite),
And sands were a ribbon of green endowing,
　　And O the sundazzle on bark and bight!

Thro' the rare red heather we danced together,
　　(O love my Willie!) and smelt for flowers:

I must mention again it was gorgeous weather,
    Rhymes are so scarce in this world of ours :—

By rises that flush'd with their purple favours,
    Thro' becks that brattled o'er grasses sheen,
We walked and waded, we two young shavers,
    Thanking our stars we were both so green.

We journeyed in parallels, I and Willie,
    In fortunate parallels !   Butterflies,
Hid in weltering shadows of daffodilly
    Or marjoram, kept making peacock eyes :

Songbirds darted about, some inky
    As coal, some snowy (I ween) as curds ;
Or rosy as pinks, or as roses pinky—
    They reck of no eerie To-come, those birds !

But they skim over bents which the millstream washes,
    Or hang in the lift 'neath a white cloud's hem ;
They need no parasols, no goloshes ;
    And good Mrs. Trimmer she feedeth them.

Then we thrid God's cowslips (as erst His heather)
    That endowed the wan grass with their golden blooms ;
And snapt—(it was perfectly charming weather)—
    Our fingers at Fate and her goddess-glooms :

And Willie 'gan sing (O, his notes were fluty ;
    Wafts fluttered them out to the white-wing'd sea)—
Something made up of rhymes that have done much duty,
    Rhymes (better to put it) of "ancientry :"

Bowers of flowers encounter'd showers
    In William's carol—(O love my Willie !)

Then he bade sorrow borrow from blithe to-morrow
    I quite forget what—say a daffodily:

A nest in a hollow, "with buds to follow,"
    I think occurred next in his nimble strain;
And clay that was "kneaden" of course in Eden—
    A rhyme most novel, I do maintain:

Mists, bones, the singer himself, love-stories,
    And all least furlable things got "furled;"
Not with any design to conceal their "glories,"
    But simply and solely to rhyme with "world."

*   *   *   *   *

O if billows and pillows and hours and flowers,
    And all the brave rhymes of an elder day,
Could be furled together, this genial weather,
    And carted, or carried on "wafts" away,
Nor ever again trotted out—ah me!
How much fewer volumes of verse there'd be!

THE COCK AND THE BULL

YOU see this pebble-stone? It 's a thing I bought
    Of a bit of a chit of a boy i' the mid o' the day—
I like to dock the smaller parts-o'-speech,
As we curtail the already cur-tail'd cur
(You catch the paronomasia, play 'po' words?)
Did, rather, i' the pre-Landseerian days.
Well, to my muttons. I purchased the concern,
And clapt it i' my poke, having given for same

By way o' chop, swop, barter or exchange—
"Chop" was my snickering dandiprat's own term—
One shilling and fourpence, current coin o' the realm.
O-n-e one and f-o-u-r four
Pence, one and fourpence—you are with me, sir?—
What hour it skills not: ten or eleven o' the clock,
One day (and what a roaring day it was
Go shop or sight-see—bar a spit o' rain!)
In February, eighteen sixty nine,
Alexandrina Victoria, Fidei
Hm—hm—how runs the jargon? being on throne.

Such, sir, are all the facts, succinctly put,
The basis or substratum—what you will—
Of the impending eighty thousand lines.
"Not much in 'em either," quoth perhaps simple Hodge.
But there's a superstructure. Wait a bit.

Mark first the rationale of the thing:
Hear logic rivel and levigate the deed.
That shilling—and for matter o' that, the pence—
I had o' course upo' me—wi' me say—
(*Mecum*'s the Latin, make a note o' that)
When I popp'd pen i' stand, scratch'd ear, wiped snout,
(Let everybody wipe his own himself)
Sniff'd—tch!—at snuffbox; tumbled up, he-heed,
Haw-haw'd (not hee-haw'd, that's another guess thing :)
Then fumbled at, and stumbled out of, door,
I shoved the timber ope wi' my omoplat;
And *in vestibulo*, i' the lobby to-wit,
(Iacobi Facciolati's rendering, sir,)
Donn'd galligaskins, antigropeloes,
And so forth; and, complete with hat and gloves,

One on and one a-dangle i' my hand,
And ombrifuge (Lord love you!), case o' rain,
I flopp'd forth, 'sbuddikins! on my own ten toes,
(I do assure you there be ten of them),
And went clump-clumping up hill and down dale
To find myself o' the sudden i' front o' the boy.
Put case I hadn't 'em on me, could I ha' bought
This sort-o'-kind-o'-what-you-might-call toy,
This pebble-thing, o' the boy-thing? Q. E. D.
That's proven without aid from mumping Pope,
Sleek porporate or bloated Cardinal.
(Isn't it, old Fatchaps? You're in Euclid now.)
So, having the shilling—having i' fact a lot—
And pence and halfpence, ever so many o' them,
I purchased, as I think I said before,
The pebble (*lapis, lapidis, -di, -dem, -de*—
What nouns 'crease short i' the genitive, Fatchaps, eh?)
O' the boy, a bare-legg'd beggarly son of a gun,
For one-and-fourpence. Here we are again.

Now Law steps in, bigwigg'd, voluminous-jaw'd;
Investigates and re-investigates.
Was the transaction illegal? Law shakes head.
Perpend, sir, all the bearings of the case.

At first the coin was mine, the chattel his.
But now (by virtue of the said exchange
And barter) *vice versa* all the coin,
Per juris operationem, vests
I' the boy and his assigns till ding o' doom;
(*In sæcula sæculo-o-o-orum;*
I think I hear the Abate mouth out that.)
To have and hold the same to him and them. . .

Confer some idiot on Conveyancing.
Whereas the pebble and every part thereof,
And all that appertaineth thereunto,
Quodcunque pertinet ad eam rem,
(I fancy, sir, my Latin's rather pat)
Or shall, will, may, might, can, could, would or should,
(*Subaudi cætera*—clap we to the close—
For what's the good of law in a case o' the kind)
Is mine to all intents and purposes.
This settled, I resume the thread o' the tale.

Now for a touch o' the vendor's quality.
He says a gen'lman bought a pebble of him,
(This pebble i' sooth, sir, which I hold i' my hand)—
And paid for't, *like* a gen'lman, on the nail.
"Did I o'ercharge him a ha'penny? Devil a bit.
Fiddlepin's end! Get out, you blazing ass!
Gabble o' the goose. Don't bugaboo-baby *me*!
Go double or quits? Yah! tittup! what's the odds?"
—There's the transaction view'd i' the vendor's light.

Next ask that dumpled hag, stood snuffling by,
With her three frowsy blowsy brats o' babes,
The scum o' the kennel, cream o' the filth-heap—Faugh!
Aie, aie, aie, aie! ὀροτοροτοροτοῖ,
('Stead which we blurt out Hoighty toighty now)—
And the baker and candlestickmaker, and Jack and Gill,
Blear'd Goody this and queasy Gaffer that.
Ask the schoolmaster. Take schoolmaster first.

He saw a gentleman purchase of a lad
A stone, and pay for it *rite*, on the square,
And carry it off *per saltum*, jauntily,
Propria quæ maribus, gentleman's property now

I

(Agreeably to the law explain'd above),
In proprium usum, for his private ends.
The boy he chuck'd a brown i' the air, and bit
I' the face the shilling: heaved a thumping stone
At a lean hen that ran cluck clucking by,
(And hit her, dead as nail i' post o' door,)
Then *abiit*—what's the Ciceronian phrase?—
Excessit, evasit, erupit—off slogs boy;
Off like bird, *avi similis*—(you observed
The dative? Pretty i' the Mantuan!)—*Anglice*
Off in three flea skips. *Hactenus*, so far,
So good, *tam bene*. *Bene, satis, male*—,
Where was I with my trope 'bout one in a quag?
I did once hitch the syntax into verse:
Verbum personale, a verb personal,
Concordat—ay, "agrees," old Fatchaps—*cum*
Nominativo, with its nominative,
Genere, i' point o' gender, *numero*,
O' number, *et persona*, and person. *Ut*,
Instance: *Sol ruit*, down flops sun, *et* and,
Montes umbrantur, out flounce mountains. Pah!
Excuse me, sir, I think I'm going mad.
You see the trick on't though, and can yourself
Continue the discourse *ad libitum*.
It takes up about eighty thousand lines,
A thing imagination boggles at:
And might, odds-bobs, sir! in judicious hands,
Extend from here to Mesopotamy.

AN EXAMINATION PAPER

"THE POSTHUMOUS PAPERS OF THE PICKWICK CLUB"

Cambridge, 1857.

1. Mention any occasions on which it is specified that the Fat Boy was *not* asleep; and that (1) Mr. Pickwick and (2) Mr. Weller, senr., ran. Deduce from expressions used on one occasion Mr. Pickwick's maximum of speed.

2. Translate into coherent English, adding a note wherever a word, a construction, or an allusion, requires it:

"Go on, Jemmy—like black-eyed Susan—all in the Downs"
—"Smart chap that cabman— handled his fives well—
but if I'd been your friend in the green jemmy—punch his head—pig's whisper—pieman, too."

Elucidate the expression, "the Spanish Traveller," and the "narcotic bedstead."

3. Who were Mr. Staple, Goodwin, Mr. Brooks, Villam, Mrs. Bunkin, "old Nobs," "cast-iron head," "young Bantam?"

4. What operation was performed on Tom Smart's chair? Who little thinks that in which pocket, of what garment, in where, he has left what, entreating him to return to whom, with how many what, and all how big?

5. Give, approximately, the height of Mr. Dubbley; and, accurately, the Christian names of Mr. Grummer, Mrs. Raddle, and the fat Boy; also the surname of the Zephyr.

6. "Mr. Weller's knowledge of London was extensive and peculiar." Illustrate this by a reference to the facts.

7. Describe the Rebellion which had irritated Mr. Nupkins on the day of Mr. Pickwick's arrest?

8. Give in full Samuel Weller's first compliment to Mary, and his father's critique upon the same young lady. What

church was on the valentine that first attracted Mr. Samuel's eye in the shop?

9. Describe the common Profeel-machine.

10. State the component parts of dog's nose; and simplify the expression "taking a grinder."

11. On finding his principal in the pound, Mr. Weller and the town-beadle varied directly. Show that the latter was ultimately eliminated, and state the number of rounds in the square which is not described.

12. "Any think for air and exercise; as the wery old donkey observed ven they voke him up from his deathbed to carry ten gen'lmen to Greenwich in a tax-cart." Illustrate this by stating any remark recorded in the Pickwick Papers to have been made by a (previously) dumb animal, with the circumstances under which he made it.

13. What kind of cigars did Mr. Ben Allen chiefly smoke, and where did he knock and take naps alternately, under the impression that it was his home?

14. What was the ordinary occupation of Mr. Sawyer's boy? whence did Mr. Allen derive the idea that there was a special destiny between Mr. S. and Arabella?

15. Describe Weller's Method of "gently indicating his presence" to the young lady in the garden; and the Form of Salutation usual among the coachmen of the period.

16. State any incidents you know in the career of Tom Martin, butcher, previous to his incarceration.

17. Give Weller's Theories for the extraction of Mr. Pickwick from the Fleet. Where was his wife's will found?

18. How did the old lady make a memorandum, and of what, at whist? Show that there were at least three times as many fiddles as harps in Muggleton at the time of the ball at Manor Farm.

19. What is a red-faced Nixon?

20. Write down the chorus to each verse of Mr. S. Weller's song, and a sketch of the mottle-faced man's excursus on it. Is there any ground for conjecturing that he (Sam) had more brothers than one?

21. How many lumps of sugar went into the Shepherd's liquor as a rule? and is any exception recorded?

22. What seal was on Mr. Winkle's letter to his father? What penitential attitude did he assume before Mr. Pickwick?

23. "She's a swelling visibly." When did the same phenomenon occur again, and what fluid caused the pressure on the body in the latter case?

24. How did Mr. Weller, senior, define the Funds, and what view did he take of Reduced Consols? In what terms is his elastic force described, when he assaulted Mr. Stiggins at the meeting? Write down the name of the meeting.

25. "Προβατογνώμων : a good judge of cattle ; hence, a good judge of character." Note on Æsch. Ag.—Illustrate the theory involved by a remark of the parent Weller.

26. Give some account of the word "fanteeg," and hazard any conjecture explanatory of the expression "My Prooshan Blue," applied by Mr. Samuel to Mr. Tony Weller.

27. In developing to P. M. his views of a proposition, what assumption did Mr. Pickwick feel justified in making?

28. Deduce from a remark of Mr. Weller, junior, the price per mile of cabs at the period.

29. What do you know of the hotel next the Bull at Rochester?

30. Who, besides Mr. Pickwick, is recorded to have worn gaiters?

KEY
TO THE 'PICKWICK' EXAMINATION PAPER

1.

See Chapters IV., VIII., XXVIII., LIV.

(1)   ,,   IV., XXX. (twice), XXXIX.

(2)   ,,   LVI.

2.

Two of Jingle's speeches are here quoted, the first being in Chapter III., and the second in Chapter II. For "Spanish traveller" see Chapter III., and for "narcotic bedstead" see Chapter XLI. "Go on, Jemmy," is Mr. Jingle's adjuration to the actor whom he has previously designated "Dismal Jemmy," urging the Commencement of the 'Stroller's Tale.' "Like black-eyed Susan—all in the Downs" has the double application to the stroller's melancholy and the first line of Gay's song of 'Black-eyed Susan'—"All in the Downs the fleet was moored." "Handled his fives well" of course refers to the "sparring" of the cabman who wanted to fight Mr. Pickwick. "Friend in the green jemmy" refers to Mr. Winkle, who, we are told in Chapter I., "wore a new green shooting-coat," &c. "Pig's whisper" is slang for a very brief space of time. Bartlett says the Americans have "pig's whistle" with the same signification.

3.

See Chapters VII., XVIII., XIX., XXII., XXVII., XXXIV., XXXVI., XLIV.

4.

See two several parts of 'The Bagman's Story' in Chapter XIV.

5.

See Chapters XXIV., XXV., XLVI., VIII., XLI.

6.

See Chapter XX.

7.

See Chapter XXIV.

8.

See Chapters XXV., LVI., XXXIII.

9.

See Chapter XXXIII.

10.

See Chapters XXXIII. and XXXI.

11.

See the end of Chapter XIX.

12.

Illustrations will be found severally in Chapters XXXIII., XXXV., XLVII.

13.

See Chapters XXX. and XXXII.

14.

See two separate passages in Chapter XXXVIII.

15.

See Chapters XXXIX. and XLIII.

16.

See Chapter XLII.

17.

See Chapters XLIII., XLV., LV.

18.

See Chapters VI. and XXVIII.

19.

See Chapter XLIII. "You've been a prophesyin' away very fine like a red-faced Nixon as the sixpenny books gives picters on." The allusion is to Robert Nixon, the Cheshire prophet. See *Notes and Queries*, first series, vol. viii., pp. 257 and 326; and fourth series, vol. xi., pp. 171 and 265. Nixon's prophecies have been frequently published in the form of chap-books, and were probably current at the time with a highly-coloured portrait.

20.

The first requisition may be complied with by reference to Chapter XLIII. The following is answered in Chapter X.

21.

See Chapters XLV. and LII.

22.

See Chapters L. and XLVII.

23.

See Chapters XXXIII. and XLV.

24.

The first two questions are answered in Chapters LII. and LV. The next is answered at the end of Chapter XXXIII.; where also is the information lastly required.

25.

The illustration required is in Chapter LV.

26.

See Chapters XXXVIII. and XXXIII. "*Fanteeg*, a worry or bustle.   Also, ill-humour.—*Various Dialects*."—HALLIWELL. "Prooshan blue" probably refers to the colour of dress-coats. "Which gentleman of your party wears a bright blue dress-coat?" inquires The Boots, in 'Pickwick,' Chapter II.   Thus Sam Weller's "Prooshan Blue" is a finely-dressed fellow of the Pickwick-Weller period.

27.

See Chapter XXIV.

28.

See the opening of Chapter XXII.

29.

See Chapter II.

30.

See Chapter XX.

MISCELLANEOUS POEMS

SONNET

WHEN o'er the world night spreads her mantle dun,
    In dreams, my love, I see those stars thine eyes
Lighting the dark ; but when the royal sun
    Looks o'er the pines and fires the orient skies,
I bask no longer in thy beauty's ray,
    And lo! my world is bankrupt of delight :
Murk night seemed lately fair-complexioned day :
    Hope-bringing day seems now most doleful night.
End, weary day, that art no day to me !
    Return, fair night, to me the best of days !
But oh, my rose, whom in my dreams I see,
    Enkindle with like bliss my waking gaze !
Replete with thee, e'en hideous night grows fair,
Then what would sweet morn be, if thou wert there !

THE BOTTLING OF THE WASP

THE wasps were one morning obtrusively gay :
    Said my true love, " I know what'll speed them away :
From a nail, or a chairback, a bottle hang down,
And they're ' tree'd '—the brave varmints that buzz round your
        crown ! "

He hath found an old bottle, I cannot say where ;
He hath bound it with skill to the back of a chair ;
Full of mild ale so yellow and sugar so brown ;
And he " tree'd " them by dozens, I bet you a crown.

They may talk of their hares, of their rabbits, and all,
Such round-headed rascals, in Westminster Hall.
But tell legislators, the things to put down
Are those queer little imps that encircle one's crown.

So here's to their health, when they next travel here :
The sugar's unrivalled, resistless the beer :
And in peace may they leave us, themselves while they drown
In the healthy malt liquor that's sold at the " Crown."

A LIFE IN THE COUNTRY

(*Stanzas for Music*)

" OH ! a life in the country how joyous,
      How ineffably charming it is ;
With no ill-mannered crowds to annoy us,
    Nor odious neighbours to quiz ! "
So murmured the beautiful Harriet
    To the fondly affectionate Brown,
As they rolled in the flame-coloured chariot
    From the nasty detestable town ;
Singing, " Oh, a life in the country how joyous,
How ineffably charming it is ! "

" I shall take a portfolio quite full
    Of the sweetest conceivable glees ;

And at times manufacture delightful
   Little odes to the doves in the trees.
There'll be dear little stockingless wretches
   In those hats that are so picturesque,
Who will make the deliciousest sketches,
   Which I'll place in my Theodore's desk ;
               And Oh, &c.

" Then how pleasant to study the habits
   Of the creatures we meet as we roam :
And perhaps keep a couple of rabbits,
   Or some fish and a bullfinch at home !
The larks, when the summer has brought 'em,
   Will sing overtures quite like Mozart's,
And the blackberries, dear, in the autumn
   Will make the most exquisite tarts !
               And Oh, &c.

" The bells of the sheep will be ringing
   All day amid sweet-scented flowers,
As we sit by some rivulet singing
   About May and her beautiful bowers.
We'll take intellectual rambles
   In those balm-laden evenings of June,
And say it reminds one of Campbell's
   (Or somebody's) lines to the moon ;
             And Oh, &c.—it is."

But these charms began shortly to pall on
   The taste of the gay Mrs. Brown :
She hadn't a body to call on,
   Nor a soul that could make up a gown.

She was yearning to see her relations ;
　And besides had a troublesome cough ;
And in fact she was losing all patience,
　And exclaimed, " We must really be off,
Though a life in the country so joyous,
So ineffably charming it is."

" But this morning I noticed a beetle
　Crawl along on the dining-room floor.
If we stay till the summer, the heat 'll
　Infallibly bring out some more.
Now, few have a greater objection
　To beetles than Harriet Brown :
And, my dear, I think, on reflection—
　I should like to go back to the town.
　　　　　　　　　　　Though, &c."

APRIL

OR, THE NEW HAT

[In deference to a prevalent taste this Poem is also a Double Acrostic]

Prologue

MY Boots had been wash'd—well wash'd—in a show'r ;
　But little I griev'd about that :
What I felt was the havock a single half-hour
　Had made with my costly new Hat.

For the Boot, tho' its lustre be dimm'd, shall assume
　Fresh sprightliness after a while :
But what art may restore its original bloom,
　When once it hath flown, to the Tile ?

I clomb to my perch, and the Horses (a bay
  And a brown) trotted off with a clatter:
The Driver look'd round in his affable way
  And said huskily "Who is your hatter?"

I was pleas'd that he'd notic'd its shape and its shine,
  And as soon as we reached the *Old Druid*
I begg'd that he'd drink to my new Four-and-nine
  In a glass of his favourite Fluid.

A gratified smile sat, I own, on my lips
  When the Landlady called to the Master
(He was standing hard by with his hands on his hips)
  To "look at the gentleman's Castor!"

I laugh'd, as an Organ-man paus'd in mid-air
  ('Twas an air that I happen'd to know
By a great foreign Maestro) expressly to stare
  At *ze gent wiz ze joli chapeau.*

Yet how swift is the transit from laughter to tears!
  Our glories, how fleeting are they!
That Hat might (with care) have adorned me for years;
  But 'twas ruin'd, alack, in a Day!

How I lov'd thee, my Bright One! I wrench in Remorse
  My hands from my Coat-tail and wring 'em:
"Why did not I, why, as a matter of course,
  When I purchas'd thee, purchase a Gingham!"

THE CUCKOO

FORTH I wandered, years ago,
　　When the summer sun was low,
And the forest all aglow
　　　With his light:
'Twas a day of cloudless skies;
When the trout neglects to rise,
And in vain the angler sighs
　　　For a bite.

And the cuckoo piped away—
How I love his simple lay,
O'er the cowslip fields of May
　　　As it floats!
May was over, and of course
He was just a little hoarse,
And appeared to me to force
　　　Certain notes.

Since Mid-April, men averred,
People's pulses, inly stirred
By the music of the bird,
　　　Had upleapt:
It was now the end of June;
I reflected that he'd soon
Sing entirely out of tune,
　　　And I wept.

Looking up, I marked a maid
Float balloon-like o'er the glade,
Casting evermore a staid
　　　Glance around:

And I thrilled with sweet surprise
When she dropt, all virgin-wise,
First a courtesy, then her eyes,
    To the ground.

Other eyes have p'raps to you
Seemed ethereally blue,
But you see you never knew
    Kate Adair.
What a mien she had ! Her hat
With what dignity it sat
On the mystery, or mat,
    Of her hair !

We were neighbours.   I had doff'd
Cap and hat to her so oft
That they both of them were soft
    In the brim :
I had gone out of my way
To bid e'en her sire good-day,
Though I wasn't, I may say,
    Fond of him :—

We had met, in streets and shops ;
But by rill or mazy copse,
Where your speech abruptly stops
    And you get
Dithyrambic ere you know it—
Where, though nothing of a poet,
You intuitively go it—
    Never yet.

So my love had ne'er been told !
Till the day when out I strolled
And the jolly cuckoo trolled
    Forth his song,

Naught had passed between us two
Save a bashful ' How d'ye do '
And a blushing ' How do *you*
  Get along ? '

But that eve (how swift it passed !)
Words of fire flew from me fast
For the first time and the last
  In my life :
Low and lower drooped her chin,
As I murmured how I'd skin
Or behead myself to win
  Such a wife.

There we stood. The squirrel leaped
Overhead : the throstle peeped
Through the leaves, all sunlight-steeped,
  Of the lime :
There we stood alone :—a third
Would have made the thing absurd :—
And she scarcely spoke a word
  All the time.

  *   *   *   *

Katie junior (such a dear !)
Has attained her thirteenth year,
And declares she feels a queer
  Sort of shock—
Not unpleasant though at all—
When she hears a cuckoo call :
So I've purchased her a small
  Cuckoo-clock.

K

THE POET AND THE FLY

PART I

ROUND the Poet, ere he slumbered,
  Sang the Fly thro' hours unnumbered;
Sauntered, if he seemed to doze,
O'er the arch that was his nose,
Darting thence to re-appear
In his subtly-chambered ear:
When at last he slept right soundly,
It transfixed him so profoundly,
Caused him agony so horrid,
That he woke and smote his forehead
(It's the course that poets take
When they're trifled with) and spake:—

"Fly! Thy brisk unmeaning buzz
Would have roused the man of Uz;
And, besides thy buzzing, I
Fancy thou'rt a stinging fly.
Fly—who'rt peering, I am certain,
At me now from yonder curtain:
Busy, curious, thirsty fly
(As thou'rt clept, I well know why)—
Cease, if only for a single
Hour, to make my being tingle!
Flee to some loved haunt of thine;
To the valleys where the kine,
Udder-deep in grasses cool,
Or the rushy-margined pool,
Strive to lash thy murmurous kin

(Vainly) from their dappled skin !
Round the steed's broad nostrils flit,
Till he foams and champs the bit,
And, reluctant to be bled,
Tosses high his lordly head.
I have seen a thing no larger
Than thyself assail a charger ;
He—who unconcerned would stand
All the braying of the band,
Who disdained trombone and drum—
Quailed before that little hum.
I have seen one flaunt his feelers
'Fore the steadiest of wheelers,
And at once the beast would bound,
Kangaroo-like, off the ground.
Lithe o'er moor and marish hie,
Like thy king, the Dragon-fly ;
With the burnished bee skim over
Sunlit uplands white with clover ;
Or, low-brooding on the lea,
Warn the swain of storms to be !
—Need I tell thee how to act ?
Do just anything in fact.
Haunt my cream ('twill make thee plump),
Filch my sugar, every lump ;
Round my matin-coat keep dodging,
In my necktie find a lodging
(Only, now that I reflect, I
Rather seldom wear a necktie) ;
Perforate my Sunday hat ;
(It's a new one—what of that ?)
Honeycomb my cheese, my favourite,
Thy researches will but flavour it ;

Spoil my dinner-beer, and sneak up
Basely to my evening tea-cup ;
Palter with my final toddy ;
But respect my face and body !
Hadst thou been a painted hornet,
Or a wasp, I might have borne it ;
But a common fly or gnat !
Come, my friend, get out of that."

Dancing down, the insect here
Stung him smartly on the ear ;
For a while—like some cheap earring—
Clung there, then retreated jeering.
(As men jeer, in prose or rhyme,
So may flies, in pantomime ;
We discern not in their buzz
Language, but the poet does.)

Long he deemed him at Death's door ;
Then sprang featly to the floor,
Seized his water-jug and drank its
Whole contents ; hung several blankets
Round his lair and pinned them fast :
" I shall rest," he moaned, " at last."
But anon a ghastlier groan
To the shuddering night made known
That with blanket and with pin
He had shut the creature IN.

PART II

WHILE unto dawn succeeded day,
  Unresting still the Victim lay ;
The many-limbed one had its way.

He heard the stair-clock's tranquil ticks ;
When it exultingly struck six,
He gave a score or so of kicks.

"Before to-morrow's sun up-climbs,"
He feebly said, "yon leafy limes,
I'll write a letter to the 'Times.'"

Haggard and wan, when noon was nigh,
He rose and flung his window high ;
He heard, beneath, an old man's cry.

He strove—but idly strove—to eat ;
Till now, to see the potted meat
Vanish before him was a treat.

He strove to write, but strove in vain ;
Dark thoughts 'gan shape them in his brain ;
He listened to that old man's strain.

It rang out, maddeningly distinct ;
As he gave ear to it he winked ;
He dropped the pen that he had inked.

(SONG OF OLD MAN BELOW.)

  "Catch-'em-alive ! Gentlemen, I've
Here such a dose as no fly can survive.

House-fly, blue-bottle,
Garden-fly—what'll
Save him when once he's got this in his throttle?
Let e'en a wasp dip his nose in the mixture,
Spread on a plate, and that wasp is a fixture.
Buy, buy; give it a try;
Don't be put down by a poor little fly.
Who'll purchase any? Only a penny
Kills you them all, if it's ever so many."

He bought, he placed some on a plate;
I wis, he had not long to wait;
They ate it at a frightful rate.

But on his friend of yesternight
(He knew the animal by sight)
His baffled gaze could ne'er alight.

At last he noticed the unfeeling
Brute in a casual manner wheeling
Round an excrescence in the ceiling.

Self-poised, it eyed the heaps of slain;
But, that it did not entertain
A thought of joining them, was plain.

It winged that upper-air till ten,
The bard's retiring-hour; and then
Descending, tackled him again.

*   *   *   *

Next morn the young man made his will;
And either shot himself at drill
Or sucked slow poison through a quill.

The Thing accurst—the Vaticide—
All wiles for snaring him defied ;
And at a good old age he died.

This tale (I guarantee it true),
Reader, I dedicate to you.
If you can find its moral, do.

LUPUS ET CANIS

MAXIMA pars hominum vitio versatur eodem,
 Qui quærunt sibi nil aliud, quam cingere luxu
Sese, et divitiis : auro famam, decus, ipsas
Permutant vitas.   "An ero locupletior," aiunt,
"Servus ?"   "Eris."   "Bene habet," respondent, "servus ero.
  Quid ?
"Esse velim liber ; libertate at melior res."
 Horum uti sermones volvo, mihi fabula quædam,
Nota quidem, in mentem venit ; at, ne te morer, audi.
 In quadam fuit urbe Canis ; Canis inclytus, acer,
Atque domus custos locupletis.   Viderat illum
Forte lupus, macer esurie, visumque salutat.
"Qui fit, amice," rogat—cupido ut miratur ocello
Corporis et decus et molem, perpastaque membra,—
"Qui fit ita ut niteas ?   Longe qui fortior, ipse
"Impastus nemora hæc noctuque dieque peragro."
Cui Canis arridens : "Vin' nostris moribus uti ?
"Elige, namque potes."   "Qui possum," ait, "oh bone? Nam
  sum
"Aspera passus multa : cibi expers atque soporis
"Montivagum caput et nivibus pulsatur et imbri ;
"Dic modo, quid faciam."   "Domus est servanda : latrones

"Arcendi a foribus." "Sum plane," ait ille, "paratus,
  "Idque libenter agam." Quid plura ? utrique placebat
Propositum, et comites peragunt iter, ipsaque tangunt
Mœnia, cum subito aspexit detrita catena
Colla lupus socii. "Quidnam hoc ?" ait. "Est nihil." "At tu
"Dic mihi, dic quæso." "Sum nempe ferocior," inquit,
"Utque vigil sim nocte, quiescam luce, catena
"Alligor : at nihil est : gratus sopor iste diurnus ;
"Vespere ubique vagor, nullo retinente, per agros,
"Frusta mihi domino lautæque obsonia mensæ
"Per totam præbente diem ; sic absque labore
"Vita beata fugit." "Si vis tamen effugere istinc,
"Num potes arbitrio ?" "Sane non id licet," inquit.
"Verum itaque est ? Equidem non tecum vivere tali
"Conditione volo : tu, re meliore potitus,
"Utere sorte tua, ac valeas ! me libera semper
"Arva juvant : nocet empta jugo, mihi crede, voluptas."
  July 4th, 1848.

ROLL ON, THOU DEEP AND DARK BLUE OCEAN, ROLL !

VOLVERE, cæruleis fundoque carentibus undis !
  Volvere ! regna virum tua littora : regna, quibus nil,
Te præter, superesse ætas dedit. O ubi Persis
Assyriæque vetus sedes ? ubi Græcia, et ingens
Gloria Romulidum ? Sopor urget ferreus omnes,
Omnes deperiere. Manes immobilis, idem,
Tu, vitreis immensus aquis, nescisque reverti
Ponte ! tot humanos quanquam miscerier æstus
Vidisti, tot sceptra retro, tot prælia ferri—

Nullæ in fronte minæ : liquido sed molle susurro
Labere qualis eras primi sub origine mundi,
Qualis in æternum labere volubilis ævum.
    1850.

PAINTING

MAGNAS artis opes, manibusque imitabile nostris
     Naturæ decus, et partos sine Marte triumphos,
Aggredior cantare.   Juvat revocasse parentum
Umbras, et simulacra modis splendentia miris
Exigua in tabula : juvat ardua cernere templa,
Æstivumque nemus, fontesque et picta Lyæo
Culta, vel ingentes hominum mirarier urbes.
Apparent lapsura nova nece Troja, ducesque
Argolici ; salit ecce ferox Romanus in hostem,
Et desolatas rursum aspectamus Athenas.
Non aliter persæpe trahunt sublustria sensus
Somnia sopitos, et imagine ludimur aurea :
Delinita tument dum pectora, voxque volentum
Dicere abest ; at mira, nova dulcedine captas,
Religio superat mentes, fruimurque priorum
Colloquio, immemoresque loci raptamur, et horæ.
    Cernis ut immensa se mole attollat in auras,
Ædes inter humo æquatas, avulsaque saxis
Saxa, Coliseum ? Sancta sub rupe morari
Musa jubet, sæclique animos revocare sepulti,
Astra ruinosas spectant ubi conscia turres,
Et campos ubi Roma fuit.   Sic omnia pictor
Rite memor servavit, inenarrabile pingens
Dextra opus, ac tabulæ dans vitam ac verba silenti.
    Hic vero instructas acie, medioque phalanges

Marte, vel in crasso revolutos pulvere currus,
Formarit, non arte rudis ; piceumque colorem
Addidit, ac multa texit formidine campum.
Ille canes, pecudumque laborantisque coloni
Pinxit opus, fecitque boves per prata vagari,
Serpere de sylvis fumum, aut sub margine rivi
Ludere ridentes pueros : aliusque domorum
Arcanos penetrat thalamos, vigilemque sub alta
Nocte senem jussit visu ardescente tueri
Argenti gazas, aurique talenta reposti.
Atque alius sacri profert miracula Libri,
Pastoris laudes, debellatumque gigantem,
Aut casum Babylonis, aquas ubi propter, inani
Fletu indulgebant, noctis per tædia longæ,
Isacidæ.   Atque alius supremi arcana reclusit
Luminis, instantemque Deum, trepidosque sub ipsis
Tartareis stantes portis denso agmine manes.
Nulli fas illis mortali excedere tectis.
Sed ne quære prius, quæ nocte teguntur acerba,
Neu scrutare Deum.   Nobis sat pandere multæ
Artis iter, quocunque ferat sacrata voluptas,
Concessamque viam cœli affectare futuri.

    1850.

PARTHENONIS RUINÆ [1]

ATLANTEA feror trans æquora, transque sonorum
    Nimbis Ionium, pastoralesque recessus
Arcadiæ : apparent candentia marmore saxa,
Prataque olivifera, et rivorum argenteus error,
Speluncæque, lacusque, et densi palmite clivi.

---

[1] Chancellor's Prize Poem, Oxford, 1851.

Hæ tibi divitiæ, musis gratissima tellus,
Attica ! quas Asiæ frustra Libyæque colonus
Optat, et auratis Hermus mercetur arenis.
Non mirum veteres hæc fortunata locorum
Nobiliore choro, formisque implesse pöetas
Ætheriis ; ipsa aura Deum spirare videtur,
Nec mortale melos ad littora volvere fluctus.
Ergo cuique jugo data numina, quaque sub umbra
Surrexere aræ : tum parva sacraria nasci,
Tum variæ paulatim artes.   Didicere colorem
Saxa pati, nec fronde sua turgescere marmor,
Et sylvæ niveis interlucere columnis.

Sed non lucorum tenebras artisque vetustæ
Prisca rudimenta, et latitantia numina sylvis,
Fert animus lustrare : vocant distantis Hymetti
Culmina, et assiduis decertans Sunion undis
Piniferum ostentat gremium camposque patentes.
Quippe hinc torva domus desolatumque videri
Palladis armatæ solium, clypeataque quondam
Effigies ; hinc hasta tremens, galeæque coruscus
Apparebat apex, et rubræ in vertice cristæ.[1]
Illas sæpe vagans Ægæo in marmore nauta,
Cum nimbi posuere, jubarque orientis Eoi
Trans Œtææ procul splendet juga, vidit aperta
Luce coruscantes, et remo innixus inerti
Substitit, optatas ut compellaret Athenas.

---

[1] Soph. Aj., 1217.

γενοίμαν ἵν᾽ ὑλᾶεν ἔπεστι πόντου
πρόβλημ᾽ ἁλίκλυστον, ἄκραν
ὑπὸ πλάκα Σουνίου,
τὰς ἱερὰς ὅπως
προσείποιμεν Ἀθάνας.

Namque ubi convulsam hanc molem, postesque tueris
Avulso capite, et longæ data saxa ruinæ ;
Stabat aprico ædes de marmore, candida partim,
Partim cæruleos cœli mentita colores,
Gaudebatque die, et sese pandebat ad ortus
Luminis, eque jugis magnam spectabat in urbem.
Quales aeriis in cautibus Apennini,
Aut nimbis involvit ubi latera ardua Parnes,
Suspendere domos aquilæ, plenoque tuentur
Solem oculo, nidosque fovent ingentibus alis.
Flore coronati postes, sertisque superbi
Auricomis ; varia lucebat tænia gutta,[1]
Mæandroque frequens circum color ibat amæno.
Quos supra, testata truces ancilia pugnas
Ordine pendebant tereti, cælataque in auro
Nomina, magnorum monumenta et munus avorum.

Necnon et varia signarat imagine frontem
Artificis manus, et lateri cælarat honores.
Hic Centaurorum rabiem Lapitheiaque arma
Aspiceres, trepidasque nurus, et Thesea raptis
Mensarum exuviis non irrita bella moventem.[2]
Illic in lucem matri non debita Pallas,[3]
Arma tenens, surgebat : eam chorus omnis Olympi
Spectabat, sobolemque pater lætatus ab alto
Veram agnoscebat solio, juxtaque locabat.
Circum antiqua Ceres, Cythereaque, Mercuriusque,
Mulciber innixus ferro, Victoriaque alis
Ardua ; nec virides texere Hyperiona fluctus,

---

[1] *Vide* Wordsworth's " Greece," description of the Metopes, Triglyphs,
etc., round the Parthenon, guttæ, festoons, and golden shields.

[2] Library of Entert. Knowledge, British Museum, p. 139. " Metopes."

[3] E. Pediment, p. 237.

Nec pallente Erebi latuit Proserpina luco.
Contra respondit tellus percussa tridenti,[1]
Et sonipes, et sylva tumens, lymphæque sequaces,
Ardentesque deum facies. Ibi regia Virgo,
Neptunusque pater, neque adhuc data victima Phœbo
Leucothea, et vitreis in curribus Amphitrite,
Herseque, Aglaurosque, et semper inops Erisicthon.
Hæc inter tranquilla maris lucebat imago,
Vivaque Callirhöe, gelidaque Ilissus in umbra,
Et nascens Erycina, fretis acclinis eburnis.
Talibus ingentem divæ splendoribus arcem
Phidiacus labor ornavit, saxoque caduco
Immortale dedit decus, et sacravit in ævum.

Quanquam, o magne parens artis, cui sculptile marmor,
Cui niveum parebat ebur, gazæque liquentes
Amnis Mæonii ; nunc o si regna revisas
Patria, dilectamque iterum spectaveris urbem,
Urbem reginam non amplius ! Exulat oris
Spirans saxum aliis, pulchri fugere colores :
Te quoque, divinæ domus ægidis, alter Ulixes[2]
Polluit ; alter, agens rubrum ipsa in limina martem,
Avulsit prædam mediis altaribus Ajax ;[3]
Quot tua funeribus nutarint saxa, quot iras
Certantum populorum, et belli incendia norint,
Testatur via clausa situ, stratæque deorum
Effigies, portæque feris hyemique patentes.
Scilicet hanc ædem Venetorum, ac turbida Sullæ
Agmina vastarunt ; hanc audivere cadentem,

---

[1] W. Pediment, p. 247.
[2] Demetrius Poliorcetes. (*Vide* Æn. i. 40, ii. 404.)
[3] Sylla dragged Aristion from the altar. Brit. Mus. p. 56. (*Vide* Æn.
ii. 164.)

Sulphuris impulsu Scythici,[1] Cephissides undæ,
Æginæque latus niveum, distansque Caphareus.
Illa nocte greges nemorosi ex arce Lycæi
Pastor agens, miro splendore rubescere cœlum
Vidit, et ex adytis non thurea nubila ferri.
Vidit, et intremuit : paucisque volantibus horis,
Templum ingens qua stabat, erat cæmenta tueri,
Et tetros cineres, caligantemque ruinam.

Atqui sæpe, cavum quo tempore sidera saxum
Frigida perspiciunt, quo rerum apparet imago
Maxima, densatæque cadunt e postibus umbræ ;
Desertis juvat ire jugis, aulaque vagari
Sub vacua, et pronis in casum hærere columnis.
Infra reliquias urbis, prostrataque passim
Templa vides, murosque ; vides, Jovis atria quondam,
Fragmina, Mavortisque jugum, lapidesque theatri :—
At circa loca mille, decus confessa parentum,
Scena nitent varia : hic Salamis se tollit ab undis
Contemptorem Asiæ, Marathonis littora longe,
Portaque Thebarum apparet, materque Pelasgæ
Ascra lyræ ; propior, sylvis aperitur Eleusin
In mediis, ac nigra quatit pineta Cithæron.
Tum flagrare faces in pectore, voxque volenti
Dicere abest ; sensusque haurit diffusa per omnes
Conscia fama loci, lapsas revocamur in horas,
Et venit in mentem, quorum cinis abditur infra.

At postquam adventum, paries ubi taxit opacus
Thesauros adytumque deæ, senisque columnis
Interclusa domus ; tum vultum atque ora parentum

---

[1] The Turks set fire to some gunpowder which the Venetians had left in the temple.   Encyl. Brit. " Athens."

Fas ipsa aspicere, et vivis miscerier umbris.
Namque hic [1] ingentem cætum, matresque, virosque,
Effusos ad sacra, senes, pallisque puellas
Extuderat longis opifex : quæ pocula ferrent,
Quæque faces, calathosque ; alias umbracula soli
Pandere, vel sacri miratas pondera pepli. [2]
Has ad pacatæ tendentes Palladis arcem
Turba sequebatur taurorum, et debita morti
Corpora : pars longo mugitu et fronte reluctans
Terribili ; tacita pars majestate superbos
Volvit ovans gressus, collique volumina in arcum
Colligit, imbelles ultro comitata magistros.
Proxima, queis gracilis testudo aut tibia curæ,
Sortiti loca, queisque merum tutarier urnis ;
Et velata silens capiebat dona sacerdos. [3]

Ast [4] alia de parte citas ardere quadrigas
Fecerat, et pubem tunicatam, ardentiaque ossa
Bellatoris equi ; quem, dorso immotus, habenis
Flexit inauratis eques, instantemque retorsit.
Ollis dissimiles habitus, grandisve cothurnus,
Aut lænæ undantes, aut Arcadis umbra galeri :
Atque alius [5] tunicam et gemmati pondera baltei
Nectit ovans, lauruque caput circumdat equinum,
Victricemque alius [6] merita cervice coronam
Accipit, aut, segnes gestu exhortatus [7] amicos,
Prona rapit spatia, et campo decurrit aperto.

Nec minus interea motus proceraque membra

[1] The Panathenaic frieze. Libr. Brit. Mus. p. 182, etc.
[2] Slabs Nos. 17-25.   [3] Nos. 84-90.
[4] Nos. 26-81. *Vide* Libr. Brit. Mus. p. 165, etc.
[5] No. 46.   [6] No. 26.   [7] No. 47.

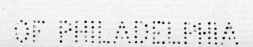

Ipsorum mirabere equum ; mirabere nares
Fulmineas, et cura modis luctantia miris,
Luminaque, osque fremens, et stantes sanguine venas.
Partem, indignantum similem, certare videres
Arrectos in frena, jubasque atque agmina caudæ
Excutere, et celsas in frontes cogere martem.[1]
Stare loco partem,[2] notamque micantibus escam
Auribus accipere,[3] aut gradientes agmine lento
Alternare pedem, plausove quiescere collo.
Talem Miltiades currum, talemve regebat
Armiger Automedon : tales invictus Achilles
Bello addebat equos, ubi Larissæa sub ipsis
Crista relucebat muris, flebantque Pelasgo
Hectora Trojanæ revolutum in pulvere matres.

Quæ vero integris species, quæ gratia formis,
Artificisque manus quantam tractata per artem,
Tum sciat, avulsos lapides direptaque si quis
Fragmina post tanto videat, simulacraque vita
Fervida, vix summo simulacra exstantia saxo.

Dicendum et peplus quales jactaret honores.
Illic arma deum, debellatosque gigantas
Cernere erat, centumque manus sublime ferentem
Enceladum, et rapto pugnantem monte Typhoea.
Hunc Pandionio de semine plurima virgo
Neverat, hunc gemmis, hunc interseverat auro
Multiplicem, et pictis dederat splendere figuris.
Qualiter Assyrii cum mercatoris ab alto
Effulgent vexilla mari, gaudentque colores
Ad solem reserare ; refert decora aureus æther,

---

[1] Nos. 32, 34, 36, etc.   [2] Nos. 44, etc.   [3] No. 58.

Fictaque purpureis in fluctibus errat imago.
Talis erat species pepli lucentis aprico
Murice; portantes pueri mollesque puellæ
Ad sonitum citharæ gradiuntur, et inclyta divæ
Facta canunt. Ut nocte satos Titanas, ut orbes
Gorgona sanguineos volventem, anguesque trilingues
Contuderit : tu, Diva, minas hominumque deumque
Sprevisti pariter : Tityum testamur, et orsis
Vulcanum irrisis, pœnamque audacis Arachnes.
Te Larissæus juvenis, te novit amicam
Inachius Perseus; tibi balsama Gallus, et Afer
Suppeditat, fusamque cremant Phœnices olivam.
Huc ades, O regina ! tuis accingimur una
Laudibus; et proprios nunquam obliviscere Graios !

Sic divam orabant varia prece.   Jamque sub ipsam
Portam adventantes, uno simul impete cuncti
Addunt in spatia, et laxis urgentur habenis.
Tum placidæ apparent facies, circaque sedentum
Ora immota deum ; Cereris tum apparet imago,
Latonæque genus duplex, et regia Juno :
Fulgida præ cunctis solium Tritonis eburnum
Pallas habet ; non ense ferox, non ægida quassans,
Sed niveis radians vittis, risuque sereno.

Talia per muros et per laquearia pictor
Atticus extuderat, gaudens revocare priorum
Gesta virum, ac tabulæ dare vitam et verba silenti.

Quanquam, ædes formosa, tibi non signifer ordo
Parietis, aut fuco diversum marmor honores
Præcipuos tribuit : tali petat arte triumphos
Barbarus, audaci attollens super æthera nisu

Pyramidum moles, et splendida mausolea.
At tibi majestas, tibi simplex gratia formæ ;
Te, dum cincta nites leviter spirantibus auris,
Et lucem simul ipsa refers, ipso æthere tractum
Visum ambire decus : circumque illustrior umbra,
Circum sancta quies, et non tua gloria fundi.
Religione nova perculsi hæremus, et alte
Evehimur : nec tantus amor percurrere visu
Singula, quam tota paulisper imagine pasci
Ardescentem animum, dum sensus impleat omnes
Nec percepta prius, nec jam intellecta voluptas.

Teque, sub auspiciis cujus jussuque secundo
Templorum redivivus honos, artesque per orbem
Surrexere novæ ; te nota in sede morantem
Fingit adhuc amor, et dulcem desiderat umbram.
Si non inscriptis titulos et nomina regum
Marte occisorum, vivit tua fama tropæis ;
Fulmina si vocis, quam mirabantur Athenæ,
Non sculpti servant lapides, non pagina chartæ ;
At patrii colles, at strata jacentibus aris
Pascua, perque altas templorum fragmina sylvas,
Te memorant, artemque tuam ; tibi vivida virtus
Clara dedit monumenta, et non mortale tropæum.

Jamque, licet vix ulla sibi monumenta vetustas
Servet adhuc, licet Italicis concesserit armis
Quisquis honos Graiorum, et nil nisi nominis umbram
Fas tanti superesse : manet tamen artis avitæ
Saltem aliquid ; manet illa patrum vestigia tardis
Passibus, et longo sectarier intervallo.
Forsitan et nostris aliquis spectarit in oris
Marmoreos apices, atque atria clausa columnis

Sole novo lucere : ast illi irrepit imago
Arcis Palladiæ ; labuntur verba per aurem
Muta diu, Graiosque juvat meminisse parentes.

CAROLUS STUART BLAYDS.
e COLL. BALLIOL.

AUSTRALIA[1]

INSULA Pacificis in fluctibus ilice multa
  Tecta jacet, pontumque jugis intercipit albis.
Supra nube vacans et nostro purior æther :
Ingentes intus campi, sectæque malignis
Tramitibus cautes, et ager non æquus aratro.
Hic ubi nunc lautas urbes, ubi rura juvenci
Fassa pedem, lætosque vides in collibus agnos ;
Barbara nuper ibi ducebat lampade luna
Gens incompositas inter querceta choreas,
Corporaque exuviis circumdabat atra ferinis.
Tantum auri vesana potest mutare cupido.

  Namque sub eluviem fluviorum et saxa repertum
Ingens pondus opum referunt : id fama per orbem
Detulit, ac resides populos accendit amore.
Huc Europææ gentes, huc Seres, et Indi
Convenere : novæ si quem telluris imago
Impulit, aut stimulis haud lenibus egit egestas.

  Ut portum[2] tetigere rates, et, læta peracti
Æquoris, in terra graditur manus : ilicet ædes
Et vici apparent nivei,[3] simulataque priscæ
Anglia, et antiquo decoratæ more tabernæ.

---

[1] University Prize Poem. Cambridge, 1853.
[2] *Portum*, sc. Port Jackson, town of Sydney.
[3] *Nivei*, the buildings being of white stone.

Cernis equos, cernis currus ; partem Area, partem
Scena trahit, magnumque forum, circusque theatri ;
Et cuidam nemorum lustranti devia Lugens [1]
Monstratur Sinus ; hic patriis e finibus exsul
Plurimus inviso terram tractabat aratro,
Fœcundumque solum pœnis, et non sua rura.
Credas littus adhuc tracta stridere catena ;
Sed fuit. Aversus petis urbem, et singula lustras ;
Præpes in æquoreas dum sol immittitur undas,
Tranquillumque nitent sub eburna carbasa luna.

Tu vero, desiderium cui suaserit ingens
Explorare sinum terræ, et rem quærere dextra,
Assurgis dum mane novum, dum flatus ab undis
Acrior, et lanæ percurrunt vellera cœlum.
Tum tauros traheamque pares : huc arma ferantur,
Huc vestes et victus ; agit secum omnia fossor.
Quadrijugos alii currus, alii esseda duro
Submittunt oneri, et meritos meliora caballos :
Inde viam faciunt. Itur per rura, per urbes ;
Quaque inculta capræ mordent juga ; quaque cadentes
Lymphæ dulce sonant, et frondea procubat umbra.

Nec tamen abruptæ cautes et fracta viarum
Offecere nihil. Sæpe acri in colle recusat
Taurus iter, nec voce potest nec verbere trudi.
Ergo alios addunt operi, gestuque minisque
Incendunt : hinc illa boum lamenta per agros,
Et gressus tenues, et noto longior ordo.
Multis auctumni pluviæ tristisque November
Obfuit : ut calido descendens imber ab Euro
Ad ver usque fremit, debacchatusque per arva
Stirpes et pecora et pavidos vi raptat agrestes.

---

[1] *Lugens Sinus*, sc. Botany Bay.

Necnon æstivis in mensibus aridus aer
Ex Arcto venit, itque ferens morbosque sitimque :
Non umbræ frigus pecori, non tecta colono
Suffecere ; furit campis equa, deque profundis
Auditur sylvis vox intempesta luparum.
Hæc metuens, sub vere viam moliris, et acres
Sæpe memor recreas ad diversoria tauros.
Ni vocet hospitiis læti te cultor agelli,
Qui lac, et tostas fruges, et poma ministret
Dulcia : multus enim placidis in vallibus ævum
Degit adhuc, nec falcis amor, nec cessit aratri.

Atque ubi longa diu circum deserta vaganti
Optati tandem incipient se prodere montes ;
Continuo saxis via crebrior, auraque tenuis
Signa dabit, clamorque virum, stridorque securis.
Mox immane vides agmen, tot moribus usos
Quot linguis armisque : riget coma, fronsque latronum
Instar habet ; sed mite genus, natumque labori.
Illi falce metunt, durisque ligonibus arvum ;
Cultro alius dirimit glebas, ac librat acerra ; [1]
Forsitan et puteos aliquis demisit in altum,
Statque inhians, si forte aurum, si forte recondant ;
Jamque solum digitis, jam forcipe prensat aheno.
Est quædam tabulis et cratibus apta supellex,
Quam cunas dixere : ferunt huc uberis arvi
Pondus, et injecta cogunt per vimina lympha.
Udæ eluctantur sordes ; quod restitit, aurum est ;
Signa palam dabit, ac digitis splendescet habendo.

Talia molitos propior sol admonet undis,
Quicquid agunt proferre vetans in majus : at illi
Addunt ligna focis, stratique in littore duro

---

[1] *Acerra*, sc. "an inspecting-pan."

Accipiunt oculis et toto pectore noctem.

    Felix, qui tantos potuit perferre labores !
Quique procellarum furiis, æstuque, fameque
Majorem se fassus, iter patefecit habendi !
Fortunatus et ille, sui qui dives, et utens
Sorte data, magnis non invidet ! Improbus illum
Fors urget labor, arcta domus, rarique sodales :
At jucunda quies, at vivæ in montibus auræ,
Et vacuus curis animus, fecere beatum.
Patris amans illi soboles, nec læta laborum
Uxor abest : non ille timet de nocte latrones,
Non auctumnalem maturis frugibus imbrem.

CARMEN GRÆCUM.[1]

COMITIIS MAXIMIS RECITATUM.

A.D. M.DCCC.LV.

Ἔσσεται ἦμαρ ὅταν πότ᾽ ὀλώλῃ Ἴλιος ἱρή.

ΑΣΤΕΩΝ πόρθητορ, ἀτειρὲς Αἰών,
  κρᾶθ᾽ ὅτῳ κισσὸς κυπαρίσσινοί τε
κλῶνες ἀμπέχουσι, μέλαν δ᾽ ὀπηδεῖ
    Δεῖμ᾽ ἀίδης δέ,

ὀστέοις λαῶν ἐπιβὰς καμόντων·
ἔργα γὰρ θνατῶν τὸ παρ᾽ οὐδὲν ἡγεῖ·
παρθένων δ᾽ εἴ τις χάρις, εἴ τις ἀνδρῶν
    γίγνεται ἀλκά,

[1] University Prize Poem. Cambridge, 1855.

πάνθ' ἅμ' ἐξόλωλεν, ὅταν δοκῇ σοι,
λευκόπεπλ' ὥσπερ ῥόδ' ἐν ἦρος ὥρα·
χἀ 'πιοῖσ' αἰὲς γενεὰ τάφοις ἐν
    τᾶσδε χορεύει.

ἢ μέγ' ὀλβία πόλις, ἑστία τε
ἦν ποκ' εὔτεκνος Πριάμω· Σκαμάνδρω δ'
ἀμφὶ δίναις ἁδὺν ἔκλαγξεν ὕμνον,
    βωκόλος ἀνήρ,

πατρίδος γαίας τότε κῦδος αἰνῶν·
νῦν δέ, δύσδαιμον πόλις, οὔ σε λέξω
τῶν ἀπορθήτων· ἀπὸ γὰρ κέκαρσαι
    ὦ ποκ' ἔχαιρες

λάϊνον πύργων στεφάνωμα· κοὔ σοι
εἶδος, οὐδ' ἥβα, κορυθαίολ' Ἕκτορ,
ἤρκεσ' ἁ θάλλοισα τὸ μὴ οὐ δαμῆναι
    δουρὶ Πελασγῷ.

ὄλβιον δὲ σ' εἶπον ὅμως, ὃς ἔγνως,
πρὶν μολεῖν, τἀπερχόμεν'· ὀλβία μοῖρ',
ὀλβία, πεπτωκέναι, οὐδ' ἰδεῖν πω
    δούλιον ἆμαρ,

ἄστυ θ' ἡμμένον πυρί, κἂν Ἀχαιαῖς
ναῦσι λευκὰς Ἀνδρομάχην παρειὰς
δάκρυσιν τέγγοισαν ἐπ' εὐρυκόλπω
    τήλοθι πόντω.

ἄλλος ὁ κρείων Βαβυλωνίας γᾶς
στᾶ ποκ' ἐν σεμνῷ θρόνω· εἵματ' ἐνδὺς
χρυσόπαστ', οἶνον δ' ἀπὸ δαιδάλω κρη
    τῆρος ἀφύσσων·

εἶπε δ' οὐκ ἐπιστάμενος τὸ μέλλον·
" φέρτερος γάρ τις θεὸς εὔχεταί μου
φῦναι ; οὐ πάντ' ἀμ' ἔσεται ; " τὸ ῥηθὲν δ'
       οὐκ ἐτέλεσσεν.

ἦλθε γάρ, λέγοντος, ἄναυδος αὐδά,
χεὶρ ὁμοία μὲν βροτῷ, οὐ δ' ὁμοία·
οἱ δ' ἄρ' ἔφριξαν τρίχα, κἀλελίχθη
       γούνατα τάρβει·

ἐκ δ' ἔφα μάντις θεῶ· " οὐ μάλα δήν,
οἷς πέποιθάς, σοι μενεῖ· ἀλλὰ κἤδη
σὸν διήρηται κράτος, ἆμαρ ἤδη
       ὕστατον ἥκει."

ἦ· τὰ δ' οὐ χαμαὶ πέσεν· οὐκ ἄκραντον
οὐδὲν ὧν εἶπεν θεός· ἠφάνισται
ἀστέων ἄνασσα, κέκευθεν ὡς ναῦν
       κῦμα θαλάσσας.

πάντα τοι μινυνθάδι' ὅσσ' ἔχει γᾶ·
κάππεσεν Ῥώμα ποκά, κάππεσεν δὲ
δαιμόνων μάτηρ ἰσοδαίμονός τε
       σπέρματος Ἑλλάς,

μυρίων Ἑλλὰς κιθαρῶν ἄγαλμα·
εἴπατ', ὦ Νυμφᾶν χοροί, ἃς Ὑμήττω
λείμακες τέρψαν, πεφιλαμέν' αἷς ἦν
       ἄντρα Λυκείω,

ποῖα δὴ δακρύσατε, τίς Κιθαιρὼν
ὕμμιν οὐ σύμφωνος, ἐπεὶ ναπαῖον
πρῶν ἰόστεπτον λίπετ', ἄμβροτοι δ' οὐκ
       ἔσσαν Ἀθᾶναι ;

δόξα ποῦ κήνων ἄρα; ποῦ ποχ' ὑμῶν,
νᾶσοι Αἰγαίας ἁλός; ἄφθιτον μὲν
ὕμμας ἀμπίσχει θέρος, ἁλίῳ δ' οὔ
πω φθινὰς αὐγά·

λοιπὰ δ' ὅσσ' ἄπαντα νέφος καλύπτει.
οὐκ ἐκεῖ χοροστασίαι καὶ ὕμνων
φθογγός, οἷς Σαπφὼ ποκα, χοῖς ἔχαιρεν
Φοῖβος Ἀπόλλων·

ἠρέμ' αὖθ' ὁδοιπόρος ἐμβατεύει
ναμάτων ὄχθας, ὄπα δ' οὐκ ἀκούει
πλὴν στενοίσης ἀχόος ἀξένῳ δὲ
τῆλε θαλάσσας.

ἴξεται δ', (ἴσμεν τόδε) κοὐχ ἑκὰς μάλ'
ἀμέρα, φθίνειν ὅτε καί σ' ἀνάγκα
Ἀλβίων, αἱ νῦν ἀδιναί τε σωπά-
σονται ἀγυιαί·

ἴξεται· τὸν μὲν χρόνον οὐκ ἐᾷ τιν'
ἱστορεῖν θνατῶν θεός· ἐν μέρει δ' ὤν
σὴ κατηφήσει χάρις, ὥστε μάτηρ
τεκνολέτειρα,

αἴλινος δ' ἔσσει σποδός. ἴσμεν ὡς γᾶ
ἐστιν ἤδη γηραλέα· καὶ ὄρφνα
ὠρανῶ κρύψει πλάκα, χἄλιος δρό-
μημα τελέσσει.

δεῖμ' ὅμως ταῦτ' οὐ φέρει ὃς καλῶς ζῇ·
τοῦτον οὐ τύμβου δνόφος, οὐ φοβάσει
ἐθνέων ἐρείπια, κἀκλιπόντες
ἀστέρες οἴμους·

στὰς δ' ἐπ' ὠχραῖς ἀϊόνεσσι θάρσος
λήψεται, καίπερ μόνος, οὐ μονωθείς·
μνάμοσιν γάρ τοι φρεσὶν ἐγγεγράπται
ῥῆμα παλαιὸν

οὐκ ἀμαυρῷ τέκτονος· "ἅλιος γὰρ
φέγγος οὐ δώσει· παρελεύσεται γᾶ
κὠρανὸς πρόπας· τὸ δ' ἐμὸν μενεῖ ῥῆμ'
ἄφθιτον αἰές."

LOCA SACRA APUD HIEROSOLYMAM [1]

O FORTUNATI colles, domus ipsius olim
Dicta Dei ; si vester honos alia exsulat ora,
Nati si periere, jacentque in pulvere turres :
At solitos circa saltus dilectaque dudum
Saxa, morantur adhuc Solymæ queis gloria cordi :
Sæpe per anfractus nemorum exaudita querela
Virginis Hebrææ, dum trunco acclinis olivæ
Cantat bella patrum, residesque recalfacit ignes.
Quin [2] (si vera fides) sub amica vesperis hora
Mira manus tangit citharam, neque cernitur ulli :
Nec carmen terrestre sonat : sed qualiter undæ
Æquoris, aut, ventis ubi mota laborat, arundo.
  Nunc in densa rapi palmis juga, nunc in apricis
Ire videmur agris, fontesque haurire sacratos :
Apparet quæ vallis aquam Cedronis opacat,
Et longæva micans inter querceta Siloe.

---

[1] University Prize Poem. Cambridge, 1855.
[2] Conf. Heber's " Palestine " :
  " For oft 'tis said in Kedron's palmy vale
  Mysterious harpings swell the midnight gale," etc.

O ubi olivarum sedes, ubi clivus amatis
Accola relliquiis ! video jam rura recludi
Bethaniæque casas procul, et qua pastor ab umbra
Regnaturus iit populorum.   Hac ille fugavit
Valle feras ; hæc antra loqui montesque docebat,
Dum labor unus oves, dum Pieris una voluptas.
Hinc persæpe Deus sera sub nocte redibat ;
Hinc ingens, Solyma, exitium, ac venientia sero
Fata tibi cecinit : tuque aspernata canentem !

Ergo inter cineres platearum ac diruta templa
Grassari permissum Italis : ergo occidit ingens
Gloria, et Isacidas matres sua forma reliquit.[1]
Tempore non alio spectatos sanguinis imbres
Dicunt, et simulacra rotis invecta coruscis,
Auditasque sonare tubas, inque aëre sudo
Fervere equum sonitus, atque arma minarier armis.
Agnovere quidem seri quid talia ferrent ;
Tunc, quum summa dies aderat, templumque vorabant
Vivi ignes :—quis Cyrus erit, qui fragmina rursus
Colligat, et patria extorres in sceptra reponat ?

Ex illo furor Europes exhaustus in urbem
Atque Asiæ : tu, Nile, truces in prælia turmas
Misisti : quid signa crucis, quid ut orbis in arma
Hesperius ruerit dicam ? Et nos fracta tuemur
Castella[2] in tumulis, famamque fovemus avorum.

Nunc in colle sacro Turcæ dominantur, et intra
Ire nefas ; clausa avertit sese advena porta.
Devenit et tandem qua sola in valle quiescunt
Ossa sepultorum vatum.   Cape[3] missile saxum

---

[1] Cf. Macc. 1. 25, 26 : "Therefore there was great mourning in Israel
. . . and the beauty of women was changed."
[2] Sc. some old castles built by Crusaders on the heights near Bethany.
[3] Alluding to the custom of casting a stone at the tomb of Absalom.

Rite manu, ac tumulum nati exsecrator iniqui.
Ast ubi Gethsemanes lucos, ubi tristia calcas
Rura, et purpureos in opaco cespite flores,
Fama loci venit in mentem crimenque priorum.
His, credo, e latebris genitor natum egit ad aram
Chaldæus ; jam ligna manu, jam ceperat ignes ;
Ibat et hinc, torvo septus grege, sanctior illo
Victima, nec dubiam in cædem : perterrita tellus
Testis qui moreretur, et intempesta ruens nox,
Mota juga, et vivi passim per littora manes.

　　Est locus [1] haud procul e muris, ubi cærulus aër,
Gleba ferax, et rubra vocant pomaria falcem :
Non uvis auctumnus eget, non ficubus æstas.
Huc olim (ut perhibent) nurus altæ stirpis origo
Venit inops : illis errabat collibus, illic
Sedit propter aquam, gremiumve replevit aristis.
Multaque præterea monstrat loca cognita famæ
Rusticus ; uxoris [2] Syriæ sub rupe sepulcrum,
Et vatis deserta domum, quæque unda, quod antrum
Regis erant desiderium, regisque latebræ.
Dein loquitur—nec genua pudet flexisse loquentem—
His ut in hospitiis, hæc inter saxa, cubarit
Ipsa Dei soboles : quo tempore sidus Eoos
Præmonuit cœleste senes, volvique per auras
Haud mortale melos pavidi sensere bubulci.

　　Inde, reliquit ubi frondentem Taboris arcem
Sol, et Iordanis collucent stagna sub astris,
Vise silens thalamum [3] ingentem qua membra jacebant

---

[1] Bethlehem.

[2] Uxoris—latebræ. Rachel's tomb, the wilderness of St. John the Baptist, the well for which David longed, the cave in which he cut off Saul's skirt.

[3] Sc. the Holy Sepulchre.

Illius, jam passa necem, jam debita cœlo.
Cernis inauratas ut præterlapsa columnas
Ingens turba virum incedat, longa oscula figens
Sæpe solo, et lacrymis humectans grandibus aras?
Fracto alios saxo videas inhiare, sedili[1]
Quondam cœlicolis; alii interiora morantur
Circum adyta, et rupem vel adhuc mirantur hiantem,[2]
Signaque[3] marmorea nondum deleta sub ara.

 Tempus[4] erit (sic fama refert) quo nomine dicti
Illius, insuetas iterum per compita pompas
Ducent, inque novos solvet se terra triumphos
Ad sonitum Pæanis, et Aurea Porta patescet.
At, famæ male credentes, ad mœnia[5] nota
Sæpe patres coëunt, et gentis quicquid ubique est
Judææ; regnumque orant, regemque morantem
Serius, atque umbra miseri oblectantur inani.
"Temnis adhuc proprios? O si, Exspectate, redires
His oculis, hac templa dares ætate renasci!"

 Scilicet et veniet, quem speravere tot anni,
Tot vatum cecinere lyræ: non ille puella
Natus matre, caput stabulis in agrestibus abdens:
Nocte latens aderit nimborum, alisque procellæ
Vectus; eum rutila stipabunt astra corona,
Atque in fronte geret non enarrabile nomen.
Ille novam ostendet Solymam, templa altera fessis
Gentibus; ipse dabit leges, ac sceptra tenebit;
Agnoscetque suos, atque agnoscetur ab illis.

---

[1] The stone where the two angels sat. [2] The marks of the earthquake.
[3] The holes where the three crosses stood are still exhibited beneath the altar.
[4] Alluding to a Turkish tradition, that the Christians will one day enter the Golden Gate in triumph.
[5] The Jews' place of mourning under the ruins of the temple wall.

TRANSLATIONS INTO ENGLISH

PREFACE (1866)

OF the following Translations, those into Latin were done for pupils at College, and a few, both of them and of the English ones, have been in print before. As they were mixed up with verses of a lighter kind, and probably did not come under the notice of most of those who will read the present volume, they have been reprinted here. On one (Horace, Book I., Ode 11) a reviewer observed that the last line was "a reminiscence of the Princess," as of course it was. To anticipate any similar criticisms it may be worth while to say a few words.

I have nowhere adopted a phrase or word of any previous translator. I had translated the first Iliad before Lord Derby's or Mr. Wright's Homer appeared, and the second before I had seen their versions. The same remark applies, *mutatis mutandis*, to Professor Conington's Horace. I did not know till I had finished the Eclogues that any translation of them existed, for Dryden's, I suppose, scarcely counts as a translation. Since then I have met with Mr. Kennedy's Virgil, and availed myself of it to correct my rendering of line 79 of Eclogue III.

On the other hand, I have taken without scruple any expression of an original writer which seemed to me to be the equivalent of the Latin or Greek with which I had to deal. And as I happen to have borrowed in all cases from well-known writers, and passages which must be familiar to every one who reads at all, I have not thought it necessary to call attention to the fact each time, by quotation commas or otherwise. Quotation commas for this purpose are, I think, open to more objections than one : and surely it would be superfluous to specify in a note that, *e.g.*, such a phrase as "catch the blossom of to-day" was caught from Tennyson.

C. S. C.

HOMER'S ILIAD. Book I

THE wrath of Peleus' son, that evil wrath
　Which on Achaia piled a myriad woes,
Oh Goddess, sing: which down to darkness hurled
Brave souls of mighty men, and made their flesh
A prey to dogs and every ravening fowl.　　　　　5
Yet Zeus his will was working: since the day
When first 'twixt Atreus' son, the King of men,
And proud Achilles there arose up war.

What god, then, bade those twain stand forth and strive?
Zeus's and Leto's son.　He, angered sore　　　　10
Against the King, sent pestilence abroad
Among the army, that the people died:
For that of Atreus' son had been disdained
His servant, Chryses.　To redeem his child
With ransom measureless had Chryses come　　　15
Ev'n to the Achaian war-ships—in his hand
The emblem of the god who smites from far,
Apollo, high upon a staff of gold.
To all the Greeks he prayed, but most of all
To Atreus' sons, twin captains of the host.　　　20

"O Atreus' sons, and bravely-harnessed Greeks!
The gods, whose dwelling is Olympus, grant
That ye may sack Priam's city, and regain
Your homes rejoicing!　Yea and unto me
May give my child, my own, and take her price,　　25
Since great is Zeus's son, the god who smites from far."

Forthwith from all the host came loud acclaim:

" Take the rich ransom, reverence the priest."
The soul of Agamemnon, Atreus' son,
Alone it liked not: scornfully he bade him   30
Begone, and laid on him a hard command.

" Let me not find thee by the hollow ships
Or lingering now, old man, or yet again
Returning! Little shall avail thee then
Apollo's staff and emblem.   For the girl,   35
I yield her not, till old age come on her
Ev'n in my home, in Argos, far away
From her own country; while she plies the loom
And tends my bed.   But go, provoke me not:
So peradventure shall we part in peace."   40

So spake he; and the old man feared, and did
His bidding.   Mute he moved along the shore,
Among the noises of the boisterous sea:
And there, apart from men, prayed many a prayer
To gold-haired Leto's son, his King, Apollo.   45

"Oh hear me, thou who standest round about
Chryse and sacred Cilla—mighty lord
Of Tenedos, who wield'st the silver bow!
Sminthian! If ever I have builded up
From floor to roof a temple in thy praise,   50
Or ever burned to thee fat flesh of goats
And oxen: then accomplish this my prayer:
And let thy shafts avenge my tears upon the Greeks."

So prayed he, and Apollo heard his prayer.
Yea from Olympus' heights he gat him down,   55
Wrath in his soul: upon his shoulder hung

The bow, and quiver covered all around.
Rang on the shoulder of the angry god
The arrows, as he stirred him : on he came
Like night : and by the ships he sate him down.   60
Twanged with a terrible twang the silver bow
As he sent forth one shaft.   And first of all
He visited the mules and swift-paced dogs :
Next at their own flesh levelling his keen dart
Smote, and for aye burned on the thick-strown pyres of slain.

Nine days his arrows went abroad among   66
The host : and on the tenth Achilles called
The folk to council.   Moved thereto was he
By Herè, white-armed goddess ; for she saw
Achaians dying, and it pitied her.   70
To whom when met, and ranged in meet conclave,
Achilles swift of foot arose and spake.

" Oh sons of Atreus !   Now, I trow, will we
Turn us again, and drift—if flee we may
From death—ev'n thither whence we came : since war   75
And pestilence at once lay low the Greeks.
But hearken.   Seek we now some seer, or priest ;
Or dream-interpreter ;—dreams come from Zeus ;—
To tell us what hath stirred Apollo thus.
If of a prayer, a sacrifice withheld,   80
He doth rebuke us : should it be his will,
Incense of lambs and goodliest of the goats
Accepting, to remove from us this plague."

He spake and sate him down.   Then rose to them
High chief of augurs, Calchas, Thestor's son,   85
Who knew what is and was and is to be,

M

Who into Ilion piloted the Greeks,
By virtue of his art, Apollo's gift.
He friendly-minded rose and spake in the midst.

"Lo! thou command'st me, oh beloved of Zeus,   90
Achilles, to declare Apollo's wrath,
The far-off-smiting King. Now therefore I
Will speak: heed thou, and swear that of a truth
Freely thou'lt aid me both with tongue and arm.
Yea, for I think to anger one who rules   95
With might the Argives; and upon him wait
The Achaians.   Now a vantage hath a King,
Let but a meaner man have angered him:
For though to-day his fury simmer down,
Yet thenceforth wrath abideth—till it work   100
Its purpose—in the bosom of the King.
Wherefore bethink thee, wilt thou succour me?"

And then Achilles swift of foot replied.
"The thing that thou dost know take heart and speak.
For by Apollo, loved of Zeus, whom thou,   105
Oh Calchas, worshipping interpretest
Unto the Danaans the things of God:—
The hand of no man out of all this host
Shall, while I live and see the light of day,
By yon broad ships be heavy upon thee: 110
Not if thou namest Agamemnon, him
Who vaunts himself this day the chiefest Greek."

Then the good prophet took him heart and spake.
"Not of a prayer or of a sacrifice
Doth he rebuke: but for his servant's sake,   115
Whom Agamemnon did disdain, nor gave

His child, nor took her price: for this, I ween,
The Smiter deals us, and shall deal us, woe.
And heavy still shall be his wasting hand,
Till to her father dear the bright-eyed maid   120
Be giv'n, unbought, unransomed; and we bear
To Chryse holy sacrifice.   This done,
It may be he will hear us and repent."

He spake, and sate him down.   Then rose to them
Broad-realmèd Agamemnon, Atreus' son,   125
A mighty man, sore angered.   Fury filled
His heart's dark places: gleamed his eyes like fires.
First Calchas, boding mischief, he bespake.

"Prophet of ill!   Thou spak'st me never yet
A fair word.   For thy soul loves evil still,   130
Nor aught good spak'st thou e'er, or brought'st to pass.
What prophesiest thou now before the host?
Sooth, that for this the Smiter works them woe;
Because I would not for rich ransom loose
The girl Chryseis.   No! at home would I   135
Possess her: I prefer her to my wife,
My first-wed wife: she is Clytemnestra's match
In stature, shape, and mind, and handicraft.
Yet will I yield her up, if this be best.
I'd liefer see my people live than die.   140
Ye deck me straight a gift, lest I alone
Of Greeks ungifted be.   That were not meet.
For see all men, my gift goes otherwhere."

And then the swift Achilles answered him.
"Most honoured, most gain-greedy of mankind!   145
How may the generous Greeks find gifts for thee?

We wot not yet of public treasury :
The spoils of cities sacked we've parted all,
And should do ill re-levying these anew.
Now yield her to the god—and threefold we   150
And fourfold will repay thee, let but Zeus
Grant us to level yon fair walls of Troy."

   And royal Agamemnon made reply.
"Brave though thou art, great chief, yet play not thus
The knave : thou shalt not dupe me nor cajole.   155
Would'st thou—so thou have honour—that I sit
With empty hands? and bidd'st me yield her up?
Now if the generous Greeks will grant a gift—
One my soul loves, a meet equivalent—
Well : but if not, I'll take with mine own arm   160
Thine, or thine, Aias, or, Odysseus, thine,
And bear it off ; and wroth mayhap he'll be
Whom I shall visit.—But of this anon.—
Launch we a dark ship on the great sea now,
Give her her tale of oars, and place on board   165
A hundred oxen, and embark therein
Fair-cheeked Briseis.   And be one, a king,
Her captain ; Aias, or Idomeneus,
Or great Odysseus, or, Achilles, thou
Most terrible of men ; that thou mayest win   170
Back with thy rites the god who smites from far."

   Answered the swift-foot chief with lowering brow :
"Oh clothed with shamelessness ! oh selfish-souled !
What Greek will do ungrudging thy behests,
Speed on thy missions, bear the brunt of war?   175
I came not for the warrior Trojans' sake
Hither to fight.   They owe no debt to me ;

Ne'er in rich Phthia, nurse of mighty men,
Spoiled they my orchards :—for betwixt us lay
Long tracts of shadowy fell and sounding sea.   180
Shameless ! 'Twas thou, thy pleasure, brought us here ;
For Menelaüs, and thee, dog, to wreak
Vengeance on Troy—which things thou heedest not
Nor reck'st of.   Lo ! thou boast'st that thou wilt seize
With thine own arm my meed, my hardwon meed,   185
Assigned me by the children of the Greeks !
My gifts are not as thy gifts, when the Greeks
Lay low some goodly-peopled town of Troy :
My hands the burden of the weary war
Must bear ; but *thy* share, when we part the spoil,   190
Is greatest ; I some small sweet morsel take
Back to my ships, when I am faint with strife.
But now I go to Phthia.   Best to wend
Home with my beakèd ships.   And scarce wilt thou—
Say I, disdainèd I—fill high thy cup   195
With treasure and with wealth, abiding here."

     Then answered Agamemnon, King of men.
" Go, if thy soul so prompts thee.   I shall not
Say ' Stay ' for my sake.   I have others near
To prize me : first of all the all-wise Zeus.   200
Of Kings, the sons of heaven, I hate thee most.
Dear to thee aye are feuds and wars and strifes.
Strong art thou ? Then 'twas heaven that gave thy strength.
Go with thy ships and with thy followers home,
Rule Myrmidons.   I care not aught for thee   205
Nor for thy wrath.   And I will tell thee this.
Chryseis Phœbus takes from me : and her
I'll send, with *my* ships, and *my* followers, back.
But to thy tent I'll go, ev'n I, and take

Thy prize, the fair Briseis : that thou learn　　　210
How I am thy better : and that others shrink
To deem themselves my mates and cope with me."

He spake.　And moved was Peleus' son : his heart
'Neath his rough breast was this way rent and that.
Should he, his keen sword drawing from his thigh,　　　215
Scatter the multitude and slay the King ?
Or curb his spirit, and forego his wrath ?
This was he turning in his brain and breast,
His great sword half unscabbarded ; when lo !
From heaven Athenè came : a messenger　　　220
From white-armed Herè, to whose soul both chiefs
Were dear and precious.　In the rear she stood,
And grasped Achilles by his yellow hair :
Seen by him only—all the rest were blind.
He marvelling, turned round : and straightway knew　　　225
Pallas Athenè ; dreadful gleamed her eyes.
And thus he spake to her with winged words.

"Why com'st thou, child of Ægis-armèd Zeus ?
To witness Agamemnon's insolence ?
This say I, and methinks 'twill come to pass.　　　230
One day he'll perish in his pride of heart."

To whom the blue-eyed goddess spake again.
"To stay thine anger, if so be thou'lt hear
My voice, I came from heaven : a messenger
From white-armed Herè, to whose soul both chiefs　　　235
Are dear and precious.　But leave off from strife,
And draw not forth the sword : but with thy tongue
Only revile him, as it needs must be.
For this *I* say, and this *shall* come to pass.

Trebled shall one day be thy rich reward   240
All through this insult.   Hear then, and be calm."

 Again Achilles swift of foot replied.
" I must abide, oh goddess, by thy word,
Though angered sore in soul: for this is right.
To him that heeds them will the gods give ear."   245

 He said, and hearkening to Athenè, stayed
Ev'n on the silver hilt, his ponderous hand.
Heavenward meanwhile she had flown, to join her peers
Up in the home of Ægis-armèd Zeus.

 Then straight Achilles spake with harmful words   250
To Atreus' son, nor put his anger by.
" Oh gorged with wine ! dog-faced, but hind at heart !
To arm thee with the people for the fray
Or with our captains crouch in ambuscade
Ne'er hadst thou courage.   That were death to thee !   255
Better no doubt to range the broad host through,
And confiscate his prize who saith thee nay.
Thou glutton King !   Thou rulest men of straw !
Else, son of Atreus, thou hadst bragged thy last.
But this I say and swear it with an oath.   260
Yea by this staff—where never leaf nor branch
May grow, since first 'twas sundered from the trunk
Upon the mountains, ne'er to blossom more—
(For that the axe hath stripped off bud and bark)—
Now in their hands the children of the Greeks   265
Bear it, who sit in judgment ; whom Zeus calls
To guard the right ; and men shall swear thereby—
The children of the Greeks shall one day long
All, for Achilles.   Thou shalt grieve, but find
No succour ; while 'neath slaughtering Hector's hand   270

Fall, and die, troops : but sit and gnash thy teeth,
Mad that thou sett'st at naught the noblest Greek."

Achilles spake : and flung to earth his staff
Studded with golden nails ; and sate him down.
The King sat o'er against him gathering wrath.   275
Then up sprang Nestor of the gracious tongue,
Clear orator of Pylos, from whose lips
Dropped music sweeter than the honeycomb.
Two generations now of speaking men
Had he seen born and bred and passed away   280
In sacred Pylos : and he ruled a third.
Who friendly-minded rose and spake in the midst.

"Lo ! a great sorrow comes upon our land.
Sure now would Priam and Priam's sons rejoice,
And every Trojan laugh within his heart,   285
Could he but learn how ye twain are at strife,
The first of Greeks in council and in war.
But hear me.   I can count more years than you.
Time was, when with a nobler race than ours
I mated : and they thought not scorn of me.   290
For ne'er yet saw I, nor shall see, their likes,
Cæneus, Pirithöus, Exadius,
Dryas, who led the people as a flock,
And Polyphemus, equal of the gods,
And Theseus, Ægeus' son, a very god.   295
These were the mightiest of the sons of earth.
Mightiest themselves, they fought with mightiest foes,
The Beasts of the Hill, and slew them horribly.
And I, to mate with these, from Pylos came,
From a far country ; for they bade me come.   300
I fought for my own hand.   No mortal man,

As men are now, would list to fight with such.
And they my counsels heard, my voice obeyed.
Ye too obey me.   To obey is good.
Nor thou, thou mighty, take the maid away,   305
But quit her, since the Greeks first made her his.
Nor thou, Achilles, stand against the King
And strive : for never honour like to his
Had sceptred King, whose glory is of Zeus.
So, son of Atreus, stay thy rage.   And him,   310
Our mighty rampart against evil war,
I do beseech to put his anger by."

   Then royal Agamemnon answered him.
"Naught hast thou said, oh sire, but what is meet.
But yonder man would overtop us all,   315
Be all men's lord and master, deal to all
Dictates, which one, at least, will scarce obey.
The gods who live for ever made him brave :
But did they thereby license him to rail?"

   Then words of warning great Achilles spake.   320
"Call me a coward and a thing of naught,
If I yield all at every word of thine.
Talk thus to others—dictate not to me :
For I shall hearken to thy words no more.
But this I tell thee—cast it in thy mind!   325
I will not draw the sword for yon girl's sake
On thee or on another ; since ye take
The thing ye gave.   But of all else that 's mine,
Treasured in my dark war-ship, not a thing
Without my licence shalt thou take or touch.   330
Doubt'st thou?   Then try, that all this host may see.
Thy blood that instant spouts around my spear."

So stood they face to face in wordy war.
And ended was the council at the ships.

Achilles to his tents and stately fleet   335
Went with Patroclus, and his followers all.
The other launched a war-ship on the main,
Manned her with twenty oars, and stowed therein
A holy hecatomb, and seated there
Fair-cheeked Chryseis: and for captain, stept   340
On board Odysseus, he of many wiles.

So they set forth and sailed the watery ways.
Then the King bade the people cleanse themselves.
They cleansed themselves, and cast into the sea
All their uncleanness: to Apollo next   345
They slew full hecatombs of bulls and goats
All by the barren waters: up to heaven
Went the sweet savour with the curling smoke.

In such wise toiled the host.   Nor aught meanwhile
Paused Agamemnon in his threatened wrath.   350
But to Talthybius and Eurybates,
His heralds twain and busy servants, spake.

"Go to Achilles' tent.   Take thence and bring
The fair Briseis.   If he say you nay,
I'll go, ev'n I, with yet a larger force,   355
And take her.   And 'twill be the worse for him."

So forth he sent them, charged with hard commands.
On, by the waters of the barren main
Unwillingly they fared: and reached at last
The vessels of the tented Myrmidons.   360

By his dark ship they found him in his tent ;—
Little Achilles joyed at seeing them ;—
Awe-struck and trembling they before the chief
Stood ; nor accosted him, nor uttered sound :
But he knew well their purpose, and began.　　　365

"Hail, heralds, messengers of Zeus and men !
Draw near.　I blame not you ; I blame the King,
Who sent you here for fair Briseis' sake.
But come, oh prince Patroclus, lead her forth,
And give her to their hand.　And be these twain　　370
My witnesses before the blessed gods
And mortal men and that untoward King :—
When one day there ariseth need of me
Their shield from foul destruction !　For the King
Raves, a doomed madman ; nor can look at once　375
Before him and behind, and see whose arm
Let the Greeks battle by the ships and live."

He said.　Patroclus his loved lord obeyed,
And led the fair Briseis from the tent,
And gave her to their hand.　And straightway they　380
Made for the Achaian ships ; and with them fared
The damsel all unwilling.　But the chief
Wept ; and from all his fellows gat apart,
And by the gray seas sate him down, and gazed
Far o'er the purpling waters : and to her　　385
Who bore him lifted up his hands and prayed.

"Mother !　Thou brought'st me forth not long to live :
Therefore should Zeus, the Thunderer, of high heaven,
Put glory in my hand.　But not a whit
Honours he me : yea, scorned am I of one,　　390

Broad-realmèd Agamemnon, Atreus' son;
With his own arm he seized, and hath, my gift."

Weeping he spake. His queenly mother heard,
'Neath ocean sitting by her ancient sire :
And rose from the gray waters as a mist,   395
And sate her down beside her weeping son,
Fondled his hand, and spake, and called him by his name.

"Why weep'st thou, Son? What grief is on thy soul?
Speak, and naught hide : that *I* too know this thing."

And with a heavy groan the swift chief spake.   400
"Shall I tell all to thee who know'st it all?
We came to sacred Thebes, Eetion's Thebes,
And spoiled her, and brought hither all the spoil.
And fairly did the children of the Greeks
Part it amongst them, and for Atreus' son   405
Chose out fair-cheeked Chryseis.   Thereupon
Came Chryses, priest of him who smites from far,
Ev'n to the war-ships of the steel-clad Greeks,
With ransom measureless to buy his child :
And in his hands Apollo's emblem sat,   410
The Smiter's, high upon a staff of gold.
To all the Greeks he prayed, but chief of all
To Atreus' sons, twin captains of the host.—
Forthwith from all the Greeks came loud acclaim :
'Take the rich ransom, reverence the priest.'   415
The soul of Agamemnon, Atreus' son,
Alone it liked not : scornfully he bade him
Begone, and laid on him a hard command.
"Back went in wrath that old man : and his prayer
Apollo heard, because he loved him well :   420
And hurled his fell shaft on us ; heaps on heaps

The people died.   Amongst Achaia's hosts
His arrows went abroad.   Then spake the seer,
Who knew it well, the Far-destroyer's will.

   "My voice first made them reconcile the god.   425
But rage seized Atreus' son.   He rose up straight,
And threatened that which, lo ! is brought to pass.
For her the keen-eyed Greeks are carrying now
To Chryse in yon war-ship : but that other,
Briseis—whom the children of the Greeks   430
Gave to my hand—the heralds from my tent
Have but this instant taken, and are gone.—
Now stand by thy brave son, if stand thou mayest.
Hie thee to heaven ; pray Zeus—if ever word
Or deed of thine made glad the soul of Zeus :—   435
For in my father's halls I have heard thee tell
Of times when of immortals thou alone
Didst shield from foul destruction him who dwells
In darkness and in clouds, Croníon named ;
When Herè, Pallas, and Poseidon—all   440
The blessed gods—would bind him.   Thou didst come,
Goddess, and loose his bonds, and summon quick
Into the broad heaven him of hundred hands—
Gods call him Briareus, Ægeon men—
He who excels in bodily force his sire.   445
By Zeus he sate down, glorying in his might.
Cowed were the blessed gods, and bound him not.

   "Remember this : sit near him : clasp his knees :
Pray that he find some way to succour Troy :
And them—the Greeks—push ev'n to their ships' sterns,   450
To die amid the waters, that all know
How much they owe their King ; and Atreus' son,
Broad-realmèd Agamemnon, learn how mad
Was he, to set at naught the noblest Greek."

And Thetis answered, letting fall a tear.   455
"Why did I rear thee, born—alas my son!—
In sorrow? Would that tearless and unpained
Thou wert sitting by thy ships: for lo! thy life
Is but a little while, a little while.
Now passing sad thy days, as passing brief: 460
Surely in evil hour I brought thee forth.
But with this tale I go to those snowpeaks,
To Zeus, whose plaything is the thunderbolt,
Will he but hear me. Thou by thy swift ships
Sit, curse the Greeks, and stay thy hand from war.   465
For Zeus to the good Æthiops yesterday,
To ocean, went, with all the gods, to feast.
The twelfth day he'll return Olympusward.
Then to his brassfloored palace will I go,
And clasp his knees; and surely he'll repent."   470

She said: and vanishing left him, vexed at heart
All for that graceful maiden, whom by force
And violence they had ta'en.

                                Odysseus reached
Chryse meanwhile, with holy sacrifice.
Now, the deep harbour gained, they furled and stowed   475
In the dark ship their sails; placed mast in crutch,
Lowered on stays all swiftly; and the rowers
Into her moorings rowed her. Anchor-stones
They cast out next, and made the hawsers fast,
And leapt out on the sea-strand; and bore forth   480
The holy sacrifice: and last stepped out
From the sea-travelling ship that damsel fair.
Whom to the altar led the wily chief,
Placed in her father's hand her hand, and spake.

"Priest! Atreus' son hath sent me, King of men,   485
To bring thy child, and holy sacrifice
Make for the Greeks; and reconcile the King,
Who now brings many sorrows on the host."

He spake, and gave her to his hand: who took
His child rejoicing.   Swiftly then they ranged   490
Round the fair altar that brave sacrifice:
Held up, with washen hands, the barley grains:
And then with lifted arm the priest made solemn prayer.

"Oh! hear me, thou who standest round about
Chryse and sacred Cilla: mighty lord   495
Of Tenedos, who wield'st the silver bow!
Surely thou heard'st me heretofore; and sore,
To honour me, didst plague Achaia's hosts.
And now accomplish this, ev'n this my prayer.
From foul destruction shield this day the Greeks."   500

So spake he: and Apollo heard his prayer.
They having knelt, and strewed the barley grains,
Drew back the victim's head, and slew, and flayed,
And cut the thighs off, and around them wrapped
The fat in layers, and sprinkled flesh thereon.   505
These the sire burned on wood; poured sparkling wine,
The warriors standing by with fivepronged forks:
They burned the thighs, and tasted of the heart,
And mashed and fixed on spits the residue,
And made roast cunningly, and drew all off.   510
At last the feast was decked. They ceased from toil,
And supped, nor aught lacked at that equal board.
And when the lust of meat and drink was gone,
The warriors filled the goblets to the brim,

And, first oblation made, they served to all.   515
With songs the livelong day they soothed the god,
Those Grecian warriors. Sweet the hymns they sang.
The Far-destroyer listened and was glad.

But when the sun set and the dusk came on,
They slept beside the cables of the ship.   520
And when Morn's daughter, rosy-fingered Dawn,
Rose, for the broad Achaian host they steered :
The Far-destroyer sent a steady gale.
They raised the mast, and spread white sails thereon.
Bellied the sails ; and purpling round the keel   525
Sounded the dark waves as the ship went on :
She scudded o'er the seas and made her way.
They, when they had reached the broad Achaian host,
Drew the dark ship to land ; high on the sands
They left her, and set great stones underneath,   530
And went home each man to his tent and ship.

Meanwhile the swift-foot chief, great Peleus' son,
By his sea-travelling ships sat nursing wrath :
To the high council went not day by day,
Went not to war : but wasted his sweet soul,   535
Abiding there, and dreamed of turmoil and of strife.

The twelfth day dawned : and to Olympus trooped,
Zeus in the van, the ever-living gods.
Thetis forgat not then her son's behests ;
But mounted on the sea-wave, and in mist   540
Rose to the great heaven and the holy mount.
Seated apart she found the All-seeing One,
On many-peaked Olympus' topmost crag :
Sat at his feet, with one hand clasped his knees,

With the other held his beard ; and prayed and spake   545
Thus to the son of Cronos, royal Zeus.

　　"Zeus !   Sire !   If ever word or deed of mine
Among the immortals welcome was to thee,
Accomplish this my prayer.   Exalt my son,
Whose days are briefer than are other men's.   550
Of Agamemnon now is he disdained ;
He took, he hath, his gift.   But thou, who dwell'st
In the high heaven, exalt him, all-wise Zeus !
Put victory on the Trojans, till the Greeks
Exalt my son, and spread abroad his praise."   555

　　She spake.   Cloud-circled Zeus said ne'er a word.
Long he sat voiceless.   Thetis to his knees
Clung as the flesh clings, and she spake again.

　　"Now bow thy head, and pledge thy changeless word,
Or else refuse—for fears come not nigh thee.   560
Say that of all the gods thou hold'st me least."

　　Spake, big with anger, then cloud-circled Zeus.
"Lo ! there is woe to be if I must strive
With Herè, whensoe'er she taunts and rails.
Ev'n now she wars with me from day to day   565
Before the gods, and saith I fight for Troy.
Now go thou hence again, lest Herè know
This thing ; and leave the issue in my hand.
Yea, that thou mayest have faith, I bow my head.
For this is my great token with the gods.   570
Irrevocable, true, each word of mine,
Sure of its purpose, when I bow my head."

　　Croníon spake : his dark brows bent, and bowed.

　　　　　　　N

From his immortal head fell rippling down
The glory of his hair.   The great rock reeled.   575

Such counsel took those twain, and parted.   She
Plunged from the bright heaven into ocean's depths,
And Zeus went homeward.   Rose up all the gods
And stood before the Sire.   None dared abide
His coming; all stood up and fronted him.   580
High on his throne he sate him.   Herè marked:
And well she knew what counsel he had ta'en
With that old sea-god's silvery-footed child.
Forthwith in bitterness she spake to Zeus.

"And which of all the gods, oh wily one,   585
Was partner in thy counsels?   Aye thou lov'st
To sit, and scheme, and settle, far from me.
And never yet didst thou of thy free-will
Deign to tell *me* one word of thy designs."

Then spake to her the sire of gods and men.   590
"Look not, oh Herè, all my mind to know.
Hard were such knowledge, though thou art my wife.
That which 'tis fit for thee to hear, nor god
Nor man shall learn before thee.   But such plans
As I may plan, and hide from every god—   595
Ask not of these things straitly nor inquire."

Then answered Herè, the gazelle-eyed Queen.
"Dread son of Cronos, have I heard thee right?
Long time too little asked I or inquired;
Thou plotting that which pleased thee, undisturbed.   600
But now sore fears my soul, lest thou be duped
By that old sea-god's silvery-footed child.

Mist-clad she sat by thee and clasped thy knees:
And thou, as I suspect, didst bow thy head,
In token that thou would'st exalt her son,　　　605
And by the Achaian ships make many fall."

Then spake in answer cloud-encircled Zeus.
"Wayward! thou wilt aye 'suspect.' I know thee well.
But all thou wilt not compass—farther still
Wilt set me from thee. All the worse for thee.　　610
Sit down, be silent, and obey my words:
Lest all the gods heaven holds avail thee naught,
Left me but lift my matchless arm on thee."

He spake; and trembled the gazelle-eyed Queen;
Silent sat down, and bent her to his will.　　　615
Then with big wrath were swelled the heavenly ones
In Zeus's palace: till Hephæstus rose,
The great Artificer, and welcome words
To white-armed Herè spake, his mother dear.

"Woe shall there be, intolerable woe,　　　　620
If ye twain battle thus for mortals' sake,
And stir up war in heaven. All joyless then
Shall seem the fair feast, since the worst prevails.
But I my mother warn (though wise is she)
To pleasure Zeus our sire: lest he should strive　625
A second time with her, and mar our feast.
What if the lord of lightning from her seat
Should choose to hurl her? for none else is strong.
But thou with softest words approach him now.
Straightway the heavenly one will smile on us."　630

He said, and leapt up, and a ponderous cup

Placed in his mother's hand, and spake to her.
" Be patient, mother, and though vexed, endure :
Lest mine eyes see her smitten whom I love.
Then shall I sorrow, yet may aid thee naught :   635
Hard 'tis to fight against the heavenly one.
Yea, for aforetime did he hurl me down,
Burning to aid thee, from the gates of heaven,
Grasped by one foot.   All day I fell and fell,
And lighted at the setting of the sun   640
In Lemnos.   Little life was in me then.
There lighting I became the Sintians' care."

  He spake.   The white-armed goddess smiled and took
The cup her son gave in her hand : while he
Filled for the others all, from left to right,   645
And poured the luscious nectar from the bowl.
Quenchless the laughter of the blessed gods,
To see him puff and pant about the hall.

  So they the live-long day, till set of sun,
Feasted, nor lacked aught at that equal board :   650
Lacked not Apollo's lovely lyre, lacked not
The Muses, whose sweet voice took up the song.

  But when the bright sun's glory had gone down,
Ready for rest they parted each to his home :
To where the Crippled Deity for each   655
Had wrought a palace with a cunning hand.
The Lord of lightning went and laid him down
Where he had slept full oft at sweet Sleep's call :
Thither ascended he, and there he slept ;
And golden-thronèd Herè by his side.   660

BOOK II.

SO all else—gods, and charioted chiefs—
 Slept the night through.   But sweet sleep bound not Zeus;
Pondering what way Achilles to exalt,
And by the Achaian ships make many fall.

This to his soul the fairest counsel seemed ;   5
To send to Atreus' son an evil Dream:
And to the Dream he spake with wingèd words.

"Go, evil Dream, to yon Greek war-ships ; seek
The tent of Agamemnon, Atreus' son ;
And tell him, truly, all I tell to thee.   10
Say, ' Arm right speedily thy unshorn Greeks ;
This hour is Ilion and her broad streets thine.
For lo ! no longer are the immortals—they
Whose home is heaven—divided.   Herè's prayer
Hath bent them all; and woes are nigh to Troy.'"   15

He spake.   The Dream, obedient, went his way;
Came swiftly to the war-ships of the Greeks,
And sought out Atreus' son :—(at rest he lay,
Divine sleep floating o'er him, in his tent :)—
And stood above his head ; in form most like   20
To Nestor, Neleus' son : of all who sat
In council Agamemnon ranked him first.
In such shape spake to him the heaven-sent Dream.

"Sleep'st thou, O son of Atreus ? son of one
At heart a warrior, tamer of the steed ?   25
Not all night long a counsellor should sleep,
A people's guard, whose cares are manifold.

Now hear me.   Zeus's messenger am I;
Who, though far off, yet cares, yet grieves for thee.
He bids thee arm in haste the unshorn Greeks;   30
Saying, ' Now is Ilion and her broad streets thine.
For lo ! no longer are the immortals—they
Whose home is heaven—divided.   Here's prayer
Hath bent them all; and woes are nigh to Troy,'
Woes which Zeus sends.   This ponder in thy mind :   35
Nor be the captive of forgetfulness,
So soon as thou shalt wake from honeyed sleep."

He spake : and parting left him there, to muse
In secret on the thing that might not be.
For in that day he thought to scale Priam's walls,   40
And knew not, simple one, the wiles of Zeus ;
How he would bring more woes, more groanings yet,
On Trojan and on Greek in hard-fought fields.
He woke : and sate erect—the heavenly voice
Still floating o'er him : donned his tunic soft   45
And fair and new : flung o'er him his great robe,
Harnessed fair sandals to his shining feet,
And o'er his shoulder swung his silver-studded sword.
And took his fathers' sceptre in his hand,
Imperishable aye : and sought therewith   50
The vessels of the brazen-coated Greeks.

At broad Olympus' gate stood sacred Dawn,
To Zeus and all the gods proclaiming light.
Then the king bade his shrill-tongued heralds go
And summon council-ward the unshorn Greeks ;   55
Who came all swiftly at their heralding.

But first a council of high elders sat

At Nestor's ship, the Pylos-nurtured king.
Thither he called them : there framed shrewd advice.

"Hear, friends ! In holy night a heaven-sent Dream   60
Came near me while I slept : in face, and form,
And bulk, it seemed great Nestor's counterpart.
Above my head it stood, and spake to me.
'Sleep'st thou, O son of Atreus ? son of one
At heart a warrior, tamer of the steed ?   65
Not all night long a counsellor should sleep,
A people's guard, whose cares are manifold.
Now hear me.   Zeus's messenger am I ;
Who, though far off, yet cares, yet grieves for thee.
He bids thee arm in haste thy unshorn Greeks ;   70
Saying, Now is Ilion and her broad streets thine.
For lo ! no longer are the immortals—they
Whose home is heaven—divided.   Here's prayer
Hath bent them all ; and woes are nigh to Troy,
Woes which Zeus sends.   This ponder in thy mind.'   75
So spake the Dream ; and spread his wings, and fled.
And sweet sleep gat from me.   But up and look
How we may arm for war Achaia's sons.
And first I will prove them, as is meet, with words,
And bid them deck for flight their oarèd ships.   80
Ye, wending separate ways, forbid their flight."

He spake, and sat him down.   Then Nestor rose,
That Nestor who in sandy Pylos reigned.
Who friendly-minded rose and spake in the midst.

"Friends ! lords and captains of the Argive hosts !   85
Now had another Greek this vision told,
We had said, 'Thou liest ;' and put us far from him.
But lo ! he saw it, of Achaians all

Who vaunts him noblest.   Nay then, up and look
How we may arm for war Achaia's sons."   90

    He spake ; and slowly from the council moved.
They rose, and followed in their leaders' wake,
Those sceptred kings ; the host flocked after them.
As when, from some rock's hollow, swarm on swarm,
Rise multitudes of thickly-thronging bees :   95
And hang in clusters o'er the flowers of spring,
And fly in myriads, this way some, some that ;
They in such multitudes from tent and ship,
Skirting the bottomless sea-sand, marched in troops
To council.   With them sped a voice of fire   100
Bidding them on : Zeus sent it : and they met.
Unquietly they met : earth groaned beneath
The trampling of the hosts as they sate down :
And there was tumult.   Then did heralds nine
Shout out, entreating them to stay their strife,   105
And listen to the kings, the sons of heaven.
In haste they sate down, halting each in his place,
And stilled their noise.   Then Agamemnon rose,
Bearing that sceptre which Hephæstus wrought,
And gave unto Croníon, royal Zeus.   110
Zeus to the courier-god, the Argus-slayer :
Hermes to Pelops, lasher of the steed :
Pelops to Atreus, shepherd of the host :
And Atreus to Thyestes rich in lambs
Dying bequeathed it.   And Thyestes last   115
Gave it to Agamemnon's arm to wield,
And be the lord of Argos and the isles.
Leaning whereon he spake before the host.

    " Friends, sons of Ares, mighty men of Greece !

Me hath Zeus bound to heaviness and woe.   120
Once (reckless one !) he swore, and bowed his head,
That I should raze Troy's walls and get me home.
But mischief doth he plot against me now :
Sends me to Argos, shamed ; for I have slain
Much people.   Thus then fare the favourites   125
Of Zeus the all-mighty : who hath bent the crests
Of many cities ; yea, and who shall bend
The crests of many more ; for strong is he.
Our sons shall one day hear it, and cry 'Shame !
Did Greece's chosen in such numbers come,   130
To battle, and to fight a bootless fight '—
(For still we see no end)—'against a few ?'
Few, say I.   For suppose we struck a truce,
Trojans and Greeks, and numbered each our hosts :
They singling all who sit beside their hearths,   135
We parting into companies of ten ;
And to each ten one Trojan served the wine :—
Unserved would sit full many a company.
So do the Greeks exceed in multitude
The Trojans in yon city.   Yet have they   140
Allies from many cities ; sworded chiefs,
Who thwart me mightily, and say me nay,
When I would level those fair walls of Troy.
Nine of the years of royal Zeus are past :
And lo ! the rigging of our ships is torn,   145
Rotted their timbers ; and our wives, I ween,
And lisping children sit within our halls,
And wait us : and our work, for which we came
To Troy, is unaccomplished.   Nay but up
And do my bidding.   Set we sail and fly   150
To our dear fatherland : for never more
May we deem Ilion and her broad streets ours."

He spake ; and stirred the inmost soul of all
The broad host : all save those who knew his wiles.
Then surged the council.   On the Icarian main   155
So surge great sea-waves, when the clouds of Zeus
Let loose upon them winds from North and East.
And as the West wind meets the standing corn,
And stirs it to its depths, and ravens on,
A hurricane ; and all the ears bow down :—   160
Ev'n so was stirred the council.   Seaward they
Rushed with a cry.   The dust rose under-foot,
In volumes.   Each called each, to lend a hand
And drag the vessels down to the great sea.
Cleared were the trenches : rose to heaven their cry,   165
As, homeward-bound, they dragged their ships from shore.

Then had the Greeks fled home before their time ;
But Herè to Athenè spake and said :
"Oh me ! oh child of Ægis-armèd Zeus,
Untiring one ! shall Argives thus flee home,   170
Riding the broad seas, to their fatherland ;
And leave, that Priam and his hosts may boast,
Helen of Argos—for whom here in Troy,
Far from his fatherland, died many a Greek ?
Now range the armies of the brass-clad Greeks :   175
And with thy soft words stay them, man by man ;
Nor seaward let them drag their rocking ships."

She spake ; the blue-eyed maid gave ear to her :
Yea, from Olympus' heights went hurrying down,
And came to the Greek war-ships speedily.   180
And there she found Odysseus, Zeus's match
In cunning, standing still.   He had not laid
A finger on his dark and oarèd ship ;

For sorrow sat upon his heart and soul.
Standing beside him spake the blue-eyed maid.   185

"Laertes' son! the man of many wiles!
What! leaping thus into your oarèd ships
Shall ye flee home unto your fatherland:
And leave, that Priam and his hosts may boast,
Helen of Argos—for whom here in Troy,   190
Far from his fatherland, died many a Greek?
Now range the armies of the brass-clad Greeks;
And with thy soft words stay them, man by man,
Nor seaward let them drag their rocking ships."

She spake.   He knew her voice who spake to him: 195
Girt him for speed, and flung his robe away.
Eurybates the herald picked it up,
That Ithacan, his servant.   He himself
Came straight to Agamemnon, Atreus' son;
And took from him the sceptre of his sires,   200
Imperishable aye; and sought therewith
The vessels of the brazen-coated Greeks.

Oft as he met a king, or foremost man,
He checked him, halting near, with softest words.

"Fair sir! thou shouldst not cower as doth a knave;   205
Now seat thyself, and likewise seat thy hosts.
Thou know'st not yet the mind of Atreus' son.
Now proves he, but anon shall plague, the Greeks.
We know not, all, the purport of his words
In council.   Should his wrath wax hot, and work   210
A mischief to the children of the Greeks!
For high the soul of kings, the sons of heaven.

Of Zeus their glory: wise Zeus loves them well."

Then when he saw, or heard uplift his voice,
One of the people: with his sceptre he   215
Would thrust at him, and shout that he might hear.

"Sirrah! sit down, and stir not, but obey
Thy betters.   Helpless and unwarlike thou,
Of none account in council or in strife.
We may not, look you, all be monarchs here.   220
The multitude of rulers bodes but ill.
Be one our lord, our king; to whom the son
Of wily Cronos gave it: sceptre gave
And sovereignty, that he should reign o'er us."

Ev'n thus he dealt his mandates through the hosts;   225
And councilward they rushed from tent and ship.
The noise was as the noise of boisterous seas,
That break on some broad beach, and ocean howls.

So all sate down, and halted each in his place.
Still one—Thersites of ungoverned tongue—   230
Brawled on.   Much store had he of scurrilous words,
Idle and scurrilous words, to hurl at kings:
Aught that he deemed the Greeks would hear and laugh.
To Troy's gates none had come so base as he.
Bow-legged he was, and halted on one foot: 235
His shoulders, hunched, encroached upon his chest;
And bore a peaked head—scant hairs grew thereon.
Achilles and Odysseus most he loathed;
At them railed aye: but Agamemnon now
He taunted in shrill treble.   All the Greeks   240
Were angered sore, and vexed within their soul.
At Agamemnon did he rail and cry.

"What lack'st thou? Why complainest, Atreus' son?
With brass thy tents abound : and in them wait
Many and peerless maidens ; whom we Greeks,   245
Whene'er we take a town, choose first for thee.
Ask'st thou yet gold ; which one mayhap shall bring—
A tamer of the steed—from Ilion,
To buy his son? whom peradventure I,
Or some Greek else hath bound and made his prize?   250
Or yet a damsel to ascend thy bed,
Kept for thine own self? Nay, unkingly 'tis
To bring this mischief on Achaia's sons.
Oh cowards! oh base and mean—not men, but maids!
Home fare we with our ships : and leave him here,   255
To gorge him with his honours—here in Troy :
And see if we will fight for him or no.
For him, who scorned one better far than he ;
For his hand took, he hath, Achilles' gift.
Yet naught Achilles frets, good easy man.   260
Else, son of Atreus, thou hadst bragged thy last."

So chode Thersites him who led the host.
But straightway was Odysseus at his side,
And, scowling, with hard words encountered him.

"Thou word-entangler! Clear thy voice and shrill :   265
Yet think not singly to contend with kings.
I say no mortal, out of all that came
With Atreus' sons to Troy, is base as thou.
Wherefore thou should'st not lift thy voice and roar
And rail at kings, thy watchword still ' Return.'   270
We know not yet the end : whether for weal
Or woe we shall return, we sons of Greece.
So thou at Agamemnon, Atreus' son,

The shepherd of the host, must sit and rail,
For that on him the mighty men of Greece   275
Heap gifts : and cut him to the heart with words.
But this I say, and this shall come to pass.
Forget thyself, as now thou hast, again :—
And—from Odysseus' shoulders drop his head,
Nor be he called Telemachus's sire,   280
If this hand strip not all thy garments off,
Mantle and tunic, and lay bare thy loins,
And send thee to the war-ships, wailing loud ;
Driven from the council with the blows of shame."

He spake : and with his sceptre smote his back   285
And shoulders. Writhed Thersites, and the tears
Came gushing : and a crimson wale appeared,
Where lit the golden sceptre, on his back.
Down sate he, trembling all and woe-begone ;
And dried his eyes ; and looked round helplessly.   290
Then laughed they fairly, tho' their souls were grieved,
And each unto his neighbour looked and said :

" Now many a brave deed hath Odysseus done ;
Fathered fair counsels, reared the crest of war :
But bravest this which he hath wrought to-day,   295
Hushing that scorner's speech, who smites with words.
Sure never more that o'er-great soul of his
Shall raise him up to gibe and scoff at kings."

So spake the people. Then Odysseus rose,
Sacker of towns, his sceptre in his hand.   300
The blue-eyed goddess in a herald's shape
Stood near : that all, both high and low, might hear
His counsel, and acquaint them with his mind.
He friendly-minded rose and spake in the midst.

" Prince ! Atreus' son ! Lo ! now they will that thou   305
Should'st do in all men's eyes a deed of shame :
Nor keep the pledge they pledged, when on their way
Hither from Argos, pasture of the steed,
That thou should'st raze yon walls and get thee home :
But ev'n as babes or widowed wives, they wail   310
Each to his fellow, ' Get we home again.'
And such indeed the toil we have toiled, that one
Might get him home in very weariness.
For let a man abide one single month,
He and his fair-oared ship—let blast and storm   315
And angry ocean keep him prisoner—
Far from his wife : and sad shall be his soul.
But we—we see the ninth year rolling on,
And abide here still.   Wherefore small blame to them
That fret beside their ships.   And yet 'twere base   320
To stay, and stay, and then go empty home.
Bear, friends : bide yet a little : till we learn
If Calchas speak true prophecies or false.
For this we know full well :—bear witness all
Not yet led captive by the Powers of death :—   325
When—'twas as yesterday,—to Aulis flocked
Achaia's ships, the messengers of woe
To Priam and to Troy ; and round about
The fountain, at the holy altar, we
Made to the immortals choicest sacrifice,   330
By the fair plane, whence glistening waters rolled :
Then saw we a great sign.   A snake whose back
Was blood-red ; sent, of him who dwells in heaven,
From darkness into light—a fearful thing—
Sprang sudden from the altar to the plane.   335
Whereon were young birds sitting, tiny things,
On the tree-top : and cowered amidst the leaves ;

Eight of them : she, who bare the brood, made nine.
He ate them ; chirping, all eight, piteously ;
And as the mother fluttered round and round   340
And wailed her offspring ; darting from his coils
He seized the shrieking creature by the wing.
And when he had eaten bird and brood, the god
Appeared, and wrought in him a miracle.
As we stood marvelling to see such things,   345
Wise Cronos' son transformed him into stone.
Such portents mingling with our sacrifice,
Then forthwith Calchas prophesied and spake.
' What struck ye speechless, oh ye unshorn Greeks?
To us this mighty sign wise Zeus hath showed,   350
Late coming, late in its accomplishment,
The fame whereof shall never pass away.
Ev'n as that serpent ate up bird and brood,
Eight of them ; she who bare the brood made nine ;—
Shall we, for years so many warring here,   355
Take Ilion and her broad streets in the ninth.'
So spake he, and behold ! it comes to pass.
Nay then, abide, O bravely-harnessed Greeks,
Here, until yon great citadel be ours."

He spake, and from the Greeks a mighty cry   360
Went up : and all the vessels round about
Rang fiercely at the shouting of the hosts,
Who liked divine Odysseus' counsel well.
To whom spake Nestor the Gerenian knight.

"Oh gods ! Your speech is as the speech of babes   365
Too young to busy them with warfare yet.
Where then our oaths, our contracts ?   Fling we now
Our plots and manly counsels to the flames,

Our pledges pledged in wine, and our right hands
Wherein we trusted.   For behold ! we strive   370
Idly with words ; and, long time tarrying here,
See yet no end.   But thou, oh Atreus' son,
Stablished of purpose ev'n as heretofore,
Lead on the Argives still through hard-fought fields :
While they drop off, those two or three, who sit   375
Aloof, and plot—(and shall accomplish naught)—
To turn them Argos-ward, or e'er we see
If Ægis-armèd Zeus keep faith or no.
Yea for I say Croníon bowed his head,
The all-mighty, in that day when first the Greeks   380
Stept on their swift ships, messengers of blood
And death to Troy—and, thundering to the right,
Signalled fair fortune.   So let none speed home,
Till each hath lain beside a Trojan wife,
And Helen's cares and anguish are avenged.   385
But whoso longs amazingly for home,
Let him upon his dark and oarèd ship
Lay hold ; and ere his fellows, drop and die.
But do thou, King, consider and obey.
Not idle are the words which Nestor speaks.   390
Tell into clans and tribes, oh King, thy men :
That clan may stand by clan, and tribe by tribe.
So shalt thou—if the Greeks obey thy voice—
See which be base, which brave, of all the host,
Leaders and led :—for singly they will fight :—   395
And know if it be Fate, or man's unskill
And cowardice, that bars thy road to Troy."

And royal Agamemnon spake again.
"Yea, and in council none is like to thee,
Old man, of all the children of the Greeks.   400

O

O Zeus, O Phœbus, and Athenè! would
I had ten such counsellors!   Soon would bow yon walls,
By our arm ta'en and sacked.   But Cronos' son
Makes woe my portion.   Ægis-armèd Zeus
Doth cast my lot in bootless feuds and strifes.   405
Lo! for a girl's sake strive with warring tongues
I and Achilles—my wrath roused the strife.
Should but we twain be one in purpose, then
Not for an hour shall linger Ilion's doom.
But break ye now your fast, and then to war.   410
Let each whet well his spear, and hold his shield
Ready, feed well his swift-foot steeds, and look,
For battle bound, his chariot o'er and o'er :
That in stern war we strive the livelong day.
For rest there shall be none, no not an hour,   415
Until night coming part the strong men's arms.
The leathern fastenings of the broad-orbed shield
Shall drip with sweat; the hands that close around
The spear-shaft falter : steeds shall drip with sweat,
Drawing their polished cars.   And should I mark   420
One, minded by his beaked ships to abide,
Aloof from battle—slender hope were his
Thenceforth, to 'scape the vulture and the dog."

He spake.   The Argives gave a mighty roar.
So roars a billow—by the South wind stirred,   425
On some high beach—against a jutting rock,
Lashed evermore by waves from every wind
Of heaven, on this side gathering and on that.
They rose, and sprang forth, parting each to his ship;
And, kindling each his tent-fire, brake their fast: 430
And to the gods who live for ever prayed,
This one or that, with sacrifice, to flee

Death and the moil of war.   An ox meanwhile
Did Agamemnon slaughter, King of men,
Fat, in its fifth year, to most mighty Zeus: 435
And called the reverend chiefs of all the Greeks,
First Nestor, and the prince Idomeneus;
Then the two Aiases, and Tydeus' son;
Odysseus sixth, in craft a match for Zeus.
Unbid the clear-voiced Menelaüs came;   440
His soul well wotted how his brother toiled.
Ranged round the ox, they raised the barley grains,
And royal Agamemnon spake in prayer.

    " Most high, most mighty, dweller in the heaven,
Zeus, hid in clouds and darkness! ere yon sun   445
Set, and the dark draw on, may I have laid
Priam's blackening palace low, and Priam's gates
Burned with avenging flame: and rent the clothes
Of Hector with the sword's edge on his breast,
And round about him seen much people fall   450
In dust, and with their teeth lay hold on earth."

    He spake.   Croníon heard not yet his prayer:
His offering took, but multiplied his woe.
They having knelt, and strewed the barley grains,
Drew back the victim's head, and slew, and flayed,   455
And cut the thighs off, and around them wrapped
The fat in layers, and sprinkled flesh thereon.
And these they burned on leafless logs; and held,
Pierced with their knives, the entrails o'er the flame.
They burned the thighs, and tasted of the heart,   460
And mashed and fixed on spits the residue,
And made roast cunningly, and drew all off.
And when the lust of meat and drink was gone,

First spake out Nestor, the Gerenian knight.

"Most glorious Agamemnon, King of men!   465
Sit we not talking here, nor still forego
The thing that lo! heaven putteth in our hand.
But up.   Let heralds of the brass-mailed Greeks
Cry, and collect the folk from ship and ship:
While through the broad host thus in multitude   470
We go, and swiftly bid keen war awake."

He spake.   Nor heedless was the King of men.
Forthwith he bade his shrill-voiced heralds go
And summon council-ward the unshorn Greeks,
Who came all swiftly at their heralding.   475
Round Atreus' son the kings, the sons of heaven,
Ranged and arrayed them.   And Athenè helped,
The blue-eyed maid, her Ægis in her hand,
That precious thing, that grows not old nor fades.
A hundred tassels hang from it, all gold,   480
All deftly wov'n; worth each a hecatomb.
Therewith she ran wild-eyed amid the host,
Bidding them on: and roused in every breast
The will to fight and cease not.   And behold!
Sweeter to them seemed warfare, than to steer   485
Their hollow ships unto their fatherland.

As on the mountain peaks destroying flame
Fires a great forest; far is seen the glare :—
From off the glorious steel the full-orbed light
Went skyward on through ether as they marched.   490

And even as great hosts of wingèd birds,
Storks, cranes, or long-necked swans, flit here and there
In Asian meadow round Caÿster's stream

On jubilant wing : and, making van-ward each,
Scream, that the whole mead rings :—so poured their hosts 495
From tent and ship into Scamander's plain.
Earth underfoot rang fiercely, to the tramp
Of warriors and of horses.   There they stood
Upon Scamander's richly-blossomed plain,
Innumerable, as flowers and leaves in spring.   500

And as great hosts of swarming flies that flit
In springtime, when the milk is in the cans,
About the herdsman's hut : so numerous stood
Before Troy's ranks the Greeks upon the plain,
And thirsted to destroy them utterly.   505

And as the goatherds sunder easily
Broad droves, as one flock feeding : even so
Their captains marshalled each his company
For war ; amidst them Atreus' royal son,
In eye and front like Zeus, Ares in bulk,   510
In chest Poseidon.   As among the herd
The bull ranks noblest, o'er the gathered kine
Preëminent : such glory in that hour
Gave Zeus to Agamemnon, to be first
And chiefest among hosts of mighty men.   515

Now name me, Muses, ye that dwell in heaven—
For ye are goddesses, see all, all know ;
We are but told a tale, and know not aught—
The captains and commanders of the Greeks.
I could not tell nor speak their multitude.   520
Had I ten tongues, ten mouths ; were this my voice
Untiring, and the heart within me brass :—
But that those children of Olympus, sprung
Of Ægis-armèd Zeus, the Muses, know

Full well what numbers came 'neath Ilion's walls.   525
Now tell I all the captains, all the ships.

Of the Bœotians Peneleus was chief,
Archesilaüs, Clonius, Leïtus,
And Prothoënor.   Some in Hyria dwelt,
Schœnus or stony Aulis, or the dells   530
Of Eteonus : in Thespeia some,
Scholus and Graia, and the broad champaign
Of Mycalessus, Harma, Eilesius,
Erythræ, Eleon, Hylè, Peneon,
Ochaleæ, and Medeon, well-walled town,   535
Copæ, Eutresis, and the haunt of doves
Thisbè.   In Coroneia, on the lawns
Of Haliartus : by Plataia, by
Glisas, and Hypothebæ, well-walled town :
Onchestus, or Poseidon's holy grove,   540
Mideia, Arnè, where the grapes grow thick,
Or sacred Cilla, or the frontier-town
Anthedon.   Fifty ships went forth of these.
A hundred men and twenty sailed in each.

They of Aspledon and Orchomenos   545
Obeyed Ascalaphus and Ialmenus,
Chiefs whom in Actor's palace, Azeus' son,
The young Astyochè to Ares bore,
Her secret bridegroom, in her maiden's tower.
Full thirty chiselled ships did these array.   550

Of Phocians Schedius and Epistrophus
Ranked foremost, sons of proud Iphitus, son
Of Nauboleus.   Of Cyparissus these
Were lords, and stony Python, Crisa's grove,

Daulis and Panopeus ; dwelt round about   555
Anemoreia and Hyampolis,
Or drank of holiest Cephissus' stream,
Or held Lilaia, whence Cephissus springs.
And forty dark ships were their retinue.
These two were captains of the Phocian lines,   560
Next the Bœotians ranging, on the left.

   The Locrian's prince, fleet Aias, Oileus' son,
Slighter than Aias, son of Telamon,
Far slighter—small and linen-corsleted—
Yet with the spear surpassed the hosts of Greece.   565
From Cynus, Opöeis, Calliarus, these,
Bessa or Scarphè, sweet Augeæ came,
Thronius, or Tarphè by Boagrius' stream.
Forty dark ships were theirs, who o'er against
The great Eubœa dwelt—the Locrians.   570

   Eubœa's hosts, the Abantians—men whose lips
Breathe war—from Chalcis, Histiaia's vines,
Cerinthus' sands, Eirethria, Dion's steep,
Or Styra or Carystus : that proud race
Brave Elephenor led, Chalcodon's son.   575
He led the fleet Abantians : warriors, shorn
Of their front locks ; with outstretched spears athirst
To rive the breastplate on the foeman's breast.
Forty dark vessels followed in his wake.

   And they who dwelt in Athens, well-walled town,   580
Land of great-souled Erechtheus—whom in days
Gone by the child of Zeus, Athenè, reared
(From bounteous Earth he sprang,) and bade him dwell
In Athens, in her own rich sanctuary :

There do Athenian warriors worship him,   585
As years roll round, with bullocks and with rams—
Their captain was Menestheus, Peteos' son.
In all the earth his like hath not arisen
To marshal steeds and shielded infantry.
Nestor alone might match him : Nestor's years   590
Were more.—And fifty dark ships followed him.

   Next, Aias brought twelve ships from Salamis ;
And moored them by the Athenian phalanxes.

   And them whom Argos reared ; from Tiryns' walls,
Hermionè and Asinè—that front   595
Each a deep bay—from Trœzen, Eïon,
And vine-clad Epidaurus : all who came
From Mases or Ægina, men of war :
Loud Diomedes ruled, and Sthenelus,
Famed Capaneus's son : Euryalus third,   600
His sire Mecisteus, *his* Talaïon.
Loud Diomedes ruled the whole array,
In eighty dark ships mustering.

                                        Those who held
Mycenæ or Cleonæ, well-walled towns,   605
Or sumptuous Corinth, Araithyria sweet,
Orneia, or where first Adrastus reigned,
Sicyon ; who dwelt on Gonoessa's steep,
Or Hyperesia ; by Pellenè dwelt
And Ægius, and all along the coast,   610
And round broad Helicè : their hundred ships
Were led by Agamemnon, Atreus' son.
Most noble as most numerous were the hosts
That followed him.   Amongst them he stood armed

In dazzling brass, exulting : and of all   615
The mighty men stood chiefest, as of all
Noblest was he, and most his following.

And those who tilled Laconia's rugged dales,
Pharis or Sparta, or the haunt of doves
Messè ; Amyclæ, Helos' sea-washed walls,   620
Laäs or Œtylus : Menelaüs led,
The king's own brother, of the ringing voice,
Full fifty ships.   They mixed not with the rest.
He moved amongst them, trusting in his might,
And urged to battle : this his heart's desire,   625
That Helen's tears and anguish be avenged.

And those from Pylos, from Arenè fair,
Thrios, the ford of Alpheus, Æpy's walls,
Cyparissëis, Helos, Pteleon,
Amphigeneia, Dorion :—where the Nine   630
Fell in with Thracian Thamyris, on his road
From Thessaly, the home of Eurytus,
And silenced all his songs : because he stood
Their vaunted conqueror, would they but appear—
Those Muses, sprung of Ægis-armèd Zeus—   635
And sing against him : they, thereat enraged,
Smote him with blindness, took away that gift
Divine, that he forgat his minstrelsy :—
Their chief was Nestor, the Gerenian knight.
And ninety chiselled ships were their array.   640

Them of Arcadia, 'neath Cyllenè's steep,
By Æpytus's tomb, where dwells a race
Of wrestlers : them of Rhipæ, Pheneüs,
Orchomenos white with sheep, and Stratia,

Wind-swept Enispè, fair Mantinea,   645
Tegea, Stymphelus, and Parrhasia :—
King Agapenor led, Anchæus' son.
Their ships were sixty : each ship furnished well
With men inured to war, Arcadia's sons.
To these did Agamemnon, King of men—   650
For they were landsmen—give of his own store
Ships and good oars, to cross the purple seas.

They of Buprasium and great Elis ; all
Whom utmost Myrsinus, Olenia's crags,
Hyrminè and Aleisium compass round ;   655
These had four chiefs—on each chief war-ships ten
Attended, with Epeans freighted well.
Part did Amphimachus, part Thalpius lead,
(Sprung, this from Cteatus, that from Eurytus
The seed of Actor ;) stout Diorès part   660
Whose sire was Amarynceus : o'er the fourth
Ruled brave Polyxenus—his sire the king
Agasthenes, who sprang from Ægeus' loins.

Them of Dulichium, and the sacred isles
That fronting Elis lie, beyond the sea,   665
The Echinæ : Meges marshalled, Phyleus' son,
In fight an Ares.   Zeus loved well the knight
Phyleus his sire ; who with his grandsire wroth
Came down unto Dulichium long ago.
Forty dark vessels followed after him.   670

The Cephalenians, haughty race, and all
Who called the quivering woods of Neritos,
Or Ithaca, or rugged Ægilips,
Their home, or Crocylæa : all who dwelt

Round Samos or Zacynthus ; and whoe'er   675
Peopled, or faced, the mainland : these obeyed
Odysseus, like in counsel unto Zeus.
And with him sailed twelve scarlet-painted ships.

   The Ætolians Thoas led, Andræmon's son;
By Pleuron, Olenus, Pylenè, reared,   680
Or Chalcis' beach, or rocky Calydon.
For Œneus' bold sons were not ; he himself
Was not, nor fair-haired Meleager, now.
So o'er Ætolia's hosts supreme command
Held Thoas.   Forty dark ships followed him.   685

   Idomeneus, brave lance, the Cretans led.
From Cnosus and Miletus, Gortyn's walls,
And Lyttus, and Lycastus, glistening white,
Phæstus and Rhytius, peopled towns, they came,
And all the parts of hundred-citied Crete.   690
Idomeneus led those, and Meriones,
Match of the war-god, when he lift his arm
For slaughter.   Eighty dark ships followed them.

   Tlepolemus, the son of Heracles,
Valiant and tall, led on nine vessels, manned   695
By noble Rhodians, dwelling round about
Rhodes in three portions : in Ielysus,
And Lindus, and Cameirus glistening white.
These did Tlepolemus, brave lance, command :
Astyocheia bare him to the might   700
Of Heracles ; who led the maid away
From Sella's stream, from Ephyrè, many a town
Of warriors, sons of heaven, laid first in dust.
He, grown to manhood in his stately home,

Slew straightway his sire's uncle, now in years,   705
Licymnius, sprung from Ares; built him ships
Forthwith, and fled, much people in his train,
O'er ocean; for he feared the other sons
And grandsons of the might of Heracles.
To Rhodes, much hardship past, the wanderer came: 710
There in three clans he settled; there obtained
The love of Zeus, whom heaven and earth obey.
Croníon's hand shed o'er them boundless wealth.

Nireus from Symè led three shapely ships:
Nireus, to Charopus and Aglaia born,   715
Nireus, of all the Greeks that came to Troy
The goodliest; all, save Peleus' noble son.
Yet poor his prowess, scant his following.

Them of Nisyrus, Crapathus, Casos, Cos,
Where reigned Eurypylus, and Calydnæ's isles,   720
Pheidippus led and Antiphus, two sons
Of Thessalus, who sprang from Heracles.
And thirty chiselled ships were their array.

Next, all who in Pelasgic Argos dwelt,
Whose home was Trachis, Alos, Alopè,   725
Phthia, and Hellas, for sweet damsels famed;—
Their fifty ships Achilles led to war:
Myrmidons, or Hellens, or Achaians hight.
Yet the dread din of battle woke not them:
For there was no man to array their hosts.   730
For in his ship their great swift leader lay,
Wroth for Briseis' sake, that fair-haired maid
Whom from Lyrnessus in hard fight he won,
When fell Lyrnessus and the walls of Thebes;

Epistrophus and Mynes, spearmen bold,   735
Smiting, Evenus' sons, of Sclepius' blood :—
For her sake lay he still—but not for long.

From Phylacè and flowery Pyrasus,
Demeter's own ; from sheep-clad Iton some,
And sea-washed Antron, and green Pteleus, came.   740
Protesilaüs was their warrior chief
Once : but the dark soil was his lodging now.
In Phylacè his widow tore her cheeks,
Unfinished stood his home : for, first of Greeks
Leaping to land, a Dardan struck him down.   745
They mourned their chief, yet were not chiefless still :
Podarces led them, bred to warfare, son
Of rich Iphiclus, son of Phylacus ;
Of proud Protesilaüs brother born :
But younger, and less brave, than that great chief   750
Protesilaüs.   Leader lacked they not ;
Yet thought, regretful, on the brave man dead.
Forty dark ships these manned.

                                And those who tilled
Pheras by Lake Bœbeis, Glaphyræ,
Or Bœbè or Iolcos, well-walled town :   755
Admetus' son led their eleven ships,
Eumelus, whom Alcestis, lady fair,
Of Pelias' daughters loveliest, bare to him.

Those whom Methonè, whom Thaumachia reared,
Or Melibœa, or Olizon's crags ;   760
Them Philoctetes led, an archer trained,
Seven ships : in each sat fifty rowers trained
Archers, in fight right valiant.   But he lay,

Racked by strong pangs, in Lemnos' sacred isle,
Abandoned of the children of the Greeks   765
To rue the fell bite of the deadly snake.
There he lay sorrowing.   But the Greeks were soon
To think of Philoctetes once again.
Chiefless they were not, though they mourned their chief.
Medon arrayed them, Rhenè's bastard child,   770
By city-sacking Oileus.

     Them who held
Œchalia, where Œchalian Eurytus
Was king, or Triccè, or Ithomè's rocks :
These Podaleirius and Machaon led,
Asclepius' two sons, of healing arts   775
Each master.   Thirty chiselled ships ranged they.

 Them from Ormenius, Hypereia's rill,
Asterius, and Titanus' white-faced cliffs ;
Euæmon's glorious son, Eurypylus,
Led forth.   And forty dark ships followed him.   780

 Argissa's, Orthè's and Gyrtona's hosts,
White Olöessa's, and Elonè's ; led
The sturdy Polypœtes, son of him
Whom deathless Zeus begat, Peirithoüs.
Him to Peirithoüs famed Hippodamè   785
Bare, when those shaggy Beasts his vengeance felt,
From Pelion unto far-off Pindus driven.
Leonteus, bred to warfare, shared his toil,
Haughty Coronus' son, of Cæneus' blood.
And forty dark ships followed after these.   790

 Gouneus from Cyphos twenty ships and two
Led.   Enienians thronged them, and the men

Whose homes were round Dodona's storm-beat crags,
Sturdy Peræbians, or who tilled the meads
Of Titaresius, that pleasant stream   795
That flows in beauty down to Penëus;
Yet with that silver-eddied river ne'er
Mingleth, but oil-like, on the surface swims:
For Peneus is an arm of that oath-witness, Styx.

    Prothoüs, Tenthredon's son, led Magnè's hosts,   800
By Peneus reared, and Pelion's quivering woods.
Forty dark ships of theirs swift Prothoüs led.

    These were the chiefs and captains of the host.
Now, tell me, Muse, who far surpassed their mates,
Horsemen or steeds, in all that chivalry   805

    Of steeds the noblest far Eumelus drave,
Driv'n once by Pheres; swift in flight as birds,
In age, hue, depth of shoulder, fairly matched.
Those mares the Monarch of the Silver Bow
Bred in Pereia, couriers of dread war.   810
    Of men far first was Aias, Telamon's son,
While Peleus' son was wroth.   For all unmatched
Was great Achilles, all unmatched his steeds.
But in his beaked sea-vessels wroth he lay
At Agamemnon, shepherd of the host.   815
His army by the breakers on the beach
With spear and quoit and bow made holiday:
While, ranged beside their several cars, their steeds
On lotus browsed and parsley of the lake.
Tented, in canvas, stood the chieftains' cars.   820
Reft of their warrior prince, they roamed at will
Among the host, and went not forth to war.

On came they : so might fire o'errun the lands.
Groaned earth beneath : as when Zeus smites in wrath,
Revelling in thunderstorm, the soil that hides   825
The Dragon, where in Arimi men show
The Dragon's grave.   Beneath their coming feet
Groaned she right sore.   They swiftly scoured the plain.

And now wind-swift to Troy fleet Iris came
From Ægis-armèd Zeus, to tell a tale   830
Of woe.   By Priam's gates assembled all
The assembly, young and old.   Then, standing near,
Spake swift-foot Iris in Polites' voice,
Priam's son, who, trusting to his feats of speed,
High upon ancient Æsyætes' tomb   835
A spy sat watching till the Achaians moved
From shipboard.   So disguised, fleet Iris spake.

"Sire ! Thou aye lov'st entanglements of words.
Thus erst in peace-time : but 'tis stern war now.
Lo ! I have looked on many a foughten field :   840
But ne'er saw yet so vast, so stout a host,
As, even like the leaves or like the sand,
March o'er the plain, to fight beneath our walls.
But, Hector, be my message first to thee.
This do.   In Priam's great city many allies   845
Dwell, late o'er earth wide-scattered, and their speech
Is diverse.   Let each captain then command,
Each head, his own troops : marshalling first his hosts."

She spake.   He knew her voice who spake to him.
And brake the assembly up.   To arms they rushed.   850
The gates flew open, and the hosts poured forth,
Horsemen and footmen.   Mighty was their din.

Far in the plain, a steep hill fronts the walls;
A man may walk all round it: called by men
The Bramble-hill, but by the gods the tomb   855
Of supple-limbed Myrinè.   There were ranged
Both Trojans and allies.

                    The Trojan host
Obeyed tall Hector of the glancing plume,
Priam's son.   Most noble as most numerous showed   860
His hosts: each spear-arm lusting for the fray.

Gallant Æneas led the Dardan lines;
Whom Aphrodite's self to Anchises bore
In Ida's glens; a goddess loved a man.
Archilochus and Acamas shared his toil,
Trained in all arts of war, Antenor's sons.   865

Seleia's dwellers, low at Ida's foot,
Rich Trojans, that drink dark Æsepus' stream,
These Pandarus led, Lycaon's brilliant son;
His very bow was great Apollo's gift.

From Adrasteia and Apæsus' realm,   870
Tereia's steep and Pityeia, came
Hosts by Adrastus and Amphius led
Of linen corslet, Merops' sons, who ruled
Percotè.   He, a seer among the seers,
Had said, "My children, go not up to war."   875
Yet recked they not—drawn on by the dark Powers of Death.

Them who round Practium and Percotè dwelt,
Sestus, Abydos, and Arisbè's grove;
Ruled Asius, prince of warriors, Asius, son

Of Hyrtacus, whom vast and fiery-hued   880
Steeds from Arisbè brought, from Sella's stream.

The fierce Pelasgian spearmen—tribes who ploughed
Larissa's rich domain—Hippothoüs led:
Hippothoüs and Pylæus, warriors, sprung
Through Lethus from Pelasgian Teutamus.   885

Peiroüs and Acamas, mighty men, from Thrace,
Led all whom Hellespont, strong-rushing, belts.
Euphemus all Ciconia's spears: his sire
Trœzenus, son of Ceas, son of heaven.

Then the Pæonians, them who bend the bow,   890
From far-off Amydon Pyræcmes brought,
From Axius: Axius, whose vast-volumed tide,
Matchless in beauty, broadens o'er the lands.

The hairy bulk of stout Pylæmenes
The Paphlagonians roused from Eneti,   895
That breeds wild mules: Cytorus, Sesamos,
Their fair homes: Cromna or Parthenia's banks,
Ægialus, or Erythinæ tall.

Odius, Epistrophus, Calydon's hosts
Led from far Alybæ.   There is silver found.   900

The Mysians Cromis led, and Ennomus
The augur. Not by augury to escape
Black death.   By fleet Achilles' hand he died
In Xanthus.   Other Trojans fell that day.

Godlike Ascanius led, and Phorcys, troops   905

From far Ascania ; Phrygians, war-athirst.
Mæonians, Antiphus and Mesthles, born
By Lake Gygeis to Talaimenes.
They led Mæonians, born at Tmolus' foot.

    The barbarous-talking Carians Nastes led,   910
These held Miletus, and Mæander's stream,
And rocky Phtheiræ's leaf-entangled shades,
And Mycalè's steep heights.   Amphimachus
Led these, and Nastes, Nomion's brilliant sons,
Amphimachus and Nastes.   Gold he had ;   915
Yet, child-like, went to war.   Poor fool ! what shield
Is gold against the bitterness of death ?
He too must die by fleet Achilles' hand
In Xanthus.   Brave Achilles took his gold.

    Sarpedon and good Glaucus Lycians led   920
From Lycia far, where whirls Scamander's stream.

FROM ILIAD I

IN HEXAMETERS

SING, O daughter of heaven, of Peleus' son, of Achilles,
   Him whose terrible wrath brought thousand woes on Achaia.
Many a stalwart soul did it hurl untimely to Hades,
Souls of the heroes of old : and their bones lay strown on the
      sea-sands,
Prey to the vulture and dog.   Yet was Zeus fulfilling a purpose ;
Since that far-off day, when in hot strife parted asunder
Atreus' sceptred son, and the chos'n of heaven, Achilles.
    Say then, which of the Gods bid arise up battle between them ?
Zeus's and Leto's son.   With the king was kindled his anger :

Then went sickness abroad, and the people died of the sickness :
For that of Atreus' son had his priest been lightly entreated, 11
Chryses, Apollo's priest.   For he came to the ships of Achaia,
Bearing a daughter's ransom, a sum not easy to number :
And in his hand was the emblem of Him, far-darting Apollo,
High on a sceptre of gold : and he prayed to the hosts of
        Achaia ;
Chiefly to Atreus' sons, twin chieftains, ordering armies.

  "Chiefs sprung of Atreus' loins ; and ye, brazen-greavèd
        Achaians !
So may the Gods this day, the Olympus-palacèd, grant you
Priam's city to raze, and return unscathed to your homesteads :
Only my own dear daughter I ask ; take ransom and yield her,
Rev'rencing His great name, son of Zeus, far-darting Apollo." 21

  Then from the host of Achaians arose tumultuous answer :
" Due to the priest is his honour ; accept rich ransom and yield
        her."

But there was war in the spirit of Atreus' son, Agamemnon ;
Disdainful he dismissed him, a right stern fiat appending :—

  "Woe be to thee, old man, if I find thee lingering longer,
Yea or returning again, by the hollow ships of Achaians !
Scarce much then will avail thee the great god's sceptre and
        emblem.
Her will I never release.   Old age must first come upon her,
In my own home, yea in Argos, afar from the land of her
        fathers,   30
Following the loom, and attending upon my bed.   But avaunt
        thee !
Go, and provoke not me, that thy way may be haply securer."

  These were the words of the king, and the old man feared
        and obeyed him :
Voiceless he went by the shore of the great dull-echoing ocean,
Thither he gat him apart, that ancient man ; and a long prayer

Prayed to Apollo his Lord, son of golden-ringleted Leto :

"Lord of the silver bow, thou whose arm girds Chryse and
    Cilla,—

Cilla beloved of the Gods,—and in might sways Tenedos,
    hearken !

Oh ! if, in days gone by, I have built from floor unto cornice,

Smintheus, a fair shrine for thee; or burned in the flames of
    the altar   40

Fat flesh of bulls and of goats; then do this thing that I ask
    thee :

Hurl on the Greeks thy shafts, that thy servant's tears be
    avengèd !"

So did he pray, and his prayer reached the ears of Phœbus
    Apollo.

Dark was the soul of the god as he moved from the heights of
    Olympus,

Shouldering a bow, and a quiver on this side fast and on that
    side.

Onward in anger he moved. And the arrows, stirred by the
    motion,

Rattled and rang on his shoulder : he came as cometh the
    midnight.

Hard by the ships he stayed him, and loosed one shaft from
    the bow-string ;

Harshly the stretched string twanged of the bow all silvery-
    shining.

First fell his wrath on the mules, and the swift-footed hound of
    the herdsman ;   50

Afterward smote he the host. With a rankling arrow he smote
    them

Aye ; and the morn and the even were red with the glare of the
    corpse-fires.

Nine days over the host sped the shafts of the god : and the
    tenth day
Dawned ; and Achilles said, " Be a council called of the people."
(Such thought came to his mind from the goddess, Hera the
    white-armed,
Hera who loved those Greeks, and who saw them dying around
    her.)
So when all were collected and ranged in a solemn assembly,
Straightway rose up amidst them and spake swift-footed
    Achilles :—
    "Atreus' son ! it were better, I think this day, that we
    wandered
Back, re-seeking our homes, (if a warfare *may* be avoided) ; 60
Now when the sword and the plague, these two things, fight
    with Achaians.
Come, let us seek out now some priest, some seer amongst us,
Yea or a dreamer of dreams—for a dream too cometh of God's
    hand—
Whence we may learn what hath angered in this wise Phœbus
    Apollo.
Whether mayhap he reprove us of prayer or of oxen unoffered ;
Whether, accepting the incense of lambs and of blemishless
    he-goats,
Yet it be his high will to remove this misery from us."
    Down sat the prince : he had spoken.   And uprose to them
    in answer
Kalchas, Thestor's son, high chief of the host of the augurs.
Well he knew what is present, what will be, and what was afore-
    time :   70
He into Ilion's harbour had led those ships of Achaia,
All by the power of the Art, which he gained from Phœbus
    Apollo.
Thus then, kindliest-hearted, arising spake he before them :

"Peleus' son! Thou demandest, a man heaven-favour'd, an
      answer
Touching the Great King's wrath, the afar-off-aiming Apollo:
Therefore I lift up my voice.   Swear thou to me, duly digesting
All,—that with right good will, by word and by deed, thou wilt
      aid me.
Surely the ire will awaken of one who mightily ruleth
Over the Argives all: and upon him wait the Achaians.
Aye is the battle the king's, when the poor man kindleth his
      anger: 80
For, if but this one day he devour his indignation,
Still on the morrow abideth a rage, that its end be accom-
      plished,
Deep in the soul of the king.   So bethink thee, wilt thou
      deliver."
    Then unto him making answer arose swift-footed Achilles:
"Fearing naught, up and open the god's will, all that is told
      thee:
For by Apollo's self, heaven's favourite, whom thou, Kalchas,
Serving aright, to the armies aloud God's oracles op'nest:
None—while as yet I breathe upon earth, yet walk in the day-
      light—
Shall, at the hollow ships, lift hand of oppression against thee,
None out of all your host—not and if thou nam'st Agamem-
      non,   90
Who now sits in his glory, the topmost flower of the armies."
    Then did the blameless prophet at last take courage and
      answer:
"Lo! He doth not reprove us of prayer or of oxen unoffered;
But for his servant's sake, the disdained of king Agamemnon,
(In that he loosed not his daughter, inclined not his ear to a
      ransom,)
Therefore the Far-darter sendeth, and yet shall send on us, evil.

Nor shall he stay from the slaughter the hand that is heavy
    upon you,
Till to her own dear father the bright-eyed maiden is yielded,
No price asked, no ransom; and ships bear hallowèd oxen
Chryse-wards:—then, it may be, will he show mercy and hear
    us."   100
    These words said, sat he down. Then rose in his place and
    addressed them
Atreus' warrior son, Agamemnon king of the nations,
Sore grieved. Fury was working in each dark cell of his bosom,
And in his eye was a glare as a burning fiery furnace:
First to the priest he addressed him, his whole mien boding a
    mischief.
    "Priest of ill luck! Never heard I aught good from thee, but
    evil.
Still doth the evil thing unto thee seem sweeter of utt'rance;
Leaving the thing which is good all unspoke, all unaccom-
    plished.
Lo! this day to the people thou say'st, God's oracles op'ning,
What, but that *I* am the cause why the god's hand worketh
    against them,   110
For that in sooth I rejected a ransom, ay and a rich one,
Brought for the girl Briseis. I did. For I chose to possess
    her,
Rather, at home: less favour hath Clytemnestra before me,
Clytemnestra my wife: unto her Briseis is equal,
Equal in form and in stature, in mind and in womanly wisdom.
Still, even thus, am I ready to yield her, so it be better:
Better is saving alive, I hold, than slaying a nation.
Meanwhile deck me a guerdon in her stead, lest of Achaians
I should alone lack honour; an unmeet thing and a shameful.
See all men, that my guerdon, I wot not whither it goeth." 120
    Then unto him made answer the swift-foot chieftain Achilles:

" O most vaunting of men, most gain-loving, offspring of Atreus !

How shall the lords of Achaia bestow fresh guerdon upon thee ?

Surely we know not yet of a treasure piled in abundance !

That which the sacking of cities hath brought to us, all hath an
      owner,

Yea it were all unfit that the host make redistribution.

Yield thou the maid to the god.   So threefold surely and four-
      fold

All we Greeks will requite thee, should that day dawn, when the
      great gods

Grant that of yon proud walls not one stone rest on another."

    *   *   *   *   *

VIRGIL'S ECLOGUES

ECLOGUE I

MELIBŒUS. TITYRUS.

M.

STRETCHED in the shadow of the broad beech, thou
    Rehearsest, Tityrus, on the slender pipe
    Thy woodland music. We our fatherland
    Are leaving, we must shun the fields we love:
    While, Tityrus, thou, at ease amid the shade,
    Bidd'st answering woods call Amaryllis 'fair.'

T. O Melibœus! 'Tis a god that made
    For me this holiday: for god I'll aye
    Account him; many a young lamb from my fold
    Shall stain his altar. Thanks to him, my kine   10
    Range, as thou seest them: thanks to him, I play
    What songs I list upon my shepherd's pipe.

M. For me, I grudge thee not; I marvel much:
    So sore a trouble is in all the land.
    Lo! feeble *I* am driving hence my goats—
    Nay *dragging*, Tityrus, one, and that with pain.
    For, yeaning here amidst the hazel-stems,
    She left her twin kids—on the naked flint
    She left them; and I lost my promised flock.
    This evil, I remember, oftentimes,   20
    (Had not my wits been wandering,) oaks foretold
    By heaven's hand smitten: oft the wicked crow
    Croaked the same message from the rifted holm.
    —Yet tell me, Tityrus, of this 'God' of thine.

T.   The city men call *Rome* my folly deemed
    Was e'en like this of ours, where week by week
    We shepherds journey with our weanling flocks.
    So whelp to dog, so kid (I knew) to dam
    Was likest: and I judged great things by small.
    But o'er all cities this so lifts her head,   30
    As doth o'er osiers lithe the cypress tree.
M.   What made thee then so keen to look on Rome?
T.   Freedom: who marked, at last, my helpless state:
    Now that a whiter beard than that of yore
    Fell from my razor: still she marked, and came
    (All late) to help me—now that all my thought
    Is Amaryllis, Galatea gone.
    While Galatea's, I despaired, I own,
    Of freedom, and of thrift.   Though from my farm
    Full many a victim stept, though rich the cheese   40
    Pressed for yon thankless city: still my hand
    Returned not, heavy with brass pieces, home.
M.   I wondered, Amaryllis, whence that woe,
    And those appeals to heav'n; for whom the peach
    Hung undisturbed upon the parent tree.
    Tityrus was gone!   Why, Tityrus, pine and rill,
    And all these copses, cried to thee, "Come home!"
T.   What could I do?   I could not step from out
    My bonds; nor meet, save there, with Pow'rs so kind.
    There, Meliboeus, I beheld that youth   50
    For whom each year twelve days my altars smoke.
    Thus answered he my yet unanswered prayer;
    "Feed still, my lads, your kine, and yoke your bulls."
M.   Happy old man!   Thy lands are yet thine own!
    Lands broad enough for thee, although bare stones
    And marsh choke every field with reedy mud.
    Strange pastures shall not vex thy teeming ewes,

Nor neighbouring flocks shed o'er them rank disease.
Happy old man !   Here, by familiar streams
And holy springs, thou'lt catch the leafy cool.   60
Here, as of old, yon hedge, thy boundary line,
Its willow-buds a feast for Hybla's bees,
Shall with soft whisperings woo thee to thy sleep.
Here, 'neath the tall cliff, shall the vintager
Sing carols to the winds : while all the time
Thy pets, the stockdoves, and the turtles make
Incessantly their moan from aëry elms.

T.   Aye, and for this shall slim stags graze in air,
And ocean cast on shore the shrinking fish ;
For this, each realm by either wandered o'er,   70
Parthians shall Arar drink, or Tigris Gauls ;
Ere from this memory shall fade that face !

M.   And we the while must thirst on Libya's sands,
O'er Scythia roam, and where the Cretan stems
The swift Oaxes ; or, with Britons, live
Shut out from all the world.   Shall I e'er see,
In far-off years, my fatherland ? the turf
That roofs my meagre hut ? see, wondering last,
Those few scant cornblades that are realms to me ?
What ! must rude soldiers hold these fallows trim ?   80
That corn barbarians ?   See what comes of strife,
Poor people—where we sowed, what hands shall reap !
Now, Melibœus, pr'ythee graft thy pears,
And range thy vines !   Nay on, my she-goats, on,
Once happy flock !   For never more must I,
Outstretched in some green hollow, watch you hang
From tufted crags, far up : no carols more
I'll sing : nor, shepherded by me, shall ye
Crop the tart willow and the clover-bloom.

T.   Yet here, this one night, thou may'st rest with me,   90

Thy bed green branches.   Chestnuts soft have I
And mealy apples, and our fill of cheese.
Already, see, the far-off chimneys smoke,
And deeper grow the shadows of the hills.

ECLOGUE II

CORYDON

FOR one fair face—his master's idol—burned
   The shepherd Corydon ; and hope had none.
Day after day he came ('twas all he could)
Where, piles of shadow, thick the beeches rose :
There, all alone, his unwrought phrases flung,
Bootless as passionate, to copse and crag.
   "Hardhearted ! Naught car'st thou for all my songs,
Naught pitiest.   I shall die, one day, for thee.
The very cattle court cool shadows now,
Now the green lizard hides beneath the thorn :   10
And for the reaper, faint with driving heat,
The handmaids mix the garlic-salad strong.
My only mates, the crickets—as I track
'Neath the fierce sun thy steps—make shrill the woods.
Better to endure the passion and the pride
Of Amaryllis : better to endure
Menalcas—dark albeit as thou art fair.
Put not, oh fair, in difference of hue
Faith overmuch : the white May-blossoms drop
And die ; the hyacinth swart, men gather it.   20
Thy scorn am I : thou ask'st not whence I am,
How rich in snowy flocks, how stored with milk.
O'er Sicily's green hills a thousand lambs

Wander, all mine : my new milk fails me not
In summer or in snow.   Then I can sing
All songs Amphion the Dircæan sang,
Piping his flocks from Attic Aracynth.
Nor am I all uncouth.   For yesterday,
When winds had laid the seas, I, from the shore,
Beheld my image.   Little need I fear   30
Daphnis, though thou wert judge, or mirrors lie.
—Oh ! be content to haunt ungentle fields,
A cottager, with me ; bring down the stag,
And with green switch drive home thy flocks of kids :
Like mine, thy woodland songs shall rival Pan's !
—'Twas Pan first taught us reed on reed to fit
With wax : Pan watches herd and herdsman too.
—Nor blush that reeds should chafe thy pretty lip.
What pains Amyntas took, this skill to gain !
I have a pipe—seven stalks of different lengths   40
Compose it—which Damœtas gave me once.
Dying he said, "At last 'tis all thine own."
The fool Amyntas heard, and grudged, the praise.
Two fawns moreover (perilous was the gorge
Down which I tracked them !)—dappled still each skin—
Drain daily two ewe-udders ; all for thee.
Long Thestylis has cried to make them hers.
Hers be they—since to thee my gifts are dross.

Be mine, oh fairest !   See ! for thee the Nymphs
Bear baskets lily-laden : Naiads bright   50
For thee crop poppy-crests and violets pale,
With daffodil and fragrant fennel-bloom :
Then, weaving casia in and all sweet things,
Soft hyacinth paint with yellow marigold.
Apples *I*'ll bring thee, hoar with tender bloom,

And chestnuts—which my Amaryllis loved,
And waxen plums: let plums too have their day.
And thee I'll pluck, oh bay, and, myrtle, thee
Its neighbour: neighboured thus your sweets shall mix.
—Pooh! Thou'rt a yokel, Corydon.   Thy love   60
Laughs at thy gifts: if gifts must win the day,
Rich is Iolas.   What thing have I,
Poor I, been asking—while the winds and boars
Ran riot in my pools and o'er my flowers?

—Yet, fool, whom fliest thou?   Gods have dwelt in woods,
And Dardan Paris.   Citadels let her
Who built them, Pallas, haunt: green woods for me.
Grim lions hunt the wolf, and wolves the kid,
And kids at play the clover-bloom.   I hunt
Thee only: each one drawn to what he loves.   70
See! trailing from their necks the kine bring home
The plough, and, as he sinks, the sun draws out
To twice their length the shadows.   Still I burn
With love.   For what can end or alter love?

Thou'rt raving, simply raving, Corydon.
Clings to thy leafy elm thy half-pruned vine.
Why not begin, at least, to plait with twigs
And limber reeds some useful homely thing?
Thou'lt find another love, if scorned by this.

ECLOGUE III

MENALCAS.   DAMŒTAS.   PALÆMON.

M.

WHOSE flock, Damœtas?   Melibœus's?
    D.   No, Ægon's.   Ægon left it in my care.
M.   Unluckiest of flocks!   Your master courts
    Neæra, wondering if she like me more:
    Meanwhile a stranger milks you twice an hour,
    Saps the flocks' strength, and robs the suckling lambs.
D.   Yet fling more charily such words at *men.*
    You—while the goats looked goatish—we know who,
    And in what chapel—(but the kind Nymphs laughed)—
M.   Then (was it?) when they saw me Micon's shrubs   10
    And young vines hacking with my rascally knife?
D.   Or when by this old beech you broke the bow
    And shafts of Daphnis: which you cried to see,
    You crossgrained lad, first given to the boy;
    And harm him somehow you must needs, or die.
M.   Where will lords stop, when knaves are come to this?
    Did not I see you, scoundrel, in a snare
    Take Damon's goat, Wolf barking all the while?
    And when I shouted, "Where's he off to?   Call,
    Tityrus, your flock,"—you skulked behind the sedge.   20
D.   Beaten in singing, should he have withheld
    The goat my pipe had by its music earned?
    That goat was mine, you mayn't p'r'aps know: and he
    Owned it himself; but said he could not pay.
M.   He beat by you?   You own a decent pipe?
    Used you not, dunce, to stand at the crossroads,
    Stifling some lean tune in a squeaky straw?

D. Shall we then try in turn what each can do?
      I stake yon cow—nay hang not back—she comes
      Twice daily to the pail, is suckling twins.   30
      Say what *you*'ll lay.

M.   I durst not wager aught
      Against you from the flock : for I have at home
      A father, I have a tyrant stepmother.
      Both count the flock twice daily, one the kids.
      But what *you*'ll own far handsomer, I'll stake
      (Since you will be so mad) two beechen cups,
      The carved work of the great Alcimedon.
      O'er them the chiseller's skill has traced a vine
      That drapes with ivy pale her wide-flung curls.
      Two figures in the centre : Conon one,   40
      And—what 's that other's name, who'd take a wand
      And show the nations how the year goes round ;
      When you should reap, when stoop behind the plough?
      Ne'er yet my lips came near them, safe hid up.

D. For *me* two cups the selfsame workman made,
      And clasped with lissom briar the handles round.
      Orpheus i' the centre, with the woods behind.
      Ne'er yet my lips came near them, safe hid up.
      —This talk of cups, if on my cow you've fixed
      Your eye, is idle.

M.   Nay you'll not this day   50
      Escape me.   Name your spot, and I'll be there.
      Our umpire be—Palæmon ; here he comes !
      I'll teach you how to challenge folks to sing.

D. Come on, if aught is in you.   I'm not loth,
      I shrink from no man.   Only, neighbour, thou
      ('Tis no small matter) lay this well to heart.

P. Say on, since now we sit on softest grass ;
      And now buds every field and every tree,

Q

And woods are green, and passing fair the year.
Damœtas, lead.   Menalcas, follow next.   60
Sing verse for verse : such songs the Muses love.

D. With Jove we open.   Jove fills everything,
      He walks the earth, he listens when I sing.

M. Me Phœbus loves.   I still have offerings meet
      For Phœbus ; bay, and hyacinth blushing sweet.

D. Me Galatea pelts with fruit, and flies
      (Wild girl) to the woods : but first would catch my eyes.

M. Unbid Amyntas comes to me, my flame ;
      With Delia's self my dogs are not more tame.

D. Gifts have I for my fair : who marked but I   70
      The place where doves had built their nest sky-high ?

M. I've sent my poor gift, which the wild wood bore,
      Ten golden apples.   Soon I'll send ten more.

D. Oft Galatea tells me—what sweet tales !
      Waft to the god's ears just a part, ye gales.

M. At heart Amyntas loves me.   Yet what then ?
      He mates with hunters, I with servingmen.

D. Send me thy Phyllis, good Iolas, now.
      To-day's my birthday.   When I slay my cow
      To help my harvest—come, and welcome, thou.   80

M. Phillis is *my* love.   When we part, she'll cry ;
      And fain would bid Iolas' self good-bye.[1]

D. Wolves kill the flocks, and storms the ripened corn ;
      And winds the tree ; and me a maiden's scorn.

---

[1] Putting the vocative "Iolla" in line 79, as Mr. Kennedy does, into
the mouth of Menalcas, not of Phyllis, I would substitute these lines for
my original ones :—

> Phillis is *my* dear love.   She wept when I—
> (Yes I, Iollas,)—left her : and "Good-bye",
> She said, "Iollas fair ; a long Good-bye".

M.   Rain is the land's delight, weaned kids' the vine ;
    Big ewes' lithe willow ; and one fair face mine.

D.   Pollio loves well this homely muse of mine.
    For a new votary fat a calf, ye Nine.

M.   Pollio *makes* songs.   For him a bull demand,
    Who butts, whose hoofs already spurn the sand.   90

D.   Who loves thee, Pollio, go where thou art gone.
    For him flow honey, thorns sprout cinnamon.

M.   Who loathes not Bavius, let him love thy notes,
    Mævius :—and yoke the fox, and milk he-goats.

D.   Flowers and ground-strawberries while your prize ye make,
    Cold in the grass—fly hence, lads—lurks the snake.

M.   Sheep, banks are treacherous : draw not over-nigh :
    See, now the lordly ram his fleece doth dry.

D.   Tityrus, yon she-goats from the river bring.
    I in due time will wash them at the spring.   100

M.   Call, lads, your sheep.   Once more our hands, should heat
    O'ertake the milk, will press in vain the teat.

D.   How rich these vetches, yet how lean my ox.
    Love kills alike the herdsman and the flocks.

M.   *My* lambs—and here love 's not in fault, you'll own—
    Witched by some jealous eye, are skin and bone.

D.   Say in what land—and great Apollo be
    To me—heaven's arch extends just cubits three.

M.   Say in what lands with kings' names grav'n are grown
    Flowers—and be Phyllis yours and yours alone.   110

P.   Not mine such strife to settle.   You have earned
    A cow, and you: and whoso else shall e'er
    Shrink from love's sweets or prove his bitterness.
    Close, lads, the springs.   The meads have drunk enough.

ECLOGUE IV

MUSES of Sicily, a loftier song
    Wake we! Some tire of shrubs and myrtles low.
Are woods our theme? Then princely be the woods.

    Come are those last days that the Sibyl sang:
The ages' mighty march begins anew.
Now comes the virgin, Saturn reigns again:
Now from high heaven descends a wondrous race.
Thou on the newborn babe—who first shall end
That age of iron, bid a golden dawn
Upon the broad world—chaste Lucina, smile: 10
Now thy Apollo reigns. And, Pollio, thou
Shalt be our Prince, when he that grander age
Opens, and onward roll the mighty moons:
Thou, trampling out what prints our crimes have left,
Shalt free the nations from perpetual fear.
While he to bliss shall waken; with the Blest
See the Brave mingling, and be seen of them,
Ruling that world o'er which his father's arm shed peace.—

    On thee, child, everywhere shall earth, untilled,
Show'r, her first baby-offerings, vagrant stems   20
Of ivy, foxglove, and gay briar, and bean;
Unbid the goats shall come big-uddered home,
Nor monstrous lions scare the herded kine.
Thy cradle shall be full of pretty flowers:
Die must the serpent, treacherous poison-plants
Must die; and Syria's roses spring like weeds.

But, soon as thou canst read of hero-deeds
Such as thy father wrought, and understand
What is true worth: the champaign day by day
Shall grow more yellow with the waving corn;   30
From the wild bramble purpling then shall hang
The grape; and stubborn oaks drop honeydew.
Yet traces of that guile of elder days
Shall linger; bidding men tempt seas in ships,
Gird towns with walls, cleave furrows in the land.
Then a new Tiphys shall arise, to man
New argosies with heroes; then shall be
New wars; and once more shall be bound for Troy,
A mightier Achilles.
                              After this,
When thou hast grown and strengthened into man,   40
The pilot's self shall range the seas no more;
Nor, each land teeming with the wealth of all,
The floating pines exchange their merchandise.
Vines shall not need the pruning-hook, nor earth .
The harrow: ploughmen shall unyoke their steers.
Nor then need wool be taught to counterfeit
This hue and that.   At will the meadow ram
Shall change to saffron, or the gorgeous tints
Of Tyre, his fair fleece; and the grazing lamb
At will put crimson on.
                              So grand an age   50
Did those three Sisters bid their spindles spin;
Three, telling with one voice the changeless will of Fate.

Oh draw—the time is all but present—near
To thy great glory, cherished child of heaven,
Jove's mighty progeny! And lo! the world,
The round and ponderous world, bows down to thee;

The earth, the ocean-tracts, the depths of heaven.
Lo! nature revels in the coming age.
Oh! may the evening of my days last on,
May breath be mine, till I have told thy deeds!   60
Not Orpheus then, not Linus, shall outsing
Me: though each vaunts his mother or his sire,
Calliopea this, Apollo that.
Let Pan strive with me, Arcady his judge;
Pan, Arcady his judge, shall yield the palm.

Learn, tiny babe, to read a mother's smile:
Already ten long months have wearied her.
Learn, tiny babe. Him, who ne'er knew such smiles,
Nor god nor goddess bids to board or bed.

ECLOGUE V

MENALCAS. MOPSUS.

Me.

MOPSUS, suppose, now two good men have met—
You at flute-blowing, as at verses I—
We sit down here, where elm and hazel mix.

Mo. Menalcas, meet it is that I obey
Mine elder. Lead, or into shade—that shifts
At the wind's fancy—or (mayhap the best)
Into some cave. See here's a cave, o'er which
A wild vine flings her flimsy foliage.

Me. On these hills one—Amyntas—vies with you.

Mo. Suppose he thought to outsing Phœbus' self?   10

Me. Mopsus, begin. If aught you know of flames
That Phyllis kindles; aught of Alcon's worth,
Or Codrus's ill-temper; then begin:

Tityrus meanwhile will watch the grazing kids.

Mo.   Ay, I will sing the song which t'other day
On a green beech's bark I cut; and scored
The music, as I wrote.   Hear that, and bid
Amyntas vie with me.

Me.   As willow lithe
Yields to pale olive; as to crimson beds
Of roses yields the lowly lavender;   20
So, to my mind, Amyntas yields to you.

Mo.   But, lad, no more: we are within the cave.

(*Sings.*) The Nymphs wept Daphnis, slain by ruthless
                death.
Ye, streams and hazels, were their witnesses:
When, clasping tight her son's unhappy corpse,
"Ruthless," the mother cried, "are gods and stars."
None to the cool brooks led in all those days,
Daphnis, his fed flocks: no four-footed thing
Stooped to the pool, or cropped the meadow-grass.
How lions of the desert mourned thy death,   30
Forests and mountains wild proclaim aloud,
'Twas Daphnis taught mankind to yoke in cars
The tiger; lead the winegod's revel on,
And round the tough spear twine the bending leaf.
Vines are the green wood's glory, grapes the vine's:
The bull the cattle's, and the rich land's corn.
Thou art thy people's.   When thou metst thy doom,
Both Pales and Apollo left our fields.
In furrows where we dropped big barley seeds,
Spring now rank darnel and the barren reed: 40
Not violet soft and shining daffodil,
But thistles rear themselves and sharp-spiked thorn.
Shepherds, strow earth with leaves, and hang the springs

With darkness!   Daphnis asks of you such rites:
And raise a tomb, and place this rhyme thereon:
"Famed in the green woods, famed beyond the skies,
A fair flock's fairer lord, here Daphnis lies."

Me.   Welcome thy song to me, oh sacred bard,
As, to the weary, sleep upon the grass:
As, in the summer-heat, a bubbling spring   50
Of sweetest water, that shall slake our thirst.
In song, as on the pipe, thy master's match,
Thou, gifted lad, shalt now our master be.
Yet will I sing in turn, in my poor way,
My song, and raise thy Daphnis to the stars—
Raise Daphnis to the stars.   He loved me too.

Mo.   Could aught in my eyes such a boon outweigh?
Song-worthy was thy theme: and Stimichon
Told me long since of that same lay of thine.

Me.   (*Sings.*)   Heaven's unfamiliar floor, and clouds and stars,
Fair Daphnis, wondering, sees beneath his feet.   61
Therefore gay revelries fill wood and field,
Pan, and the shepherds, and the Dryad maids.
Wolves plot not harm to sheep, nor nets to deer;
Because kind Daphnis makes it holiday.
The unshorn mountains fling their jubilant voice
Up to the stars: the crags and copses shout
Aloud, "A god, Menalcas, lo! a god."
Oh! be thou kind and good unto thine own!
Behold four altars, Daphnis: two for thee,   70
Two, piled for Phœbus.   Thereupon I'll place
Two cups, with new milk foaming, year by year;
Two goblets filled with richest olive-oil:
And, first with much wine making glad the feast—
At the fireside in snowtime, 'neath the trees

In harvest—pour, rare nectar, from the can
The wines of Chios.   Lyctian Ægon then
Shall sing me songs, and to Damœtas' pipe
Alphesibœus dance his Satyr-dance.
And this shalt thou lack never : when we pay   80
The Nymphs our vows, and when we cleanse the fields.
While boars haunt mountain-heights, and fishes streams,
Bees feed on thyme, and grasshoppers on dew,
Thy name, thy needs, thy glory shall abide.
As Bacchus and as Ceres, so shalt thou
Year after year the shepherd's vows receive ;
So bind him to the letter of his vow.

Mo.   What can I give thee, what, for such a song ?
Less sweet to me the coming South-wind's sigh,
The sea-wave breaking on the shore, the noise   90
Of rivers, rushing through the stony vales.

Me.   First I shall offer you this brittle pipe.
This taught me how to sing, " For one fair face : "
This taught me " Whose flock ? Melibœus's ? "

Mo.   Take thou this crook ; which oft Antigenes
Asked—and he then was loveable—in vain ;
Brass-tipped and even-knotted—beautiful !

ECLOGUE VI

*M*Y muse first stooped to trifle, like the Greek's,
    In numbers ; and, unblushing, dwelt in woods.
I sang embattled kings : but Cynthius plucked
My ear, and warned me : " Tityrus, fat should be
A shepherd's wethers, but his lays thin-drawn."
So—for enough and more will strive to tell,

Varus, thy deeds, and pile up grisly wars—
On pipe of straw will I my wood-notes sing:
I sing not all unbid. Yet oh! should one
Smit by great love, should one read this my lay—
Then with thee, Varus, shall our myrtle-groves,
And all these copses, ring. Right dearly loves
Phœbus the page that opens with thy name.

On, sisters!
                    —Chromis and Mnasylus saw
(Two lads) Silenus in a cave asleep:
As usual, swoln with yesterday's debauch.
Just where it fell his garland lay hard by;
And on worn handle hung his ponderous can.
They—for the old man oft had cheated each
Of promised songs—draw near, and make his wreaths
Fetters to bind him. Ægle makes a third,
(Ægle, the loveliest of the Naiad maids,)
To back their fears: and, as his eyes unclose,
Paints brow and temples red with mulberry.
He, laughing at the trick, cries, "Wherefore weave
These fetters? Lads, unbind me: 'tis enough
But to have seemed to have me in your power.
Ye ask a song; then listen. You I'll pay
With song: for her I've other meed in store."
And forthwith he begins. Then might you see
Move to the music Faun and forest-beast,
And tall oaks bow their heads. Not so delights
Parnassus in Apollo: not so charmed
At Orpheus Rhodope and Ismarus.

For this he sang:—How, drawn from that vast void,
Gathered the germs of earth and air and sea

10

20

30

And liquid flame.   How the Beginning sprang
Thence, and the young world waxed into a ball.
Then Earth, grown harder, walled the sea-god off
In seas, and slowly took substantial form :   40
Till on an awed world dawned the wondrous sun,
And straight from heaven, by clouds unbroken, fell
The showers : as woods first bourgeoned, here and there
A wild beast wandering over hills unknown.
Of Pyrrha casting stones, and Saturn's reign,
The stolen fire, the eagles of the rock,
He sings : and then, beside what spring last seen
The sailors called for Hylas—till the shore
All rang with ' Hylas,' ' Hylas : '—and consoles
(Happy if horned herds never had been born,)   50
With some fair bullock's love Pasiphae.
Ah ! hapless maid !   What madness this of thine ?
Once a king's daughters made believe to low,
And ranged the leas : but neither stooped to ask
Those base beasts' love : though each had often feared
To find the ploughman's gear about her neck,
And felt on her smooth brow for budding horns.
Ah ! hapless maid !   Thou roam'st from hill to hill :
He under some dark oak—his snowy side
Cushioned on hyacinths—chews the pale-green grass,   60
Or woos some favourite from the herd.   " Close, Nymphs,
Dictæan Nymphs, oh close the forest-glades !
If a bull's random footprints by some chance
Should greet me !   Lured, may be, by greener grass,
Or in the herd's wake following, vagrant kine
May bring him straight into my father's fold ! "
—Then sings he of that maid who paused to gaze
At the charmed apples :—and surrounds with moss,
Bitter tree-moss, the daughters of the Sun,

Till up they spring tall alders.—Then he sings   70
How Gallus, wandering to Parnassus' stream,
A sister led to the Aonian hills,
And, in a mortal's honour, straight uprose
The choir of Phœbus : How that priest of song,
The shepherd Linus,—all his hair with flowers
And bitter parsley shining,—spake to him.
" Take—lo ! the Muses give it thee—this pipe,
Once that Ascræan's old : to this would he
Sing till the sturdy mountain-ash came down.
Sing thou on this, whence sprang Æolia's grove,   80
Till in no wood Apollo glory more."

    So on and on he sang :—How Nisus, famed
In story, troubled the Dulichian ships ;
And in the deep seas bid her sea-dogs rend
The trembling sailors.   Tereus' tale he told,
How he was changed : what banquet Philomel,
What present, decked for him : and how she flew
To the far wilderness ; and flying paused—
(Poor thing)—to flutter round her ancient home.

    All songs which one day Phœbus sang to charmed   90
Eurotas—and the laurels learnt them off—
He sang.   The thrilled vales fling them to the stars.
Till Hesper bade them house and count their flocks,
And journeyed all unwelcome up the sky.

ECLOGUE VII

MELIBŒUS.   CORYDON.   THYRSIS.

M.

DAPHNIS was seated 'neath a murmurous oak,
    When Corydon and Thyrsis (so it chanced)
Had driv'n their two flocks—one of sheep, and one
Of teeming goats—together: herdsmen both,
Both in life's spring, and able well to sing,
Or, challenged, to reply.   To that same spot
I, guarding my young myrtles from the frost,
Find my goat strayed, the patriarch of the herd:
And straight spy Daphnis.   He, espying me
In turn, cries, "Melibœus! hither, quick!   10
Thy goat, and kids, are safe.   And if thou hast
An hour to spare, sit down beneath the shade.
Hither unbid will troop across the leas
The kine to drink: green Mincius fringes here
His banks with delicate bullrush, and a noise
Of wild bees rises from the sacred oak."

    What could I do?   Alcippe I had none,
Nor Phyllis, to shut up my new-weaned lambs:
Then, there was war on foot—a mighty war—
Thyrsis and Corydon!— So in the end   20
I made my business wait upon their sport.—
So singing verse for verse—that well the Muse
Might mark it—they began their singing-match.
Thus Corydon, thus Thyrsis sang in turn.   (*They sing.*)
C. "Ye Fountain Nymphs, my loves!   Grant me to sing
    Like Codrus:—next Apollo's rank his lines:—

Or here—if all may scarce do everything—
   I'll hang my pipe up on these sacred pines."

T.   " Swains ! a new minstrel deck with ivy now,
   Till Codrus burst with envy !   Or, should he   30
Flatter o'ermuch, twine foxglove o'er my brow,
   Lest his knave's-flattery spoil the bard to be."

C.   " 'To Dian, from young Micon : this boar's head,
   And these broad antlers of a veteran buck.'
Full-length in marble—ancle-bound with red
   Buskins—I'll rear her, should to-day bring luck."

T.   " Ask but this bowl, Priapus, and this cake
   Each year : for poor the garden thou dost keep.
Our small means made thee marble : whom we'll make
   Of gold, should lambing multiply our sheep."   40

C.   " Maid of the seas ! more sweet than Hybla's thyme,
   Graceful as ivy, white as is the swan !
When home the fed flocks wend at evening's prime,
   Then come—if aught thou car'st for Corydon."

T.   " Hark ! bitterer than wormwood may I be,
   Bristling as broom, as drifted sea-weed cheap,
If this day seem not a long year to me !
   Home, home for very shame, my o'er-fed sheep ! "

C.   " Ye mossy rills, and lawns more soft than dreams,
   Thinly roofed over by these leaves of green :   50
From the great heat—now summer's come, now teems
   The jocund vine with buds—my cattle screen."

T.   " Warm hearth, good faggots, and great fires you'll find
   In my home : black with smoke are all its planks :
We laugh, who're in it, at the chill north wind,
   As wolves at troops of sheep, mad streams at banks."

C.   " Here furry chestnuts rise and juniper :
   Heaped 'neath each tree the fallen apples lie :
All smiles.   But, once let fair Alexis stir

     From off these hills—and lo! the streams are dry."   60

T. " Thirsts in parched lands and dies the blighted grass ;
     Vines lend no shadow to the mountain-height ;
     But groves shall bloom again, when comes my lass ;
     And in glad showers Jove descend in might."

C. " Poplars Alcides likes, and Bacchus vines ;
     Fair Venus myrtle, and Apollo bay ;
     But while to hazel-leaves my love inclines,
     Nor bays nor myrtles greater are than they."

T. " Fair in woods ash ; and pine on garden-grass :
     On tall cliffs fir ; by pools the poplar-tree.   70
     But if thou come here oft, sweet Lycidas,
     Lawn-pine and mountain-ash must yield to thee."

M.   All this I've heard before : remember well
     How Thyrsis strove in vain against defeat.
     From that day forth 'twas ' Corydon ' for me.

ECLOGUE VIII

ALPHESIBŒUS'S and Damon's muse—
   Charmed by whose strife the steer forgot to graze ;
Whose notes made lynxes motionless, and bade
Rivers turn back and listen—sing we next :
Alphesibœus's and Damon's muse.

Winn'st thou the crags of great Timavus now,
Or skirtest strands where break Illyrian seas ?
I know not.   But oh when shall that day dawn
When I may tell thy deeds ? give earth thy lays,
That match alone the pomp of Sophocles ?   10
With thee began, with thee shall end, my song :
Accept what thou didst ask ; and round thy brow

Twine this poor ivy with thy victor bays.
'Twas at the hour when night's cold shadow scarce
Had left the skies ; when, blest by herdsmen, hangs
The dewdrop on the grass ; that Damon leaned
On his smooth olive-staff, and thus began.

"Wake, morning star !   Prevent warm day, and come !
While, duped and humbled, I—because I loved
Nisa with all a husband's love—complain ;   20
And call the gods, (though naught their cognizance
Availed,) at my last hour, a dying man.
Begin, my flute, a song of Arcady.

"There forests murmur aye, and pines discourse ;
And lovelorn swains, and Pan, who first reclaimed
From idleness the reed, hath audience there,
Begin, my flute, a song of Arcady.

"Nisa—is aught impossible in love ?—
Is given to Mopsus.   Griffins next will mate
With mares : our children see the coward deer   30
Come with the hound to drink.   Go, shape the torch,
Mopsus ! fling, bridegroom, nuts !   Thou lead'st a wife
Home, and o'er Œta peers the evening star.
Begin, my flute, a song of Arcady.

"Oh, mated with a worthy husband ! thou
Who scorn'st mankind—abhorr'st this pipe, these goats
Of mine, and shaggy brows, and hanging beard :
Nor think'st that gods can see what mortals do !
Begin, my flute, a song of Arcady.

"Within our orchard-walls I saw thee first,   40
A wee child with her mother—(I was sent
To guide you)—gathering apples wet with dew.

Ten years and one I scarce had numbered then;
Could scarce on tiptoe reach the brittle boughs.
I saw, I fell, I was myself no more.
Begin, my flute, a song of Arcady.

"Now know I what love is.   On hard rocks born
Tmaros, or Rhodope, or they who dwell
In utmost Africa do father him;
No child of mortal blood or lineage.   50
Begin, my flute, a song of Arcady.

"In her son's blood a mother dipped her hands
At fierce love's bidding.   Hard was her heart too—
Which harder? her heart or that knavish boy's?
Knavish the boy, and hard was her heart too.
Begin, my flute, a song of Arcady.

"Now let the wolf first turn and fly the sheep:
Hard oaks bear golden apples: daffodil
Bloom on the alder: and from myrtle-stems
Ooze richest amber.   Let owls vie with swans;   60
And be as Orpheus—Orpheus in the woods,
Arion with the dolphins—every swain,
(Begin, my flute, a song of Arcady)

"And earth become mid ocean.   Woods, farewell!
Down from some breezy mountain height to the waves
I'll fling me.   Take this last gift ere I die.
Unlearn, my flute, the songs of Arcady."

Thus Damon.   How the other made reply
Sing, sisters.   Scarce may all do everything.

A.   "Fetch water: wreathe yon altar with soft wool: 70
And burn rich vervain and brave frankincense;

R

That I may try my lord's clear sense to warp
With dark rites.   Naught is lacking save the songs.
Bring, songs, bring Daphnis from the city home.

"Songs can bring down the very moon from heaven.
Circe with songs transformed Ulysses' crew.
Songs shall in sunder burst the cold grass-snake.
Bring, songs, bring Daphnis from the city home.

"Three threads about thee, of three several hues,
I twine; and thrice—(odd numbers please the god)—   80
Carry thy image round the altar-stones.
Bring, songs, bring Daphnis from the city home.

"Weave, Amaryllis, in three knots three hues.
Just weave and say 'I'm weaving chains of love.'
Bring, songs, bring Daphnis from the city home.

"As this clay hardens, melts this wax, at one
And the same flame: so Daphnis 'neath my love.
Strew meal, and light with pitch the crackling bay.
Daphnis burns me; for Daphnis burn these bays.
Bring, songs, bring Daphnis from the city home.   90

"Be his such longing as the heifer feels,
When, faint with seeking her lost mate through copse
And deepest grove, beside some water-brook
In the green grass she sinks in her despair,
Nor cares to yield possession to the night.
Be his such longing: mine no wish to heal.
Bring, songs, bring Daphnis from the city home.

"Pledges of love, these clothes the traitor once
Bequeathed me.   I commit them, Earth, to thee

Here at my threshold.   He is bound by these.   100
Bring, songs, bring Daphnis from the city home.

"These deadly plants great Mœris gave to me,
In Pontus plucked : in Pontus thousands grow.
By their aid have I seen him skulk in woods
A wolf, unsepulchre the buried dead,
And charm to other fields the standing corn.
Bring, songs, bring Daphnis from the city home.

"Go, Amaryllis, ashes in thy hand :
Throw them—and look not backwards—o'er thy head
Into a running stream.   These next I'll try   110
On Daphnis ; who regards not gods nor songs.
Bring, songs, bring Daphnis from the city home.

"See !   While I hesitate, a quivering flame
Hath clutched the wood, self-issuing from the ash.
May this mean good !   Something—for Hylas too
Barks at the gate—it must mean.   Is it true?
Or are we lovers dupes of our own dreams ?
Cease, songs, cease.   Daphnis comes from the city home!"

ECLOGUE IX

LYCIDAS.   MŒRIS.

L.

MŒRIS, on foot ? and on the road to town ?
    M.   Oh Lycidas !—we live to tell—how one—
(Who dreamed of this ?)—a stranger—holds our farm,
And says, "'Tis mine : its ancient lords, begone ! "
Beaten, cast down—for Chance is lord of all—

We send him—bootlessly mayhap—these kids.

L.   Yet all, I heard, from where we lose yon hills,
With gradual bend down-sloping to the brook,
And those old beeches, broken columns now,
Had your Menalcas rescued by his songs.   10

M.   Thou heardst.   Fame said so.   But our songs avail,
Mœris, no more 'mid warspears than, they say,
Dodona's doves may, when the eagle stoops.
A boding raven from a rifted oak
Warned me, by this means or by that to nip
This strange strife in the bud : or dead were now
Thy Mœris ; dead were great Menalcas too.

L.   Could such curse fall on man ?   Had we so near
Lost thee, Menalcas, and thy pleasantries ?
Who then would sing the nymphs ?   Who strow with flowers
The ground, or train green darkness o'er the springs ?   21
And oh ! that song, which I (saying ne'er a word)
Copied one day—(while thou wert off to see
My darling, Amaryllis,)—from thy notes :
" Feed, while I journey but a few short steps,
Tityrus, my goats : and, Tityrus, when they've fed,
Lead them to drink : and cross not by the way
The he-goat's path : his horns are dangerous."

M.   But that to Varus, that unfinished one !
" Varus ! thy name, if Mantua still be ours—   30
(Mantua ! to poor Cremona all too near,)—
Shall tuneful swans exalt unto the stars."

L.   Begin, if in thee 's aught.   So may not yews
Of Cyrnus lure thy bees : so, clover-fed,
Thy cattle teem with milk.   Me too the muse
Hath made a minstrel : I have songs ; and me
The swains call ' poet.'   But I heed them not.
For scarce yet sing I as the great ones sing,

But, a goose, cackle among piping swans.

M. Indeed, I am busy turning o'er and o'er—   40
In hopes to recollect it—in my brain
A song, and not a mean one, Lycidas.
"Come, Galatea! sport'st thou in the waves?
Here spring is purpling; thick by river-banks
Bloom the gay flowers; white poplar climbs above
The caves, and young vines plait a roof between.
Come! and let mad seas beat against the shore."

L. What were those lines that once I heard thee sing,
All uncompanioned on a summer night—
I know the music, if I had the words.   50

M. "Daphnis! why watch those old-world planets rise?
Lo! onward marches sacred Cæsar's star,
The star that made the valleys laugh with corn,
And grapes grow ruddier upon sunny hills.
Sow, Daphnis, pears, whereof thy sons shall eat."
—Time carries all—our memories e'en—away.
Well I remember how my boyish songs
Would oft outlast the livelong summer day.
And now they're all forgot. His very voice
Hath Mœris lost: on Mœris wolves have looked.   60
—But oft thou'lt hear them from Menalcas yet.

L. Thy pleas but draw my passion out. And lo!
All hushed to listen is the wide sea-floor,
And laid the murmurings of the soughing winds.
And now we're half-way there. I can descry
Bianor's grave. Here, Mœris, where the swains
Are raking off the thick leaves, let us sing.
Or, if we fear lest night meanwhile bring up
The rain clouds, singing let us journey on—
(The way will seem less tedious)—journey on   70
Singing: and I will ease thee of thy load.

M. Cease, lad.   We'll do what lies before us now :
   Then sing our best, when comes the Master home.

ECLOGUE X

GALLUS

OH Arethuse, let this last task be mine !
   One song—a song Lycoris' self may read—
My Gallus asks : who'd grudge one song to him ?
So, when thou slid'st beneath Sicilian seas,
May ne'er salt Doris mix her stream with thine :
Begin : and sing—while yon blunt muzzles search
The underwood—of Gallus torn by love.
We lack not audience : woods take up the notes.
   Where were ye, Naiad nymphs, in grove or glen,
When Gallus died of unrequited love?   10
Not heights of Pindus or Parnassus, no
Aonian Aganippe kept ye then.
Him e'en the laurels wept and myrtle-groves.
Stretch'd 'neath the lone cliff, piny Mænalus
And chill Lycæum's stones all wept for him.
The sheep stood round.   They think not scorn of us ;
And think not scorn, O priest of song, of them.
Sheep fair Adonis fed beside the brooks.
The shepherds came.   The lazy herdsmen came.
Came, from the winter acorns dripping-wet,   20
Menalcas.   " Whence," all ask, " this love of thine ? "
Apollo came : and, " Art thou mad," he saith,
" Gallus ? Thy love, through bristling camps and snows,
Tracks now another's steps."   Silvanus came,
Crowned with his woodland glories : to and fro
Rocked the great lilies and the fennel bloom.

Pan came, Arcadia's Pan : (I have seen him, red
With elder-berries and with cinnabar :)
" Is there no end ? " quoth he : " Love heeds not this :
Tears sate not cruel Love : nor rills the leas,   30
Nor the bees clover, nor green boughs the goat."
But he rejoins sad-faced : " Yet sing this song
Upon your hills, Arcadians ! none but ye
Can sing.   Oh ! pleasantly will rest my bones,
If pipe of yours shall one day tell my loves.
Oh ! had I been as you are ! kept your flocks,
Or gleaned, a vintager, your mellow grapes !
A Phyllis, an Amyntas—whom you will—
Had been my passion—what if he be dark ?
Violets are dark and hyacinths are dark.—   40
And now should we be sitting side by side,
Willows around us and a vine o'erhead,
He carolling, or plucking garlands she.
—Here are cold springs, Lycoris, and soft lawns,
And woods : with thee I'd here decay and die.
Now, for grim war accoutred, all for love,
In the fray's centre I await the foe :
Thou, in a far land—out the very thought !—
Gazest (ah wilful !) upon Alpine snows
And the froz'n Rhine—without me—all alone !   50
May that frost harm not thee ! that jaggèd ice
Cut ne'er thy dainty feet ! I'll go, and play
My stores of music—fashioned for the lyre
Of Chalcis—on the pipe of Arcady.
My choice is made.   In woods, 'mid wild beasts' dens,
I'll bear my love, and carve it on the trees :
That with their growth, my loves may grow and grow.
Banded with nymphs I'll roam o'er Mænalus,
Or hunt swift boars ; and circle with my dogs,

Unrecking of the cold, Parthenia's glades.   60
Already over crag and ringing grove
I am borne in fancy : laugh as I let loose
The Cretan arrow from the Parthian bow :—

Pooh ! will this heal thy madness ? will that god
Learn mercy from the agonies of men ?
'Tis past : again nymphs, music, fail to please.
Again I bid the very woods begone.
No deed of mine can change him : tho' I drink
Hebrus in mid December : tho' I plunge
In snows of Thrace, the dripping winter's snows :   70
Tho', when the parched bark dies on the tall elm,
'Neath Cancer's star I tend the Æthiop's sheep.
Love's lord of all.   Let me too yield to Love.

*   *   *   *   *   *

—Sung are, oh holy ones, your minstrel's songs :
Who sits here framing pipes with slender reed.
In Gallus' eyes will ye enhance their worth :
Gallus—for whom each hour my passion grows,
As swell green alders when the spring is young.
I rise.   The shadows are the singer's bane :
Baneful the shadow of the juniper.   80
E'en the flocks like not shadow.   Go—the star
Of morning breaks—go home, my full-fed sheep.

FROM HORACE'S ODES

BOOK I

ODE 9

To Thaliarchus

ONE dazzling mass of solid snow
    Soracte stands ; the bent woods fret
  Beneath their load ; and, sharpest-set
With frost, the streams have ceased to flow.

Pile on great faggots and break up
    The ice : let influence more benign
  Enter with four-years-treasured wine,
Fetched in the ponderous Sabine cup :

Leave to the gods all else. When they
    Have once bid rest the winds that war
  Over the passionate seas, no more
Gray ash and cypress rock and sway.

Ask not what future suns shall bring.
    Count to-day gain, whate'er it chance
  To be : nor, young man, scorn the dance,
Nor deem sweet Love an idle thing,

Ere Time thy April youth hath changed
    To sourness. Park and public walk
  Attract thee now, and whispered talk
At twilight meetings pre-arranged ;

Hear now the pretty laugh that tells
In what dim corner lurks thy love;
And snatch a bracelet or a glove
From wrist or hand that scarce rebels.

ODE 11

To Leuconöe

SEEK not, for thou shalt not find it, what my end, what
  thine shall be;
Ask not of Chaldæa's science what God wills, Leuconöe:
Better far, what comes, to bear it.   Haply many a wintry blast
Waits thee still; and this, it may be, Jove ordains to be thy last,
Which flings now the flagging sea-wave on the obstinate sand-
  stone-reef.
Be thou wise: fill up the wine-cup; shortening, since the time
  is brief,
Hopes that reach into the future.   While I speak, hath stol'n
  away
Jealous Time.   Mistrust To-morrow, catch the blossom of
  To-day.

ODE 14

To a Ship

YET on fresh billows seaward wilt thou ride,
  O ship?   What dost thou?   Seek a hav'n, and there
Rest thee: for lo! thy side
  Is oarless all and bare,

And the swift south-west wind hath maimed thy mast,
And thy yards creak, and, every cable lost,
   Yield must thy keel at last
     On tyrannous sea-waves tossed

Too rudely.   Goodly canvas is not thine,
Nor gods, to hear thee when thy need is sorest :—
   True, thou—a Pontic pine,
     Child of a stately forest—

Boast'st rank and empty name : but little trust
The frightened seamen in a painted stern.
   Stay—or be mocked thou must
     By every wind in turn.

Flee—what of late sore burden was to me,
Now a sad memory and a bitter pain,—
   Those shining Cyclads flee,
     That stud the far-off main.

ODE 24

To Virgil

UNSHAMED, unchecked, for one so dear
    We sorrow.   Lead the mournful choir,
  Melpomene, to whom thy sire
Gave harp, and song-notes liquid-clear !

Sleeps He the sleep that knows no morn ?
   Oh Honour, oh twin-born with Right
   Pure Faith, and Truth that loves the light,
When shall again his like be born ?

Many a kind heart for Him makes moan ;
  Thine, Virgil, first.   But ah ! in vain
  Thy love bids heaven restore again
That which it took not as a loan :

Were sweeter lute than Orpheus given
  To thee, did trees thy voice obey ;
  The blood revisits not the clay
Which He, with lifted wand, hath driven

Into his dark assemblage, who
  Unlocks not fate to mortal's prayer.
  Hard lot !   Yet light their griefs who BEAR
The ills which they may not undo.

ODE 28

To Archytas

MEASURER of earth and ocean and the multitudinous
        sand,
  Scant the grains of tributary dust,
Lack whereof, Archytas, holds thee captive on Apulia's strand.
  Vainly in his wisdom did he trust,
Who could journey disembodied o'er the firmament, and stand
  At the gates of heaven ; for die he must.
Perished thus the sire of Pelops, messmate of the gods above :
  Thus Tithonus, caught into the air :
Minos too, the man admitted to the hidden things of Jove.
  Panthous' son himself is prisoner there—
In those shades—twice doomed to Orcus : tho' the letters on
        the shield

Proved how he had lived in Ilion's day,
Nor had aught, save skin and sinew, unto grim death deigned
    to yield.
No mean scholar he, e'en thou would'st say,
In the lore of truth and nature.   But the fate of all is sealed :
    All must tread, unlighted, death's highway.
—Into grisly War's arena some are by the Furies flung :
    'Neath the hungry sea-wave some lie dead :
Fused in undistinguished slaughter die the old man and the
    young :
    Spares not Hell's fierce queen a single head.
Me too westward-bound Orion's constant mate, the South-west-
    wind,
    Whelmed but lately in the Illyrian wave :
And, oh mariner, deny not—to a dead man's bones unkind,
    And a head that must not own a grave—
One scant heap of homeless sea-sand.   So whene'er the Eastern
    gale
    Chides the South seas, may his fury lay
Green Etruria's woods in ruin, sparing thee : so many a bale
    Drop to thee, whence only drop it may,
From great Jove, and Neptune watching o'er Tarentum's holy
    soil.
    —Wilt commit, unrecking, an offence
Which shall harm thy innocent offspring ?   On thine own head
    may recoil
    Righteous vengeance, and a recompense
That shall bow thy pride.   Abandoned, unavenged, I will not
    be :
    For such crime no offerings shall atone.
Though mayhap thy time is precious, small the boon I ask of
    thee :
    Throw three handfuls o'er me, and begone.

ODE 38

To his Slave

PERSIAN grandeur I abhor :
   Linden-wreathèd crowns, avaunt :
Boy, I bid thee not explore
   Woods which latest roses haunt :

Try on naught thy busy craft
   Save plain myrtle ; so arrayed
Thou shalt fetch, I drain, the draught
   Fitliest 'neath the scant vine-shade.

BOOK III

ODE 1

I SCORN and shun the rabble's noise.
   Abstain from idle talk.   A thing
   That ear hath not yet heard, I sing,
The Muses' priest, to maids and boys.

To Jove the flocks which great kings sway,
   To Jove great kings allegiance owe.
   Praise him : he laid the giants low :
All things that are, his nod obey.

This man may plant in broader lines
   His fruit-trees : that, the pride of race
   Enlists a candidate for place :
In worth, in fame, a third outshines

His mates; or, thronged with clients, claims
   Precedence.   Even-handed Fate
   Hath but one law for small and great:
That ample urn holds all men's names.

He o'er whose doomed neck hangs the sword
   Unsheathed, the dainties of the South
   Shall lack their sweetness in his mouth:
No note of bird or harpsichord

Shall bring him Sleep.   Yet Sleep is kind,
   Nor scorns the huts of labouring men;
   The bank where shadows play, the glen
Of Tempe dancing in the wind.

He, who but asks 'Enough,' defies
   Wild waves to rob him of his ease;
   He fears no rude shocks, when he sees
Arcturus set or Hædus rise:

When hailstones lash his vines, or fails
   His farm its promise, now of rains
   And now of stars that parch the plains
Complaining, or unkindly gales.

—In straitened seas the fish are pent;
   For dams are sunk into the deep:
   Pile upon pile the builders heap,
And he, whom earth could not content,

The Master.   Yet shall Fear and Hate
   Climb where the Master climbs: nor e'er
   From the armed trireme parts black Care;
He sits behind, the horseman's mate.

And if red marble shall not ease
　　　The heartache ; nor the shell that shines
　　　Star-bright ; nor all Falernum's vines,
All scents that charmed Achæmenes :

Why should I rear me halls of rare
　　　Design, on proud shafts mounting high ?
　　　Why bid my Sabine vale good-bye
For doubled wealth and doubled care ?

ODE 2

FRIEND ! with a poor man's straits to fight
　　　Let warfare teach thy stalwart boy :
　　　Let him the Parthian's front annoy
With lance in rest, a dreaded knight :

Live in the field, inure his eye
　　　To danger.　From the foeman's wall
　　　May the armed tyrant's dame, with all
Her damsels, gaze on him, and sigh,

" Dare not, in war unschooled, to rouse
　　　Yon Lion—whom to touch is death,
　　　To whom red Anger ever saith,
'Slay and slay on'—O prince, my spouse ! "

—Honoured and blest the patriot dies.
　　　From death the recreant may not flee :
　　　Death shall not spare the faltering knee
And coward back of him that flies.

Valour—unbeat, unsullied still—
    Shines with pure lustre : all too great
    To seize or drop the sword of state,
Swayed by a people's veering will.

Valour—to souls too great for death
    Heav'n op'ning—treads the untrodden way :
    And this dull world, this damp cold clay,
On wings of scorn, abandoneth.

—Let too the sealed lip honoured be.
    The babbler, who'd the secrets tell
    Of holy Ceres, shall not dwell
Where I dwell ; shall not launch with me

A shallop.   Heaven full many a time
    Hath with the unclean slain the just :
    And halting-footed Vengeance must
O'ertake at last the steps of crime.

ODE 3

THE just man's single-purposed mind
    Not furious mobs that prompt to ill
    May move, nor kings' frowns shake his will
Which is as rock ; not warrior winds

That keep the seas in wild unrest ;
    Nor bolt by Jove's own finger hurled :
    The fragments of a shivered world
Would crash round him still self-possest.

S

Jove's wandering son reached, thus endowed,
  The fiery bastions of the skies;
  Thus Pollux; with them Cæsar lies
Beside his nectar, radiant-browed.

Honoured for this, by tigers drawn
  Rode Bacchus, reining necks before
  Untamed; for this War's horses bore
Quirinus up from Acheron.

To the pleased gods had Juno said
  In conclave: "Troy is in the dust;
  Troy, by a judge accursed, unjust,
And that strange woman prostrated.

"The day Laomedon ignored
  His god-pledged word, resigned to me
  And Pallas ever pure, was she,
Her people, and their traitor lord.

"Now the Greek woman's guilty guest
  Dazzles no more: Priam's perjured sons
  Find not against the mighty ones
Of Greece a shield in Hector's breast:

"And, long drawn out by private jars,
  The war sleeps.   Lo! my wrath is o'er:
  And him the Trojan vestal bore
(Sprung of that hated line) to Mars,

"To Mars restore I.   His be rest
  In halls of light: by him be drained
  The nectar-bowl, his place obtained
In the calm companies of the blest.

"While betwixt Rome and Ilion raves
  A length of ocean, where they will
  Rise empires for the exiles still:
While Paris's and Priam's graves

"Are trod by kine, and she-wolves breed
  Securely there, unharmed shall stand
  Rome's lustrous Capitol, her hand
Curb with proud laws the trampled Mede.

"Wide-feared, to far-off climes be borne
  Her story; where the central main
  Europe and Libya parts in twain,
Where full Nile laves a land of corn:

"The buried secret of the mine,
  (Best left there) let her dare to spurn,
  Nor unto man's base uses turn,
Profane hands laying on things divine.

"Earth's utmost end, where'er it be,
  Let her hosts reach; careering proud
  O'er lands where watery rain and cloud,
Or where wild suns hold revelry.

"But, to the warriors of Rome,
  Tied by this law, such fates are willed;
  That they seek never to rebuild,
Too fond, too bold, their grandsires' home.

"With darkest omens, deadliest strife,
  Shall Troy, raised up again, repeat
  Her history; I the victor-fleet
Shall lead, Jove's sister and his wife.

"Thrice let Apollo rear the wall
　　　Of brass; and thrice my Greeks shall hew
　　　The fabric down: thrice matrons rue
In chains their sons', their husbands' fall."

Ill my light lyre such notes beseem.
　　　Stay, Muse; nor, wayward still, rehearse
　　　Sayings of Gods in meagre verse
That may but mar a mighty theme.

ODE 4

COME, Music's Queen, from yonder sphere:
　　　Bid thy harp speak: sing high and higher—
　　　Or take Apollo's lute and lyre,
And play, and cease not.　Did ye hear?

Or is some sweet Delusion mine?
　　　I seem to hear, to stray beside
　　　Groves that are holy; whither glide
Fair brooks, where breezes are benign.

Me, on mount Vultur once—a lad,
　　　O'ercome with sleepiness and play—
　　　(I had left Apulia miles away,
That nursed me) doves from Fayland clad

With leaflets.　Marvelled all whose nest
　　　Is Acherontia's cliff; who fell
　　　The Bantine forest trees, or dwell
On rich Ferentium's lowly breast;

How I could sleep, unharmed by bear
  Or dusky serpent.   There I lay,
  In myrtle hid and holy bay,
A lusty babe, the Great ones' care.

Yours, Sisters, yours, the Sabine hills
  I climb : at cool Præneste yours,
  Yours by flat Tibur, or the shores
Of Baiæ.   I have loved your rills,

Your choirs : for this Philippi's slaughter,
  When fled our captains, harmed not me ;
  I died not 'neath the cursed tree,
Nor sank in Palinurus' water :—

Be with me still : and, fears at rest,
  I'll launch on raving Bosphorus, stand
  Upon Assyria's sultry sand,
With Britons mate, who slay the guest,

Sit down with Spaniards, wild to sate
  Their thirst with horses' blood ; or roam
  Far o'er the quivered Scythian's home
By Tanais' banks, inviolate.

—High Cæsar ye (his war-worn braves
  Safe housed at last in thorp and town)
  Asking to lay his labours down,
Make welcome in Pierian caves.

—Kind ones !   Ye give sweet counsel, love
  Its givers.   *We* know how He slew
  The Titans, and their hideous crew,
Hurling his thunder from above,

Who the dull earth, the windy sea,
    The cities, and the realms of woe,
    And gods above, and men below,
Rules, and none other, righteously.

In truth Jove's terrors had been great ;
    So bold a front those warriors showed
    Those brethren, on his dark abode
Striving to pile all Pelion's weight.

But Mimas and Typhoëus were
    As naught, and huge Porphyrion too,
    And Rhœcus, and the arm that threw,
Undaunted, tree-trunks through the air ;

With ringing shield when Pallas met
    Their rush.   Hot Vulcan too stood there,
    And Juno sage, and he, who ne'er
Eased from the bow his shoulder yet ;

Who bathes in pure Castalian dew
    His locks ; in Lycian bowers adored,
    And his own woods,—Apollo, lord
Of Delos and of Patara too.

—Brute force its own bulk foils.   But force
    By reason led, the gods make great
    And greater ; while the strong they hate,
Whose brain revolves each evil course.

This Gyas, hundred-armed, could tell ;
    And that Orion, who with wild
    Violence assailed the Undefiled,
And by Diana's arrows fell.

　—Earth, grieved, her monster brood entombed :
　　　Mourns them, by Jove's bolts hurled to hell.
　　　Still living fires 'neath Ætna dwell,
Yet Ætna still is unconsumed :

O'er wanton Tityus' heart the bird,
　　　That miscreant's gaoler, still doth hover ;
　　　And still Pirithöus, lawless lover,
Do thrice a hundred fetters gird.

ODE 5

JOVE we call King, whose bolts rive heaven :
　　　Then a god's *presence* shall be felt
　　　In Cæsar, with whose power the Celt
And Parthian stout in vain have striven.

Could Crassus' men wed alien wives,
　　　And greet, as sons-in-law, the foe ?
　　　In the foes' land (oh Romans, oh
Lost honour !) end, in shame, their lives,

'Neath the Mede's sway ?　They, Marsians and
　　　Apulians—shields and rank and name
　　　Forgot, and that undying flame—
And Jove still reign, and Rome still stand ?

This thing wise Regulus could presage :
　　　He brooked not base conditions ; he
　　　Set not a precedent to be
The ruin of a coming age :

"No," cried he, "let the captives die,
    Spare not. I saw Rome's ensigns hung
    In Punic shrines ; with sabres, flung
Down by Rome's sons ere blood shed. I

" Saw our free citizens with hands
    Fast pinioned ; and, through portals now
    Flung wide, our soldiers troop to plough,
As once they trooped to waste, the lands.

" ' Bought by our gold, our men will fight
    But keener.' What ? To shame would you
    Add loss ? As wool, its natural hue
Once gone, may not be *painted* white ;

" True Valour, from her seat once thrust,
    Is not replaced by meaner wares.
    Do stags, delivered from the snares,
Fight ? Then shall *he* fight, who did trust

" His life to foes who spoke a lie :
    And *his* sword shatter Carthage yet,
    Around whose arms the cords have met,
A sluggard soul, that feared to die !

" Life, howe'er bought, he treasured : he
    Deemed war a thing of trade. Ah fie !—
    Great art thou, Carthage—towerest high
O'er shamed and ruined Italy ! "

As one uncitizen'd—men said—
    He puts his wife's pure kiss away,
    His little children ; and did lay
Stern in the dust his manly head :

Till those unequalled words had lent
　　Strength to the faltering sires of Rome ;
　　Then from his sorrow-stricken home
Went forth to glorious banishment.

Yet knew he, what wild tortures lay
　　Before him : knowing, put aside
　　His kin, his countrymen—who tried
To bar his path, and bade him stay :

He might be hastening on his way,—
　　A lawyer freed from business—down
　　To green Venafrum, or a town
Of Sparta, for a holiday.

ODE 6

THOU'lt rue thy fathers' sins, not thine,
　　Till built the temples be, replaced
　　The statues, foul and smoke-defaced,—
Roman,—and reared each tottering shrine.

Thou rul'st but under heaven's hand.
　　Thence all beginnings come, all ends.
　　Neglected, mark what woes it sends
On this our miserable land.

Twice Pacorus and Monæses foiled
　　Our luckless onset : huge their glee,
　　When to their necklaces they see
Hanging the wealth of Rome despoiled.

Dacian and Æthiop nigh laid low
    Our state, with civil feuds o'errun ;
    One with his fleet dismayed her, one
Smote her with arrows from his bow.

A guilty age polluted first
    Our beds, hearths, families : from that source
    Derived, the foul stream, gathering force,
O'er the broad land, a torrent, burst.

Pleased, now, the maiden learns to move
    To soft Greek airs : already knows—
    Fresh from the nursery—how to pose
Her graceful limbs ; and dreams of love :

Next, while her lord drinks deep, invites
    Her gallants in : nor singles one,
    Into whose guilty arms to run,
Stealthy and swift, when dim the lights :

No ! in her lord's sight up springs she :
    Alike at some small tradesman's beck,
    As his who walks a Spanish deck
And barters wealth for infamy.

—Were those lads of such parents bred
    Who dyed the seas with Punic blood ?
    Pyrrhus, Antiochus withstood,
And Hannibal, the nation's dread ?

Rude soldiers' sons, a rugged kind,
    They brake the soil with Sabine spade :
    Or shouldered stakes their axe had made
To a right rigorous mother's mind,

What time the shadows of the rocks
    Change, as the sun's departing car
    Sends on the hours that sweetest are,
And men unyoke the wearied ox.

Time mars not—what?   A spoiler he.
    Our sires were not so brave a breed
    As *their* sires: we, a worse, succeed;
To raise up sons more base than we.

ODE 13

To the Fountain of Bandusia

BANDUSIA, stainless mirror of the sky!
    Thine is the flower-crown'd bowl, for thee shall die,
      When dawns yon sun, the kid;
      Whose horns, half-seen, half-hid,

Challenge to dalliance or to strife—in vain!
Soon must the firstling of the wild herd be slain,
      And those cold springs of thine
      With blood incarnadine.

Fierce glows the Dogstar, but his fiery beam
Toucheth not thee: still grateful thy cool stream
      To labour-wearied ox,
      Or wanderer from the flocks:

And henceforth thou shalt be a royal fountain:
My harp shall tell how from yon cavernous mountain,
      Where the brown oak grows tallest,
      All babblingly thou fallest.

ODE 18

To a Faun

WOOER of young Nymphs who fly thee,
　　Lightly o'er my sunlit lawn,
Trip, and go, nor injured by thee
　　Be my weanling herds, O Faun:

If the kid his doomed head bows, and
　　Brims with wine the loving cup,
When the year is full; and thousand
　　Scents from altars hoar go up.

Each flock in the rich grass gambols
　　When the month comes which is thine;
And the happy village rambles
　　Fieldward with the idle kine:

Lambs play on, the wolf their neighbour:
　　Wild woods deck thee with their spoil;
And with glee the sons of labour
　　Stamp upon their foe the soil.

BOOK IV

ODE 13

To Lyce

LYCE, the gods have listened to my prayer:
The gods have listened, Lyce.   Thou art gray
 And still would'st thou seem fair;
  Still unshamed drink, and play,

And, wine-flushed, woo slow-answering Love with weak
Shrill pipings.   With young Chia He doth dwell,
 Queen of the harp; her cheek
  Is his sweet citadel:—

He marked the withered oak, and on he flew
Intolerant; shrank from Lyce grim and wrinkled,
 Whose teeth are ghastly-blue,
  Whose temples snow-besprinkled:—

Not purple, not the brightest gem that glows,
Brings back to her the years which, fleeting fast,
 Time hath once shut in those
  Dark annals of the Past.

Oh, where is all thy loveliness? soft hue
And motions soft?   Oh, what of Her doth rest,
 Her, who breathed love, who drew
  My heart out of my breast?

Fair, and far-famed, and subtly sweet, thy face
    Ranked next to Cinara's.   But to Cinara fate
        Gave but a few years' grace ;
          And lets live, all too late,

Lyce, the rival of the beldam crow :
    That fiery youth may see with scornful brow
        The torch that long ago
          Beamed bright, a cinder now.

EPODE 2

" HAPPY—who far from turmoil, like the men
      That lived in days gone by,
With his own oxen ploughs his native glen,
    Nor dreams of usury !
Him the fierce clarion summons not to war ;
    He dreads not angry seas :
The courts—the stately citizens' proud door—
    He gets him far from these.
His maiden-vines it is his gentle craft
    With poplars tall to wed :
Or the rank outgrowth lopping off, ingraft
    Fair branches in its stead ;
To watch his kine, that wander, lowing, far
    Into the valley deep :
Store the prest honey in the taintless jar,
    Or shear his tender sheep.
And soon as Autumn, with fair fruitage tricked,
    Peeps o'er the fallows bare ;
Then with what glee his purpling grape is picked,
    And newly-grafted pear,

For you, Priapus and Silvanus—strict
　　Guard of his land—to share.
—Now 'neath an ancient oak, entangled now
　　In green grass, will he lie ;
Where streams go by bank-hidden ; from the bough
　　Is heard the wood-birds' cry ;
And brawls the clear brook, as if seeking how
　　To sing him lullaby.
—But when the wintry skies Jove's thunder rives,
　　And down the snow-storms pour ;
Towards the set pit-fall, doubling oft, he drives
　　The hound-encompassed boar :
Or with smooth rods his web of nets prepares,
　　The fat thrush to surprise ;
Or nooses stranger cranes, or frightened hares—
　　Either a glorious prize !
Who, with such pleasures round him, for the cares
　　That fret a lover sighs ?

" Does a pure wife his household cares divide,
　　Watch his sweet little ones ;—
(The Sabine's thus and swift Apulian's bride
　　Toiled 'neath Apulia's suns ;)—
The sacred hearth with seasoned faggots heap,
　　When her tired lord draws nigh ;
And hurdling, nothing loth, her folded sheep,
　　Drain their great udders dry :
Then the last vintage draw from the sweet cask,
　　To grace the home-made feast ?—
For Lucrine purple-fish I shall not ask,
　　Nor turbots from the East :
Not char, which—thundering first o'er other seas—
　　Storms carried to our shore,

Not woodcocks from Ionia would please,
    Or hens from Guinea, more
My taste; than oil that, in the rich boughs hid,
    Her hands did thence obtain;
And meadow-dock, and mallow that can rid
    Our suffering frames from pain,
With lamb that bled for Terminus; and kid
    By wolves so nearly slain!

" So banqueting, how sweet to notice how
    The fed ewes homeward fare:
How oxen, half asleep, the inverted plough
    On drooping shoulders bear;
And slaves—sure signs of wealth—ranged idle now,
    Swarm round the glad hearth's glare!"

So did the money-lender Appius speak,
    Resolved to be a swain,
And got his money in. Within a week
    Would put it out again.

THE DEAD OX

From Virgil, Georg. III

LO! smoking in the stubborn plough, the ox
    Falls, from his lip foam gushing crimson-stained,
And sobs his life out. Sad of face the ploughman
Moves, disentangling from his comrade's corpse
The lone survivor: and its work half-done,
Abandoned in the furrow stands the plough.
Not shadiest forest-depths, not softest lawns,
May move him now: not river amber-pure,
That tumbles o'er the cragstones to the plain.

Powerless the broad sides, glazed the rayless eye,
And low and lower sinks the ponderous neck.
What thank hath he for all the toil he toiled,
The heavy-clodded land in man's behoof
Upturning? Yet the grape of Italy,
The stored-up feast hath wrought no harm to him:
Green leaf and taintless grass are all their fare;
The clear rill or the travel-freshened stream
Their cup: nor one care mars their honest sleep.

SPEECH OF AJAX

SOPHOCLES, AJAX, 645

ALL strangest things the multitudinous years
Bring forth, and shadow from us all we know.
Falter alike great oath and steeled resolve;
And none shall say of aught, "This may not be."
Lo! I myself, but yesterday so strong,
As new-dipt steel am weak and all unsexed
By yonder woman: yea I mourn for them,
Widow and orphan, left amid their foes.
But I will journey seaward—where the shore
Lies meadow-fringed—so haply wash away
My sin, and flee that wrath that weighs me down.
And, lighting somewhere on an untrodden way,
I will bury this my lance, this hateful thing,
Deep in some earth-hole where no eye shall see—
Night and Hell keep it in the underworld!
For never to this day, since first I grasped
The gift that Hector gave, my bitterest foe,
Have I reaped aught of honour from the Greeks.

T

So true that byword in the mouths of men,
" A foeman's gifts are no gifts, but a curse."
    Wherefore henceforward shall I know that God
Is great ; and strive to honour Atreus' sons.
Princes they are, and should be obeyed. How else ?
Do not all terrible and most puissant things
Yet bow to loftier majesties ? The Winter,
Who walks forth scattering snows, gives place anon
To fruitage-laden Summer ; and the orb
Of weary Night doth in her turn stand by,
And let shine out, with his white steeds, the Day.
Stern tempest-blasts at last sing lullaby
To groaning seas : even the archtyrant, Sleep,
Doth loose his slaves, not hold them chained for ever.
And shall not mankind too learn discipline ?
I know, of late experience taught, that him
Who is my foe I must but hate as one
Whom I may yet call Friend : and him who loves me
Will I but serve and cherish as a man
Whose love is not abiding. Few be they
Who, reaching Friendship's port, have there found rest.
    But, for these things, they shall be well. Go thou,
Lady, within, and there pray that the Gods
May fill unto the full my heart's desire.
And ye, my mates, do unto me with her
Like honour : bid young Teucer, if he come,
To care for me, but to be *your* friend still.
For where my way leads, thither I shall go :
Do ye my bidding ; haply ye may hear,
Though now is my dark hour, that I have peace.

FROM LUCRETIUS. Book II

SWEET, when the great sea's water is stirred to his depths
  by the storm-winds,
Standing ashore to descry one afar-off mightily struggling :
Not that a neighbour's sorrow to you yields dulcet enjoyment ;
But that the sight hath a sweetness, of ills ourselves are exempt
  from.
Sweet 'tis too to behold, on a broad plain mustering, war-hosts
Arm them for some great battle, one's self unscathed by the
  danger :—
Yet still happier this :—To possess, impregnably guarded,
Those calm heights of the sages, which have for an origin Wisdom ;
Thence to survey our fellows, observe them this way and that way
Wander amidst Life's paths, poor stragglers seeking a highway :
Watch mind battle with mind, and escutcheon rival escutcheon ;
Gaze on that untold strife, which is waged 'neath the sun and
  the starlight,
Up as they toil on the surface whereon rest Riches and Empire.
 O race born unto trouble ! O minds all lacking of eyesight !
'Neath what a vital darkness, amidst how terrible dangers,
Move ye thro' this thing, Life, this fragment ! Fools, that ye
  hear not
Nature clamour aloud for the one thing only ; that, all pain
Parted and past from the Body, the Mind too bask in a blissful
Dream, all fear of the future and all anxiety over !
 Now, as regards Man's Body, a few things only are needful,
(Few, tho' we sum up all,) to remove all misery from him ;
Aye, and to strew in his path such a lib'ral carpet of pleasures,
That scarce Nature herself would at times ask happiness
  ampler.

Statues of youth and of beauty may not gleam golden around
  him,
(Each in his right hand bearing a great lamp lustrously
  burning,
Whence to the midnight revel a light may be furnishèd
  always) ;
Silver may not shine softly, nor gold blaze bright, in his
  mansion,
Nor to the noise of the tabret his halls gold-cornicèd echo :—
Yet still he, with his fellow, reposed on the velvety green-
  sward,
Near to a rippling stream, by a tall tree canopied over,
Shall, though they lack great riches, enjoy all bodily pleasure.
Chiefliest then, when above them a fair sky smiles, and the
  young year
Flings with a bounteous hand over each green meadow the
  wild-flowers :—
Not more quickly depart from his bosom fiery fevers,
Who beneath crimson hangings and pictures cunningly
  broidered
Tosses about, than from him who must lie in beggarly raiment.

Therefore, since to the Body avail not Riches, avails not
Heraldry's utmost boast, nor the pomp and the pride of an
  empire ;
Next shall you own, that the Mind needs likewise nothing of
  these things.
Unless—when, peradventure, your armies over the champaign
Spread with a stir and a ferment, and bid War's image
  awaken,
Or when with stir and with ferment a fleet sails forth upon
  Ocean—
Cowed before these brave sights, pale Superstition abandon

Straightway your mind as you gaze, Death seem no longer
    alarming,
Trouble vacate your bosom, and Peace hold holiday in you.
  But, if (again) all this be a vain impossible fiction;
If of a truth men's fears, and the cares which hourly beset
    them,
Heed not the jav'lin's fury, regard not clashing of broad-
    swords;
But all-boldly amongst crowned heads and the rulers of empires
Stalk, not shrinking abashed from the dazzling glare of the red
    gold,
Not from the pomp of the monarch, who walks forth purple-
    apparelled:
These things show that at times we are bankrupt, surely, of
    Reason;
Think too that all Man's life through a great Dark laboureth
    onward.
For, as a young boy trembles, and in that mystery, Darkness,
Sees all terrible things: so do we too, ev'n in the daylight,
Ofttimes shudder at that which is not more really alarming
Than boys' fears, when they waken, and say some danger is
    o'er them.
  So this panic of mind, these clouds which gather around us,
Fly not the bright sunbeam, nor the ivory shafts of the Day-
    star:
Nature, rightly revealed, and the Reason only, dispel them.

  Now, how moving about do the prime material atoms
Shape forth this thing and that thing; and, once shaped, how
    they resolve them;
What power says unto each, This must be; how an inherent
Elasticity drives them about Space vagrantly onward;
I shall unfold: thou simply give all thyself to my teaching.

Matter mingled and massed into indissoluble union
Does not exist. For we see how wastes each separate sub-
 stance;
So flow piecemeal away, with the length'ning centuries, all
 things,
Till from our eye by degrees that old self passes, and is not.
Still Universal Nature abides unchanged as aforetime.
Whereof this is the cause. When the atoms part from a sub-
 stance,
That suffers loss; but another is elsewhere gaining an increase:
So that, as one thing wanes, still a second bursts into blossom,
Soon, in its turn, to be left. Thus draws this Universe always
Gain out of loss; thus live we mortals one on another.
Bourgeons one generation, and one fades. Let but a few years
Pass, and a race has arisen which was not: as in a racecourse,
One hands on to another the burning torch of Existence.

* * * * *

FROM CATULLUS

SONNET TO THE ISLAND OF SIRMIO

GEM of all isthmuses and isles that lie,
 Fresh or salt water's children, in clear lake
Or ampler ocean: with what joy do I
 Approach thee, Sirmio! Oh! am I awake,
Or dream that once again mine eye beholds
Thee, and has looked its last on Thracian wolds?
 Sweetest of sweets to me that pastime seems,
When the mind drops her burden: when—the pain
Of travel past—our own cot we regain,
 And nestle on the pillow of our dreams!

'Tis this one thought that cheers us as we roam.
Hail, O fair Sirmio! Joy, thy lord is here!
Joy too, ye waters of the Golden Mere!
And ring out, all ye laughter-peals of home!

FROM ILIAD VIII

LL. 555-565

As in the heights of heaven the moon gleams clear, and around her
Shine in their beauty the stars, nor is one cloud moving in ether;
Shines forth every cliff, and the jutting peaks of the headlands,
Forest and glen: then,—as opens the rifting firmament heaven-wards,—
Star is revealed upon star: and gay is the heart of the herds-man:—
Not in less number than they, from the Xanthus' stream to the sea sands,
Glimmered the red watchfires that encompassed Ilion alway;—
Glimmered amid Troy's host as a thousand stars; and at each one
There sat threescore and ten, their face lighted up by the fire-brand.
Meanwhile, each at his car, till crowned in her glory the morning
Roused them, their good steeds stood, white oats and barley before them.

FROM HEINE[1]

"So far from agreeable were his [Heine's] recollections of Hamburg, that when, in 1830, Mrs. Moscheles asked him to write in her album, he treated her to a satire on her native town, which we here give in the original, and an English version of the same."—*Life of Moscheles*, vol. i., p. 195.

I CRAVE an ampler, worthier sphere:
　　I'd liefer bleed at every vein
Than stifle 'mid these hucksters here,
　　These lying slaves of paltry gain.

They eat, they drink; they're every whit
　　As happy as their type, the mole;
Large are their bounties—as the slit
　　Through which they drop the poor man's dole.

With pipe in mouth they go their way,
　　With hands in pockets; they are blest
With grand digestions : only *they*
　　Are such hard morsels to digest !

The hand that's red with some dark deed,
　　Some giant crime, were white as wool
Compared with these sleek saints, whose creed
　　Is paying all their debts in full.

Ye clouds that sail to far-off lands,
　　O waft me to what clime ye will;

[1] This and the two following translations were written for A. D. Coleridge's "Life of Moscheles" (itself an adaptation from the German).

To Lapland's snows, to Libya's sands,
  To the world's end—but onward still!

Take me, O clouds! They ne'er look down;
  But (proof of a discerning mind)
One moment hang o'er Hamburg town,
  The next they leave it leagues behind.

FROM J. F. CASTELLI [1]

AT BEETHOVEN'S GRAVE

FROM the high rock I marked a fountain breaking;
  It poured its riches forth o'er glade and plain;
Where'er they streamed I saw new life awaking,
  The grandam world was in her prime again;
To the charmed spot the tribes of earth came thronging,
And stoopt to that pure wave with eager longing.

Yet of these hosts few only, keener-sighted
  Than were their fellows, all its glamour knew:
The simple multitude surveyed, delighted,
  Its diamond glitter and its changing hue;
But—save unto those few that saw more clearly—
That wondrous fountain was a fountain merely.

At last its source dried up, its torrent dwindled;
  And all mankind discerned its virtue then;
In minstrel's breast and bard's a fire was kindled,
  And brush and chisel vied with harp and pen:

[1] In "Life of Moscheles," vol. i., p. 167.

But wild desire, and minstrelsy, and wailing,
  To call it back to life were unavailing.

*   *   *   *

Thou who sleep'st here, thy toil, thy bondage ended !
  Lo ! in that fountain's tale is told thine own.
Marvelled at oft, more oft misapprehended,
  By the few only thou wast truly known.
All shall exalt thee, now that low thou liest :
That thou may'st live, O deathless one, thou diest.

FROM J. F. CASTELLI[1]

AT BEETHOVEN'S FUNERAL

E V'RY tear that is shed by the mourner is holy ;
    When the dust of the mighty to earth is consigned,
When those he held dearest move sadly and slowly
    To the grave of the friend in whose heart they were shrined.

But our grief-stricken train is a wild sea that surges,
    That spreads to yon starry pavilion o'erhead
And girdles the globe : for all nature sings dirges,
    Where'er rings an echo, to-day o'er the dead.

But weep not for him : for yourselves sorrow only :
    Though proud was his place in the hierarchy here,
This Earth might not hold him ; his spirit was lonely,
    And yearned for a home in a loftier sphere.

So Heaven to the minstrel its portal uncloses ;
    The Muse thither calls him, to sit by her side

---

[1] In " Life of Moscheles," vol. i., p. 166.

And hear, from the throne where in bliss she reposes,
　His own hallow'd harmonies float far and wide.

Yet here, in our memories homed, he abideth ;
　Round his name lives a glory that ne'er may grow dim ;
Time fain would o'ertake him, but time he derideth ;
　The grisly Destroyer is distanced by him.

[Bei Ludwig van Beethoven's Leichenbegangniss (am 29 März, 1827).]

TRANSLATIONS OF HYMNS

(FROM "THE HYMNARY"[1])

EASTER

Concinet orbis cunctus, Alleluia.　A Sequence.　SARUM MISSAL

ALLELUIA let the nations
　　Sing to-day from West to East ;
As they solemnize with praises
　　And with prayers the Paschal feast.

And ye little ones be joyful,
　　Whom the Holy Font hath made
White as snow : the lake that burneth
　　Shall not make your ranks afraid.

We, with you, to measured music
　　Fain would tune the slackened string ;

---

[1] "The Hymnary ; a Book of Church Song ;" published by Novello,
Ewer and Co.　To each hymn the number in "The Hymnary" is
appended.

And in subtly-cadenced anthems
   Bid our voices rise and ring.

Since for us, a mute meek Victim,
   Christ endured the cross and shame :
He, the Living Life, a captive
   Unto death for us became :

For our sakes He deigned to carry
   To His lip the cup of gall :
Nail and spear, and pain and wounding,
   In our cause He braved them all :

So through suffering He descended,
   Laden with our sins, to hell ;
Whence He comes with many a trophy,
   Telling that He triumphed well :

Death o'erthrown, He brake the weapons
   Of His ancient foe in twain;
And the third day lo ! He riseth,
   In His flesh, to life again.

Sing we then to Him glad anthems,
   Who spread wide the heavenly door,
And to man gave life eternal :
   His be praise for evermore. [271.]

EASTER

Victimæ paschali laudes immolent Christiani. A Sequence of the 12th Century

O UR salvation to obtain
   Christ our Passover is slain :
Unto Christ we Christians raise
This our sacrifice of praise.

By the Lamb the sheep were bought ;
By the Pure the guilty sought :
With their God were made at one
Sinners by the sinless Son.

In a dark mysterious strife
Closed the powers of Death and Life,
And the Lord of Life was slain :
Yet He liveth and doth reign.

" Say what saw'st thou, Mary, say,
As thou wentest on thy way."
" Christ's, the Living's, tomb ; the throes
Earth was torn with as He rose :

And the angels twain who bare
Witness that He was not there ;
And the grave-clothes of the Dead,
And the cloth that bound His head :

Christ our Hope is risen, and He
Goes before to Galilee."

Trust we Mary: she is true;
Heed we not the faithless Jew.

Conqueror, King, to Thee we raise
This our sacrifice of praise:
We believe Thee risen indeed;
Hear us, help us in our need.   [275.]

EASTER

Panditur saxo tumulus remoto.   JEAN BAPTISTE SANTEUIL.
Paris Breviary

THE stone is rolled away;
    The grave is bid display
Her secrets; through her charnel-chambers rings
    A voice; and lo, the dead
    Lifts his awakened head,
Lo, the deaf hearkens to the King of kings.

O wondrous sight!   Again
    Life throbs in every vein:
Bound hand and foot and blindfold, on his way
    The dead goes forth alive;
    Doomed haply to survive
The multitude who mourn for him to-day.

Thus Death himself, our foe,
    At last shall be laid low;
His chains rent piecemeal, and his slaves set free.
    That, which Thy Sovereign Power
    Hath wrought, O Christ, this hour
Is but an emblem of the things to be.

Now to the Father, Son,
And Spirit, ever One,
Be power ascribed by all things that have breath.
In Thee, O Christ, we trust:
When we return to dust,
Save us, we pray Thee, from the second Death.   [622.]

THE TRANSFIGURATION

Quam nos potenter allicis.   JEAN BAPTISTE SANTEUIL.
Paris Breviary

O CHRIST, how potent is Thy grace!
    Ne'er doth Thy loving-kindness fail,
Whether we see Thee through a veil,
    Or face to face.

Now his adopted sons are we
Who called Thee Son: our Surety thus
Gives His unfailing pledge to us
    Of bliss to be.

O Father, Son, what then was shown,
Upon the Mount, the cloud dispelled?
The types are gone; the three beheld
    Truth stand alone.

O feebly tracked by Faith's dim ray,
Lord, may we one day share Thy bliss;
See Thee; enjoy Thee; bursting this
    Our prison of clay.

To Him Who said, the bright cloud riven,
"This is My Son"; and, Son, to Thee;
To Thee, Blest Spirit; One in Three,
All praise be given.   [368.]

THE TRANSFIGURATION

Cœlestis formam gloriæ.   14th Century

THE shadow of the glory which one day
    Christ's church on earth stands waiting to put on,
This morn did Christ upon the Mount display:
    There as the sun He shone.

That tale shall ages yet unborn record,
    How those three chosen gazed with awe-struck eye,
While Moses and Elias with the Lord
    Awhile held converse high.

The three great witnesses are gathered there
    Of Grace, Law, Prophecy: and, hark, aloud
To God the Son doth God the Father bear
    His witness from the cloud.

His Face aglow, His garments glistering white,
    So Christ foreshows what guerdon He prepares
For faith; so tells them who in God delight
    What glory shall be theirs.

That mystery supreme, which they beheld
    Who saw the vision, lifts to heaven our gaze;
And year by year, O Lord, our hearts are swelled
    With wonder and with praise.

O Father, from Thy sole-begotten Son
 And gracious Spirit separable ne'er;
Dwell Thou within us, that, the battle won,
 Thy glory we may share. [367.]

ASCENSION

Felix dies mortalibus. JEAN BAPTISTE SANTEUIL.
Paris Breviary

FOR aye shall mortals bless the day
 When with His Blood Christ won the way,
Incarnate God, to Heaven, and passed
Through its bright gates unbarred at last.

We are the members, He the Head:
We follow where our Prince hath led
And, one with Him on earth in love,
Shall share His throne in heaven above.

Gone hence, His own yet deem Him near,
For by His Spirit He is here:
As on the head depend the parts,
So rules one influence all our hearts.

But O that Day, that dreadful Day!
Whither shall sinners flee away
When, armed with vengeance, He shall come
Down from His throne to strike them dumb?

The just One, by the guilty called
Unjust, shall see them stand appalled,
Who once condemned Him, and resume
His Judgeship to pronounce their doom.

U

Man to redeem, whose due was death,
Christ freely yielded up His breath :
And, ah, what woe must they sustain
For whom His Blood was shed in vain !

Thou Who one day our Judge shalt be,
Jesu, all glory be to Thee :
All glory to the Father, Son,
And Holy Spirit, Three in One.   [317.]

ASCENSION

Rector omnipotens die hodierno.   HARTMANN, a Monk of
St. Gall

LORD of all power and might,
  Mankind redeemèd, Who dost this day soar
Back to those realms of light
    Where Thou satt'st throned before :

Ere skyward Thou didst rise
Thou badst Apostles to the world proclaim
God's pardon, and baptize
    All in the Triune Name.

Nor didst Thou let depart,
Lord, from the holy city Thine eleven,
Till poured into their heart
    Was that last gift of heaven.

" Lo ! but a few days hence
Ye shall no more be comfortless : I go
To heaven, to send you thence
    One Who shall soothe your woe :

"And in Samaria ye,
And in Judæa and in Jerusalem,
My witnesses shall be."
So spake the Lord to them.

He spake: and as they gazed
A cloud received Him, marvellously bright;
With wistful eyes upraised
They watched Him fade from sight:

Behold, two men stood near
Arrayed in white apparel; and they said—
"Why stand ye gazing here
Into the heaven o'erhead?

"This Jesus, to His Throne
Who this day riseth upon God's right hand,
Shall come again, His own
With usury to demand."

O God of earth, sea, sky;
Man, whom Thou madest, whom the Foe erewhile
From Eden forced to fly,
By craftiness and guile,

And dragged him to the night
Of death and darkness: and whom Thou, O Lord,
With Thine own Blood to light
And freedom hast restored:

Man yet again may win
The bliss he fell from: Thou hast paid the price;
Thou bidd'st him enter in
Once more to Paradise.

Thou shalt return: and men
Hear from Thy lips their doom or their release.
Grant, we beseech Thee, then
To us eternal peace.   [305.]

WHITSUNTIDE

Sancti Spiritus adsit nobis gratia.   KING ROBERT OF
FRANCE, OR ST. NOTKER

COME, O Holy Ghost, within us; and, removing by Thy
    grace
Every taint and tinge of evil, make our hearts Thy dwelling
    place.

Be with us, O quickening Spirit; Thou canst pierce the deepest
    night:
Cleanse our base imaginations, change our darkness into light.

O Thou Holy One Who lovest wisdom always, be Thou kind,
By Thy mystical anointing heal the blindness of our mind.

Thou That purifiest all things, as none else beside Thee can,
Purify the clouded eyesight, Spirit, of our inner man;

That by us our Heavenly Father may at last be seen and
    known:
For the pure in heart shall see Him, and the pure in heart
    alone.

Fired by Thee the holy Prophets sang, of old, Messiah's birth;
By Thee fortified, Apostles bore Christ's banner o'er the earth.

When God spake, and as a fabric rose up earth and sea and
    sky,
Thou wast brooding on the waters, Blessed Spirit, fosteringly.

Still at thy command the waters bring forth life, to quicken
    hearts ;
Still Thy sacred inspiration unto man new life imparts.

Lord, Thou makest tongues of Babel one in worship and in
    speech :
Truth to them who bowed to idols, mighty Master, Thou dost
    teach.

Therefore when we kneel before Thee hear us, gracious Spirit,
    hear ;
Prayers are all in vain without Thee, shall not reach the Father's
    ear.

Spirit, Who through all the ages hast instructed in Thy lore
Souls of Saints that felt Thy presence like a shadow hovering
    o'er,

Dwelling now in Christ's Apostles, in a new and wondrous way,
And the gift of gifts bestowing, Thou hast glorified this day.
                                  [322.]

WHITSUNTIDE

Veni superne Spiritus. CHARLES COFFIN. Paris Breviary

COME, O Spirit, from on high ;
    Earth awaits Thee, parched and dry :
Dwell, O Lord, these souls within,
Which Christ's Blood hath cleansed from sin.

O redeem the pledge He gave
Ere the lustrous cloud He clave:
Dwell with us, no more to part,
And with fire baptize each heart.

For a Father lost we mourn;
Look upon us, left forlorn;
Heal our sorrows: only Thou
Canst give hope; O give it now.

Things that Christ in days of old
Did from simple babes withhold,
Things that they might hardly learn,
Let our riper minds discern.

Let the truths, which once a few.
Priests and Prophets dimly knew,
Now be published by Thy grace
Freely among every race.

Let Thy holy influence draw
All men to Thee; let the Law,
Once on dumb stones graven, be
In our hearts writ legibly.

To the Father, glory be,
And the Son eternally,
And the Spirit, ever One
With the Father and the Son.   [320.]

WHITSUNTIDE

Lux jucunda, lux insignis.   ADAM OF ST. VICTOR

DAY all jubilant, all splendid,
    When from heaven the fire descended
    On the chosen of the Lord !
Heart is full, and tongue rejoices :
Yea, our hearts invite our voices
    To sing praise with one accord.

He who ne'er His promise breaketh,
Thus His chosen Bride retaketh,
    On the Pentecostal day.
From the Rock, with honey teeming
Once, a gracious oil is streaming ;
    Never shall that Rock decay.

Writ on stone, not preached by flamèd
Tongues, the Law was once proclaimèd
    From the mount in all men's view :
Hearts in Christ created newly,
Tongues in love united truly,
    Here are granted to a few.

O the joy, the exultation
Of that day when the foundation
    Of Christ's Holy Church was laid !
When she gave to God thanksgiving
For three thousand souls, her living
    Firstfruits, as they kneeled and prayed !

This the two wave-loaves portended
Of the Law :—two peoples, blended
 Into one—One God adore.
They were twain : until united
By the Stone the builders slighted,
 Never to be sundered more.

Not in vessels that are olden
Is the new wine meetly holden :
 Like Elisha, to the brim
All the widow's vessels filling,
Christ with sacred dew is willing
 To fill all who trust in Him.

Not to hearts by discord riven,
Shall these sacred gifts be given
 Precious dew, nor oil, nor wine :
Ne'er the Paraclete abideth
Within hearts which sin divideth,
 Shutting out the light divine.

Comforter, possess and cheer us !
Venom then shall not draw near us ;
 Hate shall flee before Thy face.
There is no delight, no sweetness,
Health, nor comfort, nor completeness,
 Where Thou dost withhold Thy grace.

Oil of gladness, Lamp uplifted,
Heavenly Bread, by Whom are gifted
 With strange power the springs and brooks ;
New-create and pure, we render
Thus our thanks, on whom with tender
 Love, not hate, the Saviour looks.

Gift, and Giver of all blessing,
Evermore be we addressing
   Praise, with lip and heart, to Thee.
Cleanse our sins; in Christ renew us;
And, when perfected, give to us
   Our eternal jubilee.   [324.]

WHITSUNTIDE

Audimur: almo Spiritus.   CHARLES COFFIN.   Paris Breviary

L O, the father hears our prayer:
   Unto failing hearts to bear
All Christ promised ere He rose,
Forth to-day the Spirit goes.

As the Lord of Life draws nigh,
Signs and wonders multiply:
First through all the house there past
Sounds, as of a rushing blast;

Flakes of fire fell fast, and hung,
Each one like a burning tongue,
In the pure thin air, and shed
Lustre upon every head.

Then the flames that lit each brow,
Passing thence—we know not how—
To their inmost spirit pour
Light and strength unknown before.

Marvelling much the nations heard
Preached in every tongue the word;

All that seers had e'er discerned,
Told again in words that burned.

On the hearers then was poured
Forth the Spirit of the Lord :
Thick as sheaves at harvest-tide
They arose and prophesied.

Praise the Father, praise the Son :
Equal honour, too, be done
Unto Him, Who can inspire
Human hearts with flaming fire.   [321.]

THE VIGIL OF WHITSUNTIDE

O Christe qui noster poli.   Paris Breviary

O CHRIST, Who dost, our herald, rise
Into the mansions of the skies :
Call, lift us, whom Thou here dost see
Prostrate and downcast, up to Thee.

Make us to haste with purest love
Unto the joys that are above,
Undreamed of by the earthly mind :
Faith can alone that treasure find.

There, the reward of labours past,
God gives His own Himself at last :
Their all in all is He, to bless
Their souls with perfect happiness.

Lord, from high heaven this holy tide
Send down Thy Spirit, Who shall guide
Us, by His all-prevailing grace,
To Thy most glorious dwelling-place.

Jesu, for ever glorified
Thou sittest by the Father's side ;
All glory be to Father, Son,
And Spirit, while the ages run.   [318.]

WHITSUNTIDE

Supreme Rector cœlitum.   Paris Breviary

SOVEREIGN of Heaven, Who didst prevail
O'er death, and with Thy life-blood dye
The path by which we hope to scale
        Yon starry sky :

Look down in mercy from Thy throne
    At God's right hand, O Lord, and see
Us who are lingering here alone,
        Orphaned of Thee.

Hear us, O Christ, for we were born
    Out of the travail of Thy soul ;
When by the spear Thy side was torn
        To make us whole.

Thy toils and anguish at an end,
    Thou wearest now a glorious crown :
The hour is come ; send, Saviour, send
        Thy Spirit down.

O Jesu, glory be to Thee,
　　To God's right hand Who didst ascend:
Glory to God, the One and Three
　　　　World without end. [319.]

TRINITY

Benedicta sit beata Trinitas.   A Sequence.   SARUM MISSAL

ALL blessing to the Blessed Three!
　Hail, co-eternal Deity,
In glory equal, Father, Son,
And Spirit; ever Three in One.

Ruling o'er all things, One in Will,
Three Persons, yet One Substance still:
The Uncreated Unity,
In Godhead One, in Persons Three.

This faith can souls from sin release,
And bring them to that land of peace,
Where by the bright celestial throng
Is poured for aye triumphant song.

White-robed in Jesus' steps they tread,
Who sits enthroned above their head;
Their day of suffering past and gone,
Lo, they have put new raiment on.

Let us, in whom God's grace doth glow,
Pay now to God the debt we owe:
So, when to this world we have died,
Our place may still in heaven abide.

So, peradventure, when the last
Fight hath been fought and overpast,
We shall behold fair mansions rise,
To be our dwelling, in the skies ;

Where evermore a wondrous Light
Shines, inextinguishably bright :
It is the Vision of the blest,
The Lord Himself made manifest.

Its beams on angels' breasts it throws,
As on the Source from which it flows
They gaze,—the Form of Him Who trod
Erewhile this earth, Incarnate God.

On Him they gaze with burning thirst :
So shall the righteous burn, when first
They see the infinite reward
Assigned them by their Judge, the Lord.   [336.]

S. JOHN BAPTIST

Præcursor altus luminis.   VENERABLE BEDE

HAIL, harbinger of Morn :
    Thou that art this day born,
And heraldest the Word with clarion voice !
    Ye faithful ones, in him
    Behold the dawning dim
Of the bright Day, and let your hearts rejoice.

    John ;—by that chosen name
    To call him, Gabriel came
By God's appointment from his home on high :

What deeds that babe should do
To manhood when he grew,
God sent His angel forth to testify.

Yet in his mother's womb,
To Him Who should illume
With light the nations John his witness bore:
And when he came to birth,
John first proclaimed to earth
That witness, and is glorious evermore.

There hath none greater, none,
Than Zachariah's son
Ris'n among those that are of woman born;
A prophet, he may claim
More than a prophet's fame;
Sublimer deeds than theirs his front adorn.

Enough: can human speech
Unto his glory reach,
Meetly may mortals herald forth his praise,
For whom, in time of old,
God bade His seer unfold
The mighty work ordained in after-days?

"Lo, to prepare Thy way,"
Did God the Father say,
"Before Thy face My messenger I send,
Thy coming to forerun;
As on the orient sun
Doth the bright daystar morn by morn attend."

Praise therefore God most High;
Praise Him Who came to die
For us, His Son That liveth evermore;

And to the Spirit raise,
The Comforter, like praise,
While time endureth and when time is o'er.   [361.]

MARTYRS

Supernæ matris gaudia.   ADAM OF ST. VICTOR

CHRIST'S Church in heaven to-day
   Rejoiceth : and rejoice, Christ's Church on earth.
We have our times of mourning and of mirth ;
   Their tears are wiped away.

Succour Thy children, Lord,
Thy Church that in this joyless valley dwells :
Peopling the air, let angel sentinels
   Keep o'er her watch and ward.

The world, the flesh, hell's powers
Wage differing war around us ; aye upstart
New phantom-hosts ; the sabbath of the heart,
   O Lord, it is not ours.

On earth we know no calm :
Fear succeeds Hope, Grief banishes Delight ;
In heaven they sing, and pause not day or night,
   Their never-ending psalm.

O happy City ! Life
Is there but one long day of jubilee !
O happy citizens, for ever free
   From turmoil and from strife !

They wax not old, nor faint :
They fear no treachery, flee before no foe ;
Gladness alone doth in each bosom glow ;
    One joy fills every saint.

The blest one whom we sing
This day, now into Paradise received,
Beholds His Face in Whom he has believed ;
    He sees, unveiled, His King.

May we too find a place
Among the habitations of the just
This hour of anguish over ; as our trust,
    O Lord, is in Thy grace.   [403.]

FESTIVALS OF APOSTLES

Supreme, quales, Arbiter.   JEAN BAPTISTE SANTEUIL.
Paris Breviary

O LORD, through instruments how weak
    Thou workest out Thy sovereign will !
Frail earthen vessels Thou dost seek,
    And with Thy choicest treasure fill.

And in due time the pitchers, charged
    With light, Thou dost in pieces dash ;
And thence the light breaks forth, enlarged,
    As from the cloud the prisoned flash.

O'er earth Thy messengers are heard ;
    They haste like clouds before the gale ;
Fraught with the Word, the sacred Word,
    They pour forth thunder, lightning, hail.

Christ is their war-cry: at its sound
    Are hell's proud citadels laid low:
So, while the trumpets clanged around,
    Fell once the walls of Jericho.

Lord, let these trumpet blasts divine
    From treacherous sleep awake mankind;
And let these lights, erst lit at Thine,
    Disperse the darkness of our mind.

To Thee, on Thy Apostle's day,
    We pay all worship, God of might:
For thou hast callèd us that lay
    In darkness to Thy Glorious light.   [389.]

BETHANY

Intrante Christo Bethanicam domum.   Paris Breviary

TO Bethany Christ comes, the leper's guest.
    Speed we then thither: Simon spreads for all
        The banquet: with the rest
        We flock to Simon's hall.

While Lazarus feasts, and Martha decks the board,
A box of odorous oil doth Mary take,
        Right costly; to be poured
        Forth for her Master's sake.

She bathes His feet, and wipes them with her hair;
She breaks the box, and all the oil is spilled
        Over His head: the air
        Seems with new fragrance filled.

X

O why do scornful hands at Mary point?
Proud was her task; this treasure did she save,
    Beforehand to anoint
        Christ's Body for the grave.

And, as His Faith is preached in every tongue,
And far-off lands to His allegiance won,
    Still shall o'er earth be sung
        This deed which she hath done.

Now to the Father and the Son uplift
High praise for ever; Praise, and never cease,
    The Spirit; through whose gift
        Christ's Bride hath perfect peace.   [625.]

DE DIE JUDICII [1]

(Translated almost literally into the same metre as the original, with a rhyme added to make it an English metre, from an alphabetical hymn by Thomasius, published in Archbishop Trench's " Sacred Latin Poetry.")

CONCERNING THE DAY OF JUDGMENT.

A S a thief, who falls at midnight on his unsuspecting prey,
    When we think not shall o'ertake us the Almighty's Judg-
    ment Day.

B rief shall seem to men the pleasures that they prized in times
    of yore,
    When they know that as a moment Time hath past, and is
    no more.

C langing over Earth's four quarters shall the sudden trumpet-call
    Summon unto Christ's tribunal, dead or living, one and all:

---

[1] This Translation is the last thing Calverley wrote for the press. It was finished a few weeks before his death.—ED.

D own from highest heaven descended, shining angels hovering near,

Shall the Judge in all the brightness of His majesty appear.

E arth from pole to pole shall tremble, paling stars shall shrink from sight;

And the sun himself be darkened, and the round moon lose her light.

F ire shall execute, unbidden, his all-righteous Lord's decree,

Sky and lands in flame devouring, and the great unfathomed sea.

G lorious shall the King be seated then upon His throne on high,

The attendant choirs of angels standing awed and trembling by:

H is elect upon His right hand shall He bid their station take;

While as goats of evil savour on His left the wicked quake.

" I nto heavenly mansions enter," to the first shall say the Son,

"Which My Father's love prepared you ere the ages had begun;

K indly ye did once as brethren succour in His need your Lord;

Of your kindness of aforetime take ye now the rich reward."

' L ord," they shall exclaim, all joyous, "when beheld we thee in need?

When to us didst thou for succour, thou the King most mighty, plead?"

M ark the Judge Almighty's answer:—"When ye heard the poor man's plea;

Fed, clad, housed him; lo, ye did it in your lowliness to Me."

N ext to those upon His left hand the All-Just their doom shall tell:

"Hence ye cursed from My presence to the fiery flames of hell!

O nce I craved your ear a beggar, and ye mocked at My hard lot;

I was sick, and ye forsook Me ; naked, and ye clothed Me
  not."

P iteously shall ask the wicked : "Lord, when dealt we with
  Thee thus ?

  Sick or poor, when wast Thou mocked at, O most mighty
  King, by us ? "

Q uickly shall reply the High One : " When ye scorned the
  beggar's cry,

  Lo, the man whom ye thought scorn of in your wantonness
  was I."

R eeling back, shall then the wicked sink into the fiery glare,

  Where abides the worm that dies not, and the flames are
  quenchèd ne'er.

S atan with his servants lieth chained those darksome depths
  beneath,

  Where for ever must the damnèd weep, and wail, and gnash
  the teeth.

T hen on wings shall mount the faithful, led by many an angel-
  band,

  To the realm of joy and gladness, to their heavenly Fatherland :

U pon them in perfect brilliance Light and Peace shall shine
  from them

  Veiled no more shall be that City, that supreme Jerusalem

¹ X ᵗ the King, in all the brightness of His Father's splendour
  decked,

  Face to face shall then be gazed on by the hosts of His elect

---

¹ There is an apparent hiatus in the alphabet of Thomasius here, U and
V, like I and J, being treated as one letter. The claim, however, of V to
be a distinct letter is so far recognized that it begins the next line in the
couplet in the original as in the translation. There is no W in Latin, and
no available X : so the author had to content himself with Xᵗᵘˢ, and the
translator has followed him.

Y e beware then of the Serpent and his wiles : uphold the weak,
   Heed not gold, and flee vain pleasures, if the stars ye fain
      would seek :
Z one with Chastity's pure girdle day by day your loins, and
      turn,
   When the Master comes, to meet Him, bearing with you
      lamps that burn.

THEOCRITUS

[TRANSLATED INTO ENGLISH VERSE]

PREFACE

I HAD intended translating all or nearly all these Idylls into blank verse, as the natural equivalent of Greek or of Latin hexameters; only deviating into rhyme where occasion seemed to demand it. But I found that other metres had their special advantages: the fourteen-syllable line in particular has that, among others, of containing about the same number of syllables as an ordinary line of Theocritus. And there is also no doubt something gained by variety.

Several recent writers on the subject have laid down that every translation of Greek poetry, especially bucolic poetry, must be in rhyme of some sort. But they have seldom stated, and it is hard to see, why. There is no rhyme in the original, and *primâ facie* should be none in the translation. Professor Blackie has, it is true, pointed out the "assonances, alliterations, and rhymes," which are found in more or less abundance in Ionic Greek.[1] These may of course be purely accidental, like the hexameters in Livy or the blank-verse lines in Mr. Dickens's prose: but accidental or not (it may be said) they are there, and ought to be recognized. May we not then recognize them by introducing similar assonances, etc., here and there into the English version? or by availing ourselves of what Professor Blackie again calls attention to, the "compensating powers"[2] of English? I think with him that it was hard to speak of our language as one which "transforms *boos megaloio boeién* into 'great ox's hide.'" Such phrases as 'The Lord is a man of war,' 'The trumpet spake not to the armed throng,' are to my ear quite as grand as Homer: and it would be equally fair to ask what we are to make of a language which transforms Milton's line into ἡ σάλπιγξ οὐ προσέφη τόν ὡπλισμένον ὄχλον.[3] But be this as it may, these phenomena are surely too rare and too arbitrary to be adequately repre-

---

[1] BLACKIE'S *Homer*, vol. i., pp. 413, 414.
[2] *Ibid.*, page 377, etc.   [3] Professor Kingsley.

sented by any regularly recurring rhyme : and the question remains, what is there in the unrhymed original to which rhyme answers ?

To me its effect is to divide the verse into couplets, triplets, or (if the word may include them all) *stanzas* of some kind. Without rhyme we have no apparent means of conveying the effect of stanzas. There are of course devices such as repeating a line or part of a line at stated intervals, as is done in ' Tears, idle tears ' and elsewhere : but clearly none of these would be available to a translator. Where therefore he has to express stanzas, it is easy to see that rhyme may be admissible and even necessary. Pope's couplet may (or may not) stand for elegiacs, and the "In Memoriam" stanza for some one of Horace's metres. Where the heroes of Virgil's Eclogues sing alternately four lines each, Gray's quatrain seems to suggest itself : and where a similar case occurs in these Idylls (as for instance in the ninth) I thought it might be met by taking whatever received English stanza was nearest the required length. Pope's couplet again may possibly best convey the pomposity of some Idylls and the point of others. And there may be divers considerations of this kind. But, speaking generally, where the translator has not to intimate stanzas—where he has on the contrary to intimate that there are none—rhyme seems at first sight an intrusion and a *suggestio falsi*.

No doubt (as has been observed) what ' Pastorals ' we have are mostly written in what is called the heroic measure. But the reason is, I suppose, not far to seek. Dryden and Pope wrote ' heroics,' not from any sense of their fitness for bucolic poetry, but from a sense of their universal fitness : and their followers copied them. But probably no scholar would affirm that any poem, original or translated, by Pope or Dryden or any of their school, really resembles in any degree the bucolic poetry of the Greeks. Mr. Morris, whose poems appear to me to resemble it more almost than anything I have ever seen, of course writes what is technically Pope's metre, and equally of course is not of Pope's school. Whether or no Pope and Dryden *intended* to resemble the old bucolic poets in style is, to say the least, immaterial. If they did not, there is no reason whatever why any of us who do should adopt their metre : if they did and failed, there is every reason why we should select a different one.

Professor Conington has adduced one cogent argument against blank verse : that is, that hardly any of us can write it.[1] But if this is so—if the ' blank verse ' which we write is virtually prose in disguise—the addition of rhyme would only make it rhymed prose, and we should be as far as ever from "verse really deserving the name."[2] Unless (which I can

---

[1] Preface to CONINGTON'S *Æneid*, p. ix.   [2] *Ibid.*

hardly imagine) the mere incident of 'terminal consonance' can constitute that verse which would not be verse independently, this argument is equally good against attempting verse of any kind : we should still be writing disguised, and had better write undisguised, prose. Prose translations are of course tenable, and are (I am told) advocated by another very eminent critic. These considerations against them occur to one : that, among the characteristics of his original which the translator is bound to preserve, one is that he wrote metrically ; and that the prattle which passes muster, and sounds perhaps rather pretty than otherwise, in metre, would in plain prose be insufferable. Very likely some exceptional sort of prose may be meant, which would dispose of all such difficulties : but this would be harder for an ordinary writer to evolve out of his own brain, than to construct any species of verse for which he has at least a model and a precedent.

These remarks are made to show that my metres were not selected, as it might appear, at hap-hazard. Metre is not so unimportant as to justify that. For the rest, I have used Briggs's edition [1] ("Poetæ Bucolici Græci"), and have never, that I am aware of, taken refuge in any various reading where I could make any sense at all of the text as given by him. Sometimes I have been content to put down what I felt was a wrong rendering rather than omit ; but only in cases where the original was plainly corrupt, and all suggested emendations seemed to me hopelessly wide of the mark. What, for instance, may be the true meaning of βολβός τις κοχλίας in the fourteenth Idyll I have no idea. It is not very important. And no doubt the sense of the last two lines of the "Death of Adonis" is very unlikely to be what I have made it. But no suggestion that I met with seemed to me satisfactory or even plausible : and in this and a few similar cases I have put down what suited the context. Occasionally also, as in the Idyll here printed last—the one lately discovered by Bergk, which I elucidated by the light of Fritzsche's conjectures—I have availed myself of an opinion which Professor Conington somewhere expresses, to the effect that, where two interpretations are tenable, it is lawful to accept for the purposes of translation the one you might reject as a commentator. τετορταῖος has I dare say nothing whatever to do with 'quartan fever.'

On one point, rather a minor one, I have ventured to dissent from Professor Blackie and others : namely, in retaining the Greek, instead of adopting the Roman, nomenclature. Professor Blackie says [2] that there are

---

[1] Since writing the above lines I have had the advantage of seeing Mr. Paley's "Theocritus," which was not out when I made my version.

[2] BLACKIE'S *Homer*, Preface, pp. xii, xiii.

some men by whom "it is esteemed a grave offence to call Jupiter Jupiter," which begs the question : and that Jove "is much more musical" than Zeus, which begs another. Granting (what might be questioned) that *Zeus*, *Aphrodite*, and *Eros* are as absolutely the same individuals with *Jupiter*, *Venus*, and *Cupid* as *Odysseus* undoubtedly is with *Ulysses*—still I cannot see why, in making a version of (say) Theocritus, one should not use by way of preference those names by which he invariably called them, and which are characteristic of him : why, in turning a Greek author into English, we should begin by turning all the proper names into Latin. Professor Blackie's authoritative statement [1] that "there are whole idylls in Theocritus which would sound ridiculous in any other language than that of Tam o' Shanter" I accept of course unhesitatingly, and should like to see it acted upon by himself or any competent person. But a translator is bound to interpret all as best he may : and an attempt to write Tam o' Shanter's language by one who was not Tam o' Shanter's countryman would, I fear, result in something more ridiculous still.

C. S. C.

IDYLL I

The Death of Daphnis

Thyrsis.   A Goatherd.

Thyrsis.

SWEET are the whispers of yon pine that makes
 Low music o'er the spring, and, Goatherd, sweet
Thy piping; second thou to Pan alone.
Is his the hornèd ram? then thine the goat.
Is his the goat? to thee shall fall the kid ;
And toothsome is the flesh of unmilked kids.
  Goatherd. Shepherd, thy lay is as the noise of streams
Falling and falling aye from yon tall crag.

---

[1] BLACKIE'S *Homer*, vol. i., page 384.

If for their meed the Muses claim the ewe,
Be thine the stall-fed lamb ; or if they choose
The lamb, take thou the scarce less-valued ewe.

    Thyrsis. Pray, by the Nymphs, pray, Goatherd, seat thee
        here
Against this hill-slope in the tamarisk shade,
And pipe me somewhat, while I guard thy goats.

    Goatherd. I durst not, Shepherd, O I durst not pipe
At noontide; fearing Pan, who at that hour
Rests from the toils of hunting. Harsh is he ;
Wrath at his nostrils aye sits sentinel.
But, Thyrsis, thou canst sing of Daphnis' woes ;
High is thy name for woodland minstrelsy :
Then rest we in the shadow of the elm
Fronting Priapus and the Fountain-nymphs.
There, where the oaks are and the Shepherd's seat,
Sing as thou sang'st erewhile, when matched with him
Of Libya, Chromis ; and I'll give thee, first,
To milk, ay thrice, a goat—she suckles twins,
Yet ne'ertheless can fill two milkpails full ;—
Next, a deep drinking-cup, with sweet wax scoured,
Two-handled, newly-carven, smacking yet
O' the chisel. Ivy reaches up and climbs
About its lip, gilt here and there with sprays
Of woodbine, that enwreathed about it flaunts
Her saffron fruitage. Framed therein appears
A damsel ('tis a miracle of art)
In robe and snood : and suitors at her side
With locks fair-flowing, on her right and left,
Battle with words, that fail to reach her heart.
She, laughing, glances now on this, flings now
Her chance regards on that : they, all for love
Wearied and eye-swoln, find their labour lost.

Carven elsewhere an ancient fisher stands
On the rough rocks : thereto the old man with pains
Drags his great casting-net, as one that toils
Full stoutly : every fibre of his frame
Seems fishing ; so about the gray-beard's neck
(In might a youngster yet) the sinews swell.
Hard by that wave-beat sire a vineyard bends
Beneath its graceful load of burnished grapes ;
A boy sits on the rude fence watching them.
Near him two foxes : down the rows of grapes
One ranging steals the ripest ; one assails
With wiles the poor lad's scrip, to leave him soon
Stranded and supperless.   He plaits meanwhile
With ears of corn a right fine cricket-trap,
And fits it on a rush : for vines, for scrip,
Little he cares, enamoured of his toy.
     The cup is hung all round with lissom briar,
Triumph of Æolian art, a wondrous sight.
It was a ferryman's of Calydon :
A goat it cost me, and a great white cheese.
Ne'er yet my lips came near it, virgin still
It stands.   And welcome to such boon art thou,
If for my sake thou'lt sing that lay of lays.
I jest not : up, lad, sing : no songs thou'lt own
In the dim land where all things are forgot.
     Thyrsis [*sings*]. *Begin, sweet Maids, begin the woodland song.*
The voice of Thyrsis.   Ætna's Thyrsis I.
Where were ye, Nymphs, oh where, while Daphnis pined ?
In fair Penëus' or in Pindus' glens ?
For great Anapus' stream was not your haunt,
Nor Ætna's cliff, nor Acis' sacred rill.
     Begin, sweet Maids, begin the woodland song.
O'er him the wolves, the jackals howled o'er him ;

The lion in the oak-copse mourned his death.
  Begin, sweet Maids, begin the woodland song.
The kine and oxen stood around his feet,
The heifers and the calves wailed all for him.
  Begin, sweet Maids, begin the woodland song.
First from the mountain Hermes came, and said,
"Daphnis, who frets thee? Lad, whom lov'st thou so?"
  Begin, sweet Maids, begin the woodland song.
Came herdsmen, shepherds came, and goatherds came ;
All asked what ailed the lad. Priapus came
And said, " Why pine, poor Daphnis? while the maid
Foots it round every pool and every grove,
  (*Begin, sweet Maids, begin the woodland song*)
"O lack-love and perverse, in quest of thee ;
Herdsman in name, but goatherd rightlier called.
With eyes that yearn the goatherd marks his kids
Run riot, for he fain would frisk as they :
  (*Begin, sweet Maids, begin the woodland song*)
"With eyes that yearn dost thou too mark the laugh
Of maidens, for thou may'st not share their glee."
Still naught the herdsman said : he drained alone
His bitter portion, till the fatal end.
  Begin, sweet Maids, begin the woodland song.
Came Aphroditè, smiles on her sweet face,
False smiles, for heavy was her heart, and spake :
"So, Daphnis, thou must try a fall with Love !
But stalwart Love hath won the fall of thee."
  Begin, sweet Maids, begin the woodland song.
Then "Ruthless Aphroditè," Daphnis said,
"Accursed Aphroditè, foe to man !
Say'st thou mine hour is come, my sun hath set ?
Dead as alive, shall Daphnis work Love woe."
  Begin, sweet Maids, begin the woodland song.

" Fly to Mount Ida, where the swain (men say)
And Aphroditè—to Anchises fly :
There are oak-forests ; here but galingale,
And bees that make a music round the hives.
> *Begin, sweet Maids, begin the woodland song.*

" Adonis owed his bloom to tending flocks
And smiting hares, and bringing wild beasts down.
> *Begin, sweet Maids, begin the woodland song.*

" Face once more Diomed : tell him ' I have slain
The herdsman Daphnis ; now I challenge thee.'
> *Begin, sweet Maids, begin the woodland song.*

" Farewell, wolf, jackal, mountain-prisoned bear !
Ye'll see no more by grove or glade or glen
Your herdsman Daphnis !   Arethuse, farewell,
And the bright streams that pour down Thymbris' side.
> *Begin, sweet Maids, begin the woodland song.*

" I am that Daphnis, who lead here my kine,
Bring here to drink my oxen and my calves.
> *Begin, sweet Maids, begin the woodland song.*

" Pan, Pan, oh whether great Lyceum's crags
Thou haunt'st to-day, or mightier Mænalus,
Come to the Sicel isle !   Abandon now
Rhium and Helicè, and the mountain-cairn
(That e'en gods cherish) of Lycaon's son !
> *Forget, sweet Maids, forget your woodland song.*

" Come, king of song, o'er this my pipe, compact
With wax and honey-breathing, arch thy lip :
For surely I am torn from life by Love.
> *Forget, sweet Maids, forget your woodland song.*

" From thicket now and thorn let violets spring,
Now let white lilies drape the juniper,
And pines grow figs, and nature all go wrong :
For Daphnis dies.   Let deer pursue the hounds,

And mountain-owls outsing the nightingale.
  Forget, sweet Maids, forget your woodland song."

So spake he, and he never spake again.
Fain Aphroditè would have raised his head ;
But all his thread was spun.   So down the stream
Went Daphnis : closed the waters o'er a head
Dear to the Nine, of nymphs not unbeloved.
    Now give me goat and cup ; that I may milk
The one, and pour the other to the Muse.
Fare ye well, Muses, o'er and o'er farewell !
I'll sing strains lovelier yet in days to be.
    Goatherd. Thrysis, let honey and the honeycomb
Fill thy sweet mouth, and figs of Ægilus :
For ne'er cicala trilled so sweet a song.
Here is the cup : mark, friend, how sweet it smells :
The Hours, thou'lt say, have washed it in their well.
Hither, Cissætha ! Thou, go milk her ! Kids,
Be steady, or your pranks will rouse the ram.

IDYLL II

THE SORCERESS

WHERE are the bay-leaves, Thestylis, and the charms ?
    Fetch all ; with fiery wool the caldron crown ;
Let glamour win me back my false lord's heart !
Twelve days the wretch hath not come nigh to me,
Nor made inquiry if I die or live,
Nor clamoured (oh unkindness !) at my door.
Sure his swift fancy wanders otherwhere,

The slave of Aphroditè and of Love.
I'm off to Timagetus' wrestling-school
At dawn, that I may see him and denounce
His doings ; but I'll charm him now with charms.
So shine out fair, O moon ! To thee I sing
My soft low song : to thee and Hecatè
The dweller in the shades, at whose approach
E'en the dogs quake, as on she moves through blood
And darkness and the barrows of the slain.
All hail, dread Hecatè : companion me
Unto the end, and work me witcheries
Potent as Circè or Medea wrought,
Or Perimedè of the golden hair !
    Turn, magic wheel, draw homeward him I love.
First we ignite the grain.   Nay, pile it on :
Where are thy wits flown, timorous Thestylis ?
Shall I be flouted, I, by such as thou ?
Pile, and still say, ' This pile is of his bones.'
    Turn, magic wheel, draw homeward him I love.
Delphis racks me : I burn him in these bays.
As, flame-enkindled, they lift up their voice,
Blaze once, and not a trace is left behind :
So waste his flesh to powder in yon fire !
    Turn, magic wheel, draw homeward him I love.
E'en as I melt, not uninspired, the wax,
May Mindian Delphis melt this hour with love :
And, swiftly as this brazen wheel whirls round,
May Aphroditè whirl him to my door.
    Turn, magic wheel, draw homeward him I love.
Next burn the husks.   Hell's adamantine floor
And aught that else stands firm can Artemis move.
Thestylis, the hounds bay up and down the town :
The goddess stands i' the crossroads : sound the gongs.

Turn, magic wheel, draw homeward him I love.
Hushed are the voices of the winds and seas;
But O not hushed the voice of my despair.
He burns my being up, who left me here
No wife, no maiden, in my misery.

Turn, magic wheel, draw homeward him I love.
Thrice I pour out; speak thrice, sweet mistress, thus:
"What face soe'er hangs o'er him be forgot
Clean as, in Dia, Theseus (legends say)
Forgat his Ariadne's locks of love."

Turn, magic wheel, draw homeward him I love.
The coltsfoot grows in Arcady, the weed
That drives the mountain-colts and swift mares wild.
Like them may Delphis rave: so, maniac-wise,
Race from his burnished brethren home to me.

Turn, magic wheel, draw homeward him I love.
He lost this tassel from his robe; which I
Shred thus, and cast it on the raging flames.
Ah baleful Love! why, like the marsh-born leech,
Cling to my flesh, and drain my dark veins dry?

Turn, magic wheel, draw homeward him I love.
From a crushed eft to-morrow he shall drink
Death! But now, Thestylis, take these herbs and smear
That threshold o'er, whereto at heart I cling
Still, still—albeit he thinks scorn of me—
And spit, and say, ''Tis Delphis' bones I smear.'

Turn, magic wheel, draw homeward him I love.

[*Exit Thestylis.*

Now, all alone, I'll weep a love whence sprung
When born? Who wrought my sorrow? Anaxo came,
Her basket in her hand, to Artemis' grove.
Bound for the festival, troops of forest beasts
Stood round, and in the midst a lioness.

Bethink thee, mistress Moon, whence came my love.
Theucharidas' slave, my Thracian nurse now dead
Then my near neighbour, prayed me and implored
To see the pageant : I, the poor doomed thing,
Went with her, trailing a fine silken train,
And gathering round me Clearista's robe.

Bethink thee, mistress Moon, whence came my love.
Now, the mid-highway reached by Lycon's farm,
Delphis and Eudamippus passed me by.
With beards as lustrous as the woodbine's gold
And breasts more sheeny than thyself, O Moon,
Fresh from the wrestler's glorious toil they came.

Bethink thee, mistress Moon, whence came my love.
I saw, I raved, smit (weakling) to my heart.
My beauty withered, and I cared no more
For all that pomp ; and how I gained my home
I know not : some strange fever wasted me.
Ten nights and days I lay upon my bed.

Bethink thee, mistress Moon, whence came my love.
And wan became my flesh, as 't had been dyed,
And all my hair streamed off, and there was left
But bones and skin.   Whose threshold crossed I not,
Or missed what grandam's hut who dealt in charms ?
For no light thing was this, and time sped on.

Bethink thee, mistress Moon, whence came my love.
At last I spake the truth to that my maid :
"Seek, an thou canst, some cure for my sore pain.
Alas, I am all the Mindian's ! But begone,
And watch by Timagetus' wrestling-school :
There doth he haunt, there soothly take his rest.

Bethink thee, mistress Moon, whence came my love.
"Find him alone : nod softly : say, 'she waits' ;
And bring him."   So I spake : she went her way,

And brought the lustrous-limbed one to my roof.
And I, the instant I beheld him step
Lightfooted o'er the threshold of my door,
　　(*Bethink thee, mistress Moon, whence came my love,*)
Became all cold like snow, and from my brow
Brake the damp dewdrops : utterance I had none,
Not e'en such utterance as a babe may make
That babbles to its mother in its dreams ;
But all my fair frame stiffened into wax.
　　Bethink thee, mistress Moon, whence came my love.
He bent his pitiless eyes on me ; looked down,
And sate him on my couch, and sitting, said :
"Thou hast gained on me, Simætha, (e'en as I
Gained once on young Philinus in the race,)
Bidding me hither ere I came unasked.
　　Bethink thee, mistress Moon, whence came my love.
"For I had come, by Eros I had come,
This night, with comrades twain or may-be more,
The fruitage of the Wine-god in my robe,
And, wound about my brow with ribands red,
The silver leaves so dear to Heracles.
　　Bethink thee, mistress Moon, whence came my love.
"Had ye said 'Enter,' well : for 'mid my peers
High is my name for goodliness and speed :
I had kissed that sweet mouth once and gone my way.
But had the door been barred, and I thrust out,
With brand and axe would we have stormed ye then.
　　Bethink thee, mistress Moon, whence came my love.
"Now be my thanks recorded, first to Love,
Next to thee, maiden, who didst pluck me out,
A half-burned helpless creature, from the flames,
And badst me hither.   It is Love that lights
A fire more fierce than his of Lipara ;

(*Bethink thee, mistress Moon, whence came my love.*)
"Scares, mischief-mad, the maiden from her bower,
The bride from her warm couch."   He spake: and I,
A willing listener, sat, my hand in his,
Among the cushions, and his cheek touched mine,
Each hotter than its wont, and we discoursed
In soft low language.   Need I prate to thee,
Sweet Moon, of all we said and all we did?
Till yesterday he found no fault with me,
Nor I with him.   But lo, to-day there came
Philista's mother—hers who flutes to me—
With her Melampo's; just when up the sky
Gallop the mares that chariot rose-limbed Dawn:
And divers tales she brought me, with the rest
How Delphis loved, she knew not rightly whom:
But this she knew; that of the rich wine aye
He poured 'to Love;' and at the last had fled,
To line, she deemed, the fair one's hall with flowers.
Such was my visitor's tale, and it was true:
For thrice, nay four times, daily he would stroll
Hither, leave here full oft his Dorian flask:
Now—'tis a fortnight since I saw his face.
Doth he then treasure something sweet elsewhere?
Am I forgot?   I'll charm him now with charms.
But let him try me more, and by the Fates
He'll soon be knocking at the gates of hell.
Spells of such power are in this chest of mine,
Learned, lady, from mine host in Palestine.

Lady, farewell: turn ocean-ward thy steeds:
As I have purposed, so shall I fulfil.
Farewell, thou bright-faced Moon! Ye stars, farewell,
That wait upon the car of noiseless Night.

IDYLL III

THE SERENADE

I PIPE to Amaryllis; while my goats,
  Tityrus their guardian, browse along the fell.
O Tityrus, as I love thee, feed my goats:
And lead them to the spring, and, Tityrus, 'ware
The lifted crest of yon gray Libyan ram.
  Ah winsome Amaryllis! Why no more
Greet'st thou thy darling, from the caverned rock
Peeping all coyly? Think'st thou scorn of him?
Hath a near view revealed him satyr-shaped
Of chin and nostril? I shall hang me soon.
See here ten apples: from thy favourite tree
I plucked them: I shall bring ten more anon.
Ah witness my heart-anguish! Oh were I
A booming bee, to waft me to thy lair,
Threading the fern and ivy in whose depths
Thou nestlest! I have learned what Love is now:
Fell god, he drank the lioness's milk,
In the wild woods his mother cradled him,
Whose fire slow-burns me, smiting to the bone.
O thou whose glance is beauty and whose heart
All marble: O dark-eyebrowed maiden mine!
Cling to thy goatherd, let him kiss thy lips,
For there is sweetness in an empty kiss.
Thou wilt not? Piecemeal I will rend the crown,
The ivy-crown which, dear, I guard for thee,
Inwov'n with scented parsley and with flowers:
Oh I am desperate—what betides me, what?—

Still art thou deaf?   I'll doff my coat of skins
And leap into yon waves, where on the watch
For mackerel Olpis sits : tho' I 'scape death,
That I have all but died will pleasure thee.
That learned I when (I murmuring ' loves she me ? ')
The *Love-in-absence*, crushed, returned no sound,
But shrank and shrivelled on my smooth young wrist.
I learned it of the sieve-divining crone
Who gleaned behind the reapers yesterday :
' Thou'rt wrapt up all,' Agraia said, ' in her ;
She makes of none account her worshipper.'
    Lo ! a white goat, and twins, I keep for thee :
Mermnon's lass covets them : dark she is of skin :
But yet hers be they ; thou but foolest me.
    She cometh, by the quivering of mine eye.
I'll lean against the pine-tree here and sing.
She may look round : she is not adamant.
[*Sings*] Hippomenes, when he a maid would wed,
    Took apples in his hand and on he sped.
    Famed Atalanta's heart was won by this ;
    She marked, and maddening sank in Love's abyss.

    From Othrys did the seer Melampus stray
    To Pylos with his herd : and lo there lay
    In a swain's arms a maid of beauty rare ;
    Alphesibœa, wise of heart, she bare.

    Did not Adonis rouse to such excess
    Of frenzy her whose name is Loveliness,
    (He a mere lad whose wethers grazed the hill)
    That, dead, he 's pillowed on her bosom still ?

    Endymion sleeps the sleep that changeth not :

And, maiden mine, I envy him his lot !
Envy Iasion's : his it was to gain
Bliss that I dare not breathe in ears profane.

My head aches. What reck'st thou? I sing no more :
E'en where I fell I'll lie, until the wolves
Rend me—may that be honey in thy mouth !

IDYLL IV

The Herdsmen

Battus. Corydon.

Battus.

WHO owns these cattle, Corydon? Philondas? Prythee
say.

Corydon. No, Ægon : and he gave them me to tend while
he 's away.

Battus. Dost milk them in the gloaming, when none is nigh
to see?

Corydon. The old man brings the calves to suck, and keeps
an eye on me.

Battus. And to what region then hath flown the cattle's
rightful lord?

Corydon. Hast thou not heard? With Milo he vanished
Elisward.

Battus. How ! was the wrestler's oil e'er yet so much as seen
by him?

Corydon. Men say he rivals Heracles in lustiness of limb.

Battus. I'm Polydeuces' match (or so my mother says) and
more.

Corydon. —So off he started; with a spade, and of these
　　ewes a score.

Battus. This Milo will be teaching wolves how they should
　　raven next.

Corydon. —And by these bellowings his kine proclaim how
　　sore they're vexed.

Battus. Poor kine! they've found their master a sorry knave
　　indeed.

Corydon. They're poor enough, I grant you: they have not
　　heart to feed.

Battus. Look at that heifer! sure there's naught, save bare
　　bones, left of her.

Pray, does she browse on dewdrops, as doth the grasshopper?

Corydon. Not she, by heaven! She pastures now by Æsarus'
　　glades,

And handfuls fair I pluck her there of young and green grass-
　　blades;

Now bounds about Latymnus, that gathering-place of shades.

Battus. That bull again, the red one, my word but he is
　　lean!

I wish the Sybarite burghers aye may offer to the queen

Of heaven as pitiful a beast: those burghers are so mean!

Corydon. Yet to the Salt Lake's edges I drive him, I can
　　swear;

Up Physcus, up Neæthus' side—he lacks not victual there,

With dittany and endive and foxglove for his fare.

Battus. Well, well! I pity Ægon. His cattle, go they must

To rack and ruin, all because vain-glory was his lust.

The pipe that erst he fashioned is doubtless scored with rust?

Corydon. Nay, by the Nymphs! That pipe he left to me,
　　the selfsame day

He made for Pisa: I am too a minstrel in my way:

Well the flute-part in '*Pyrrhus*' and in '*Glauca*' can I play.

I sing too '*Here's to Croton*' and '*Zacynthus O 'tis fair,*'
And '*Eastward to Lacinium :*'—the bruiser Milo there
His single self ate eighty loaves ; there also did he pull
Down from its mountain-dwelling, by one hoof grasped, a bull,
And gave it Amaryllis : the maidens screamed with fright ;
As for the owner of the bull he only laughed outright.

> *Battus.* Sweet Amaryllis ! thou alone, though dead, art un-
> forgot.

Dearer than thou, whose light is quenched, my very goats are
not.

Oh for the all-unkindly fate that 's fallen to my lot !

> *Corydon.* Cheer up, brave lad ! to-morrow may ease thee of
> thy pain :

Aye for the living are there hopes, past hoping are the slain :
And now Zeus sends us sunshine, and now he sends us rain.

> *Battus.* I'm better. Beat those young ones off ! E'en now
> their teeth attack

That olive's shoots, the graceless brutes ! Back, with your
white face, back !

> *Corydon.* Back to thy hill, Cymætha ! Great Pan, how deaf
> thou art !

I shall be with thee presently, and in the end thou'lt smart.
I warn thee, keep thy distance. Look, up she creeps again !
Oh were my hare-crook in my hand, I'd give it to her then !

> *Battus.* For heaven's sake, Corydon, look here ! Just now
> a bramble-spike

Ran, there, into my instep—and oh how deep they strike,
Those lancewood-shafts ! A murrain light on that calf, I say !
I got it gaping after her. Canst thou discern it, pray ?

> *Corydon.* Ay, ay ; and here I have it, safe in my finger-nails.
> *Battus.* Eh ! at how slight a matter how tall a warrior quails !
> *Corydon.* Ne'er range the hill-crest, Battus, all sandal-less and
> bare :

Because the thistle and the thorn lift aye their plumed heads
    there.

    Battus. —Say, Corydon, does that old man we wot of (tell me,
        please !)

Still haunt the dark-browed little girl whom once he used to
    tease ?

    Corydon. Ay my poor boy, that doth he : I saw them yesterday

Down by the byre ; and, trust me, loving enough were they.

    Battus. Well done, my veteran light-o'-love ! In deeming
        thee mere man,

I wronged thy sire : some Satyr he, or an uncouth-limbed Pan.

IDYLL V

THE BATTLE OF THE BARDS

Comatas. Lacon. Morson.

Comatas.

GOATS, from a shepherd who stands here, from Lacon,
    keep away :

Sibyrtas owns him ; and he stole my goatskin yesterday.

    Lacon. Hi ! lambs ! avoid yon fountain. Have ye not eyes
        to see

Comatas, him who filched a pipe but two days back from me ?

    Comatas. Sibyrtas' bondsman own a pipe ? whence gotst thou
        that, and how ?

Tootling through straws with Corydon mayhap 's beneath thee
    now ?

    Lacon. 'Twas Lycon's gift, your highness. But pray,
        Comatas, say,

What is that skin wherewith thou saidst that Lacon walked
    away ?

Why, thy lord's self had ne'er a skin whereon his limbs to lay.

   Comatas. The skin that Crocylus gave me, a dark one streaked
      with white,

The day he slew his she-goat.   Why, thou wert ill with spite,

Then, my false friend ; and thou would'st end by beggaring me
      quite.

   Lacon. Did Lacon, did Calæthis' son purloin a goatskin ? No,

By Pan that haunts the sea-beach !   Lad, if I served thee so,

Crazed may I drop from yon hill-top to Crathis' stream below !

   Comatas. Nor pipe of thine, good fellow—the Ladies of the
      Lake

So be still kind and good to me—did e'er Comatas take.

   Lacon. Be Daphnis' woes my portion, should that my cred-
      ence win !

Still, if thou list to stake a kid—that surely were no sin—

Come on, I'll sing it out with thee—until thou givest in.

   Comatas. ' *The hog he braved Athene.*'   As for the kid, 'tis
      there :

You stake a lamb against him—that fat one—if you dare.

   Lacon. Fox ! were that fair for either ?   At shearing who'd
      prefer

Horsehair to wool ? or when the goat stood handy, suffer her

To nurse her firstling, and himself go milk a blatant cur ?

   Comatas. The same who deemed his hornet's-buzz the true
      cicala's note,

And braved—like you—his better.   And so forsooth you vote

My kid a trifle ?   Then come on, fellow !   I stake the goat.

   Lacon. Why be so hot ?   Art thou on fire ?   First prythee
      take thy seat

'Neath this wild woodland olive : thy tones will sound more
      sweet.

Here falls a cold rill drop by drop, and green grass-blades
      uprear

Their heads, and fallen leaves are thick, and locusts prattle
here.

   Comatas. Hot I am not; but hurt I am, and sorely, when I
think

That thou canst look me in the face and never bleach nor
blink—

Me, thine own boyhood's tutor! Go, train the she-wolf's
brood:

Train dogs—that they may rend thee! This, this is gratitude!

   Lacon. When learned I from thy practice or thy preaching
aught that's right,

Thou puppet, thou misshapen lump of ugliness and spite?

   Comatas. When? When I beat thee, wailing sore: yon goats
looked on with glee,

And bleated; and were dealt with e'en as I had dealt with thee.

   Lacon. Well, hunchback, shallow be thy grave as was thy
judgment then!

But hither, hither! Thou'lt not dip in herdsman's lore again.

   Comatas. Nay, here are oaks and galingale: the hum of
housing bees

Makes the place pleasant, and the birds are piping in the trees.

And here are two cold streamlets; here deeper shadows fall

Than yon place owns, and look what cones drop from the pine-
tree tall.

   Lacon. Come hither, and tread on lambswool that is soft as
any dream:

Still more unsavoury than thyself to me thy goatskins seem.

Here will I plant a bowl of milk, our ladies' grace to win;

And one, as huge, beside it, sweet olive-oil therein.

   Comatas. Come hither, and trample dainty fern and poppy-
blossom: sleep

On goatskins that are softer than thy fleeces piled three deep.

Here will I plant eight milkpails, great Pan's regard to gain,

Round them eight cups : full honeycombs shall every cup
    contain.
    Lacon. Well! there essay thy woodcraft : thence fight me,
    never budge
From thine own oak ; e'en have thy way. But who shall be
    our judge ?
Oh, if Lycopas with his kine should chance this way to trudge !
    Comatas. Nay, I want no Lycopas. But hail yon woods-
    man, do :
'Tis Morson—see ! his arms are full of bracken—there, by you.
    Lacon. We'll hail him.
    Comatas.   Ay, you hail him.
    Lacon.   Friend, 'twill not take thee long :
We're striving which is master, we twain, in woodland song :
And thou, my good friend Morson, ne'er look with favouring
    eyes
On me ; nor yet to yonder lad be fain to judge the prize.
    Comatas. Nay, by the Nymphs, sweet Morson, ne'er for
    Comatas' sake
Stretch thou a point ; nor e'er let *him* undue advantage take.
Sibyrtas owns yon wethers ; a Thurian is he :
And here, my friend, Eumares' goats, of Sybaris, you may
    see.
    Lacon. And who asked thee, thou naughty knave, to whom
    belonged these flocks,
Sibyrtas, or (it might be) me ? Eh, thou'rt a chatterbox !
    Comatas. The simple truth, most worshipful, is all that I
    allege :
I'm not for boasting. But thy wit hath all too keen an edge.
    Lacon. Come sing, if singing 's in thee—and may our friend
    get back
To town alive ! Heaven help us, lad, how thy tongue doth
    clack !

Comatas. [*Sings*] Daphnis the mighty minstrel was less
  precious to the Nine

Than I.   I offered yesterday two kids upon their shrine.

  Lacon. [*Sings*] Ay, but Apollo fancies me hugely : for him
    I rear

A lordly ram : and, look you, the Carnival is near.

  Comatas. Twin kids hath every goat I milk, save two.   My
    maid, my own,

Eyes me and asks 'At milking time, rogue, art thou all alone ? '

  Lacon. Go to ! nigh twenty baskets doth Lacon fill with
    cheese :

Hath time to woo a sweetheart too upon the blossomed leas.

  Comatas. Clarissa pelts her goatherd with apples, should he
    stray

By with his goats; and pouts her lip in a quaint charming way.

  Lacon. Me too a darling smooth of face notes as I tend my
    flocks :

How maddeningly o'er that fair neck ripple those shining
    locks !

  Comatas. Tho' dogrose and anemone are fair in their degree

The rose that blooms by garden-walls still is the rose for me.

  Lacon. Tho' acorns' cups are fair, their taste is bitterness,
    and still

I'll choose, for honeysweet are they, the apples of the hill.

  Comatas. A cushat I will presently procure and give to her

Who loves me : I know where it sits ; up in the juniper.

  Lacon. Pooh ! a soft fleece, to make a coat, I'll give the day
    I shear

My brindled ewe—(no hand but mine shall touch it)—to my
    dear.

  Comatas. Back, lambs, from that wild-olive : and be content
    to browse

Here on the shoulder of the hill, beneath the myrtle boughs.

Lacon. Run, (will ye ?) Ball and Dogstar, down from that oak
    tree, run :
And feed where Spot is feeding, and catch the morning sun.

  Comatas. I have a bowl of cypress-wood : I have besides a
    cup :
Praxiteles designed them : for *her* they're treasured up.

  Lacon. I have a dog who throttles wolves : he loves the sheep,
    and they
Love him : I'll give him to my dear, to keep wild beasts at bay.

  Comatas. Ye locusts that o'erleap my fence, oh let my vines
    escape
Your clutches, I beseech you : the bloom is on the grape.

  Lacon. Ye crickets, mark how nettled our friend the goat-
    herd is !
I ween, ye cost the reapers pangs as acute as his.

  Comatas. Those foxes with their bushy tails, I hate to see
    them crawl
Round Micon's homestead and purloin his grapes at evenfall.

  Lacon. *I* hate to see the beetles that come warping on the
    wind,
And climb Philondas' trees, and leave never a fig behind.

  Comatas. Have you forgot that cudgelling I gave you ? At
    each stroke
You grinned and twisted with a grace, and clung to yonder oak.

  Lacon. That I've forgot—but I have not, how once Eumares
    tied
You to that selfsame oak-trunk, and tanned your unclean hide.

  Comatas. There's some one ill—of heartburn. You note it,
    I presume,
Morson ? Go quick, and fetch a squill from some old beldam's
    tomb.

  Lacon. I think I'm stinging somebody, as Morson too per-
    ceives—

Go to the river and dig up a clump of sowbread-leaves.

Comatas. May Himera flow, not water, but milk : and may'st
    thou blush,
Crathis, with wine ; and fruitage grow upon every rush.

Lacon. For me may Sybaris' fountain flow, pure honey : so
    that you,
My fair, may dip your pitcher each morn in honey-dew.

Comatas. My goats are fed on clover and goat's-delight :
    they tread
On lentisk leaves; or lie them down, ripe strawberries o'er their
    head.

Lacon. My sheep crop honeysuckle bloom, while all around
    them blows
In clusters rich the jasmine, as brave as any rose.

Comatas. I scorn my maid; for when she took my cushat,
    she did not
Draw with both hands my face to hers and kiss me on the spot.

Lacon. I love my love, and hugely : for, when I gave my
    flute,
I was rewarded with a kiss, a loving one to boot.

Comatas. Lacon, the nightingale should scarce be challenged
    by the jay,
Nor swan by hoopoe : but, poor boy, thou aye wert for a fray.

Morson. I bid the shepherd hold his peace. Comatas, unto
    you
I, Morson, do adjudge the lamb. You'll first make offering
    due
Unto the nymphs : then savoury meat you'll send to Morson
    too.

Comatas. By Pan I will ! Snort, all my herd of he-goats : I
    shall now
O'er Lacon, shepherd as he is, crow ye shall soon see how.
I've won, and I could leap sky-high ! Ye also dance and skip,

My hornèd ewes : in Sybaris' fount to-morrow all shall dip.
Ho ! you, sir, with the glossy coat and dangerous crest; you
　　　dare
Look at a ewe, till I have slain my lamb, and ill you'll fare.
What ! is he at his tricks again ?　He is, and he will get
(Or my name 's not Comatas), a proper pounding yet.

IDYLL VI

The Drawn Battle

Daphnis. Damœtas.

DAPHNIS the herdsman and Damœtas once
　　　Had driven, Aratus, to the selfsame glen.
One chin was yellowing, one showed half a beard.
And by a brookside on a summer noon
The pair sat down and sang ; but Daphnis led
The song, for Daphnis was the challenger.
　Daphnis. "See ! Galatea pelts thy flock with fruit,
And calls their master 'Lack-love,' Polypheme.
Thou mark'st her not, blind, blind, but pipest aye
Thy wood-notes.　See again, she smites thy dog :
Sea-ward the fleeced flocks' sentinel peers and barks,
And, through the clear wave visible to her still,
Careers along the gently babbling beach.
Look that he leap not on the maid new-risen
From her sea-bath and rend her dainty limbs.
She fools thee, near or far, like thistle-waifs
In hot sweet summer : flies from thee when wooed,
Unwooed pursues thee : risks all moves to win ;
For, Polypheme, things foul seem fair to Love."

And then, due prelude made, Damœtas sang.

Damœtas. " I marked her pelt my dog, I was not blind,
By Pan, by this my one my precious eye
That bounds my vision now and evermore !
But Telemus the Seer, be his the woe,
His and his children's, that he promised me !
Yet do I too tease her ; I pass her by,
Pretend to woo another :—and she hears
(Heaven help me !) and is faint with jealousy ;
And hurrying from the sea-wave as if stung,
Scans with keen glance my grotto and my flock.
'Twas I hissed on the dog to bark at her ;
For, when I loved her, he would whine and lay
His muzzle in her lap.   These things she'll note
Mayhap, and message send on message soon :
But I will bar my door until she swear
To make me on this isle fair bridal-bed.
And I am less unlovely than men say.
I looked into the mere (the mere was calm),
And goodly seemed my beard, and goodly seemed
My solitary eye, and, half-revealed,
My teeth gleamed whiter than the Parian marl.
Thrice for good luck I spat upon my robe :
That learned I of the hag Cottytaris—her
Who fluted lately with Hippocoön's mowers."

Damœtas then kissed Daphnis lovingly :
One gave a pipe and one a goodly flute.
Straight to the shepherd's flute and herdsman's pipe
The younglings bounded in the soft green grass :
And neither was o'ermatched, but matchless both.

z

IDYLL VII

HARVEST-HOME

ONCE on a time did Eucritus and I
   (With us Amyntas) to the riverside
Steal from the city.   For Lycopeus' sons
Were that day busy with the harvest-home,
Antigenes and Phrasidemus, sprung
(If aught thou holdest by the good old names)
By Clytia from great Chalcon—him who erst
Planted one stalwart knee against the rock,
And lo, beneath his foot Burinè's rill
Brake forth, and at its side poplar and elm
Showed aisles of pleasant shadow, greenly roofed
By tufted leaves.   Scarce midway were we now,
Nor yet descried the tomb of Brasilas :
When, thanks be to the Muses, there drew near
A wayfarer from Crete, young Lycidas.
The horned herd was his care : a glance might tell
So much : for every inch a herdsman he.
Slung o'er his shoulder was a ruddy hide
Torn from a he-goat, shaggy, tangle-haired,
That reeked of rennet yet : a broad belt clasped
A patched cloak round his breast, and for a staff
A gnarled wild-olive bough his right hand bore.
Soon with a quiet smile he spoke—his eye
Twinkled, and laughter sat upon his lip :
" And whither ploddest thou thy weary way
Beneath the noontide sun, Simichidas ?
For now the lizard sleeps upon the wall,

The crested lark folds now his wandering wing.
Dost speed, a bidden guest, to some reveller's board?
Or townward to the treading of the grape?
For lo! recoiling from thy hurrying feet
The pavement-stones ring out right merrily."
Then I: "Friend Lycid, all men say that none
Of haymakers or herdsmen is thy match
At piping: and my soul is glad thereat.
Yet, to speak sooth, I think to rival thee.
Now look, this road holds holiday to-day:
For banded brethren solemnise a feast
To richly-dight Demeter, thanking her
For her good gifts: since with no grudging hand
Hath the boon goddess filled the wheaten floors.
So come: the way, the day, is thine as mine:
Try we our woodcraft—each may learn from each.
I am, as thou, a clarion-voice of song;
All hail me chief of minstrels. But I am not,
Heaven knows, o'ercredulous: no, I scarce can yet
(I think) outvie Philetas, nor the bard
Of Samos, champion of Sicilian song.
They are as cicadas challenged by a frog."

I spake to gain mine ends; and laughing light
He said: "Accept this club, as thou'rt indeed
A born truth-teller, shaped by heaven's own hand!
I hate your builders who would rear a house
High as Oromedon's mountain-pinnacle:
I hate your song-birds too, whose cuckoo-cry
Struggles (in vain) to match the Chian bard.
But come, we'll sing forthwith, Simichidas,
Our woodland music: and for my part I—
List, comrade, if you like the simple air

I forged among the uplands yesterday.

[*Sings*] Safe be my true-love convoyed o'er the main
To Mitylenè—though the southern blast
Chase the lithe waves, while westward slant the Kids,
Or low above the verge Orion stand—
If from Love's furnace she will rescue me,
For Lycidas is parched with hot desire.
Let halcyons lay the sea-waves and the winds,
Northwind and Westwind, that in shores far-off
Flutters the seaweed—halcyons, of all birds
Whose prey is on the waters, held most dear
By the green Nereids : yea let all things smile
On her to Mitylenè voyaging,
And in fair harbour may she ride at last.
I on that day, a chaplet woven of dill
Or rose or simple violet on my brow,
Will draw the wine of Pteleas from the cask
Stretched by the ingle.   They shall roast me beans,
And elbow-deep in thyme and asphodel
And quaintly-curling parsley shall be piled
My bed of rushes, where in royal ease
I sit and, thinking of my darling, drain
With stedfast lip the liquor to the dregs.
I'll have a pair of pipers, shepherds both,
This from Acharnæ, from Lycopè that ;
And Tityrus shall be near me and shall sing
How the swain Daphnis loved the stranger-maid ;
And how he ranged the fells, and how the oaks
(Such oaks as Himera's banks are green withal)
Sang dirges o'er him waning fast away
Like snow on Athos, or on Hæmus high,
Or Rhodopè, or utmost Caucasus.

And he shall sing me how the big chest held
(All through the maniac malice of his lord)
A living goatherd : how the round-faced bees,
Lured from their meadow by the cedar-smell,
Fed him with daintiest flowers, because the Muse
Had made his throat a well-spring of sweet song.
Happy Comatas, this sweet lot was thine !
Thee the chest prisoned, for thee the honey-bees
Toiled, as thou slavedst out the mellowing year :
And oh hadst thou been numbered with the quick
In my day !   I had led thy pretty goats
About the hill-side, listening to thy voice :
While thou hadst lain thee down 'neath oak or pine,
Divine Comatas, warbling pleasantly."

    He spake and paused ; and thereupon spake I.
" I too, friend Lycid, as I ranged the fells,
Have learned much lore and pleasant from the Nymphs,
Whose fame mayhap hath reached the throne of Zeus.
But this wherewith I'll grace thee ranks the first :
Thou listen, since the Muses like thee well.

[*Sings*] On me the young Loves sneezed : for hapless I
Am fain of Myrto as the goats of Spring.
But my best friend Aratus inly pines
For one who loves him not.   Aristis saw—
(A wondrous seer is he, whose lute and lay
Shrinèd Apollo's self would scarce disdain)—
How love had scorched Aratus to the bone.
O Pan, who hauntest Homolè's fair champaign,
Bring the soft charmer, whosoe'er it be,
Unbid to his sweet arms—so, gracious Pan,
May ne'er thy ribs and shoulderblades be lashed

With squills by young Arcadians, whensoe'er
They are scant of supper! But should this my prayer
Mislike thee, then on nettles mayest thou sleep,
Dinted and sore all over from their claws!
Then mayest thou lodge amid Edonian hills
By Hebrus, in midwinter; there subsist,
The Bear thy neighbour: and, in summer, range
With the far Æthiops 'neath the Blemmyan rocks
Where Nile is no more seen! But O ye Loves,
Whose cheeks are like pink apples, quit your homes
By Hyetis, or Byblis' pleasant rill,
Or fair Dionè's rocky pedestal,
And strike that fair one with your arrows, strike
The ill-starred damsel who disdains my friend.
And lo, what is she but an o'er-ripe pear?
The girls all cry 'Her bloom is on the wane.'
We'll watch, Aratus, at that porch no more,
Nor waste shoe-leather: let the morning cock
Crow to wake others up to numb despair!
Let Molon, and none else, that ordeal brave:
While we make ease our study, and secure
Some witch, to charm all evil from our door."

I ceased. He smiling sweetly as before,
Gave me the staff, 'the Muses' parting gift,'
And leftward sloped tow'rd Pyxa. We the while
Bent us to Phrasydeme's, Eucritus and I,
And baby-faced Amyntas: there we lay
Half-buried in a couch of fragrant reed
And fresh-cut vineleaves, who so glad as we?
A wealth of elm and poplar shook o'erhead;
Hard by, a sacred spring flowed gurgling on
From the Nymphs' grot, and in the sombre boughs

The sweet cicada chirped laboriously.
Hid in the thick thorn-bushes far away
The treefrog's note was heard; the crested lark
Sang with the goldfinch; turtles made their moan,
And o'er the fountain hung the gilded bee.
All of rich summer smacked, of autumn all:
Pears at our feet, and apples at our side
Rolled in luxuriance; branches on the ground
Sprawled, overweighed with damsons; while we brushed
From the cask's head the crust of four long years.
Say, ye who dwell upon Parnassian peaks,
Nymphs of Castalia, did old Chiron e'er
Set before Heracles a cup so brave
In Pholus' cavern—did as nectarous draughts
Cause that Anapian shepherd, in whose hand
Rocks were as pebbles, Polypheme the strong,
Featly to foot it o'er the cottage lawns:—
As, ladies, ye bid flow that day for us
All by Demeter's shrine at harvest-home?
Beside whose cornstacks may I oft again
Plant my broad fan: while she stands by and smiles,
Poppies and cornsheaves on each laden arm.

IDYLL VIII

The Triumph of Daphnis

Daphnis. Menalcas. A Goatherd.

DAPHNIS, the gentle herdsman, met once, as legend tells,
   Menalcas making with his flock the circle of the fells.
Both chins were gilt with coming beards: both lads could sing
   and play:

Menalcas glanced at Daphnis, and thus was heard to say :
" Art thou for singing, Daphnis, lord of the lowing kine ?
I say my songs are better, by what thou wilt, than thine."
Then in his turn spake Daphnis, and thus he made reply :
" O shepherd of the fleecy flock, thou pipest clear and high ;
But come what will, Menalcas, thou ne'er wilt sing as I."

> *Menalcas.* This art thou fain to ascertain, and risk a bet with
> me ?
> *Daphnis.* This I full fain would ascertain, and risk a bet with
> thee.
> *Menalcas.* But what, for champions such as we, would seem
> a fitting prize ?
> *Daphnis.* I stake a calf : stake thou a lamb, its mother's self
> in size.

Menalcas. A lamb I'll venture never : for aye at close of day
Father and mother count the flock, and passing strict are they.

> *Daphnis.* Then what shall be the victor's fee ? What wager
> wilt thou lay ?

Menalcas. A pipe discoursing through nine mouths I made,
full fair to view ;
The wax is white thereon, the line of this and that edge true.
I'll risk it : risk my father's own is more than I dare do.

> *Daphnis.* A pipe discoursing through nine mouths, and fair,
> hath Daphnis too :

The wax is white thereon, the line of this and that edge true.
But yesterday I made it : this finger feels the pain
Still, where indeed the rifted reed hath cut it clean in twain.
But who shall be our umpire ? who listen to our strain ?

> *Menalcas.* Suppose we hail yon goatherd ; him at whose
> horned herd now

The dog is barking—yonder dog with white upon his brow.

> Then out they called : the goatherd marked them, and up
> came he ;

Then out they sang; the goatherd their umpire fain would be.
To shrill Menalcas' lot it fell to start the woodland lay:
Then Daphnis took it up. And thus Menalcas led the way.

> *Menalcas.* "Rivers and vales, a glorious birth! Oh if
>   Menalcas e'er
> Piped aught of pleasant music in your ears:
> Then pasture, nothing loth, his lambs; and let young Daphnis
>   fare
> No worse, should he stray hither with his steers."

> *Daphnis.* "Pastures and rills, a bounteous race! If Daphnis
>   sang you e'er
> Such songs as ne'er from nightingale have flowed;
> Then to his herd your fatness lend; and let Menalcas share
> Like boon, should e'er he wend along this road."

> *Menalcas.* "'Tis spring, 'tis greenness everywhere; with milk
>   the udders teem,
> And all things that are young have life anew,
> Where my sweet maiden wanders: but parched and withered
>   seem,
> When she departeth, lawn and shepherd too."

> *Daphnis.* "Fat are the sheep, the goats bear twins, the hives
>   are thronged with bees,
> Rises the oak beyond his natural growth,
> Where falls my darling's footstep: but hungriness shall seize,
> When she departeth, herd and herdsman both."

> *Menalcas.* "Come, ram, with thy blunt-muzzled kids and
>   sleek wives at thy side,
> Where winds the brook by woodlands myriad-deep:
> There is *her* haunt. Go, Stump-horn, tell her how Proteus
>   plied
> (A god) the shepherd's trade, with seals for sheep."

> *Daphnis.* "I ask not gold, I ask not the broad lands of a
>   king;

I ask not to be fleeter than the breeze;
But 'neath this steep to watch my sheep, feeding as one, and
    fling
  (Still clasping *her*) my carol o'er the seas."
  Menalcas. "Storms are the fruit-tree's bane; the brook's, a
    summer hot and dry;
The stag's a woven net, a gin the dove's;
Mankind's, a soft sweet maiden. Others have pined ere I:
Zeus! Father! hadst not thou thy lady-loves?"

Thus far, in alternating strains, the lads their woes rehearst:
Then each one gave a closing stave. Thus sang Menalcas
    first:
  Menalcas. "O spare, good wolf, my weanlings! their milky
    mothers spare!
Harm not the little lad that hath so many in his care!
What, Firefly, is thy sleep so deep? It ill befits a hound,
Tending a boyish master's flock, to slumber over-sound.
And, wethers, of this tender grass take, nothing coy, your fill:
So, when it comes, the after-math shall find you feeding still.
So! so! graze on, that ye be full, that not an udder fail:
Part of the milk shall rear the lambs, and part shall fill my
    pail."

Then Daphnis flung a carol out, as of a nightingale:
  Daphnis. "Me from her grot but yesterday a girl of haughty
    brow
Spied as I passed her with my kine, and said, "How fair art
    thou!"
I vow that not one bitter word in answer did I say,
But, looking ever on the ground, went silently my way.
The heifer's voice, the heifer's breath, are passing sweet to me;
And sweet is sleep by summer-brooks upon the breezy lea:

As acorns are the green oak's pride, apples the apple-bough's;
So the cow glorieth in her calf, the cowherd in his cows."

Thus the two lads; then spoke the third, sitting his goats
　　　　among:
　　Goatherd. "O Daphnis, lovely is thy voice, thy music sweetly
　　　　sung;
Such song is pleasanter to me than honey on my tongue.
Accept this pipe, for thou hast won.　And should there be
　　　　some notes
That thou couldst teach me, as I plod alongside with my goats,
I'll give thee for thy schooling this ewe, that horns hath none:
Day after day she'll fill the can, until the milk o'errun."

Then how the one lad laughed and leaped and clapped his
　　　　hands for glee!
A kid that bounds to meet its dam might dance as merrily.
And how the other inly burned, struck down by his disgrace!
A maid first parting from her home might wear as sad a face.

Thenceforth was Daphnis champion of all the country side:
And won, while yet in topmost youth, a Naiad for his bride.

IDYLL IX

Pastorals

Daphnis.　Menalcas.　A Shepherd.

Shepherd.

A SONG from Daphnis!　Open he the lay,
He open: and Menalcas follow next:
While the calves suck, and with the barren kine

The young bulls graze, or roam knee-deep in leaves,
And ne'er play truant. But a song from thee,
Daphnis—anon Menalcas will reply.
   Daphnis. Sweet is the chorus of the calves and kine,
     And sweet the herdsman's pipe. But none may vie
With Daphnis; and a rush-strown bed is mine
     Near a cool rill, where carpeted I lie
     On fair white goatskins. From a hill-top high
The westwind swept me down the herd entire,
     Cropping the strawberries: whence it comes that I
     No more heed summer, with his breath of fire,
Than lovers heed the words of mother and of sire.

Thus Daphnis: and Menalcas answered thus:
   Menalcas. O Ætna, mother mine! A grotto fair,
     Scooped in the rocks, have I: and there I keep
All that in dreams men picture! Treasured there
     Are multitudes of she-goats and of sheep,
     Swathed in whose wool from top to toe I sleep.
The fire that boils my pot, with oak or beech
     Is piled—dry beech-logs when the snow lies deep;
     And storm and sunshine, I disdain them each
As toothless sires a nut, when broth is in their reach.

I clapped applause, and straight produced my gifts:
   A staff for Daphnis—'twas the handiwork
Of nature, in my father's acres grown:
Yet might a turner find no fault therewith.
I gave his mate a goodly spiral-shell:
We stalked its inmate on the Icarian rocks
And ate him, parted fivefold among five.
He blew forthwith the trumpet on his shell.
Tell, woodland Muse—and then farewell—what song

I, the chance-comer, sang before those twain.
  Shepherd. Ne'er let a falsehood scarify my tongue!
  Crickets with crickets, ants with ants agree,
And hawks with hawks : and music sweetly sung,
  Beyond all else, is grateful unto me.
  Filled aye with music may my dwelling be!
Not slumber, not the bursting forth of Spring
  So charms me, nor the flowers that tempt the bee,
As those sweet Sisters.   He, on whom they fling
One gracious glance, is proof to Circè's blandishing.

IDYLL X

THE TWO WORKMEN

Milo.   Battus.

WHAT now, poor o'erworked drudge, is on thy mind?
    No more in even swathe thou layest the corn :
Thy fellow-reapers leave thee far behind,
  As flocks a ewe that's footsore from a thorn.
By noon and midday what will be thy plight
If now, so soon, thy sickle fails to bite?
  Battus. Hewn from hard rocks, untired at set of sun,
Milo, didst ne'er regret some absent one?
  Milo. Not I. What time have workers for regret?
  Battus. Hath love ne'er kept thee from thy slumbers yet?
  Milo. Nay, heaven forbid! If once the cat taste cream!
  Battus. Milo, these ten days love hath been my dream.
  Milo. You drain your wine, while vinegar's scarce with me.
  Battus. —Hence since last spring untrimmed my borders be.
  Milo. And what lass flouts thee?

Battus.   She whom we heard play
Amongst Hippocoön's reapers yesterday.

Milo. Your sins have found you out—you're e'en served right:
You'll clasp a corn-crake in your arms all night.

Battus. You laugh: but headstrong Love is blind no less
Than Plutus: talking big is foolishness.

Milo. I talk not big.   But lay the corn-ears low
And trill the while some love-song—easier so
Will seem your toil: you used to sing, I know.

Battus. Maids of Pieria, of my slim lass sing!
One touch of yours ennobles everything.

> [*Sings*] Fairy Bombyca! thee do men report
>   Lean, dusk, a gipsy: I alone nut-brown.
> Violets and pencilled hyacinths are swart,
>   Yet first of flowers they're chosen for a crown.
> As goats pursue the clover, wolves the goat,
> And cranes the ploughman, upon thee I dote.

> Had I but Crœsus' wealth, we twain should stand
>   Gold-sculptured in Love's temple; thou, thy lyre
> (Ay or a rose or apple) in thy hand,
>   I in my brave new shoon and dance-attire.
> Fairy Bombyca! twinkling dice thy feet,
> Poppies thy lips, thy ways none knows how sweet!

Milo. Who dreamed what subtle strains our bumpkin wrought?
How shone the artist in each measured verse!
Fie on the beard that I have grown for naught!
Mark, lad, these lines by glorious Lytierse.

> [*Sings*] O rich in fruit and cornblade: be this field
> Tilled well, Demeter, and fair fruitage yield!

> Bind the sheaves, reapers: lest one, passing, say—
> 'A fig for these, they're never worth their pay.'

Let the mown swathes look northward, ye who mow,
Or westward—for the ears grow fattest so.

Avoid a noontide nap, ye threshing men:
The chaff flies thickest from the corn-ears then.

Wake when the lark wakes; when he slumbers, close
Your work, ye reapers: and at noontide doze.

Boys, the frogs' life for me! They need not him
Who fills the flagon, for in drink they swim.

Better boil herbs, thou toiler after gain,
Than, splitting cummin, split thy hand in twain.

Strains such as these, I trow, befit them well
Who toil and moil when noon is at its height:
Thy meagre love-tale, bumpkin, thou shouldst tell
Thy grandam as she wakes up ere 'tis light.

IDYLL XI

The Giant's Wooing

METHINKS all nature hath no cure for Love,
Plaster or unguent, Nicias, saving one;
And this is light and pleasant to a man,
Yet hard withal to compass—minstrelsy.
As well thou wottest, being thyself a leech,
And a prime favourite of those Sisters nine.
'Twas thus our Giant lived a life of ease,
Old Polyphemus, when, the down scarce seen

On lip and chin, he wooed his ocean nymph:
No curlypated rose-and-apple wooer,
But a fell madman, blind to all but love.
Oft from the green grass foldward fared his sheep
Unbid: while he upon the windy beach,
Singing his Galatea, sat and pined
From dawn to dusk, an ulcer at his heart:
Great Aphroditè's shaft had fixed it there.
Yet found he that one cure: he sate him down
On the tall cliff, and seaward looked, and sang:

"White Galatea, why disdain thy love?
White as a pressed cheese, delicate as the lamb,
Wild as the heifer, soft as summer grapes!
If sweet sleep chain me, here thou walk'st at large;
If sweet sleep loose me, straightway thou art gone,
Scared like a sheep that sees the gray wolf near.
I loved thee, maiden, when thou cam'st long since,
To pluck the hyacinth-blossom on the fell,
Thou and my mother, piloted by me.
I saw thee, see thee still, from that day forth
For ever; but 'tis naught, ay naught, to thee.
I know, sweet maiden, why thou art so coy:
Shaggy and huge, a single eyebrow spans
From ear to ear my forehead, whence one eye
Gleams, and an o'erbroad nostril tops my lip.
Yet I, this monster, feed a thousand sheep
That yield me sweetest draughts at milking-tide:
In summer, autumn, or midwinter, still
Fails not my cheese; my milkpail aye o'erflows.
Then I can pipe as ne'er did Giant yet,
Singing our loves—ours, honey, thine and mine—
At dead of night: and hinds I rear eleven

(Each with her fawn) and bearcubs four, for thee.
Oh come to me—thou shalt not rue the day—
And let the mad seas beat against the shore!
'Twere sweet to haunt my cave the livelong night:
Laurel, and cypress tall, and ivy dun,
And vines of sumptuous fruitage, all are there:
And a cold spring that pine-clad Ætna flings
Down from the white snow's midst, a draught for gods!
Who would not change for this the ocean-waves?

"But thou mislik'st my hair? Well, oaken logs
Are here, and embers yet aglow with fire.
Burn (if thou wilt) my heart out, and mine eye,
Mine only eye wherein is my delight.
Oh why was I not born a finny thing,
To float unto thy side and kiss thy hand,
Denied thy lips—and bring thee lilies white
And crimson-petalled poppies' dainty bloom!
Nay—summer hath his flowers and autumn his;
I could not bring all these the selfsame day.
Lo, should some mariner hither oar his road,
Sweet, he shall teach me straightway how to swim,
That haply I may learn what bliss ye find
In your sea-homes. O Galatea, come
Forth from yon waves, and coming forth forget
(As I do, sitting here) to get thee home:
And feed my flocks and milk them, nothing loth,
And pour the rennet in to fix my cheese!

"The blame's my mother's; she is false to me;
Spake thee ne'er yet one sweet word for my sake,
Though day by day she sees me pine and pine.
I'll feign strange throbbings in my head and feet

To anguish her—as I am anguished now."

O Cyclops, Cyclops, where are flown thy wits?
Go plait rush-baskets, lop the olive-boughs
To feed thy lambkins—'twere the shrewder part.
Chase not the recreant, milk the willing ewe:
The world hath Galateas fairer yet.

"—Many a fair damsel bids me sport with her
The livelong night, and smiles if I give ear.
On land at least I still am somebody."

Thus did the Giant feed his love on song,
And gained more ease than may be bought with gold.

IDYLL XII

THE COMRADES

THOU art come, lad, come! Scarce thrice hath dusk to-
        day
Given place—but lovers in an hour grow gray.
As spring's more sweet than winter, grapes than thorns,
The ewe's fleece richer than her latest-born's;
As young girls' charms the thrice-wed wife's outshine,
As fawns are lither than the ungainly kine,
Or as the nightingale's clear notes outvie
The mingled music of all birds that fly;
So at thy coming passing glad was I.
I ran to greet thee e'en as pilgrims run
To beechen shadows from the scorching sun:
Oh if on us accordant Loves would breathe,
And our two names to future years bequeath!

' These twain '—let men say—' lived in olden days.
This was a *yokel* (in their country-phrase),
That was his *mate* (so talked these simple folk) :
And lovingly they bore a mutual yoke.
The hearts of men were made of sterling gold,
When troth met troth, in those brave days of old.'

O Zeus, O gods who age not nor decay !
Let e'en two hundred ages roll away,
But at the last these tidings let me learn,
Borne o'er the fatal pool whence none return :—
" By every tongue thy constancy is sung,
Thine and thy favourite's—chiefly by the young."
But lo, the future is in heaven's high hand :
Meanwhile thy graces all my praise demand,
Not false lip-praise, not idly bubbling froth—
For though thy wrath be kindled, e'en thy wrath
Hath no sting in it : doubly I am caressed,
And go my way repaid with interest.

Oarsmen of Megara, ruled by Nisus erst !
Yours be all bliss, because ye honoured first
That true child-lover, Attic Diocles.
Around his gravestone with the first spring-breeze
Flock the bairns all, to win the kissing-prize :
And whoso sweetliest lip to lip applies
Goes crown-clad home to its mother.   Blest is he
Who in such strife is named the referee :
To brightfaced Ganymede full oft he'll cry
To lend his lip the potencies that lie
Within that stone with which the usurers
Detect base metal, and which never errs.

IDYLL XIII

HYLAS

NOT for us only, Nicias, (vain the dream,)
    Sprung from what god soe'er, was Eros born :
Not to us only grace doth graceful seem,
    Frail things who wot not of the coming morn.
No—for Amphitryon's iron-hearted son,
Who braved the lion, was the slave of one :—

A fair curled creature, Hylas was his name.
    He taught him, as a father might his child,
All songs whereby himself had risen to fame ;
    Nor ever from his side would be beguiled
When noon was high, nor when white steeds convey
Back to heaven's gates the chariot of the day,

Nor when the hen's shrill brood becomes aware
    Of bed-time, as the mother's flapping wings
Shadow the dust-browned beam.   'Twas all his care
    To shape unto his own imaginings
And to the harness train his favourite youth,
Till he became a man in very truth.

Meanwhile, when kingly Jason steered in quest
    Of the Gold Fleece, and chieftains at his side
Chosen from all cities, proffering each her best,
    To rich Iolchos came that warrior tried,
And joined him unto trim-built Argo's crew ;
And with Alcmena's son came Hylas too.

Through the great gulf shot Argo like a bird—
 And by-and-by reached Phasis, ne'er o'erta'en
By those in-rushing rocks, that have not stirred
 Since then, but bask, twin monsters, on the main.
But now, when waned the spring, and lambs were fed
In far-off fields, and Pleiads gleamed o'erhead,

That cream and flower of knighthood looked to sail.
 They came, within broad Argo safely stowed,
(When for three days had blown the southern gale)
 To Hellespont, and in Propontis rode
At anchor, where Cianian oxen now
Broaden the furrows with the busy plough.

They leapt ashore, and, keeping rank, prepared
 Their evening meal : a grassy meadow spread
Before their eyes, and many a warrior shared
 (Thanks to its verdurous stores) one lowly bed.
And while they cut tall marigolds from their stem
And sworded bulrush, Hylas slipt from them.

Water the fair lad went to seek and bring
 To Heracles and stalwart Telamon,
(The comrades aye partook each other's fare,)
 Bearing a brazen pitcher.   And anon,
Where the ground dipt, a fountain he espied,
And rushes growing green about its side.

There rose the sea-blue swallow-wort, and there
 The pale-hued maidenhair, with parsley green
And vagrant marsh-flowers ; and a revel rare
 In the pool's midst the water-nymphs were seen
To hold, those maidens of unslumbrous eyes
Whom the belated peasant sees and flies.

And fast did Malis and Eunica cling,
   And young Nychea with her April face,
To the lad's hand, as stooping o'er the spring
   He dipt his pitcher.   For the young Greek's grace
Made their soft senses reel ; and down he fell,
All of a sudden, into that black well.

So drops a red star suddenly from sky
   To sea—and quoth some sailor to his mate :
" Up with the tackle, boy ! the breeze is high."
   Him the nymphs pillowed, all disconsolate,
On their sweet laps, and with soft words beguiled ;
But Heracles was troubled for the child.

Forth went he ; Scythian-wise his bow he bore
   And the great club that never quits his side ;
And thrice called ' Hylas '—ne'er came lustier roar
   From that deep chest.   Thrice Hylas heard and tried
To answer, but in tones you scarce might hear ;
The water made them distant though so near.

And as a lion, when he hears the bleat
   Of fawns among the mountains far away,
A murderous lion, and with hurrying feet
   Bounds from his lair to his predestined prey :
So plunged the strong man in the untrodden brake—
(Lovers are maniacs)—for his darling's sake.

He scoured far fields—what hill or oaken glen
   Remembers not that pilgrimage of pain ?
His troth to Jason was forgotten then.
   Long time the good ship tarried for those twain
With hoisted sails ; night came and still they cleared
The hatches, but no Heracles appeared.

On he was wandering, reckless where he trod,
    So mad a passion on his vitals preyed :
While Hylas had become a blessèd god.
    But the crew cursed the runaway who had stayed
Sixty good oars, and left him there to reach
Afoot bleak Phasis and the Colchian beach.

IDYLL XIV

The Love of Æschines

Thyonichus.   Æschines.

Æschines.

HAIL, sir Thyonichus.
    Thyonichus.   Æschines, to you.
    Æschines. I have missed thee.
    Thyonichus.   Missed me ! Why what ails him now ?
    Æschines. My friend, I am ill at ease.
    Thyonichus.   Then this explains
Thy leanness, and thy prodigal moustache
And dried-up curls. Thy counterpart I saw,
A wan Pythagorean, yesterday.
He said he came from Athens : shoes he had none :
He pined, I'll warrant,—for a quartern loaf.
    Æschines. Sir, you will joke—But I've been outraged sore,
And by Cynisca. I shall go stark mad
Ere you suspect—a hair would turn the scale.
    Thyonichus. Such thou wert always, Æschines my friend.
In lazy mood or trenchant, at thy whim
The world must wag. But what 's thy grievance now ?
    Æschines. That Argive, Apis the Thessalian Knight,
Myself, and gallant Cleonicus, supped

Within my grounds.   Two pullets I had slain,
And a prime pig : and broached my Biblian wine ;
'Twas four years old, but fragrant as when new.
Truffles were served to us : and the drink was good.
Well, we got on, and each must drain a cup
To whom he fancied ; only each must name.
We named, and took our liquor as ordained ;
But she sate silent—this before my face.
Fancy my feelings !   " Wilt not speak ?   Hast seen
A wolf ? " some wag said.   "Shrewdly guessed," quoth she,
And blushed—her blushes might have fired a torch.
A wolf *had* charmed her : Wolf her neighbour's son,
Goodly and tall, and fair in divers eyes :
For his illustrious sake it was she pined.
This had been breathed, just idly, in my ear :
Shame on my beard, I ne'er pursued the hint.
Well, when we four were deep amid our cups,
The Knight must sing ' The Wolf' (a local song)
Right through for mischief.   All at once she wept
Hot tears as girls of six years old might weep,
Clinging and clamouring round their mother's lap.
And I, (you know my humour, friend of mine,)
Drove at his face, one, two !   She gathered up
Her robes and vanished straightway through the door.
" And so I fail to please, false lady mine ?
Another lies more welcome in thy lap ?
Go warm that other's heart : he'll say thy tears
Are liquid pearls."   And as a swallow flies
Forth in a hurry, here or there to find
A mouthful for her brood among the eaves :
From her soft sofa passing-swift she fled
Through folding-doors and hall, with random feet :
' *The stag had gained his heath*' : you know the rest.

Three weeks, a month, nine days and ten to that,
To-day's the eleventh : and 'tis just two months
All but two days, since she and I were two.
Hence is my beard of more than Thracian growth.
Now Wolf is all to her : Wolf enters in
At midnight ; I am a cypher in her eyes ;
The poor Megarian, nowhere in the race.
All would go right, if I could once *unlove* :
But now, you wot, the rat hath tasted tar.
And what may cure a swain at his wit's end
I know not : Simus, (true,) a mate of mine,
Loved Epichalcus' daughter, and took ship
And came home cured.   I too will sail the seas.
Worse men, it may be better, are afloat,
I shall still prove an average man-at-arms.

 Thyonichus. Now may thy love run smoothly, Æschines !
But should'st thou really mean a voyage out,
The freeman's best paymaster's Ptolemy.

 Æschines. What is he else ?

 Thyonichus.   A gentleman : a man
Of wit and taste ; the top of company ;
Loyal to ladies ; one whose eye is keen
For friends, and keener still for enemies.
Large in his bounties, he, in kingly sort,
Denies a boon to none : but, Æschines,
One should not ask too often.   This premised,
If thou wilt clasp the military cloak
O'er thy right shoulder, and with legs astride
Await the onward rush of shielded men :
Hie thee to Egypt.   Age o'ertakes us all ;
Our temples first ; then on o'er cheek and chin,
Slowly and surely, creep the frosts of Time.
Up and do somewhat, ere thy limbs are sere.

IDYLL XV

THE FESTIVAL OF ADONIS

Gorgo. Praxinoä.

Gorgo.

PRAXINOÄ in?
    Praxinoä.   Yes, Gorgo dear!   At last!
That you're here now's a marvel!   See to a chair,
A cushion, Eunoä!
    Gorgo.   I lack naught.
    Praxinoä.   Sit down.
    Gorgo. Oh, what a thing is spirit!   Here I am,
Praxinoä, safe at last from all that crowd
And all those chariots—every street a mass
Of boots and uniforms!   And the road, my dear,
Seemed endless—you live now so far away!
    Praxinoä. This land's-end den—I cannot call it house—
My madcap hired to keep us twain apart
And stir up strife.   'Twas like him, odious pest!
    Gorgo. Nay call not, dear, your lord, your Deinon, names
To the babe's face.   Look how it stares at you!
There, baby dear, she never meant Papa!
It understands, by'r lady!   Dear Papa!
    Praxinoä. Well, yesterday (that means what day you like)
'Papa' had rouge and hair-powder to buy;
He brought back salt!   this oaf of six-foot-one!
    Gorgo. Just such another is that pickpocket
My Diocleides.   He bought t' other day
Six fleeces at seven drachms, his last exploit.

What were they? scraps of worn-out pedlar's-bags,
Sheer trash.—But put your cloak and mantle on;
And we'll to Ptolemy's, the sumptuous king,
To see the *Adonis*. As I hear, the queen
Provides us something gorgeous.

 Praxinoä.   Ay, the grand
Can do things grandly.

 Gorgo.   When you've seen yourself,
What tales you'll have to tell to those who've not.
'Twere time we started!

 Praxinoä.   All time's holiday
With idlers! Eunoä, pampered minx, the jug!
Set it down here—you cats would sleep all day
On cushions—Stir yourself, fetch water, quick!
Water 's our first want. How she holds the jug!
Now, pour—not, cormorant, in that wasteful way—
You've drenched my dress, bad luck t' you! There, enough:
I have made such toilet as my fates allowed.
Now for the key o' the plate-chest. Bring it, quick!

 Gorgo. My dear, that full pelisse becomes you well.
What did it stand you in, straight off the loom?

 Praxinoä. Don't ask me, Gorgo: two good pounds and
   more.
Then I gave all my mind to trimming it.

 Gorgo. Well, 'tis a great success.

 Praxinoä.   I think it is.
My mantle, Eunoä, and my parasol!
Arrange me nicely. Babe, you'll bide at home!
Horses would bite you—Boo!—Yes, cry your fill,
But we won't have you maimed. Now let 's be off.
You, Phrygia, take and nurse the tiny thing:
Call the dog in: make fast the outer door!

          [Exeunt.

Gods! what a crowd!   How, when shall we get past
This nuisance, these unending ant-like swarms?
Yet, Ptolemy, we owe thee thanks for much
Since heaven received thy sire!   No miscreant now
Creeps Thug-like up, to maul the passer-by.
What games men played erewhile—men shaped in crime,
Birds of a feather, rascals every one!
—We're done for, Gorgo darling—here they are,
The Royal horse!   Sweet sir, don't trample me!
That bay—the savage!—reared up straight on end!
Fly, Eunoä, can't you?   Doggedly she stands.
He'll be his rider's death!—How glad I am
My babe's at home.

    Gorgo.   Praxinoä, never mind!
See, we're before them now, and they're in line.

    Praxinoä. There, I'm myself.   But from a child I feared
Horses, and slimy snakes.   But haste we on:
A surging multitude is close behind.

    Gorgo [*to Old Lady*].   From the palace, mother?

    Old Lady.   Ay, child.

    Gorgo.   Is it fair
Of access?

    Old Lady. Trying brought the Greeks to Troy.
Young ladies, they must try who would succeed.

    Gorgo. The crone hath said her oracle and gone.
Women know all—how Adam married Eve.
—Praxinoä, look what crowds are round the door!

    Praxinoä. Fearful!   Your hand, please, Gorgo.   Eunoä, you
Hold Eutychis—hold tight or you'll be lost.
We'll enter in a body—hold us fast!
Oh dear, my muslin dress is torn in two,
Gorgo, already!   Pray, good gentleman,
(And happiness be yours) respect my robe!

Stranger. I could not if I would—nathless I will.

Praxinoä. They come in hundreds, and they push like
    swine.

Stranger. Lady, take courage : it is all well now.

Praxinoä. And now and ever be it well with thee,
Sweet man, for shielding us !   An honest soul
And kindly.   Oh ! they're smothering Eunoä :
Push, coward !   That 's right !   'All in,' the bridegroom said,
And locked the door upon himself and bride.

Gorgo. Praxinoä, look !   Note well this broidery first.
How exquisitely fine—too good for earth !
Empress Athenè, what strange sempstress wrought
Such work ?   What painter painted, realized
Such pictures ?   Just like life they stand or move,
Facts and not fancies !   What a thing is man !
How bright, how lifelike on his silvern couch
Lies, with youth's bloom scarce shadowing his cheek,
That dear Adonis, lovely e'en in death !

A Stranger. Bad luck t' you, cease your senseless pigeon's
    prate !
Their brogue is killing—every word a drawl !

Gorgo. Where did he spring from ?   Is our prattle aught
To you, Sir ?   Order your own slaves about :
You're ordering Syracusan ladies now !
Corinthians bred (to tell you one fact more)
As was Bellerophon : islanders in speech,
For Dorians may talk Doric, I presume ?

Praxinoä. Persephonè ! none lords it over me,
Save one !   No scullion's-wage for us from *you !*

Gorgo. Hush, dear.   The Argive's daughter 's going to sing
The *Adonis :* that accomplished vocalist
Who has no rival in " *The Sailor's Grave.*"
Observe her attitudinizing now.

Song. Queen, who lov'st Golgi and the Sicel hill
　　And Ida; Aphroditè radiant-eyed;
The stealthy-footed Hours from Acheron's rill
　　Brought once again Adonis to thy side
How changed in twelve short months! They travel slow,
　　Those precious Hours: we hail their advent still,
For blessings do they bring to all below.
　　O Sea-born! thou didst erst, or legend lies,
Shed on a woman's soul thy grace benign,
　　And Berenicè's dust immortalize.
O called by many names, at many a shrine!
　　For thy sweet sake doth Berenicè's child
(Herself a second Helen) deck with all
　　That's fair, Adonis. On his right are piled
Ripe apples fallen from the oak-tree tall;
　　And silver caskets at his left support
Toy-gardens, Syrian scents enshrined in gold
　　And alabaster, cakes of every sort
That in their ovens the pastrywomen mould,
　　When with white meal they mix all flowers that bloom,
Oil-cakes and honey-cakes. There stand portrayed
　　Each bird, each butterfly; and in the gloom
Of foliage climbing high, and downward weighed
　　By graceful blossoms, do the young Loves play
Like nightingales, and perch on every tree,
　　And flit, to try their wings, from spray to spray.
Then see the gold, the ebony! Only see
　　The ivory-carven eagles, bearing up
To Zeus the boy who fills his royal cup!
Soft as a dream, such tapestry gleams o'erhead
　　As the Milesian's self would gaze on, charmed.
But sweet Adonis hath his own sweet bed:
　　Next Aphroditè sleeps the roseate-armed,

A bridegroom of eighteen or nineteen years.
  Kiss the smooth boyish lip—there's no sting there!
The bride hath found her own: all bliss be hers!
  And him at dewy dawn we'll troop to bear
Down where the breakers hiss against the shore:
  There, with dishevelled dress and unbound hair,
Bare-bosomed all, our descant wild we'll pour:

"Thou haunt'st, Adonis, earth and heaven in turn,
  Alone of heroes.   Agamemnon ne'er
Could compass this, nor Aias stout and stern:
  Not Hector, eldest-born of her who bare
Ten sons, not Patrocles, nor safe-returned
From Ilion Pyrrhus, such distinction earned:
  Nor, elder yet, the Lapithæ, the sons
Of Pelops and Deucalion; or the crown
  Of Greece, Pelasgians.   Gracious may'st thou be,
Adonis, now: pour new-year's blessings down!
  Right welcome dost thou come, Adonis dear:
  Come when thou wilt, thou'lt find a welcome here."

Gorgo. 'Tis fine, Praxinoä! How I envy her
Her learning, and still more her luscious voice!
We must go home: my husband's supperless:
And, in that state, the man's just vinegar.
Don't cross his path when hungry! So farewell,
Adonis, and be housed 'mid welfare aye!

IDYLL XVI

THE VALUE OF SONG

WHAT fires the Muse's, what the minstrel's lays?
　　Hers some immortal's, ours some hero's praise,
Heaven is her theme, as heavenly was her birth :
We, of earth earthy, sing the sons of earth.
Yet who, of all that see the gray morn rise,
Lifts not his latch and hails with eager eyes
My Songs, yet sends them guerdonless away?
Barefoot and angry homeward journey they,
Taunt him who sent them on that idle quest,
Then crouch them deep within their empty chest,
(When wageless they return, their dismal bed)
And hide on their chill knees once more their patient head.
Where are those good old times?　Who thanks us, who,
For our good word?　Men list not now to do
Great deeds and worthy of the minstrel's verse :
Vassals of gain, their hand is on their purse,
Their eyes on lucre : ne'er a rusty nail
They'll give in kindness ; this being aye their tale :
" Kin before kith ; to prosper is my prayer ;
Poets, we know, are heaven's peculiar care.
We've Homer ; and what other 's worth a thought ?
I call him chief of bards who costs me naught."

Yet what if all your chests with gold are lined?
Is this enjoying wealth?　Oh fools and blind !
Part on your heart's desire, on minstrels spend
Part ; and your kindred and your kind befriend :.
And daily to the gods bid altar-fires ascend.

Nor be ye churlish hosts, but glad the heart
Of guests with wine, when they must needs depart:
And reverence most the priests of sacred song:
So, when hell hides you, shall your names live long;
Not doomed to wail on Acheron's sunless sands,
Like some poor hind, the inward of whose hands
The spade hath gnarled and knotted, born to groan,
Poor sire's poor offspring, hapless Penury's own!

Their monthly dole erewhile unnumbered thralls
Sought in Antiochus', in Aleuas' halls;
On to the Scopadæ's byres in endless line
The calves ran lowing with the hornèd kine;
And, marshalled by the good Creondæ's swains
Myriads of choice sheep basked on Crannon's plains.
Yet had their joyaunce ended, on the day
When their sweet spirit dispossessed its clay,
To hated Acheron's ample barge resigned.
Nameless, their stored-up luxury left behind,
With the lorn dead through ages had they lain,
Had not a minstrel bade them live again :—
Had not in woven words the Ceïan sire
Holding sweet converse with his full-toned lyre
Made even their swift steeds for aye renowned,
When from the sacred lists they came home crowned.
Forgot were Lycia's chiefs, and Hector's hair
Of gold, and Cycnus femininely fair;
But that bards bring old battles back to mind.
Odysseus—he who roamed amongst mankind
A hundred years and more, reached utmost hell
Alive, and 'scaped the giant's hideous cell—
Had lived and died: Eumæus and his swine;
Philœtius, busy with his herded kine;

And great Laërtes' self, had passed away,
Were not their names preserved in Homer's lay.
Through song alone may man true glory taste ;
The dead man's riches his survivors waste.

But count the waves, with yon gray wind-swept main
Borne shoreward : from a red brick wash his stain
In some pool's violet depths : 'twill task thee yet
To reach the heart on baleful avarice set.
To such I say 'Fare well' : let theirs be store
Of wealth ; but let them always crave for more :
Horses and mules inferior things *I* find
To the esteem and love of all mankind.

But to what mortal's roof may I repair,
I and my Muse, and find a welcome there ?
I and my Muse : for minstrels fare but ill,
Reft of those maids, who know the mightiest's will.
The cycle of the years, it flags not yet ;
In many a chariot many a steed shall sweat :
And one, to manhood grown, my lays shall claim,
Whose deeds shall rival great Achilles' fame,
Who from stout Aias might have won the prize
On Simois' plain, where Phrygian Ilus lies.
Now, in their sunset home on Libya's heel,
Phœnicia's sons unwonted chillness feel :
Now, with his targe of willow at his breast,
The Syracusan bears his spear in rest,
Amongst these Hiero arms him for the war,
Eager to fight as warriors fought of yore ;
The plumes float darkling o'er his helmèd brow.
O Zeus, the sire most glorious ; and O thou,

Empress Athenè; and thou, damsel fair,
Who with thy mother wast decreed to bear
Rule o'er rich Corinth, o'er that city of pride
Beside whose walls Anapus' waters glide :—
May ill winds waft across the Southern sea
(Of late a legion, now but two or three,)
Far from our isle, our foes; the doom to tell,
To wife and child, of those they loved so well;
While the old race enjoy once more the lands
Spoiled and insulted erst by alien hands !

And fair and fruitful may their cornlands be !
Their flocks in thousands bleat upon the lea,
Fat and full-fed; their kine, as home they wind,
The lagging traveller of his rest remind !
With might and main their fallows let them till :
Till comes the seedtime, and cicalas trill
(Hid from the toilers of the hot midday
In the thick leafage) on the topmost spray !
O'er shield and spear their webs let spiders spin,
And none so much as name the battle-din !
Then Hiero's lofty deeds may minstrels bear
Beyond the Scythian ocean-main, and where
Within those ample walls, with asphalt made
Time-proof, Semiramis her empire swayed.
I am but a single voice; but many a bard
Beside me do those heavenly maids regard :
May those all love to sing, 'mid earth's acclaim,
Of Sicel Arethuse, and Hiero's fame.

O Graces, royal nurselings, who hold dear
The Minyæ's city, once the Theban's fear :

Unbidden I tarry, whither bidden I fare
My Muse my comrade.   And be ye too there,
Sisters divine ! Were ye and song forgot,
What grace had earth ? With you be aye my lot !

IDYLL XVII

THE PRAISE OF PTOLEMY

WITH Zeus begin, sweet sisters, end with Zeus,
   When ye would sing the sovereign of the skies :
But first among mankind rank Ptolemy ;
First, last, and midmost ; being past compare.
Those mighty ones of old, half men half gods,
Wrought deeds that shine in many a subtle strain ;
I, no unpractised minstrel, sing but him ;
Divinest ears disdain not minstrelsy.
But as a woodman sees green Ida rise
Pine above pine, and ponders which to fell
First of those myriads ; even so I pause
Where to begin the chapter of his praise :
For thousand and ten thousand are the gifts
Wherewith high heaven hath graced the kingliest king.

Was not he born to compass noblest ends,
Lagus' own son, so soon as he matured
Schemes such as ne'er had dawned on meaner minds ?
Zeus doth esteem him as the blessèd gods ;
In the sire's courts his golden mansion stands.
And near him Alexander sits and smiles,
The turbaned Persian's dread ; and, fronting both,
Rises the stedfast adamantine seat

Erst fashioned for the bull-slayer Heracles.
Who there holds revels with his heavenly mates,
And sees, with joy exceeding, children rise
On children ; for that Zeus exempts from age
And death their frames who sprang from Heracles :
And Ptolemy, like Alexander, claims
From him ; his gallant son their common sire.
And when, the banquet o'er, the Strong Man wends,
Cloyed with rich nectar, home unto his wife,
This kinsman hath in charge his cherished shafts
And bow ; and that his gnarled and knotted club ;
And both to white-limbed Hebè's bower of bliss
Convoy the bearded warrior and his arms.

Then how among wise ladies—blest the pair
That reared her !—peerless Berenicè shone !
Dionè's sacred child, the Cyprian queen,
O'er that sweet bosom passed her taper hands :
And hence, 'tis said, no man loved woman e'er
As Ptolemy loved her. She o'er-repaid
His love ; so, nothing doubting, he could leave
His substance in his loyal children's care,
And rest with her, fond husband with fond wife.
She that loves not bears sons, but all unlike
Their father : for her heart was otherwhere.

O Aphroditè, matchless e'en in heaven
For beauty, thou didst love her ; wouldst not let
Thy Berenicè cross the wailful waves :
But thy hand snatched her—to the blue lake bound
Else, and the dead's grim ferryman—and enshrined
With thee, to share thy honours. There she sits,
To mortals ever kind, and passion soft

Inspires, and makes the lover's burden light.
The dark-browed Argive, linked with Tydeus, bare
Diomed the slayer, famed in Calydon:
And deep-veiled Thetis unto Peleus gave
The javelineer Achilles.   Thou wast born
Of Berenicè, Ptolemy by name
And by descent, a warrior's warrior child.
Cos from its mother's arms her babe received,
Its destined nursery, on its natal day:
'Twas there Antigonè's daughter in her pangs
Cried to the goddess that could bid them cease:
Who soon was at her side, and lo ! her limbs
Forgat their anguish, and a child was born
Fair, its sire's self.   Cos saw, and shouted loud;
Handled the babe all tenderly, and spake:

" Wake, babe, to bliss: prize me, as Phœbus doth
His azure-spherèd Delos: grace the hill
Of Triops, and the Dorians' sister shores,
As king Apollo his Rhenæa's isle."

So spake the isle.   An eagle high o'erhead
Poised in the clouds screamed thrice, the prophet-bird
Of Zeus, and sent by him.   For awful kings
All are his care, those chiefliest on whose birth
He smiled: exceeding glory waits on them:
Theirs is the sovereignty of land and sea.
But if a myriad realms spread far and wide
O'er earth, if myriad nations till the soil
To which heaven's rain gives increase: yet what land
Is green as low-lying Egypt, when the Nile
Wells forth and piecemeal breaks the sodden glebe?
Where are like cities, peopled by like men?

Lo he hath seen three hundred towns arise,
Three thousand, yea three myriad ; and o'er all
He rules, the prince of heroes, Ptolemy.
Claims half Phœnicia, and half Araby,
Syria and Libya, and the Æthiops murk ;
Sways the Pamphylian and Cilician braves,
The Lycian and the Carian trained to war,
And all the isles : for never fleet like his
Rode upon ocean : land and sea alike
And sounding rivers hail king Ptolemy.
Many are his horsemen, many his targeteers,
Whose burdened breast is bright with clashing steel :
Light are all royal treasuries, weighed with his.
For wealth from all climes travels day by day
To his rich realm, a hive of prosperous peace.
No foeman's tramp scares monster-peopled Nile,
Waking to war her far-off villages :
No armèd robber from his war-ship leaps
To spoil the herds of Egypt. Such a prince
Sits throned in her broad plains, in whose right arm
Quivers the spear, the bright-haired Ptolemy.
Like a true king, he guards with might and main
The wealth his sires' arm won him and his own.
Nor strown all idly o'er his sumptuous halls
Lie piles that seem the work of labouring ants.
The holy homes of gods are rich therewith ;
Theirs are the firstfruits, earnest aye of more.
And freely mighty kings thereof partake,
Freely great cities, freely honoured friends.
None entered e'er the sacred lists of song,
Whose lips could breathe sweet music, but he gained
Fair guerdon at the hand of Ptolemy.
And Ptolemy do music's votaries hymn

For his good gifts—hath man a fairer lot
Than to have earned much fame among mankind?
The Atridæ's name abides, while all the wealth
Won from the sack of Priam's stately home
A mist closed o'er it, to be seen no more.
Ptolemy, he only, treads a path whose dust
Burns with the footprints of his ancestors,
And overlays those footprints with his own.
He raised rich shrines to mother and to sire,
There reared their forms in ivory and gold,
Passing in beauty, to befriend mankind.
Thighs of fat oxen oftentimes he burns
On crimsoning altars, as the months roll on,
Ay he and his staunch wife.   No fairer bride
E'er clasped her lord in royal palaces:
And her heart's love her brother-husband won.
In such blest union joined the immortal pair
Whom queenly Rhea bore, and heaven obeys:
One couch the maiden of the rainbow decks
With myrrh-dipt hands for Hera and for Zeus.

Now farewell, prince! I rank thee aye with gods:
And read this lesson to the afterdays,
Mayhap they'll prize it: 'Honour is of Zeus.'

IDYLL XVIII

THE BRIDAL OF HELEN

WHILOM, in Lacedæmon,
    Tript many a maiden fair
To gold-tressed Menelaus' halls,
    With hyacinths in her hair:

Twelve to the Painted Chamber,
　　The queenliest in the land,
The clustered loveliness of Greece,
　　Came dancing hand in hand.
For Helen, Tyndarus' daughter,
　　Had just been wooed and won,
Helen the darling of the world,
　　By Atreus' younger son :
With woven steps they beat the floor
　　In unison, and sang
Their bridal-hymn of triumph
　　Till all the palace rang.

" Slumberest so soon, sweet bridegroom ?
　　Art thou o'erfond of sleep ?
Or hast thou leadenweighted limbs ?
　　Or hadst thou drunk too deep
When thou didst fling thee to thy lair ?
　　Betimes thou should'st have sped,
If sleep were all thy purpose,
　　Unto thy bachelor's bed :
And left her in her mother's arms
　　To nestle, and to play
A girl among her girlish mates
　　Till deep into the day :—
For not alone for this night,
　　Nor for the next alone,
But through the days and through the years
　　Thou hast her for thine own.

" Nay ! heaven, O happy bridegroom,
　　Smiled as thou enteredst in

To Sparta, like thy brother kings,
    And told thee thou should'st win !
What hero son-in-law of Zeus
    Hath e'er aspired to be ?
Yet lo ! one coverlet enfolds
    The child of Zeus, and thee.
Ne'er did a thing so lovely
    Roam the Achaian lea.

" And who shall match her offspring,
    If babes are like their mother ?
For we were playmates once, and ran
    And raced with one another
(All varnished, warrior fashion)
    Along Eurotas' tide,
Thrice eighty gentle maidens,
    Each in her girlhood's pride :
Yet none of all seemed faultless,
    If placed by Helen's side.

" As peers the nascent Morning
    Over thy shades, O Night,
When Winter disenchains the land,
    And Spring goes forth in white :
So Helen shone above us,
    All loveliness and light.

" As climbs aloft some cypress,
    Garden or glade to grace ;
As the Thessalian courser lends
    A lustre to the race :
So bright o'er Lacedæmon
    Shone Helen's rosebud face.

" And who into the basket e'er
    The yarn so deftly drew,
Or through the mazes of the web
    So well the shuttle threw,
And severed from the framework
    As closelywov'n a warp :—
And who could wake with masterhand
    Such music from the harp,
To broadlimbed Pallas tuning
    And Artemis her lay—
As Helen, Helen in whose eyes
    The Loves for ever play ?

" O bright, O beautiful, for thee
    Are matron-cares begun.
We to green paths and blossomed meads
    With dawn of morn must run,
And cull a breathing chaplet ;
    And still our dream shall be,
Helen, of thee, as weanling lambs
    Yearn in the pasture for the dams
That nursed their infancy.

" For thee the lowly lotus-bed
    We'll spoil, and plait a crown
To hang upon the shadowy plane ;
    For thee will we drop down
('Neath that same shadowy platan)
    Oil from our silver urn ;
And carven on the bark shall be
    This sentence, ' HALLOW HELEN'S TREE ' ;
In Dorian letters, legibly
    For all men to discern.

" Now farewell, bride, and bridegroom
  Blest in thy new-found sire !
May Leto, mother of the brave,
  Bring babes at your desire,
And holy Cypris either's breast
  With mutual transport fire :
And Zeus the son of Cronos
  Grant blessings without end,
From princely sire to princely son
  For ever to descend.

" Sleep on, and love and longing
  Breathe in each other's breast ;
But fail not when the morn returns
  To rouse you from your rest :
With dawn shall we be stirring,
  When, lifting high his fair
And feathered neck, the earliest bird
  To clarion to the dawn is heard.
    O god of brides and bridals,
      Sing ' Happy, happy pair ! ' "

IDYLL XIX

LOVE STEALING HONEY

ONCE thievish Love the honeyed hives would rob,
    When a bee stung him : soon he felt a throb
Through all his finger-tips, and, wild with pain,
Blew on his hands and stamped and jumped in vain.
To Aphroditè then he told his woe :
' How can a thing so tiny hurt one so ? '
She smiled and said : ' Why, thou'rt a tiny thing,
As is the bee ; yet sorely thou canst sting.'

IDYLL XX

TOWN AND COUNTRY

ONCE I would kiss Eunicè. "Back," quoth she,
  And screamed and stormed ; "a sorry clown kiss me ?
Your country compliments, I like not such ;
No lips but gentles' would I deign to touch.
Ne'er dream of kissing me : alike I shun
Your face, your language, and your tigerish fun.
How winning are your tones, how fine your air !
Your beard how silken and how sweet your hair !
Pah ! you've a sick man's lips, a blackamoor's hand :
Your breath's defilement.   Leave me, I command."

Thrice spat she on her robe, and, muttering low,
Scanned me, with half-shut eyes, from top to toe :
Brought all her woman's witcheries into play,
Still smiling in a set sarcastic way,
Till my blood boiled, my visage crimson grew
With indignation, as a rose with dew :
And so she left me, inly to repine
That such as she could flout such charms as mine.

O shepherds, tell me true !   Am I not fair ?
Am I transformed ?   For lately I did wear
Grace as a garment ; and my cheeks, o'er them
Ran the rich growth like ivy round the stem.
Like fern my tresses o'er my temples streamed ;
O'er my dark eyebrows, white my forehead gleamed :
My eyes were of Athenè's radiant blue,
My mouth was milk, its accents honeydew.

Then I could sing—my tones were soft indeed !—
To pipe or flute or flageolet or reed :
And me did every maid that roams the fell
Kiss and call fair : not so this city belle.
She scorns the herdsman ; knows not how divine
Bacchus ranged once the valleys with his kine ;
How Cypris, maddened for a herdsman's sake,
Deigned upon Phrygia's mountains to partake
His cares : and wooed, and wept, Adonis in the brake.
What was Endymion, sweet Selenè's love ?
A herdsman's lad.   Yet came she from above,
Down to green Latmos, by his side to sleep.
And did not Rhea for a herdsman weep ?
Didst not thou, Zeus, become a wandering bird,
To win the love of one who drove a herd ?
Selenè, Cybelè, Cypris, all loved swains :
Eunicè, loftier-bred, their kiss disdains.
Henceforth, by hill or hall, thy love disown,
Cypris, and sleep the livelong night alone.

IDYLL XXI

THE FISHERMEN

Asphalion.   A Comrade.

WANT quickens wit : Want's pupils needs must work,
   O Diophantus : for the child of toil
Is grudged his very sleep by carking cares :
Or, if he taste the blessedness of night,
Thought for the morrow soon warns slumber off.

Two ancient fishers once lay side by side
On piled-up sea-wrack in their wattled hut,

Its leafy wall their curtain.   Near them lay
The weapons of their trade, basket and rod,
Hooks, weed-encumbered nets, and cords and oars,
And, propped on rollers, an infirm old boat.
Their pillow was a scanty mat, eked out
With caps and garments : such the ways and means,
Such the whole treasury of the fishermen.
They knew no luxuries : owned nor door nor dog ;
Their craft their all, their mistress Poverty :
Their only neighbour Ocean, who for aye
Round their lorn hut came floating lazily.

Ere the moon's chariot was in mid-career,
The fishers girt them for their customed toil,
And banished slumber from unwilling eyes,
And roused their dreamy intellects with speech :

Asphalion. "They say that soon flit summer-nights away,
Because all lingering is the summer day :
Friend, it is false ; for dream on dream have I
Dreamed, and the dawn still reddens not the sky.
How ? am I wandering ? or does night pass slow ?"

His Comrade. "Asphalion, scout not the sweet summer so.
'Tis not that wilful seasons have gone wrong,
But care maims slumber, and the nights seem long.

Asphalion. "Didst thou e'er study dreams ?   For visions fair
I saw last night ; and fairly thou should'st share
The wealth I dream of, as the fish I catch.
Now, for sheer sense, I reckon few thy match ;
And, for a vision, he whose motherwit
Is his sole tutor best interprets it.
And now we've time the matter to discuss :
For who could labour, lying here (like us)
Pillowed on leaves and neighboured by the deep,

Or sleeping amid thorns no easy sleep?
In rich men's halls the lamps are burning yet;
But fish come alway to the rich man's net."

    Comrade. "To me the vision of the night relate;
Speak, and reveal the riddle to thy mate."

    Asphalion. "Last evening, as I plied my watery trade,
(Not on an o'erfull stomach—we had made
Betimes a meagre meal, as you can vouch,)
I fell asleep; and lo! I seemed to crouch
Among the boulders, and for fish to wait,
Still dangling, rod in hand, my vagrant bait.
A fat fellow caught it: (e'en in sleep I'm bound
To dream of fishing, as of crusts the hound:)
Fast clung he to the hooks; his blood outwelled;
Bent with his struggling was the rod I held:
I tugged and tugged: my efforts made me ache:
'How, with a line thus slight, this monster take?'
Then gently, just to warn him he was caught,
I twitched him once; then slacked and then made taut
My line, for now he offered not to run;
A glance soon showed me all my task was done.
'Twas a gold fish, pure metal every inch
That I had captured.   I began to flinch:
'What if this beauty be the sea-king's joy,
Or azure Amphitritè's treasured toy!'
With care I disengaged him—not to rip
With hasty hook the gilding from his lip:
And with a tow-line landed him, and swore
Never to set my foot on ocean more,
But with my gold live royally ashore.
So I awoke: and, comrade, lend me now
Thy wits, for I am troubled for my vow."

    Comrade. "Ne'er quake: you're pledged to nothing, for no prize

You gained or gazed on. Dreams are naught but lies.
Yet may this dream bear fruit; if, wide-awake
And not in dreams, you'll fish the neighbouring lake.
Fish that are meat you'll there mayhap behold,
Not die of famine, amid dreams of gold."

IDYLL XXII

The Sons of Leda

THE pair I sing, that Ægis-armèd Zeus
    Gave unto Leda; Castor and the dread
Of bruisers Polydeuces, whensoe'er
His harnessed hands were lifted for the fray.
Twice and again I sing the manly sons
Of Leda, those Twin Brethren, Sparta's own:
Who shield the soldier on the deadly scarp,
The horse wild-plunging o'er the crimson field,
The ship that, disregarding in her pride
Star-set and star-rise, meets disastrous gales:—
Such gales as pile the billows mountain-high,
E'en at their own wild will, round stem or stern:
Dash o'er the hold, the timbers rive in twain,
Till mast and tackle dangle in mid-air
Shivered like toys, and, as the night wears on,
The rain of heaven falls fast, and, lashed by wind
And iron hail, broad ocean rings again.
Then can they draw from out the nether abyss
Both craft and crew, each deeming he must die:
Lo the winds cease, and o'er the burnished deep
Comes stillness; this way flee the clouds and that;
And shine out clear the Great Bear and the Less,

c c

And, 'twixt the Asses dimly seen, the Crib
Foretells fair voyage to the mariner.
O saviours, O companions of mankind,
Matchless on horse or harp, in lists or lay;
Which of ye twain demands my earliest song?
Of both I sing; of Polydeuces first.

Argo, escaped the two inrushing rocks,
And snow-clad Pontus with his baleful jaws,
Came to Bebrycia with her heaven-sprung freight;
There by one ladder disembarked a host
Of Heroes from the decks of Jason's ship.
On the low beach, to leeward of the cliff,
They leapt, and piled their beds, and lit their fires:
Castor meanwhile, the bridler of the steed,
And Polydeuces of the nut-brown face,
Had wandered from their mates; and, wildered both,
Searched through the boskage of the hill, and found
Hard by a slab of rock a bubbling spring
Brimful of purest water.   In the depths
Below, like crystal or like silver gleamed
The pebbles: high above it pine and plane
And poplar rose, and cypress tipt with green;
With all rich flowers that throng the mead, when wanes
The Spring, sweet workshops of the furry bee.
There sat and sunned him one of giant bulk
And grisly mien: hard knocks had stov'n his ears:
Broad were his shoulders, vast his orbèd chest:
Like a wrought statue rose his iron frame:
And nigh the shoulder on each brawny arm
Stood out the muscles, huge as rolling stones
Caught by some rain-swoln river and shapen smooth
By its wild eddyings: and o'er nape and spine

Hung, balanced by the claws, a lion's skin.
Him Leda's conquering son accosted first :

> *Polydeuces.* Luck to thee, friend unknown ! Who own this
> shore ?
> *Amycus.* Luck, quotha, to see men ne'er seen before !
> *Polydeuces.* Fear not, no base or base-born herd are we.
> *Amycus.* Nothing I fear, nor need learn this from thee.
> *Polydeuces.* What art thou ? brutish churl, or o'erproud king ?
> *Amycus.* E'en what thou see'st : and I am not trespassing.
> *Polydeuces.* Visit our land, take gifts from us, and go.
> *Amycus.* I seek naught from thee and can naught bestow.
> *Polydeuces.* Not e'en such grace as from yon spring to sip ?
> *Amycus.* Try, if parch'd thirst sits languid on thy lip.
> *Polydeuces.* Can silver move thee ? or if not, what can ?
> *Amycus.* Stand up and fight me singly, man with man.
> *Polydeuces.* With fists ? or fist and foot, eye covering eye ?
> *Amycus.* Fall to with fists ; and all thy cunning try.
> *Polydeuces.* This arm, these gauntlets, who shall dare with-
> stand ?
> *Amycus.* I : and " the Bruiser" lifts no woman's-hand.
> *Polydeuces.* Wilt thou, to crown our strife, some meed assign ?
> *Amycus.* Thou shalt be called my master, or I thine.
> *Polydeuces.* By crimson-crested cocks such games are won.
> *Amycus.* Lions or cocks, we'll play this game or none.

He spoke, and clutched a hollow shell, and blew
His clarion.   Straightway to the shadowy pine
Clustering they came, as loud it pealed and long,
Bebrycia's bearded sons ; and Castor too,
The peerless in the lists, went forth and called
From the Magnesian ship the Heroes all.

Then either warrior armed with coils of hide

His hands, and round his limbs bound ponderous bands,
And, breathing bloodshed, stept into the ring.
First there was much manœuvring, who should catch
The sunlight on his rear : but thou didst foil,
O Polydeuces, valour by address ;
And full on Amycus' face the hot noon smote.
He in hot wrath strode forward, threatening war ;
Straightway the Tyndarid smote him, as he closed,
Full on the chin : more furious waxed he still,
And, earthward bent, dealt blindly random blows.
Bebrycia shouted loud, the Greeks too cheered
Their champion : fearing lest in that scant space
This Tityus by sheer weight should bear him down.
But, shifting yet still there, the son of Zeus
Scored him with swift exchange of left and right,
And checked the onrush of the sea-god's child
Parlous albeit : till, reeling with his wounds,
He stood, and from his lips spat crimson blood.
Cheered yet again the princes, when they saw
The lips and jowl all seamed with piteous scars,
And the swoln visage and the half-closed eyes.
Still the prince teased him, feinting here or there
A thrust ; and when he saw him helpless all,
Let drive beneath his eyelids at his nose,
And laid it bare to the bone.   The stricken man
Measured his length supine amid the fern.
Keen was the fighting when he rose again,
Deadly the blows their sturdy gauntlets dealt.
But while Bebrycia's chieftain sparred round chest
And utmost shoulder, the resistless foe
Made his whole face one mass of hideous wounds.
While the one sweated all his bulk away,
And, late a giant, seemed a pigmy now,

The other's limbs waxed ever as he fought
In semblance and in size.   But in what wise
The child of Zeus brought low that man of greed,
Tell, Muse, for thine is knowledge : I unfold
A secret not mine own : at thy behest
Speak or am dumb, nor speak but as thou wilt.

Amycus, athirst to do some doughty deed,
Stooping aslant from Polydeuces' lunge
Locked their left hands ; and, stepping out, upheaved
From his right hip his ponderous other-arm.
And hit and harmed had been Amyclæ's king ;
But, ducking low, he smote with one stout fist
The foe's left temple—fast the life-blood streamed
From the grim rift—and on his shoulder fell.
While with his left he reached the mouth, and made
The set teeth tingle ; and, redoubling aye
His plashing blows, made havoc of his face
And crashed into his cheeks, till all abroad
He lay, and throwing up his arms disclaimed
The strife, for he was even at death's door.
No wrong the vanquished suffered at thy hands,
O Polydeuces ; but he sware an oath,
Calling his sire Poseidon from the depths,
Ne'er to do violence to a stranger more.

Thy tale, O prince, is told.   Now sing I thee,
Castor the Tyndarid, lord of rushing horse
And shaking javelin, corsleted in brass.

PART II

The sons of Zeus had borne two maids away,
Leucippus' daughters.   Straight in hot pursuit

Went the two brethren, sons of Aphareus,
Lynceus and Idas bold, their plighted lords.
And when the tomb of Aphareus was gained,
All leapt from out their cars, and front to front
Stood, with their ponderous spears and orbèd shields.
First Lynceus shouted loud from 'neath his helm :

"Whence, sirs, this lust for strife? Why, sword in hand,
Raise ye this coil about your neighbours' wives?
To us Leucippus these his daughters gave,
Long ere ye saw them : they are ours on oath.
Ye, coveting (to your shame) your neighbour's bed
And kine and asses and whate'er is his,
Suborned the man and stole our wives by bribes.
How often spake I thus before your face,
Yea I myself, though scant I am of phrase :
'Not thus, fair sirs, do honourable men
Seek to woo wives whose troth is given elsewhere.
Lo, broad is Sparta, broad the hunting-grounds
Of Elis : fleecy Arcady is broad,
And Argos and Messenè and the towns
To westward, and the long Sisyphian reach.
There 'neath her parents' roof dwells many a maid
Second to none in godliness or wit :
Wed of all these, and welcome, whom ye will,
For all men court the kinship of the brave ;
And ye are as your sires, and they whose blood
Runs in your mother's veins, the flower of war.
Nay, sirs, but let us bring this thing to pass ;
Then, taking counsel, choose meet brides for you.'
So I ran on ; but o'er the shifting seas
The wind's breath blew my words, that found no grace
With you, for ye defied the charmer's voice.

Yet listen to me now if ne'er before :
Lo ! we are kinsmen by the father's side.
But if ye lust for war, if strife must break
Forth among kin, and bloodshed quench our feud,
Bold Polydeuces then shall hold his hands
And his cousin Idas from the abhorrèd fray :
While I and Castor, the two younger-born,
Try war's arbitrement ; so spare our sires
Sorrow exceeding. In one house one dead
Sufficeth : let the others glad their mates,
To the bride-chamber passing, not the grave,
And o'er yon maids sing jubilee.   Well it were
At cost so small to lay so huge a strife."

   He spoke—his words heaven gave not to the winds.
They, the two first-born, disarrayed and piled
Their arms, while Lynceus stept into the ring,
And at his shield's rim shook his stalwart spear.
And Castor likewise poised his quivering lance ;
High waved the plume on either warrior's helm.
First each at other thrust with busy spear
Where'er he spied an inch of flesh exposed :
But lo ! both spearpoints in their wicker shields
Lodged ere a blow was struck, and snapt in twain.
Then they unsheathed their swords, and framed new modes
Of slaughter : pause or respite there was none.
Oft Castor on broad shield and plumèd helm
Lit, and oft keen-eyed Lynceus pierced his shield,
Or grazed his crest of crimson.   But anon,
As Lynceus aimed his blade at Castor's knee,
Back with the left sprang Castor and struck off
His fingers : from the maimed limb dropped the sword.
And, flying straightway, for his father's tomb

He made, where gallant Idas sat and saw
The battle of the brethren.   But the child
Of Zeus rushed in, and with his broadsword drave
Through flank and navel, sundering with swift stroke
His vitals : Lynceus tottered and he fell,
And o'er his eyelids rushed the dreamless sleep.
Nor did their mother see her elder son
Come a fair bridegroom to his Cretan home.
For Idas wrenched from off the dead man's tomb
A jutting slab, to hurl it at the man
Who had slain his brother.   Then did Zeus bring aid,
And struck the marble fabric from his grasp,
And with red lightning burned his frame to dust.
So doth he fight with odds who dares provoke
The Tyndarids, mighty sons of mighty sire.
Now farewell, Leda's children : prosper aye
The songs I sing.   What minstrel loves not well
The Tyndarids, and Helen, and the chiefs
That trod Troy down for Meneläus' sake ?
The bard of Chios wrought your royal deeds
Into his lays, who sang of Priam's state,
And fights 'neath Ilion's walls ; of sailor Greeks,
And of Achilles towering in the strife.
Yet take from me whate'er of clear sweet song
The Muse accords me, even all my store !
The gods' most precious gift is minstrelsy.

IDYLL XXIII

Love Avenged

A LAD deep-dipt in passion pined for one
    Whose mood was froward as her face was fair.
Lovers she loathed, for tenderness she had none :
    Ne'er knew what Love was like, nor how he bare
A bow, and arrows to make young maids smart :
Proof to all speech, all access, seemed her heart.

So he found naught his furnace to allay ;
    No quiver of lips, no lighting of kind eyes,
Nor rose-flushed cheek ; no talk, no lover's play
    Was deigned him : but as forest-beasts are shy
Of hound and hunter, with this wight dealt she ;
Fierce was her lip, her eyes gleamed ominously.

Her tyrant's-heart was imaged in her face,
    That flushed, then altering put on blank disdain.
Yet, even then, her anger had its grace,
    And made her lover fall in love again.
At last, unable to endure his flame,
To the fell threshold all in tears he came :

Kissed it, and lifted up his voice and said :
    "O heart of stone, O curst and cruel maid
Unworthy of all love, by lions bred,
    See, my last offering at thy feet is laid,
The halter that shall hang me ! So no more
For my sake, lady, need thy heart be sore.

"Whither thou doom'st me, thither must I fare.
     There is a path, that whoso treads hath ease
(Men say) from love; Forgetfulness is there.
     But if I drain that chalice to the lees,
I may not quench the love I have for you;
Now at your gates I cast my long adieu.

"Your future I foresee.   The rose is gay,
     And passing-sweet the violet of the spring:
Yet time despoils them, and they soon decay.
     The lily droops and dies, that lustrous thing;
The solid-seeming snowdrift melts full fast;
And maiden's bloom is rare, but may not last.

"The time shall come, when you shall feel as I;
     And, with seared heart, weep many a bitter tear.
But, maiden, grant one farewell courtesy.
     When you come forth, and see me hanging here,
E'en at your door, forget not my hard case;
But pause and weep me for a moment's space.

"And drop one tear, and cut me down, and spread
     O'er me some garment, for a funeral pall,
That wrapped thy limbs: and kiss me—let the dead
     Be privileged thus highly—last of all.
You need not fear me: not if your disdain
Changed into fondness could I live again.

"And scoop a grave, to hide my loves and me:
     And thrice, at parting, say, 'My friend's no more:'
Add if you list, 'a faithful friend was he;'
     And write this epitaph, scratched upon your door:
*Stranger, Love slew him.   Pass not by, until
Thou hast paused and said, 'His mistress used him ill.'*"

This said, he grasped a stone : that ghastly stone
  At the mid threshold 'neath the wall he laid,
And o'er the beam the light cord soon was thrown,
  And his neck noosed.   In air the body swayed,
Its footstool spurned away.   Forth came once more
The maid, and saw him hanging at her door.

No struggle of heart it cost her, ne'er a tear
  She wept o'er that young life, nor shunned to soil,
By contact with the corpse, her woman's-gear.
  But on she went to watch the athletes' toil,
Then made for her loved haunt, the riverside :
And there she met the god she had defied.

For on a marble pedestal Eros stood
  Fronting the pool : the statue leaped, and smote
And slew that miscreant.   All the stream ran blood ;
  And to the top a girl's cry seemed to float.
Rejoice, O lovers, since the scorner fell ;
And, maids, be kind ; for Love deals justice well.

IDYLL XXIV

The Infant Heracles

ALCMENA once had washed and given the breast
  To Heracles, a babe of ten months old,
And Iphicles his junior by a night ;
And cradled both within a brazen shield,
A gorgeous trophy, which Amphitryon erst
Had stript from Pterelaüs fall'n in fight.
She stroked their baby brows, and thus she said :

  "Sleep, children mine, a light luxurious sleep,

Brother with brother : sleep, my boys, my life :
Blest in your slumber, in your waking blest ! "

    She spake and rocked the shield ; and in his arms
Sleep took them.   But at midnight, when the Bear
Wheels to his setting, in Orion's front
Whose shoulder then beams broadest ; Hera sent,
Mistress of wiles, two huge and hideous things,
Snakes with their scales of azure all on end,
To the broad portal of the chamber-door,
All to devour the infant Heracles.
They, all their length uncoiled upon the floor,
Writhed on to their blood-feast ; a baleful light
Gleamed in their eyes, rank venom they spat forth.
But when with lambent tongues they neared the cot,
Alcmena's babes (for Zeus was watching all)
Woke, and throughout the chamber there was light.
Then Iphicles—so soon as he descried
The fell brutes peering o'er the hollow shield,
And saw their merciless fangs—cried lustily,
And kicked away his coverlet of down,
Fain to escape.   But Heracles, he clung
Round them with warlike hands, in iron grasp
Prisoning the two : his clutch upon their throat,
The deadly snake's laboratory, where
He brews such poisons as e'en heaven abhors.
They twined and twisted round the babe that, born
After long travail, ne'er had shed a tear
E'en in his nursery ; soon to quit their hold,
For powerless seemed their spines.   Alcmena heard,
While her lord slept, the crying, and awoke.

    " Amphitryon, up : chill fears take hold on me.

Up : stay not to put sandals on thy feet.
Hear'st thou our child, our younger, how he cries ?
Seest thou yon walls illumed at dead of night,
But not by morn's pure beam ?   I know, I know,
Sweet lord, that some strange thing is happening here."

She spake ; and he, upleaping at her call,
Made swiftly for the sword of quaint device
That aye hung dangling o'er his cedarn couch :
And he was reaching at his span-new belt,
The scabbard (one huge piece of lotus-wood)
Poised on his arm ; when suddenly the night
Spread out her hands, and all was dark again.
Then cried he to his slaves, whose sleep was deep :
" Quick, slaves of mine ; fetch fire from yonder hearth :
And force with all your strength the doorbolts back !
Up, loyal-hearted slaves : the master calls."

Forth came at once the slaves with lighted lamps.
The house was all astir with hurrying feet.
But when they saw the suckling Heracles
With the two brutes grasped firm in his soft hands,
They shouted with one voice.   But he must show
The reptiles to Amphitryon ; held aloft
His hands in childish glee, and laughed and laid
At his sire's feet the monsters still in death.

Then did Alcmena to her bosom take
The terror-blanched and passionate Iphicles :
Cradling the other in a lambswool quilt,
Her lord once more bethought him of his rest.

Now cocks had thrice sung out that night was o'er.
Then went Alcmena forth and told the thing
To Teiresias the seer, whose words were truth,

And bade him rede her what the end should be :—
"And if the gods bode mischief, hide if not,
Pitying, from me : man shall not thus avoid
The doom that Fate upon her distaff spins.
Son of Eueres, thou hast ears to hear."

Thus spake the queen, and thus he made reply :
"Mother of monarchs, Perseus' child, take heart ;
And look but on the fairer side of things.
For by the precious light that long ago
Left tenantless these eyes, I swear that oft
Achaia's maidens, as when eve is high
They mould the silken yarn upon their lap,
Shall tell Alcmena's story : blest art thou
Of women.   Such a man in this thy son
Shall one day scale the star-encumbered heaven :
His amplitude of chest bespeaks him lord
Of all the forest beasts and all mankind.
Twelve tasks accomplished he must dwell with Zeus ;
His flesh given over to Trachinian fires ;
And son-in-law be hailed of those same gods
Who sent yon skulking brutes to slay thy babe.
Lo ! the day cometh when the fawn shall couch
In the wolf's lair, nor fear the spiky teeth
That would not harm him.   But, O lady, keep
Yon smouldering fire alive ; prepare you piles
Of fuel, bramble-sprays or fern or furze
Or pear-boughs dried with swinging in the wind :
And let the kindled wild-wood burn those snakes
At midnight, when they looked to slay thy babe.
And let at dawn some handmaid gather up
The ashes of the fire, and diligently
Convey and cast each remnant o'er the stream

Faced by clov'n rocks, our boundary: then return
Nor look behind.   And purify your home
First with sheer sulphur, rain upon it then,
(Chaplets of olive wound about your heads,)
Innocuous water, and the customed salt.
Lastly, to Zeus almighty slay a boar :
So shall ye vanquish all your enemies."

Spake Teiresias, and wheeling (though his years
Weighed on him sorely) gained his ivory car.
And Heracles as some young orchard-tree
Grew up, Amphitryon his reputed sire.
Old Linus taught him letters, Phœbus' child,
A dauntless toiler by the midnight lamp.
Each fall whereby the sons of Argos fell,
The flingers by cross-buttock, each his man
By feats of wrestling : all that boxers e'er,
Grim in their gauntlets, have devised, or they
Who wage mixed warfare and, adepts in art,
Upon the foe fall headlong : all such lore
Phocian Harpalicus gave him, Hermes' son :
Whom no man might behold while yet far off
And wait his armèd onset undismayed :
A brow so truculent roofed so stern a face.
To launch, and steer in safety round the goal,
Chariot and steed, and damage ne'er a wheel,
This the lad learned of fond Amphitryon's self.
Many a fair prize from listed warriors he
Had won on Argive racegrounds ; yet the car
Whereon he sat came still unshattered home,
What gaps were in his harness time had made.
Then with couched lance to reach the foe, his targe
Covering his rear, and bide the biting sword ;

Or, on the warpath, place his ambuscade,
Marshal his lines and rally his cavaliers;
This knightly Castor learned him, erst exiled
From Argos, when her realms with all their wealth
Of vineyards fell to Tydeus, who received
Her and her chariots at Adrastus' hand.
Amongst the Heroes none was Castor's match
Till age had dimmed the glory of his youth.

Such tutors this fond mother gave her son.
The stripling's bed was at his father's side,
One after his own heart, a lion's skin.
His dinner, roast meat, with a loaf that filled
A Dorian basket, you might soothly say
Had satisfied a delver; and to close
The day he took, sans fire, a scanty meal.
A simple frock went halfway down his leg:

*   *   *   *   *

IDYLL XXV

HERACLES THE LION SLAYER

*   *   *   *   *

TO whom thus spake the herdsman of the herd,
    Pausing a moment from his handiwork:
"Friend, I will solve thy questions, for I fear
The angry looks of Hermes of the roads.
No dweller in the skies is wroth as he,
With him who saith the asking traveller nay.

"The flocks Augéas owns, our gracious lord,
One pasture pastures not, nor one fence bounds.
They wander, look you, some by Elissus' banks

Or god-beloved Alphéus' sacred stream,
Some by Buprasion, where the grape abounds,
Some here: their folds stand separate. But before
His herds, though they be myriad, yonder glades
That belt the broad lake round lie fresh and fair
For ever: for the low-lying meadows take
The dew, and teem with herbage honeysweet,
To lend new vigour to the hornèd kine.
Here on thy right their stalls thou canst descry
By the flowing river, for all eyes to see:
Here, where the platans blossom all the year,
And glimmers green the olive that enshrines
Rural Apollo, most august of gods.

Hard by, fair mansions have been reared for us
His herdsmen; us who guard with might and main
His riches that are more than tongue may tell:
Casting our seed o'er fallows thrice upturn'd
Or four times by the share; the bounds whereof
Well do the delvers know, whose busy feet
Troop to his wine-vats in fair summer-time.

Yea, all these acres wise Augéas owns,
These corn-clad uplands and these orchards green,
Far as yon ledges whence the cataracts leap.
Here do we haunt, here toil, as is the wont
Of labourers in the fields, the livelong day.
But prythee tell me thou—so shalt thou best
Serve thine own interests—wherefore art thou here?
Seeking Augéas, or mayhap some slave
That serves him? I can tell thee and I will
All thou would'st know: for of no churlish blood
Thou camest, nor wert nurtured as a churl:
That read I in thy stateliness of form;
The sons of heaven move thus among mankind."

Then answered him the warrior son of Zeus.
"Yea, veteran, I would see the Epéan King
Augéas ; surely for this end I came.
If he bides there amongst his citizens,
Ruling the folk, determining the laws,
Look, father; bid some serf to be my guide,
Some honoured master-worker in the fields,
Who to shrewd questions shrewdly can reply.
Are not we made dependent each on each ? "

To him the good old swain made answer thus :
"Stranger, some god hath timed thy visit here,
And given thee straightway all thy heart's desire.
Hither Augéas, offspring of the Sun,
Came, with young Phyleus splendid in his strength,
But yesterday from the city, to review
(Not in one day) his multitudinous wealth,
Methinks e'en princes say within themselves,
'The safeguard of the flock 's the master's eye.'
But haste, we'll seek him : to my own fold I
Will pilot thee ; there haply find the King."

He said and went in front : but pondered much
(As he surveyed the lion-skin and the club,
Itself an armful) whence this stranger came ;
And fain had asked. But fear recalled the words
That trembled on his lip, the fear to say
Aught that his fiery friend might take amiss.
For who can fathom all his fellow's mind ?

The dogs perceived their coming, yet far off :
They scented flesh, they heard the thud of feet :
And with wild gallop, baying furiously,
Ran at Amphitryon's son : but feebly whined

And fawned upon the old man at his side.
Then Heracles, just lifting from the ground
A pebble, scared them home, and with hard words
Cursed the whole pack ; and having stopped their din
(Inly rejoiced, nathless, to see them guard
So well an absent master's house) he spake :

"Lo ! what a friend the royal gods have given
Man in the dog ! A trusty servant he !
Had he withal an understanding heart,
To teach him when to rage and when forbear,
What brute could claim like praise ? But, lacking wit,
'Tis but a passionate random-raving thing."

He spake : the dogs ran scurrying to their lairs.
And now the sun wheeled round his westering car
And led still evening on : from every field
Came thronging the fat flocks to bield and byre.
Then in their thousands, drove on drove, the kine
Came into view ; as rainclouds, onward driven
By stress of gales, the west or mighty north,
Come up o'er all the heaven ; and none may count
And naught may stay them as they sweep through air ;
Such multitudes the storm's strength drives ahead,
Such multitudes climb surging in the rear—
So in swift sequence drove succeeded drove,
And all the champaign, all the highways swarmed
With tramping oxen ; all the sumptuous leas
Rang with their lowing. Soon enough the stalls
Were populous with the laggard-footed kine,
Soon did the sheep lie folded in their folds.
Then of that legion none stood idle, none
Gaped listless at the herd, with naught to do :

But one drew near and milked them, binding clogs
Of wood with leathern thongs around their feet :
One brought, all hungering for the milk they loved,
The longing young ones to the longing dams.
One held the pail, one pressed the dainty cheese,
Or drove the bulls home, sundered from the kine.
Pacing from stall to stall, Augéas saw
What revenue his herdsman brought him in.
With him his son surveyed the royal wealth,
And, strong of limb and purpose, Heracles.
Then, though the heart within him was as steel,
Framed to withstand all shocks, Amphitryon's son
Gazed in amazement on those thronging kine ;
For none had deemed or dreamed that one, or ten,
Whose wealth was more than regal, owned those tribes :
Such huge largess the Sun had given his child,
First of mankind for multitude of flocks.
The Sun himself gave increase day by day
To his child's herds : whate'er diseases spoil
The farmer, came not there ; his kine increased
In multitude and value year by year :
None cast her young, or bear unfruitful males.
Three hundred bulls, white-pasterned, crumple-horned,
Ranged amid these, and eke two hundred roans,
Sires of a race to be : and twelve besides
Herded amongst them, sacred to the Sun.
Their skin was white as swansdown, and they moved
Like kings amid the beasts of laggard foot.
Scorning the herd in uttermost disdain
They cropped the green grass in untrodden fields :
And when from the dense jungle to the plain
Leapt a wild beast, in quest of vagrant cows ;
Scenting him first, the twelve went forth to war.

Stern was their bellowing, in their eye sat death,
Foremost of all for mettle and for might
And pride of heart loomed Phaeton : him the swains
Regarded as a star ; so bright he shone
Among the herd, the cynosure of eyes.
He, soon as he descried the sun-dried skin
Of the grim lion, made at Heracles
(Whose eye was on him)—fain to make his crest
And sturdy brow acquainted with his flanks.
Straight the prince grasped him with no tender grasp
By the left horn, and bowed that giant bulk
To earth, neck foremost : then, by pressure brought
To bear upon his shoulder, forced him back.
The web of muscles that enwraps the nerves
Stood out from the brute's fore-arm plain to see.
Marvelled the King, and Phyleus his brave son,
At the strange prowess of Amphitryon's child.

Then townwards, leaving straight that rich champaign,
Stout Heracles his comrade, Phyleus fared ;
And soon as they had gained the paven road,
Making their way hotfooted o'er a path
(Not o'er-conspicuous in the dim green wood)
That left the farm and threaded through the vines,
Out-spake unto the child of Zeus most high,
Who followed in his steps, Augéas' son,
O'er his right shoulder glancing pleasantly.

" O stranger, as some old familiar tale
I seem to cast thy history in my mind.
For there came one to Argos, young and tall,
By birth a Greek from Helicè-on-seas,
Who told this tale before a multitude :

How that an Argive in his presence slew
A fearful lion-beast, the dread and death
Of herdsmen ; which inhabited a den
Or cavern by the grove of Nemean Zeus.
He may have come from sacred Argos' self,
Or Tiryns, or Mycenæ : what know I ?
But thus he told his tale, and said the slayer
Was (if my memory serves me) Perseus' son.
Methinks no islander had dared that deed
Save thee : the lion's skin that wraps thy ribs
Argues full well some gallant feat of arms.
But tell me, warrior, first—that I may know
If my prophetic soul speak truth or not—
Art thou the man of whom that stranger Greek
Spoke in my hearing ?   Have I guessed aright ?
How slew you single-handed that fell beast ?
How came it among rivered Nemea's glens ?
For none such monster could the eagerest eye
Find in all Greece : Greece harbours bear and boar,
And deadly wolf : but not this larger game.
'Twas this that made his listeners marvel then :
They deemed he told them travellers' tales, to win
By random words applause from standers-by."

Then Phyleus from the mid-road edged away,
That both might walk abreast, and he might catch
More at his ease what fell from Heracles :
Who journeying now alongside thus began :

" On the prior matter, O Augéas' child,
Thine own unaided wit hath ruled aright.
But all that monster's history, how it fell,
Fain would I tell thee who hast ears to hear,

Save only whence it came : for none of all
The Argive host could read that riddle right.
Some god, we dimly guessed, our niggard vows
Resenting, had upon Phoroneus' realm
Let loose this very scourge of humankind.
On peopled Pisa plunging like a flood
The brute ran riot : notably it cost
Its neighbours of Bembina woes untold.
And here Eurystheus bade me try my first
Passage of arms, and slay that fearsome thing.
So with my buxom bow and quiver lined
With arrows I set forth : my left hand held
My club, a beetling olive's stalwart trunk
And shapely, still environed in its bark :
This hand had torn from holiest Helicon
The tree entire, with all its fibrous roots.
And finding soon the lion's whereabouts,
I grasped my bow, and on the bent horn slipped
The string, and laid thereon the shaft of death.
And, now all eyes, I watched for that fell thing,
In hopes to view him ere he spied out me.
But midday came, and nowhere could I see
One footprint of the beast or hear his roar :
And, trust me, none appeared of whom to ask,
Herdsman or labourer, in the furrowed lea ;
For wan dismay kept each man in his hut.
Still on I footed, searching through and through
The leafy mountain-passes, till I saw
The creature, and forthwith essayed my strength.
Gorged from some gory carcass, on he stalked
At eve towards his lair ; his grizzled mane,
Shoulders, and grim glad visage, all adrip
With carnage ; and he licked his bearded lips.

I, crouched among the shadows of the trees
On the green hill-top, waited his approach,
And as he came I aimed at his left flank.
The barbèd shaft sped idly, nor could pierce
The flesh, but glancing dropped on the green grass.
He, wondering, raised forthwith his tawny head,
And ran his eyes o'er all the vicinage,
And snarled and gave to view his cavernous throat.
Meanwhile I levelled yet another shaft,
Ill pleased to think my first had fled in vain.
In the mid-chest I smote him, where the lungs
Are seated: still the arrow sank not in,
But fell, its errand frustrate, at his feet.
Once more was I preparing, sore chagrined,
To draw the bowstring, when the ravenous beast
Glaring around espied me, lashed his sides
With his huge tail, and opened war at once.
Swelled his vast neck, his dun locks stood on end
With rage: his spine moved sinuous as a bow,
Till all his weight hung poised on flank and loin.
And e'en as, when a chariot-builder bends
With practised skill his shafts of splintered fig,
Hot from the fire, to be his axle-wheels;
Flies the tough-rinded sapling from the hands
That shape it, at a bound recoiling far:
So from far-off the dread beast, all of a heap,
Sprang on me, hungering for my life-blood. I
Thrust with one hand my arrows in his face
And my doffed doublet, while the other raised
My seasoned cudgel o'er his crest, and drave
Full at his temples, breaking clean in twain
On the fourfooted warrior's hairy scalp
My club; and ere he reached me, down he fell.

Headlong he fell, and poised on tremulous feet
Stood, his head wagging, and his eyes grown dim;
For the shrewd stroke had shattered brain and bone.
I, marking him beside himself with pain,
Fell, ere recovering he should breathe again,
At vantage on his solid sinewy neck,
My bow and woven quiver thrown aside.
With iron clasp I gripped him from the rear
(His talons else had torn me) and, my foot
Set on him, forced to earth by dint of heel
His hinder parts, my flanks intrenched the while
Behind his fore-arm; till his thews were stretched
And strained, and on his haunches stark he stood
And lifeless; hell received his monstrous ghost.
Then with myself I counselled how to strip
From off the dead beast's limbs his shaggy hide,
A task full onerous, since I found it proof
Against all blows of steel or stone or wood.
Some god at last inspired me with the thought,
With his own claws to rend the lion's skin.
With these I flayed him soon, and sheathed and armed
My limbs against the shocks of murderous war.
Thus, sir, the Nemean lion met his end,
Erewhile the constant curse of beast and man."

IDYLL XXVI

The Bacchanals

AGAVÈ of the vermeil-tinted cheek
   And Ino and Autonoä marshalled erst
Three bands of revellers under one hill-peak.
   They plucked the wild-oak's matted foliage first,

Lush ivy then, and creeping asphodel;
And reared therewith twelve shrines amid the untrodden fell:

To Semelè three, to Dionysus nine.
    Next, from a vase drew offerings subtly wrought,
And prayed and placed them on each fresh green shrine;
    So by the god, who loved such tribute, taught.
Perched on the sheer cliff, Pentheus could espy
All, in a mastick hoar ensconced that grew thereby.

Autonoä marked him, and with frightful cries
    Flew to make havoc of those mysteries weird
That must not be profaned by vulgar eyes.
    Her frenzy frenzied all. Then Pentheus feared
And fled: and in his wake those damsels three,
Each with her trailing robe up-gathered to the knee.

"What will ye, dames?" quoth Pentheus. "Thou shalt guess
    At what we mean, untold," Autonoä said.
Agavè moaned—so moans a lioness
    Over her young one—as she clutched his head:
While Ino on the carcass fairly laid
Her heel, and wrenched away shoulder and shoulder-blade.

Autonoä's turn came next: and what remained
    Of flesh their damsels did among them share,
And back to Thebes they came all carnage-stained,
    And planted not a king but aching there.
Warned by this tale, let no man dare defy
Great Bacchus; lest a death more awful he should die,

And when he counts nine years or scarcely ten,
    Rush to his ruin. May I pass my days
Uprightly, and be loved of upright men !
    And take this motto, all who covet praise :

('Twas Ægis-bearing Zeus that spake it first :)
" The godly seed fares well: the wicked's is accurst."

Now bless ye Bacchus, whom on mountain snows,
 Prisoned in his thigh till then, the Almighty laid.
And bless ye fairfaced Semelè, and those
 Her sisters, hymned of many a hero-maid,
Who wrought, by Bacchus fired, a deed which none
May gainsay—who shall blame that which a god hath done?

IDYLL XXVII

A Countryman's Wooing

Daphnis.   A Maiden.

The Maiden.

*H*OW fell sage Helen? through a swain like thee.
 Daphnis. Nay the true Helen's just now kissing me.
The Maiden. Satyr, ne'er boast : " what's idler than a kiss?"
Daphnis. Yet in such pleasant idling there is bliss.
The Maiden. I'll wash my mouth : where go thy kisses then?
Daphnis. Wash, and return it—to be kissed again.
The Maiden. Go kiss your oxen, and not unwed maids.
Daphnis. Ne'er boast ; for beauty is a dream that fades.
The Maiden. Past grapes are grapes : dead roses keep their
 smell.
Daphnis. Come to yon olives : I have a tale to tell.
The Maiden. Not I : you fooled me with smooth words
 before.
Daphnis. Come to yon elms, and hear me pipe once more.
The Maiden. Pipe to yourself : your piping makes me cry.
Daphnis. A maid, and flout the Paphian? Fie, oh fie!

The Maiden. She's naught to me, if Artemis' favour last.

Daphnis. Hush, ere she smite you and entrap you fast.

The Maiden. And let her smite me, trap me as she will!

Daphnis. Your Artemis shall be your saviour still?

The Maiden. Unhand me! What, again? I'll tear your lip.

Daphnis. Can you, could damsel e'er, give Love the slip?

The Maiden. You are his bondslave, but not I, by Pan!

Daphnis. I doubt he'll give thee to a worser man.

The Maiden. Many have wooed me, but I fancied none.

Daphnis. Till among many came the destined *one*.

The Maiden. Wedlock is woe. Dear lad, what can I do?

Daphnis. Woe it is not, but joy and dancing too.

The Maiden. Wives dread their husbands: so I've heard it said.

Daphnis. Nay, they rule o'er them. What does woman dread?

The Maiden. Then children—Eileithya's dart is keen.

Daphnis. But the deliverer, Artemis, is your queen.

The Maiden. And bearing children all our grace destroys.

Daphnis. Bear them and shine more lustrous in your boys.

The Maiden. Should I say yea, what dower awaits me then?

Daphnis. Thine are my cattle, thine this glade and glen.

The Maiden. Swear not to wed, then leave me in my woe?

Daphnis. Not I, by Pan, though thou should'st bid me go.

The Maiden. And shall a cot be mine, with farm and fold?

Daphnis. Thy cot's half-built, fair wethers range this wold.

The Maiden. What, what to my old father must I say?

Daphnis. Soon as he hears my name he'll not say nay.

The Maiden. Speak it: by e'en a name we're oft beguiled.

Daphnis. I'm Daphnis, Lycid's and Nomæa's child.

The Maiden. Well-born indeed: and not less so am I.

Daphnis. I know—Menalcas' daughter may look high.

The Maiden. That grove, where stands your sheepfold, show
  me, please.
Daphnis. Nay look, how green, how tall my cypress-trees.
The Maiden. Graze, goats: I go to learn the herdsman's trade.
Daphnis. Feed, bulls : I show my copses to my maid.
The Maiden. Satyr, what mean you ? You presume o'ermuch.
Daphnis. This waist is round, and pleasant to the touch.
The Maiden. By Pan, I'm like to swoon ! Unhand me pray !
Daphnis. Why be so timorous ? Pretty coward, stay.
The Maiden. This bank is wet : you've soiled my pretty gown.
Daphnis. See, a soft fleece to guard it I put down.
The Maiden. And you've purloined my sash. What can this
  mean ?
Daphnis. This sash I'll offer to the Paphian queen.
The Maiden. Stay, miscreant—some one comes—I heard a
  noise.
Daphnis. 'Tis but the green trees whispering of our joys.
The Maiden. You've torn my plaidie, and I am half unclad.
Daphnis. Anon I'll give you a yet ampler plaid.
The Maiden. Generous just now, you'll one day grudge me
  bread.
Daphnis. Ah ! for thy sake my life-blood I could shed.
The Maiden. Artemis, forgive ! Thy eremite breaks her vow.
Daphnis. Love, and Love's mother, claim a calf and cow.
The Maiden. A woman I depart, my girlhood o'er.
Daphnis. Be wife, be mother ; but a girl no more.

Thus interchanging whispered talk the pair,
Their faces all aglow, long lingered there.
At length the hour arrived when they must part.
With downcast eyes, but sunshine in her heart,
She went to tend her flock ; while Daphnis ran
Back to his herded bulls, a happy man.

IDYLL XXVIII

THE DISTAFF

DISTAFF, blithely whirling distaff, azure-eyed Athena's gift
To the sex the aim and object of whose lives is house-
hold thrift,
Seek with me the gorgeous city raised by Neilus, where a plain
Roof of palm-green rush o'er-arches Aphroditè's hallowed fane.
Thither ask I Zeus to waft me, fain to see my old friend's face,
Nicias, o'er whose birth presided every passion-breathing Grace;
Fain to meet his answering welcome; and anon deposit thee
In his lady's hands, thou marvel of laborious ivory.
Many a manly robe ye'll fashion, much translucent maiden's gear;
Nay, should e'er the fleecy mothers twice within the selfsame
year
Yield their wool in yonder pasture, Theugenis of the dainty feet
Would perform the double labour: matron's cares to her are
sweet.
To an idler or a trifler I had verily been loth
To resign thee, O my distaff, for the same land bred us both:
In the land Corinthian Archias built aforetime, thou hadst birth,
In our island's core and marrow, whence have sprung the kings
of earth:
To the home I now transfer thee of a man who knows full well
Every craft whereby men's bodies dire diseases may repel:
There to live in sweet Miletus.   Lady of the Distaff she
Shall be named, and oft reminded of her poet-friend by thee:
Men shall look on thee and murmur to each other, "Lo! how
small
Was the gift, and yet how precious!   Friendship's gifts are price-
less all."

IDYLL XXIX

Loves

"SINCERITY comes with the wine-cup," my dear:
Then now o'er our wine-cups let us be sincere.
My soul's treasured secret to you I'll impart;
It is this; that I never won fairly your heart.
One half of my life, I am conscious, has flown;
The residue lives on your image alone.
You are kind, and I dream I'm in paradise then;
You are angry, and lo! all is darkness again.
It is right to torment one who loves you? Obey
Your elder; 'twere best; and you'll thank me one day.
Settle down in one nest on one tree (taking care
That no cruel reptile can clamber up there);
As it is with your lovers you're fairly perplext;
One day you choose one bough, another the next.
Whoe'er at all struck by your graces appears,
Is more to you straight than the comrade of years;
While he's like the friend of a day put aside;
For the breath of your nostrils, I think, is your pride.
Form a friendship, for life, with some likely young lad;
So doing, in honour your name shall be had.
Nor would Love use you hardly; though lightly can he
Bind strong men in chains, and as wrought upon me
Till the steel is as wax—but I'm longing to press
That exquisite mouth with a clinging caress.

No? Reflect that you're older each year than the last;
That we all must grow gray, and the wrinkles come fast.
Reflect, ere you spurn me, that youth at his sides

Wears wings; and once gone, all pursuit he derides:
Nor are men over keen to catch charms as they fly.
Think of this and be gentle, be loving as I:
When your years are maturer, we two shall be then
The pair in the Iliad over again.
But if you consign all my words to the wind
And say, "Why annoy me? you're not to my mind,"
I—who lately in quest of the Gold Fruit had sped
For your sake, or of Cerberus guard of the dead—
Though you called me, would ne'er stir a foot from my door,
For my love and my sorrow thenceforth will be o'er.

IDYLL XXX

THE DEATH OF ADONIS

CYTHERA saw Adonis
    And knew that he was dead;
She marked the brow, all grisly now,
    The cheek no longer red;
And "Bring the boar before me"
    Unto her Loves she said.

Forthwith her winged attendants
    Ranged all the woodland o'er,
And found and bound in fetters
    Threefold the grisly boar:
One dragged him at a rope's end
    E'en as a vanquished foe;
One went behind and drave him
    And smote him with his bow:

On paced the creature feebly;
   He feared Cythera so.

To him said Aphroditè:
  "So, worst of beasts, 'twas you
Who rent that thigh asunder,
   Who him that loved me slew?"
And thus the beast made answer:
  "Cythera, hear me swear
By thee, by him that loved thee,
   And by these bonds I wear,
And them before whose hounds I ran—
I meant no mischief to the man
   Who seemed to thee so fair.

"As on a carven statue
  Men gaze, I gazed on him;
I seemed on fire with mad desire
   To kiss that offered limb:
My ruin, Aphroditè,
   Thus followed from my whim.

"Now therefore take and punish
  And fairly cut away
These all unruly tusks of mine;
   For to what end serve they?
And if thine indignation
  Be not content with this,
Cut off the mouth that ventured
  To offer him a kiss"—

But Aphroditè pitied
  And bade them loose his chain.

E E

The boar from that day forward
　　Still followed in her train ;
Nor ever to the wildwood
　　Attempted to return,
But in the focus of Desire
　　Preferred to burn and burn.

IDYLL XXXI

Loves

AH for this the most accursed, unendurable of ills !
　　Nigh two months a fevered fancy for a maid my bosom fills.
Fair she is, as other damsels : but for what the simplest swain
Claims from the demurest maiden, I must sue and sue in vain.
Yet doth now this thing of evil my longsuffering heart beguile,
Though the utmost she vouchsafes me is the shadow of a smile :
And I soon shall know no respite, have no solace e'en in sleep.
Yesterday I watched her pass me, and from down-dropt eyelids
　　peep
At the face she dared not gaze on—every moment blushing
　　more—
And my love took hold upon me as it never took before.
Home I went a wounded creature, with a gnawing at my heart;
And unto the soul within me did my bitterness impart.

"Soul, why deal with me in this wise ? Shall thy folly know
　　no bound ?
Canst thou look upon these temples, with their locks of silver
　　crowned,
And still deem thee young and shapely ? Nay, my soul, let us
　　be sage ;

Act as they that have already sipped the wisdom-cup of age.
Men have loved and have forgotten. Happiest of all is he
To the lover's woes a stranger, from the lover's fetters free:
Lightly his existence passes, as a wild-deer fleeting fast:
Tamed, it may be, he shall voyage in a maiden's wake at last:
Still to-day 'tis his to revel with his mates in boyhood's flowers.
As to thee, thy brain and marrow passion evermore devours,
Prey to memories that haunt thee e'en in visions of the night;
And a year shall scarcely pluck thee from thy miserable plight."

Such and divers such reproaches did I heap upon my soul.
And my soul in turn made answer:—"Whoso deems he can control
Wily love, the same shall lightly gaze upon the stars of heaven
And declare by what their number overpasses seven times seven.
Will I, nill I, I may never from my neck his yoke unloose.
So, my friend, a god hath willed it: he whose plots could out-wit Zeus,
And the queen whose home is Cyprus. I, a leaflet of to-day,
I whose breath is in my nostrils, am I wrong to own his sway?"

FRAGMENT FROM THE "BERENICE"

YE that would fain net fish and wealth withal,
    For bare existence harrowing yonder mere,
To this our Lady slay at even-fall
    That holy fish, which, since it hath no peer
    For gloss and sheen, the dwellers about here
Have named the Silver Fish. This done, let down
    Your nets, and draw them up, and never fear
To find them empty * * * *

EPIGRAMS AND EPITAPHS

I.

YOURS be yon dew-steep'd roses, yours be yon
 Thick-clustering ivy, maids of Helicon :
Thine, Pythian Pæan, that dark-foliaged bay ;
With such thy Delphian crags thy front array.
This horn'd and shaggy ram shall stain thy shrine,
Who crops e'en now the feathering turpentine.

II.

TO Pan doth white-limbed Daphnis offer here
 (He once piped sweetly on his herdsman's flute)
His reeds of many a stop, his barbèd spear,
 And scrip, wherein he held his hoards of fruit.

III.

DAPHNIS, thou slumberest on the leaf-strown lea,
 Thy frame at rest, thy springes newly spread
O'er the fell-side.   But two are hunting thee :
 Pan, and Priapus with his fair young head
Hung with wan ivy.   See ! they come, they leap
Into thy lair—fly, fly,—shake off the coil of sleep !

IV.

FOR yon oaken avenue, swain, you must steer,
 Where a statue of figwood, you'll see, has been set :
It has never been barked, has three legs and no ear ;
 But I think there is life in the patriarch yet.

He is handsomely shrined within fair chapel-walls ;
   Where, fringed with sweet cypress and myrtle and bay,
A stream ever-fresh from the rock's hollow falls,
   And the ringleted vine her ripe store doth display :
And the blackbirds, those shrill-piping songsters of spring,
   Wake the echoes with wild inarticulate song :
And the notes of the nightingale plaintively ring,
   As she pours from her dun throat her lay sweet and strong.
Sitting there, to Priapus, the gracious one, pray
   That the lore he has taught me I soon may unlearn :
Say I'll give him a kid, and in case he says nay
   To this offer, three victims to him will I burn ;
A kid, a fleeced ram, and a lamb sleek and fat ;
He will listen, mayhap, to my prayers upon that.

v.

PRYTHEE, sing something sweet to me—you that can
    play
First and second at once.   Then I too will essay
To croak on the pipes : and yon lad shall salute
Our ears with a melody breathed through his flute.
In the cave by the green oak our watch we will keep,
And goatish old Pan we'll defraud of his sleep.

vi.

POOR Thyrsis !   What boots it to weep out thine eyes ?
    Thy kid was a fair one, I own :
But the wolf with his cruel claw made her his prize,
   And to darkness her spirit hath flown.
Do the dogs cry ?   What boots it ?   In spite of their cries
   There is left of her never a bone.

VII.

For a Statue of Æsculapius

FAR as Miletus travelled Pæan's son;
    There to be guest of Nicias, guest of one
Who heals all sickness; and who still reveres
Him, for his sake this cedarn image rears.
The sculptor's hand right well did Nicias fill;
And here the sculptor lavished all his skill.

VIII.

Ortho's Epitaph

FRIEND, Ortho of Syracuse gives thee this charge:
    Never venture out, drunk, on a wild winter's night.
I did so and died. My possessions were large;
    Yet the turf that I'm clad with is strange to me quite.

IX.

Epitaph of Cleonicus

MAN, husband existence: ne'er launch on the sea
    Out of season: our tenure of life is but frail.
Think of poor Cleonicus: for Phasos sailed he
From the valleys of Syria, with many a bale:
With many a bale, ocean's tides he would stem
When the Pleiads were sinking; and he sank with them.

X.

FOR A STATUE OF THE MUSES

TO you this marble statue, maids divine,
    Xenocles raised, one tribute unto nine.
Your votary all admit him : by this skill
He gat him fame : and you he honours still.

XI

EPITAPH OF EUSTHENES

HERE the shrewd physiognomist Eusthenes lies,
    Who could tell all your thoughts by a glance at your
    eyes.
A stranger, with strangers his honoured bones rest ;
They valued sweet song, and he gave them his best.
All the honours of death doth the poet possess :
If a small one, they mourned for him nevertheless.

XII.

FOR A TRIPOD ERECTED BY DAMOTELES TO BACCHUS

THE precentor Damoteles, Bacchus, exalts
    Your tripod, and, sweetest of deities, you.
He was champion of men, if his boyhood had faults ;
And he ever loved honour and seemliness too.

XIII.

FOR A STATUE OF ANACREON

THIS statue, stranger, scan with earnest gaze;
    And, home returning, say "I have beheld
Anacreon, in Teos; him whose lays
    Were all unmatched among our sires of eld."
Say further: "Youth and beauty pleased him best;"
    And all the man will fairly stand exprest.

XIV.

EPITAPH OF EURYMEDON

THOU hast gone to the grave, and abandoned thy son
    Yet a babe, thy own manhood but scarcely begun.
Thou art throned among gods: and thy country will take
Thy child to her heart, for his brave father's sake.

XV.

ANOTHER

PROVE, traveller, now, that you honour the brave
    Above the poltroon, when he's laid in the grave,
By murmuring "Peace to Eurymedon dead."
The turf should lie light on so sacred a head.

XVI.

For a Statue of the Heavenly Aphrodite

APHRODITE stands here; she of heavenly birth;
  Not that base one who's wooed by the children of earth.
'Tis a goddess; bow down.   And one blemishless all,
Chrysogonè, placed her in Amphicles' hall:
Chrysogonè's heart, as her children, was his,
And each year they knew better what happiness is.
For, Queen, at life's outset they made thee their friend;
Religion is policy too in the end.

XVII.

To Epicharmus

READ these lines to Epicharmus.   They are Dorian, as
    was he
      The sire of Comedy.
Of his proper self bereavèd, Bacchus, unto thee we rear
      His brazen image here;
We in Syracuse who sojourn, elsewhere born.   Thus much we
    can
      Do for our countryman,
Mindful of the debt we owe him.   For, possessing ample store
      Of legendary lore,
Many a wholesome word, to pilot youths and maids thro' life,
    he spake:
      We honour him for their sake.

XVIII.

Epitaph of Cleita, Nurse of Medeius

THE babe Medeius to his Thracian nurse
　　This stone—inscribed *To Cleita*—reared in the mid-
highway.
Her modest virtues oft shall men rehearse;
Who doubts it? is not "Cleita's worth" a proverb to this day?

XIX.

To Archilochus

PAUSE, and scan well Archilochus, the bard of elder days,
　　　　By east and west
　　　　Alike's confest
　　　The mighty lyrist's praise.
Delian Apollo loved him well, and well the sister-choir:
　　　　His songs were fraught
　　　　With subtle thought,
　　　And matchless was his lyre.

XX.

Under a Statue of Peisander,

who wrote the labours of heracles

HE whom ye gaze on was the first
　　That in quaint song the deeds rehearsed
Of him whose arm was swift to smite,
Who dared the lion to the fight:

That tale, so strange, so manifold,
Peisander of Cameirus told.
For this good work, thou may'st be sure,
   His country placed him here,
In solid brass that shall endure
Through many a month and year.

XXI.

EPITAPH OF HIPPONAX

BEHOLD Hipponax' burialplace,
   A true bard's grave.
Approach it not, if you're a base
   And base-born knave.
But if your sires were honest men
   And unblamed you,
Sit down thereon serenely then,
   And eke sleep too.

———

Tuneful Hipponax rests him here.
Let no base rascal venture near.
Ye who rank high in birth and mind
Sit down—and sleep, if so inclined.

XXII.

ON HIS OWN BOOK

NOT my namesake of Chios, but I, who belong
   To the Syracuse burghers, have sung you my song.
I'm Praxagoras' son by Philinna the fair,
And I never asked praise that was owing elsewhere.

TRANSLATIONS INTO LATIN

LYCIDAS

E N ! iterum laurus, iterum salvete myricæ
   Pallentes, nullique hederæ quæ ceditis ævo.
Has venio baccas, quanquam sapor asper acerbis,
Decerptum, quassumque manu folia ista proterva,
Maturescentem prævortens improbus annum.
Causa gravis, pia causa, subest, et amara deûm lex;
Nec jam sponte mea vobis rata tempora turbo.
Nam periit Lycidas, periit superante juventa
Imberbis Lycidas, nec par manet illius alter.
Quis cantare super Lycida neget? Ipse quoque artem
Nôrat Apollineam, versumque imponere versu.
Non nullo vitreum fas innatet ille feretrum
Flente, voluteturque arentes corpus ad auras,
Indotatum adeo et lacrymæ vocalis egenum.

   Quare agite, o sacri fontis queis cura, sorores,
Cui sub inaccessi sella Jovis exit origo:
Incipite, et sonitu graviore impellite chordas.
Lingua procul male prompta loqui, suasorque morarum
Sit pudor: alloquiis ut mollior una secundis
Pieridum faveat, cui mox ego destiner, urnæ:
Et gressus prætergrediens convertat, et " Esto,"
Dicat, "amœna quies atra tibi veste latenti":
Uno namque jugo duo nutribamur; eosdem

Pavit uterque greges ad fontem et rivulum et umbram.
  Tempore nos illo, nemorum convexa priusquam,
Aurora reserante oculos, cœpere videri,
Urgebamus equos ad pascua : novimus horam
Aridus audiri solitus qua clangor asili ;
Rore recente greges passi pinguescere noctis
Sæpius, albuerat donec quod vespere sidus
Hesperios axes prono inclinasset Olympo.
At pastorales non cessavere camœnæ,
Fistula disparibus quas temperat apta cicutis :
Saltabant Satyri informes, nec murmure læto
Capripedes potuere diu se avertere Fauni ;
Damœtasque modos nostros longævus amabat.
  Jamque, relicta tibi, quantum mutata videntur
Rura—relicta tibi, cui non spes ulla regressûs !
Te sylvæ, teque antra, puer, deserta ferarum,
Incultis obducta thymis ac vite sequaci,
Decessisse gemunt ; gemitusque reverberat Echo.
Non salices, non glauca ergo coryleta videbo
Molles ad numeros lætum motare cacumen.
Quale rosis scabies ; quam formidabile vermis
Depulso jam lacte gregi, dum tondet agellos ;
Sive quod, indutis verna jam veste, pruinæ
Floribus, albet ubi primum paliurus in agris :
Tale fuit nostris, Lycidam periisse, bubulcis.
  Qua, Nymphæ, latuistis, ubi crudele profundum
Delicias Lycidam vestras sub vortice torsit ?
Nam neque vos scopulis tum ludebatis in illis [1]

---

[1] The following alternative rendering was found amongst the author's
papers :

> Quæ mora vos tenuit, Nymphæ, quum immitibus æquor
> Delicias Lycidam vestras submergeret undis ?
> Nam neque tunc scopulis colludebatis in illis

Quos veteres, Druidæ, vates, illustria servant
Nomina; nec celsæ setoso in culmine Monæ,
Nec, quos Deva locos magicis amplectitur undis.
Væ mihi! delusos exercent somnia sensus:
Venissetis enim; numquid venisse juvaret?
Numquid Pieris ipsa parens interfuit Orphei,
Pieris ipsa suæ sobolis, qui carmine rexit
Corda virum, quem terra olim, quam magna, dolebat,
Tempore quo, dirum auditu strepitante caterva,
Ora secundo amni missa, ac fœdata cruore,
Lesbia præcipitans ad litora detulit Hebrus?
  Eheu quid prodest noctes instare diesque
Pastorum curas spretas humilesque tuendo,
Nilque relaturam meditari rite Camœnam?
Nonne fuit satius lusus agitare sub umbra,
(Ut mos est aliis,) Amaryllida sive Neæram
Sectanti, ac tortis digitum impediisse capillis?
Scilicet ingenuum cor Fama, novissimus error
Illa animi majoris, uti calcaribus urget
Spernere delicias ac dedi rebus agendis.
Quanquam—exoptatam jam spes attingere dotem;
Jam nec opinata remur splendescere flamma:—
Cæca sed invisa cum forfice venit Erinnys,
Quæ resecet tenui hærentem subtemine vitam.
"At Famam non illa," refert, tangitque trementes
Phœbus Apollo aures. "Fama haud, vulgaris ad instar
Floris, amat terrestre solum, fictosque nitores
Queis inhiat populus, nec cum Rumore patescit.
Vivere dant illi, dant increbrescere late
Puri oculi ac vox summa Jovis, cui sola Potestas.
Fecerit ille semel de facto quoque virorum
Arbitrium: tantum famæ manet æthera nactis."
  Fons Arethusa! sacro placidus qui laberis alveo,

Frontem vocali prætextus arundine, Minci!
Sensi equidem gravius carmen. Nunc cetera pastor
Exsequor. Adstat enim missus pro rege marino,
Seque rogâsse refert fluctus, ventosque rapaces,
Quæ sors dura nimis tenerum rapuisset agrestem.
Compellasse refert alarum quicquid ab omni
Spirat, acerba sonans, scopulo, qui cuspidis instar
Prominet in pelagus; fama haud pervenerat illuc.
Hæc ultro pater Hippotades responsa ferebat:
"Nulli sunt nostro palati carcere venti.
Straverat æquor aquas, et sub Jove compta sereno
Lusum exercebat Panope nymphæque sorores.
Quam Furiæ struxere per interlunia, leto
Fœtam ac fraude ratem,—malos velarat Erinnys,—
Credas in mala tanta caput mersisse sacratum."
    Proximus huic tardum senior se Camus agebat;
Cui setosa chlamys, cui pileus ulva: figuris
Idem intertextus dubiis erat, utque cruentos
Quos perhibent flores, inscriptus margine luctum.
"Nam quis," ait, "prædulce meum me pignus ademit?"
    Post hos, qui Galilæa regit per stagna carinas,
Post hos venit iturus: habet manus utraque clavim,
(Queis aperit clauditque) auro ferrove gravatam.
Mitra tegit crines; quassis quibus, acriter infit:
"Scilicet optassem pro te dare corpora leto
Sat multa, o juvenis: quod serpunt ventribus acti,
Vi quot iter faciunt spretis in ovilia muris.
Hic labor, hoc opus est, pecus ut tondente magistro
Præripiant epulas, trudatur dignior hospes.
Capti oculis, non ore! pedum tractare nec ipsi
Norunt; quotve bonis sunt upilionibus artes.
Sed quid enim refert, quove est opus, omnia nactis?
Fert ubi mens, tenue ac deductum carmen avenam

Radit stridentem stipulis. Pastore negato
Suspicit ægra pecus : vento gravis ac lue tracta
Tabescit ; mox fœda capit contagia vulgus.
Quid dicam, stabulis ut clandestinus oberrans
Expleat ingluviem tristis lupus, indice nullo ?
Illa tamen bimanus custodit machina portam,
Stricta, paratque malis plagam non amplius unam."

En, Alphee, redi ! Quibus ima cohorruit unda
Voces præteriere : redux quoque Sicelis omnes
Musa voca valles ; huc pendentes hyacinthos
Fac jaciant, teneros huc flores mille colorum.
O nemorum depressa, sonant ubi crebra susurri
Umbrarum, et salientis aquæ, Zephyrique protervi ;
Queisque virens gremium penetrare Canicula parcit :
Huc oculos, totidem mirandas vertite gemmas,
Mellitos imbres queis per viridantia rura
Mos haurire, novo quo tellus vere rubescat.
Huc ranunculus, ipse arbos, pallorque ligustri,
Quæque relicta perit, vixdum matura feratur
Primula : quique ebeno distinctus, cætera flavet
Flos, et qui specie nomen detrectat eburna.
Ardenti violæ rosa proxima fundat odores ;
Serpyllumque placens, et acerbo flexile vultu
Verbascum, ac tristem si quid sibi legit amictum.
Quicquid habes pulcri fundas, amarante : coronent
Narcissi lacrymis calices, sternantque feretrum
Tectus ubi lauro Lycidas jacet : adsit ut oti
Saltem aliquid, ficta ludantur imagine mentes.
Me miserum ! Tua nam litus, pelagusque sonorum
Ossa ferunt, queiscunque procul jacteris in oris ;
Sive procellosas ultra Symplegadas ingens
Jam subter mare visis, alit quæ monstra profundum ;
Sive (negarit enim precibus te Jupiter udis)
Cum sene Bellero, veterum qui fabula, dormis,

Qua custoditi montis prægrandis imago
Namancum atque arces longe prospectat Iberas.
Verte retro te, verte deum, mollire precando :
Et vos infaustum juvenem delphines agatis.
    Ponite jam lacrymas, sat enim flevistis, agrestes.
Non periit Lycidas, vestri mœroris origo,
Marmorei quanquam fluctus hausere cadentem.
Sic et in æquoreum se condere sæpe cubile
Luciferum videas ; nec longum tempus, et effert
Demissum caput, igne novo vestitus ; et aurum
Ceu rutilans, in fronte poli splendescit Eoi.
Sic obiit Lycidas, sic assurrexit in altum ;
Illo, quem peditem mare sustulit, usus amico.
Nunc campos alios, alia errans stagna secundum
Rorantesque lavans integro nectare crines,
Audit inauditos nobis cantari Hymenæos,
Fortunatorum sedes ubi mitis amorem
Lætitiamque affert.   Hic illum, quotquot Olympum
Prædulces habitant turbæ, venerabilis ordo,
Circumstant : aliæque canunt, interque canendum
Majestate sua veniunt abeuntque catervæ,
Illius ex oculis lacrymas arcere paratæ.
Ergo non Lycidam jam lamentantur agrestes.
Divus eris ripæ, puer, hoc ex tempore nobis,
Grande, nec immerito, veniens in munus ; opemque
Poscent usque tuam, dubiis quot in æstubus errant.
    Hæc incultus aquis puer ilicibusque canebat ;
Processit dum mane silens talaribus albis.
Multa manu teneris discrimina tentat avenis,
Dorica non studio modulatus carmina segni :
Et jam sol abiens colles extenderat omnes,
Jamque sub Hesperium se præcipitaverat alveum.
Surrexit tandem, glaucumque retraxit amictum ;
Cras lucos, reor, ille novos, nova pascua quæret.

BOADICEA

W HEN the British warrior-queen,
  Bleeding from the Roman rods,
Sought with an indignant mien,
  Counsel of her country's gods ;

Sage beneath the spreading oak
  Sat the Druid, hoary chief ;
Every burning word he spoke,
  Full of rage and full of grief.

" Princess ! if our aged eyes
  Weep upon thy matchless wrongs,
'Tis because resentment ties
  All the terrors of our tongues.

" Rome shall perish—write that word
  In the blood that she has spilt :
Perish, hopeless and abhorred,
  Deep in ruin as in guilt.

" Rome for empire far renowned,
  Tramples on a thousand states ;
Soon her pride shall kiss the ground—
  Hark ! the Gaul is at her gates !

" Other Romans shall arise,
  Heedless of a soldier's name ;
Sounds, not arms, shall win the prize,
  Harmony the path to fame.

"*Furens quid femina possit*"

QUO secta virgis tempore Romulis,
　Fastidiosa fronte, Britanniæ
Regina bellatrix ad aras
　　Indigetûm steterat deorum :

Quercu sedebat sub patula senex
Vates, nivali rex Druidûm coma ;
　In carmen exarsurus ira
　　Implacidum, implacidumque luctu.

"Natæne regum nil nisi lacrymam
Senes inanem reddimus, haud prius
　Vulgata perpessæ?　Minaces
　　Stringit enim dolor ipse linguas.

"Cadet—rubescant sanguine literæ,
Quem fudit, istæ—Roma ; carens cadet
　Spe quaque, detestata terris ;
　　Mersa pari scelerum ruina.

"Late tyranno sub pede proterit
Jam mille gentes, ipsa tamen solo
　Æquanda.　Nunc (adverte !) portas
　　Gallus habet.　Nova nequiores

"Ætas Quirites, pejor avis, feret,
Queis vile nomen militiæ ; sonis,
　Non marte, quæsturos honorem ;
　　Voce viam reserante famæ.

"Then the progeny that springs
    From the forests of our land,
Armed with thunder, clad with wings,
    Shall a wider world command.

"Regions Cæsar never knew
    Thy posterity shall sway ;
Where his eagles never flew :
    None invincible as they."

Such the bard's prophetic words,
    Pregnant with celestial fire,
Bending as he swept the chords
    Of his sweet but awful lyre.

She, with all a monarch's pride,
    Felt them in her bosom glow ;
Rushed to battle, fought and died ;
    Dying hurled them at the foe.

"Ruffians, pitiless as proud,
    Heaven awards the vengeance due ;
Empire is on us bestowed,
    Shame and ruin wait for you."

                                        COWPER.

COME LIVE WITH ME

COME, live with me, and be my love,
    And we will all the pleasures prove,
That valleys, groves, or hills, or field,
Or woods and steepy mountains yield.

"Exinde silvæ quam sobolem sinu
Gestant avitæ, fulmineis potens
    Pennis et alarum capesset
      Remigio populum ampliorem.

"Quas ipse nescit Cæsar, aheneus
Quas ales oras non adiit, tuos,
    Regina, fas torquere natos,
      Indocilem numerum repulsæ."

Hæc elocutus cælitus edito
Scatebat igni fatidicus senex :
    Dum, pronus in chordas, sonantem
      Dulce lyram modulatur iræ.

Queis illa sentit non humilis calens
Regina dictis : queis—ruerat nova
    In arma—bellatrix sub ipsum
      Funus adhuc premit acris hostes :—

"At, durior grex omnibus, omnium
Contemptor ! æqui di quoque vindices
    Regnare nos optant : probrosa
      Vos perimi placitum ruina."

" Et nos cedamus amori "

MOPSUS.

TRANSFER, amantis amans, laribus te, Lydia nostris—
    Ruris uti cunctas experiamur opes :
Quot vallis, juga, saltus, ager, quot amœna ministret
    Mons gravis ascensu, quot vel amœna nemus.

And we will sit upon the rocks,
Seeing the shepherds feed their flocks
By shallow rivers, to whose falls
Melodious birds sing madrigals.

And I will make thee beds of roses
And a thousand fragrant posies :
A gown made of the finest wool,
Which from our pretty lambs we'll pull.

The shepherd swains shall dance and sing
For thy delight each May morning :
If these delights thy mind may move,
Then live with me and be my love.

MARLOW.

IF all the world and love were young ;
   And truth in every shepherd's tongue,
These pretty pleasures might me move
To live with thee and be thy love.

Time drives the flocks from field to fold,
When rivers rage and rocks grow cold ;
And Philomel becometh dumb,
The rest complain of cares to come.

But could youth last and love still breed,
Had joys no date nor age no need,
Then these delights my mind might move
To live with thee and be thy love.

RALEIGH.

Sæpius acclines saxo spectare juvarit
    Ducat uti pastum Thyrsis herile pecus ;
Sub vada rivorum, queis adsilientibus infra
    Concordes avibus suave loquantur aves.

Ipse rosas, queis fulta cubes caput, ipse recentum
    Quidquid alant florum pascua mille, feram :
Pro læna tibi vellus erit, neque tenuior usquam,
    Me socio teneras quo spoliaris oves.

Cantabunt salientque tibi pastoria pubes,
    Maia novum quoties jusserit ire diem :
Quæ si forte tibi sint oblectamina cordi,
    Vive comes Mopsi, Lydia, amantis amans.

LYDIA

FINGE nec huic mundo nec amoribus esse senectam ;
    Pastorumque labris usque subesse fidem :
His forte illecebris (est his sua namque venustas)
    Mota comes Mopsi viverem, amantis amans.

Tempus agit pecudes campis in ovile relictis ;
    Fitque ferox fluvius frigidiusque jugum.
Dediscit Philomela modos et conticet ultro
    Venturis querimur cætera turba malis.

Sin amor assidua subolesceret usque juventa,
    Nec joca cessarent, pluris egeret anus :
His equidem illecebris (est his sua namque venustas)
    Mota comes Mopsi viverem, amantis amans.

WHILE MUSING THUS

WHILE musing thus, with contemplation fed
　　And thousand fancies buzzing in my brain,
The sweet-tongued Philomel perched o'er my head,
　　And chanted forth a most melodious strain,
Which rapt me so with wonder and delight,
　　I judged my hearing better than my sight,
And wished me wings with her awhile to take my flight.

"O merry bird!" said I, "that fears no snares,
　　That neither toils, nor hoards up in thy barns,
Feels no sad thought, nor cruciating cares
　　To gain more good, or shun what might thee harm;
Thy clothes ne'er wear, thy meat is every where,
　　Thy bed a bough, thy drink the water clear,
Remind'st not what is past, nor what's to come dost fear."

"The dawning morn with songs thou dost prevent,
　　Set'st hundred notes unto thy feathered crew,
So each one tunes his pretty instrument,
　　And warbling out the old, begins anew.
And thus they pass their youth in summer season,
　　Then follow thee into a better region,
Where winter's never felt by that sweet airy legion."

ANNE BRADSTREET.

SWEET DAY

SWEET day, so cool, so calm, so bright,
　　The bridal of the earth and sky:
The dew shall weep thy fall to-night;
　　For thou must die.

" Avis in ramo tecta laremque parat "

STABAM multa movens, studio sic pastus inani,
  Somnia per vacuum dum fervent mille cerebrum :
Jamque canora mihi supra caput adstitit ales,
Et liquido Philomela modos e gutture fudit.
Obstupui ; raptusque nova dulcedine dixi,
"Quanto oculis potior, quam traximus aure, voluptas."
Meque simul volui sumtis quatere æthera pennis.

"Fortunata nimis ! Tibi retia nulla timori,
Te nullus labor urget, agis nec in horrea messes ;
Nil conscire tibi, nulla tabescere culpa,
Sorte datum, quo plura petas, quo noxia vites.
At passim cibus, at sordent velamina nunquam :
Pocula sunt fontes liquidi tibi, fronsque cubile,
Nec memori veterum, nec mox ventura timenti.

Ante dies quam lucet ades, modulansque catervæ
Dividis aligeræ centum discrimina vocum.
Continuo ad cantum præludunt oribus illæ
Suavisonis ; peragunt opus instaurantque peracta.
Hisque modis superante fovent æstate juventam.
Te duce dein abeunt in fortunatius arvum
Blanda volans legio, nulli penetrabile brumæ."

" Parcent animæ fata superstiti "

LUX dulcis, cui tanta quies et frigus et ardor,
      Terræ polique nuptiæ,
At flebit tua fata tamen sub vesperis horam
      Ros, quippe leto debitæ.

Sweet rose, whose hue, angry and brave,
　　Bids the rash gazer wipe his eye :
　　　Thy root is ever in its grave ;
　　　　And thou must die.

Sweet Spring, full of sweet days and roses,
　　A box where sweets compacted lie,
　　My music shows ye have your closes,
　　　　And all must die.

Only a sweet and virtuous soul,
　　Like seasoned timber, never gives ;
　　But though the whole world turn to coal,
　　　　Then chiefly lives.

　　　　　　　　　　　　GEO. HERBERT.

IN MEMORIAM

CVI.

THE time admits not flowers or leaves
　　　To deck the banquet.　Fiercely flies
　　The blast of North and East, and ice
Makes daggers at the sharpen'd eaves,

And bristles all the brakes and thorns
　　　To yon hard crescent, as she hangs
　　　Above the wood which grides and clangs
Its leafless ribs and iron horns

Together, in the drifts that pass,
　　　To darken on the rolling brine
　　　That breaks the coast.　But fetch the wine,
Arrange the board and brim the glass ;

Tuque, color cujus forti similisque minanti
    Temere tuentum lumina
Præstringit ; radice lates tenus usque sepulcro ;
    Et te perire fas, Rosa.

Dulces Maia refers hilaris lucesque rosasque,
    Thesaurus ingens dulcium.
Has sed in occasum me vergere disce magistro ;
    Perire nam fas omnia.

Dulces ergo animæ demum et virtutis amantes
    Durant, ut ilex arida ;
In fumum ac cinerem vertatur mundus : at illæ
    Tunc enitescent clarius.

In memoriam

NON hora myrto, non violis sinit
    Nitere mensas.   Trux Aquilo foras
  Bacchatus inspicavit hastas
      E foribus glacies acutis ;

Horretque saltus spinifer, algidæ
Sub falce lunæ ; dum nemori imminet,
  Quod stridet illiditque costis
      Cornua, jam vacuis honorum,

Ferrata ; nimbis prætereuntibus,
Ut incubent tandem implacido sali
  Qui curvat oras.   Tu Falernum
      Prome, dapes strue, dic coronent

Bring in great logs and let them lie,
   To make a solid core of heat;
    Be cheerful-minded, talk and treat
Of all things ev'n as he were by:

We keep the day with festal cheer,
   With books and music.   Surely we
    Will drink to him whate'er he be,
And sing the songs he loved to hear.

TENNYSON.

TEARS, IDLE TEARS

TEARS, idle tears, I know not what they mean,
   Tears from the depth of some divine despair
Rise in the heart, and gather to the eyes,
In looking on the happy Autumn-fields,
And thinking of the days that are no more.

Fresh as the first beam glittering on a sail,
That brings our friends up from the underworld,
Sad as the last which reddens over one
That sinks with all we love below the verge;
So sad, so fresh, the days that are no more.

Ah, sad and strange as in dark Summer dawns
The earliest pipe of half-awaken'd birds
To dying ears, when unto dying eyes
The casement slowly grows a glimmering square;
So sad, so strange, the days that are no more.

TENNYSON.

Crateras : ignis cor solidum, graves
Repone ramos.   Jamque doloribus
   Loquare securus fugatis
     Quæ socio loquereris illo ;

Hunc dedicamus lætitiæ diem
Lyræque musisque.   Illius, illius
   Da, quicquid audit : nec silebunt
     Qui numeri placuere vivo.

Surgit amari aliquid

SCILICET et lacrymas—quis dixerit unde profectas ?—
  Nescio quod desiderium divinius imo
Nil profecturas e pectore cogit, et udi
Stant oculi : quoties autumni aprica tuemur
Rura, diesque animo qui præteriere recursant.

Dulce jubar, candent quo primo vela carinæ,
Altero ab orbe tuos tibi summittentis amicos :
Triste, quod in freta longa rubet condentibus isdem
Teque tuæque animæ partem.   Tam dulcis imago
Tam te tristis obit, qui præteriere, dierum.

Ægrum, ac tanquam aliunde, sonat morientis in aure
Excutientum avium sublustri mane sopores
Æstivus canor, incipiunt ubi languida circa
Lumina majores noto trepidare fenestræ.
Tanquam aliunde, dies qui præteriere revortunt.

PSALM LV. v. 4.

MY heart is disquieted within me : and
The fear of death is fallen upon me.

Fearfulness and trembling are come upon me :
And an horrible dread hath overwhelmed me.

And I said, O that I had wings like a dove :
For then would I flee away, and be at rest.

Lo, then would I get me away far off ;
And remain in the wilderness.

I would make haste to escape ;
Because of the stormy wind and tempest.

OF HOLIER JOY

OF holier joy he sang, more true delight,
    In other happier isles for them reserved,
Who, faithful here, from constancy and right
    And truth have never swerved ;

How evermore the tempered ocean-gales
    Breathe round those hidden islands of the blest,
Steeped in the glory spread, when day-light fails,
    Far in the sacred West.

How unto them, beyond our mortal night,
    Shines ever more in strength the golden day ;

" Præsaga mali mens "

COR concitatum, quassaque senseram
    Instante leto pectora ; senseram
  Terrore pallescens, et artus
    Auguriis tremefactus atris :

Dixique tandem : " Verterer alitem
Nunc in columbam ! scilicet in loca
  Longinqua deportarer, almæ
    Pacis amans ; et inhospitales

Inter Gelonos, his fugiens procul
Terris, manerem. Nulla fugam mora
  Tardaret, exosi procellæ
    Sævitiem, pluviosque ventos."

" Arva, beata
Petamus arva "

TUM graviore canit vera oblectamina plectro,
    Beatiore queis in insula frui
Integros maneat vitæ ; quæ fasque fidesque
    Diuque culta veritas det assequi.

Utque marina supra secretos usque piorum
    Agros susurret aura temperatius ;
Agros, occidui saturet quos gloria Phœbi,
    Sacris in Occidentis ultimi locis.

Utque procul nobis, tenebris procul omnibus, illos
    Inauret usque vividus micans dies ;

And meadows with purpureal roses bright
    Bloom round their feet alway ;

And how 'twas given thro' virtue to aspire
    To golden seats in ever-calm abodes ;
Of mortal men, admitted to the quire
    Of high immortal Gods.

TRENCH.

FROM THE ANALOGY, Ch. I.

AND it is certain, that the bodies of all animals are in a constant flux, from that never-ceasing attrition which there is in every part of them. Now things of this kind unavoidably teach us to distinguish between these living agents ourselves, and large quantities of matter in which we are very nearly interested : since these may be alienated, and actually are in a daily course of succession, and changing their owners ; while we are assured, that each living agent remains one and the same permanent being. And this general observation leads us to the following ones.

First ; that we have no way of determining by experience what is the certain bulk of the living being each man calls himself : and yet, till it be determined that it is larger in bulk than the solid elementary particles of matter, which there is no ground to think any natural power can dissolve, there is no sort of reason to think death to be the dissolution of it, of the living being, even though it should not be absolutely indiscerptible.

BUTLER.

Purpureis distincta rosis ubi gleba perenni
  Nitore crura condat ambulantium.

Tanta dari castis. Utque affectetur ab isdem
  In aureis serena sedibus domus;
Mortalesque viros tandem immortalis in altum
  Receperit sedile numinum chorus.

"Non omnis moriar"

ID quoque constat, uti, quot corpora sunt animantum,
  Non cessent fluere, assiduis quippe obvia plagis
Omni ex parte. Quibus monito distare fatendumst
Te qui vivis agisque, et molem materiai
Quantamvis, quacum sis nexus conque ligatus.
Has alienari quoniam vulgoque videmus
Trudi alias aliis, nec demum addicier ulli.
At, qui vivis agisque, manes certe unus et idem.
Queis animadversis audi quæ deinde sequantur.
  Principio, nunquam cognoveris experiundo
Mole sit id vivum quanta, quam quisque vocet se.
Quod tamen incerto sit majus mole minusve
Quam solida illa fuant corpuscula materiai,
(Quæ quis enim reputet natura posse resolvi?)
Nulla patet ratio cur solvi morte putaris
Hoc vivum, sit et hocce licet delebile tandem.

FOUNTAIN THAT SPARKLEST

FOUNTAIN, that sparklest through the shady place,
Making a soft sad murmur o'er the stones
That strew thy lucid way!   Oh, if some guest
Should haply wander near, with slow disease
Smitten, may thy cold springs the rose of health
Bring back, and the quick lustre to his eye!
The ancient oaks that on thy margin wave,
The song of birds, and through the rocky cave
The clear stream gushing, their according sounds
Should mingle, and like some strange music steal
Sadly, yet soothing, o'er his aching breast.
And thou pale exile from thy native shores
Here drink (O could'st thou! as of Lethe's stream!)
Nor friends, nor bleeding country, nor the views
Of hills or streams beloved, nor vesper's bell,
Heard in the twilight vale, remember more!

FROM THE CHRISTIAN YEAR

GO up and watch the new-born rill
Just trickling from its mossy bed,
Streaking the heath-clad hill
With a bright emerald thread.

Canst thou her bold career foretell,
What rocks she shall o'erleap or rend,
How far in Ocean's swell
Her freshening billows send?

"juvat integros accedere fontes
    Atque haurire"

O QUI umbrosa micas inter loca, perque notantes
    Lucidum iter lapides, Fons, ita molle canis;
Molle quidem sed triste tamen :—si forte quis hospes
    Erret ad has, lenta tabe peractus, aquas;
Tu, precor, huic roseam gelido refer amne salutem,
    Inque oculo saliat, qualiter ante, nitor!
Scilicet antiquæ, riparum insignia, quercus,
    Puraque per durum quæ specus unda salit,
Voxque avium carmen poterunt sociare, quod illi
    Serpat ut insuetæ corda per ægra lyræ.
Sunt etenim mulcent quos tristia. Tuque paternis
    Qui procul ex oris pallidus exsul abes,
Hinc bibe—si posses Lethæum flumen! amici
    Nec tibi, nec moriens Roma sit ipsa moræ;
Non juga, non dulces fluvii, campana nec actum
    Sub ferruginea valle locuta diem.

" Parva metu primo "

I NUPER ortum suspice rivulum,
    Vix e virenti qua trepidat toro,
      Clivumque vestitum genista
        Cærulei notat instar auri.

Dic quo feratur scilicet insolens?
    Quæ scindet aut quæ transiliet juga?
      Quorsumve, dic, fluctus tumentem
        Mittet in Oceanum salubres?

Perchance that little brook shall flow
    The bulwark of some mighty realm,
      Bear navies to and fro
        With monarchs at their helm.

Or canst thou guess, how far away
    Some sister nymph, beside her urn
      Reclining night and day,
        'Mid reeds and mountain fern,

Nurses her store, with thine to blend
    When many a moor and glen are past,
      Then in the wide sea end
        Their spotless lives at last.

                        KEBLE.

WINTER

LOW the woods
    Bow their hoar head; and ere the languid sun
Faint from the west emits his evening ray,
Earth's universal face, deep hid and chill,
Is one wild dazzling waste, that buries wide
The works of man. Drooping, the labourer-ox
Stands cover'd o'er with snow, and then demands
The fruit of all his toil. The fowls of heaven,
Tamed by the cruel season, crowd around
The winnowing store, and claim the little boon
Which Providence assigns them. One alone,
The redbreast, sacred to the household gods,
Wisely regardful of the embroiling sky,
In joyless fields and thorny thickets, leaves
His shivering mates, and pays to trusted man

Quem cernis est ut rivulus, imperi
Factus potentis præsidium, rates
   Hinc inde sit vecturus, ipsis
     Consulibus ratium magistris.

An scire fas est te, quibus in jugis
Acclinis urnæ nympha soror die
   Noctuque, montanaque tecta
     Carice arundineaque ripa,

Quodcunque apud se est pascat? At aviis
Elapsa silvis mox sociabitur
   Tecum, sub Ægæo patenti
     Innocuam positura vitam.

" Aspera venit hiems "

CANA laborantes demittunt culmina silvæ.
  Sol quoque languidior.   Necdum jubar illius orto
Vespere ab Hesperiis trepidum se prodidit oris,
At tellus, quam magna, latet: stant frigore campi,
Ferales late campi candore maligno,
Obruiturque labos hominum.   Stat taurus arator
Languida colla gravis multa nive: quid labor illum
Aut benefacta juvant?   Domat inclementia cœli
Aerias volucres; vannumque frequenter Iacchi
Stipantes, quæ parva pater munuscula parvis
Donet habere Deus, poscunt.   Deque omnibus una,
Rubro nota sinu, (propriam dixere Penates,)
Haud Jovis imprudens cœlum miscentis, in arvis
Illætabilibus et spinifero dumeto
Frigentes linquit socios, ac visit in annum

His annual visit. Half afraid, he first
Against the window beats ; then, brisk, alights
On the warm hearth ; then, hopping o'er the floor,
Eyes all the smiling family askance,
And pecks, and starts, and wonders where he is ;
Till more familiar grown, the table crumbs
Attract his slender feet. The foodless wilds
Pour forth their brown inhabitants. The hare,
Though timorous of heart, and hard beset
By death in various forms, dark snares and dogs,
And more unpitying men, the garden seeks,
Urged on by fearless want. The bleating kind
Eye the bleak heaven, and next the glistening earth,
With looks of dumb despair ; then, sad dispersed,
Dig for the wither'd herbs through heaps of snow.

THOMSON.

"LEAVES HAVE THEIR TIME TO FALL"

LEAVES have their time to fall,
     And flowers to wither at the North-wind's breath,
And stars to set : but all,
     Thou hast all seasons for thine own, O Death !

Day is for mortal care,
     Eve for glad meetings at the joyous hearth,
Night for the dreams of sleep, the voice of prayer :
     But all for thee, thou mightiest of the earth !

The banquet has its hour,
     The feverish hour of mirth and song and wine :
There comes a day for grief's o'erwhelming shower,
     A time for softer tears : but all are thine.

Tecta virum, fidens animi. Primumque fenestram
Spemque metumque inter, pulsat; mox acriter almum
Invasura focum. Dein interiora per aulæ
(Ridentes transversa tuens) it passibus æquis,
Quaque sit admirans, rostro petit et tremit alas.
Jamque levi pede, rebus ubi se assuevit, in ipsa
Frusta legit mensa. Furvum genus aspera mittunt
(Defit enim cibus) arva. Lepus, cui pectus inaudax,
Quam plaga quamque canes et plurima mortis imago,
Quamque premit cunctis homo durior, ipsa propinquat
(Vim dedit esuries) hortos. Videt æthera tristem
Balantum pecus, arva videt splendentia, muto
Spem positam fassum obtutu. Tum tristiter imo
E nive marcentes effossum spargitur herbas.

" *Debemur morti nos nostraque* "

FRONDES est ubi decidant,
   Marcescantque rosæ flatu Aquilonio:
  Horis astra cadunt suis;
Sed, Mors, cuncta tibi tempora vindicas.

  Curis nata virum dies;
Vesper colloquiis dulcibus ad focum;
  Somnis nox magis, et preci:
Sed nil, Terrigenum maxima, non tibi.

  Festis hora epulis datur,
(Fervens hora jocis, carminibus, mero;)
  Fusis altera lacrymis
Aut fletu tacito: quæque tamen tua.

Youth and the opening rose
　　May look like things too glorious for decay,
And smile at thee !—but thou art not of those
　　That wait the ripen'd bloom to seize their prey !

FELICIA HEMANS.

MY BROTHER

MY boyish days are nearly gone,
　　My breast is not unsullied now ;
And worldly cares and woes will soon
　　Cut their deep furrows on my brow.

And life will take a darker hue
From ills my brother never knew :
And human passions o'er my soul
Now hold their dark and fell control :
And fear and envy, hate and rage,
Proclaim approaching manhood's age.

And I have made me bosom friends,
　　And loved and linked my heart with others ;
But who with mine his spirit blends
　　As mine was blended with my brother's ?

When years of rapture glided by,
　　The spring of life's unclouded weather,
Our souls were knit ; and thou and I,
　　My brother, grew in love together.
The chain is broke that bound us then.
When shall I find its like again ?

MOULTRIE.

Virgo, seu rosa pullulans,
Tantum quippe nitent ut nequeant mori ?
Rident te ? Neque enim soles
Prædæ parcere, dum flos adoleverit.

" Ille meos, primum qui me sibi junxit, amores
Abstulit.   Ille habeat secum servetque sepulcro"

PRÆTEREUNT nostræ, vel præteriere, juventæ
Tempora ; nec maculam nescit, ut ante, sinus.
Mox venient rerum curæ rerumque dolores ;
Et fronte in juveni ruga senilis erit.
Caligare mihi mox ipsa videbitur ætas,
Tincta novis (frater nesciit illa) malis.
Nunc etiam quicunque viris solet esse libido
Torva regunt animum truxque caterva meum :
Nunc livorque odiumque et mista timoribus ira
Exagitant trepidum, Virque, loquuntur, eris.
Unanimos equidem legi coluique sodales ;
Fovi equidem multos interiore sinu :
Qua vero partem illam animæ, pars altera, quæram ?
Frater erat nostri pars ita, fratris ego.
Tunc, ubi felices labi non sensimus annos,
Fulsit ubi verno sol sine nube polo ;
Frater, erant nobis animi per mutua nexi ;
Par tibi tunc annis, par et amore fui.
Copula dissiluit qua nectebamur : at illi
Dic quibus in latebris, qua sequar arte, parem ?

"LET US TURN HITHERWARD OUR BARK"

"LET us turn hitherward our bark," they cried,
 "And, 'mid the blisses of this happy isle,
Past toil forgetting and to come, abide
 In joyfulness awhile.

And then, refreshed, our tasks resume again,
 If other tasks we yet are bound unto,
Combing the hoary tresses of the main
 With sharp swift keel anew."

O heroes, that had once a nobler aim,
 O heroes, sprung from many a god-like line,
What will ye do, unmindful of your fame,
 And of your race divine?

But they, by these prevailing voices now
 Lured, evermore draw nearer to the land,
Nor saw the wrecks of many a goodly prow,
 That strewed that fatal strand;

Or seeing, feared not—warning taking none
 From the plain doom of all who went before,
Whose bones lay bleaching in the wind and sun,
 And whitened all the shore.

TRENCH.

Ὦ πέπονες, κάκ' ἐλέγχε', Ἀχαιΐδες, οὐκέτ' Ἀχαιοί.

"QUIN huc," fremebant, "dirigimus ratem:
  Hic, dote læti divitis insulæ,
Paullisper hæremus, futuri
    Nec memores operis, nec acti:

"Curas refecti cras iterabimus,
Si qua supersunt emeritis novæ:
    Pexisse pernices acuta
      Canitiem pelagi carina."

O rebus olim nobilioribus
Pares: origo Dî quibus ac Deæ
    Heröes! oblitine famæ
      Hæc struitis, generisque summi?

Atqui propinquant jam magis ac magis,
Ducti magistra voce, solum: neque
    Videre prorarum nefandas
      Fragmina nobilium per oras;

Vidisse seu non pœnitet—ominis
Incuriosos tot præëuntium,
    Quorum ossa sol siccantque venti,
      Candet adhuc quibus omnis ora.

ŒNONE

O MOTHER, hear me yet before I die.
　　Hear me, O earth.　I will not die alone,
Lest their shrill happy laughter come to me
Walking the cold and starless road of Death
Uncomforted, leaving my ancient love
With the Greek woman.　I will rise and go
Down into Troy, and ere the stars come forth
Talk with the wild Cassandra, for she says
A fire dances before her, and a sound
Rings ever in her ears of armed men.
What this may be I know not, but I know
That, wheresoe'er I am by night and day,
All earth and air seem only burning fire.

TENNYSON.

THE SOLDIER'S DREAM

O UR bugles sang truce, for the night clouds had lowered,
　　And the sentinel stars kept a watch in the sky ;
And thousands had sunk on the ground overpowered,
　　The weary to sleep and the wounded to die.

When reposing that night on my pallet of straw,
　　By the wolf-scaring faggot that guarded the slain,
At the dead of the night a sweet vision I saw,
　　And thrice ere the morning I dreamt it again.

Methought from the battle-field's dreadful array,
　　Far, far I had roamed on a desolate track :
'Twas autumn—and sunshine arose on my way
　　To the home of my father, that welcomed me back.

" longam incomitata videtur
Ire viam "

QUAS moriens loquor, Ida parens, en accipe voces :
   Accipe tu, tellus. Non ibo sola sub umbras ;
Fortunatorum risus ne verberet aurem,
Dum caligantes campos, jam frigida, Leti,
Jam nullo comitante, tero, priscumque maritum
Pellex Graia tenet. Quin ibo ac Dorica castra
Deveniam : necdum surgentibus adloquar astris
Amentem Cassandram animi. Nam lumina coram
Scintillare refert ignes, et murmur ad aurem
Tanquam armatorum nunquam cessare rotari.
Quæ quid monstra ferant, non auguror : id mihi demum
Nosse satis : quocunque feror noctuque dieque,
Igni stare mero tellusque videtur et aer.

" Cur hæc ego somnia vidi ? "

NOX jam densa ruit : vigil undique sidus in æthra
   Excubat. Auditis ponimus arma tubis.
Mille peracta virum fluxerunt corpora campo,
   Occupet ut letum saucia, fessa sopor.

At mihi quem fultum custodit stramine parco
   Præsidium cæsis flamma lupisque metus,
Nocte super media dulcissima venit imago,
   Somniaque ante ortum ter rediere diem.

Arma feramque aciem mihi deseruisse videbar,
   Et desolatis longum iter ire viis.
Venerat auctumnus : desideriumque meorum
   Ad patrios ieram, sole favente, lares.

I flew to the pleasant fields traversed so oft
  In life's morning march, when my bosom was young;
I heard my own mountain-goats bleating aloft,
  And I knew the sweet strain that the corn-reapers sung.

Then pledged we the wine-cup, and fondly I swore
  From my home and my weeping friends never to part;
My little ones kissed me a thousand times o'er,
  And my wife sobbed aloud in her fulness of heart.

" Stay, stay with us—rest; thou art weary and worn: "
  And fain was the war-broken soldier to stay:
But sorrow returned with the dawning of morn,
  And the voice in my dreaming ear melted away.

CAMPBELL.

THE BUTTERFLY

AS rising on its purple wing
  The insect-queen of eastern spring,
O'er emerald meadows of Kashmeer
Invites the young pursuer near,
And leads him on from flower to flower
A weary chase and wasted hour,
Then leaves him, as it soars on high,
With panting heart and tearful eye:
So Beauty lures the full-grown child,
With hue as bright, and wing as wild;
A chase of idle hopes and fears,
Begun in folly, closed in tears,
If won, to equal ills betray'd,
Woe waits the insect and the maid;
A life of pain, the loss of peace,

Quos jam in procinctu vitæ, jamque inscius ævi,
　　Lustrabam toties, transferor ales agris :
Audieram balare meas in rupe capellas ;
　　Fallebat veteri carmine messor opus.

Sum quoque pollicitus, socia inter pocula, nunquam
　　Flentibus a sociis ire, meaque domo.
Oscula dant centum parvi, dein altera, nati :
　　Uxoris gremium rumpit anhelus amor :—

" Fessus et æger ades, nobis ades usque," susurrat.
　　Fractus idem bellis miles et ipse volo.
Nequicquam.　Redeunte die rediere dolores.
　　Audieram voces : sed sopor illud erat.

" Neque enim levia aut ludicra petuntur "

PENNIS ut ostro tollitur æmulis
　　Quæ ver Eoüm papilio regit,
Per gramen invitans smaragdo
　　Lucidius puerum sequacem ;
Vel has vel illas detinet ad rosas
Fessum vagandi, nec bene prodigum
　　Horæ ; relinquens dein anhelo
　　　Ore, genis, abit ales, udis :
Per spes adultum sic puerum rapit
Metusque vanos, sic vario nitens
　　Splendore, sic pennata, virgo ;
　　　Cœpta miser flet inepta sero.
Vincas :—ad unum virgine prodita
Vermique fatum, par superest dolor
　　Utrique ; seu lascivus infans,

From infant's play and man's caprice :
The lovely toy so fiercely sought
Hath lost its charm by being caught,
For every touch that woo'd its stay
Hath brush'd its brightest hues away,
Till charm, and hue, and beauty gone
'Tis left to fly or fall alone.

BYRON.

GLENIFFER

KEEN blaws the wind o'er the braes o' Gleniffer,
   The auld castle turrets are cover'd wi' snaw,
How changed frae the time when I met wi' my lover,
   Amang the broom bushes by Stanley green shaw.
The wild flowers o' simmer were spread a' sae bonnie,
   The mavis sang sweet frae the green birken tree ;
But far to the camp they ha'e march'd my dear Johnnie,
   And now it is winter wi' nature and me.

Then ilk thing around us was blythesome and cheerie,
   Then ilk thing around us was bonnie and braw ;
Now naething is heard but the wind whistling drearie,
   And naething is seen but the wide-spreading snaw.
The trees are a' bare, and the birds mute and dowie,
   They shake the cauld drift frae their wings as they flee ;
And chirp out their plaints, seeming wae for my Johnnie ;
   'Tis winter wi' them and 'tis winter wi' me.

TANNAHILL.

Sive virum dederit libido
Vitam inquietam, ac mille gravem malis.
Sectamur acres dulcia : quæ simul
   Prensaris, amisere formam ;
     Suasor enim digitus morarum
Sensim colores proterit aureos ;
Donec recessit forma, color, venus :
   Te deinde securo, volarint
     Seu jaceant viduata campo.

" Versa loci facies "

RADIT Aricinæ vallis latus acriter aura,
   Nix grave longævis turribus hæret onus :
Non erat illa loci facies, ubi tecta genista
   Ad lucum viridem fabar, Amate veni.
Injussas jucunda rosas ibi pandidit æstas ;
   Cantanti merulæ betula tegmen erat :
Nunc ad castra meus procul exsulat actus Amyntas :
   Nunc eadem terris et mihi venit hiems.

Plurima lætitiæ tunc undique risit imago,
   Cuique erat in gremio vis, et in ore nitor :
Nunc nihil audieris nisi mæsti sibila venti,
   Nunc nihil aspicias hinc nisi et inde nivem.
Arbos muta ; silent pavefactæ, interque volandum
   Excutiunt alis sessile frigus, aves ;
Voce loqui visæ blanda, Ploramus Amyntam.
   Venit hiems illis : et mihi venit hiems.

H H

HE sung what spirit thro' the whole mass is spread,
Everywhere all: how Heavens God's laws approve
And think it rest eternally to move:
How the kind Sun usefully comes and goes,
Wants it himself, yet gives to Man repose:
He sung how Earth blots the Moon's gilded wane
Whilst foolish men beat sounding brass in vain,
Why the great waters her slight horns obey,
Her changing horns not constanter than they:
He sung how grisly comets hung in air,
Why swords and plagues attend their fatal hair,
God's beacons for the world, drawn up so far
To publish ills, and raise all earth to war:
What radiant pencil draws the watery bow,
What ties up hail, and picks the fleecy snow;
What palsy of the Earth here shakes fix'd hills
From off her brows, and here whole rivers spills.
Thus did this Heathen Nature's secrets tell,
And sometimes missed the cause, but sought it well.

COWLEY.

THE NEREIDS

THE Nereid maids in days of yore
Saw the lost pilot loose the helm,
Saw the wreck blacken all the shore,
And every wave some head o'erwhelm.

Afar the youngest of the train
Beheld (but fear'd and aided not)
A minstrel from the billowy main
Borne breathless near her coral grot:

"*Est Deus in nobis : agitante calescimus illo*"

NAMQUE canebat uti, penetrans omnem undique, totam
    Spiritus intus agat molem : confirmet ut æther
Jura Dei, requiemque putet sine fine moveri.
Sol ut eat redeatque suos iter almus in usus,
Detque viris, quanquam desideret ipse, soporem.
Aureaque ut lucem premat objice Cynthia terra,
At stulti temere æra viri crepitantia plangant :
Unde regat parvis eadem mare cornubus ingens,
Queis mare non levius, non inconstantius, ipsum.
Cur visæ in cœlo tristes pendere cometæ,
Fatalemque comam morbique ensesque sequantur.
Illa deos dare signa viris, et figere cœlo,
Quo vulgent mala, quove vocent in prælia gentes.
Quis radio pluvium describat gentibus arcum,
Vellera quid pectet nivis, ac tortum alliget imbrem.
Unde tremens tellus, nunc deturbarit in ipsa
Fronte sitos montes, nunc totum effuderit amnem.
Barbarus explicuit sic rerum arcana ; latentes
Impar sæpe loqui, par semper quærere, causas.

"*Sedet æternumque sedebit*"

NEREIDES (sic fama refert) videre puellæ
    Rector ut excideret puppe, subactus aquis :
Litus uti fractis nigresceret omne carinis,
    Omnis et abreptum volveret unda caput.

At procul a pelago stans una, novissima natu
    (Ni metus obstaret, forte tulisset opem),
Semanimum vatem spumosis vidit ab undis
    Ad se—curalio tecta latebat—agi.

Then terror fled, and pity rose,
  "Ah me," she cried, "I come too late !
Rather than not have soothed his woes,
  I would, but may not, share his fate."

She raised his hand.   "What hand like this
  Could reach the heart athwart the lyre ?
What lips like these return my kiss,
  Or breathe, incessant, soft desire ? "

From eve to morn, from morn to eve,
  She gazed his features o'er and o'er,
And those who love and who believe,
  May hear her sigh along the shore.

                                W. S. LANDOR.

WEEP NO MORE

WEEP no more, nor sigh, nor groan ;
    Sorrow calls no time that 's gone ;
Violets plucked, the sweetest rain
Makes not fresh nor grow again :
Trim thy locks, look cheerfully ;
Fate's hidden ends eyes cannot see :
Joys as winged dreams fly fast ;
Why should sadness longer last ?
Grief is but a wound to woe ;
Gentlest fair, mourn, mourn no mo.

                                FLETCHER.

Tum retro metus omnis iit, miserataque casum
    "Veni ego," conclamat, "væ mihi ! sera nimis.
"Mallem equidem, tantos quam non mulsisse dolores,
    "Ipsa pari—possem si modo—sorte mori."

Inde levans dextram, "Num par," ait, "illius unquam
    "Perveniet tacta cordis ad ima lyra?
"Talibus aut quisquam mihi dividet oscula labris,
    "Dum tenerum id numquam dicere cessat, Amo ?"

Jamque dies nocti subit altera, noxque diei,
    At sedet, at vultum perlegit illa viri.
Illam, si quis amans et non incredulus idem est,
    Audiat ut circa litus anhelet adhuc.

"*Ne doleas plus nimio*"

FLENDI jam satis, et satis gemendi.
    Nec tempus lacrymis vocaris actum,
Carptis nec violis benigna quamvis
Nasci dat pluvia ac virere rursum.
Quin crines colis explicasque vultum?
Fati cæca nefas videre nobis.
Somni par fugit alitis voluptas:
Quidni tristitiæ modus sit idem?
Fletu nil nisi prorogas dolorem.
Sat, dulcissima Philli, sat dolendi.

GLUMDALCLITCH'S LAMENT

WHY did I trust thee with that giddy youth?
  Who from a page can ever learn the truth?
Versed in court-tricks, that money-loving boy
To some lord's daughter sold the living toy;
Or rent him limb from limb in cruel play,
As children tear the wings of flies away.
From place to place o'er Brobdingnag I'll roam,
And never will return, or bring thee home.
But who hath eyes to trace the passing wind?
How these thy fairy footsteps can I find?
Dost thou bewilder'd wander all alone
In the green thicket of a mossy stone;
Or, tumbled from the toadstool's slippery round,
Perhaps, all maim'd, lie grovelling on the ground?
Dost thou, embosom'd in the lovely rose,
Or sunk, within the peach's down, repose?
Within the kingcup if thy limbs are spread,
Or in the golden cowslip's velvet head,
O show me Flora, 'midst those sweets, the flower
Where sleeps my Grildrig in the fragrant bower?

But ah! I fear thy little fancy roves
On little females, and on little loves;
Thy pigmy children, and thy tiny spouse,
The baby playthings that adorn thy house,
Doors, windows, chimneys, and the spacious rooms,
Equal in size to cells of honeycombs:
Hast thou for these now ventured from the shore,
Thy bark a bean-shell and a straw thy oar?

                                        POPE.

" Illum absens absentem auditque videtque"

MENS levis est juvenum.   Quid te commisimus illi?
    Quisve putet famulo cuilibet esse fidem?
Tene, ut Tulliolis esses ludibria vivus,
    Vendidit aularum doctus amansque lucri?
Ceuve solent pueri pennas avellere muscis,
    Ossibus horribili distulit ossa joco?
At Cyclopeas errabo hinc inde per oras:
    At referar nunquam, te nisi nacta, domum.
Sed quis enim celeres oculo deprenderit auras?
    Qua Lemurum similes prosequar arte pedes?
Muscosusne lapis, frondens te silva, fatigat,
    Quærentem socios exanimemque metu?
An teretis nimium lapsus de vertice fungi,
    Cernuus incumbis membraque truncus humi?
Purpureine lates tectus lanugine mali?
    An rosa te gremio dulce soporat onus?
Si calice in calthi totus jam extenderis, aut si
    Aureus in molli te vehit axe crocus:
Monstra, Flora, mihi, qui flos e millibus unus
    Silvula delicias condit odora meas!

Quanquam ah! quam vereor ne parvi forsan amores,
    Duxerit et parvum femina parva sinum.
Pigmæi pueri, veraque minutior uxor,
    Quotque tuos ornent frivola cunque lares:
Porta, fenestra, foci, spatiosæ scilicet aulæ,
    Mole pares cellis qua thyma condit apis;
Hæccine sunt litus pro queis abscondere nostrum
    Ausus eras, remo stramine, lintre faba?

LAURA MATILDA'S DIRGE

From "Rejected Addresses"

BALMY zephyrs, lightly flitting,
    Shade me with your azure wing;
On Parnassus' summit sitting,
    Aid me, Clio, while I sing.

Softly slept the dome of Drury
    O'er the empyreal crest,
When Alecto's sister-fury
    Softly slumb'ring sunk to rest.

Lo! from Lemnos limping lamely,
    Lags the lowly Lord of Fire,
Cytherea yielding tamely
    To the Cyclops dark and dire.

Clouds of amber, dreams of gladness,
    Dulcet joys and sports of youth,
Soon must yield to haughty sadness;
    Mercy holds the veil to Truth.

See Erostratus the second
    Fires again Diana's fane;
By the Fates from Orcus beckon'd
    Clouds envelop Drury Lane.

Where is Cupid's crimson motion?
    Billowy ecstasy of woe,
Bear me straight, meandering ocean,
    Where the stagnant torrents flow.

Nænia.

O QUOT odoriferi volitatis in aëre venti,
　　Cæruleum tegmen vestra sit ala mihi :
Tuque sedens Parnassus ubi caput erigit ingens,
　　Dextra veni, Clio : teque docente canam.

Jam suaves somnos Tholus affectare Theatri
　　Cœperat, igniflui trans laqueare poli :
Alectûs consanguineam quo tempore Erinnyn,
　　Suave soporatam, cœpit adire quies.

Lustra sed ecce labans claudo pede Lemnia linquit
　　Luridus (at lente lugubriterque) Deus :
Amisit veteres, amisit inultus, amores ;
　　Teter habet Venerem terribilisque Cyclops.

Electri nebulas, potioraque somnia vero ;
　　Quotque placent pueris gaudia, quotque joci ;
Omnia tristitiæ fas concessisse superbæ :
　　Admissum Pietas scitque premitque nefas.

Respice ! Nonne vides ut Erostratus alter ad ædem
　　Rursus agat flammas, spreta Diana, tuam ?
Mox, Acheronteis quas Parca eduxit ab antris,
　　Druriacum nubes corripuere domum.

O ubi purpurei motus pueri alitis ? o qui
　　Me mihi turbineis surripis, angor, aquis !
Duc, labyrintheum, duc me, mare, tramite recto
　　Quo rapidi fontes, pigra caterva, ruunt !

Blood in every vein is gushing,
 Vixen vengeance lulls my heart;
See the Gorgon gang is rushing!
 Never, never let us part.

HERRICK. AMARILLIS.

Herrick.

MY dearest love, since thou wilt go,
 And leave me here behind thee;
For love or pitie, let me know
 The place where I may find thee.

Am. In country meadowes, pearled with dew,
 And set about with lilies:
There, filling maunds with cowslips, you
 May find your Amarillis.

Her. What have the meades to do with thee,
 Or with thy youthfull houres?
Live thee at court where thou may'st be
 The Queen of men, not flowers.

Let country wenches make 'em fine
 With posies, since 'tis fitter
For thee with richest jemmes to shine,
 And like the starres to glitter.

HERRICK.

Jamque—soporat enim pectus Vindicta Virago;
  Omnibus a venis sanguinis unda salit;
Gorgoneique greges præceps (adverte!) feruntur—
  Sim, precor, o! semper sim tibi junctus ego.

In pratis studiosa florum

Hor.

O QUÆ sola places mihi,
  Si vis ire tamen, nosque relinquere,
  Dic te—si quis amor mei,
Si restat pietas—quo repetam loco?

Am.   Inter pascua, ros ubi
  Par gemmæ rutilat, dædala liliis,
    Implentem calathos, tuam
  Illic invenias fors Amaryllida.

Hor.   Quid te pascua detinent
  Annis te teneris? I pete Cæsaris
    Aulam; non ibi flosculos
  Flectes imperiis, sed potius viros.

    Certet rustica Phidyle
  Se jactare rosis: te decorarier
    Gemmis rectius Indiæ
  Et lucere parem sideris aurei.

CA' THE EWES

AS I gaed down the waterside,
　There I met my shepherd lad,
He row'd me sweetly in his plaid,
　　And he ca'd me his dearie.

Chor. Ca' the ewes to the knowes,
　　Ca' them where the heather grows,
　　Ca' them where the burnie flows,
　　　My bonnie dearie.

Will ye gang down the waterside,
And see the waves sae sweetly glide,
Beneath the hazels spreading wide?
　　The moon it shines fu' clearly.

I was bred up at nae sic school,
My shepherd lad, to play the fool,
And a' the day to sit in dool,
　　And naebody to see me.

Ye shall get gowns and ribbons meet,
Cauf-leather shoon upon your feet,
And in my arms ye's lie and sleep,
　　And ye shall be my dearie.

If ye'll but stand to what you've said,
I's gang wi' you, my shepherd lad,
And ye may rowe me in your plaid,
　　And I sall be your dearie.

Pastor, Virgo

Virgo

PASTOR erranti mihi propter amnem
  Obvius venit meus, ambiensque
Suaviter palla, "Mihi," dixit, "una es,
    Phylli, voluptas."

Ambo. Duc ad acclives tumulos, genista
  Duc ubi frondent juga, rivulusque
  Volvitur, matres gregis, o meorum
    Finis amorum!

Pas. An libet ferri tibi propter amnem;
  Cernere et fluctus ut eant amœni
  Subter umbrosas corylos, nec abdant
    Nubila lunam?

Vir. Non erat primis mihi mos ab annis
  Prosequi lusus, puer, inficetos;
  Non queri, quam longa, diem, nec unquam
    Cernier ulli.

Pas. Coaque, et vittæ tibi, quasque tergum
  Det juvencorum soleæ ambulanti,
  Dos erunt, nostris et onus lacertis
    Dulce quiesces.

Vir. Hæreas istis modo rite dictis,
  Tum libens tecum, bone pastor, ibo;
  Pallium obduces mihi, meque dices
    Unus amatam.

While waters wimple to the sea,
While day blinks in the lift sae hie,
Till clay-cauld death sall blind my eye
 Ye shall be my dearie.

Burns.

THE GENTLE SHEPHERD

Peg.

O PATIE, let me gang, I mauna stay:
 We're baith cry'd hame, and Jeanie she's away.

Pat. I'm laith to part sae soon; now we're alane,
And Roger he's away wi' Jeanie gane:
They're as content, for aught I hear or see,
To be alane themselves, I judge, as we.
Here, where primroses thickest paint the green,
Hard by this little burnie let us lean:
Hark! how the lav'rocks chant aboon our heads,
How saft the westlin' winds sough through the reeds.

Peg. The scented meadow-birds and healthy breeze,
For aught I ken, may mair than Peggy please.

Pat. Ye wrang me sair to doubt my being kind;
In speaking sae, ye ca' me dull and blind,
Gif I could fancy aught's sae sweet and fair
As my sweet Meg, or worthy of my care.
Thy breath is sweeter than the sweetest briar,
Thy cheek and breast the finest flowers appear:
Thy words excel the maist delightfu' notes
That warble through the merle or mavis' throats:
With thee I tent nae flowers that busk the field,
Or ripest berries that our mountains yield;
The sweetest fruits that hing upon the tree
Are far inferior to a kiss of thee.

Ramsay.

Pas. Dum patens amnes trepident in æquor,
    Rideat dum sol super arce cœli,
    Te, premet donec mea frigus Orci
        Lumina, amabo.

Delia, Mopsus.

D.

DECEDAM sine, Mopse; nefas mihi, Mopse, morari :
    Phyllis abest, poscuntque domi me teque parentes.
M. Tam propere piget avelli ; nunc denique nulli
    Cernimur, et Corydon cum Phyllide cessit in agros.
    Si qua fides oculis aut auribus, haud minus illis
    Quam mihi quamque tibi solis, reor, esse voluntas.
    Hic, narcissus ubi viridem densissimus agrum
    Pingit, ad hunc tenuem flectamus corpora rivum.
    Audis quem cantum supra det alauda, notique
    Ut per arundineam suspirent leniter ulvam ?
D. Suavis odor prati, volucresque auræque salubres,
    Credo equidem sunt, Mopse, magis quam Delia cordi.
M. Non equidem hoc merui : nostro diffidis amori ?
    Istud ais ? Nimirum oculis et mente vacarem,
    Fingere si possem tam dulce et amabile quidquam,
    Tamve meæ dignum, quam dulcis Delia, curæ.
    Ora halant tua suave magis quocunque roseto ;
    Flos sinus, ac florum splendent par nobile malæ :
    At vox præcellit quod jucundissimum ab ullo
    Aut turdi aut merulæ stillatur gutture murmur.
    Me nulli alliciunt, pratorum insignia, flores,
    Bacca nec in clivis quamvis matura paternis,
    Sis modo tu mecum : prædulcia sustinet arbos
    Poma ; tamen pomis tua dulcius oscula Mopso.

"POOR TREE"

POOR tree; a gentle mistress placed thee here,
　　To be the glory of the glade around.
Thy life has not survived one fleeting year,
　　And she too sleeps beneath another mound.

But mark what differing terms your fates allow,
　　Though like the period of your swift decay;
Thine are the sapless root and wither'd bough;
　　Hers the green memory and immortal day.

CARLISLE.

SONG

"FAITHLESS SWALLOW"

FAITHLESS Swallow, fly away,
　　To purer air and brighter day;
But when spring shall deck the plain,
　　Swallow, come again!

Thou could'st not brook the changing sky,
Or autumn winds that sadly sigh,
Too soon my fost'ring care forgot—
　　And thou hast left my cot.

Flebilis Arbor

TE dominæ pia cura solo, miseranda, locarat
    Patentis, arbor, ut fores agri decus.
At mansit tua vita brevem non amplius annum;
    At ipsa dormit extero sub aggere.
Quam diversa tamen sors est (adverte) duarum!
    Fugax utramque vexit hora; sed tibi,
Arbor, truncus iners, frons arida restat: at illi
    Perenne lumen ac virens adhuc amor.

Idem aliter redditum

MOLLIS huc hera quam tulit caducam
    Ut saltus decus, arbor, emineres
Anno non superas brevi peracto;
    At cespes procul ambit arctus illam.
Pares funere (dispares eædem
    Quanto discite) marcuistis ambæ.
Frons restat tibi passa, sicca radix;
    Illi lux nova jugiter virenti.

CŒLUM ubi candidius te, perfida, defer, hirundo;
    Cœlum ubi candidius, splendidiorque dies:
Tempus erit tamen, arva redux quo pinget Aprilis;
    Illud ubi veniet, perfida, rursus ades.

Scilicet impatiens cœli mutabilis, et qui
    Triste sub auctumnum ventus anhelat, eras:
Hæc metuens, oblita manus quæ fovit egentem,
    A laribus nostris post breve tempus abis.

I I

When, thy weary wand'rings o'er,
Shelter thou shalt claim once more,
Smiles alone shall greet thee here,
    Swallow, do not fear !

Again I'll watch thy pinions light,
Around my head in airy flight,
Again thy faithless love forget,
    And give thee welcome yet !

Faithless Swallow, fly away,
To purer air and brighter day ;
But when spring shall deck the plain,
    Swallow, come again !

HYMN TO THE MORNING

(*Written in the Vale of Chamouni*)

AWAKE, my soul ! not only passive praise
    Thou owest ! not alone these swelling tears,
Mute thanks and secret ecstasy ! Awake,
Voice of sweet song ! Awake, my heart, awake !
Green vales and icy cliffs, all join my song !
  Thou first and chief, sole sovran of the Vale !
O struggling with the darkness all the night,
And visited all night by troops of stars,
Or when they climb the sky or when they sink :
Companion of the morning star at dawn,
Thyself Earth's rosy star, and of the dawn
Co-herald : wake, O wake, and utter praise !

At cum fessa viæ, jam tandem erroribus actis,
  Hospitis officium, qualiter ante, petes,
Huc redeas ! reducem nos excipiemus, hirundo,
  Risibus assuetis ; exue quemque metum,

Tecta levi rursus circumvectabere penna,
  Aeriumque oculis rite tuebor iter :
Utque prius spretos ultro obliviscar amores,
  Utque prius dicam, Sit tua nostra domus.

Ergo aliis infida locis te transfer hirundo,
  Lucet ubi cœlo candidiore dies :
At cum prata, novum jam ver induta, nitescent,
  Ne dubites nostrum rursus adire larem.

RUMPE moras, mea mens ! non tantum laudibus istis
    Nunc opus ! haud lacrymis satis est turgescere, cæca
Fervere lætitia, ac tacitas persolvere grates :
Excute, cor, somnos ! vosque adspirate canenti
Gramineæ valles, glacieque rigentia saxa !
Incipe, vox arguta, melos !
                    Te, maxime regum,
Te primum aggredior, vallis decus : humida cujus
Nox caput invadit tenebris ; quem plurima longas
Sidera per noctes, nunc sero orientia cœlo,
Nunc obitura, petunt : rosei qui sideris instar,
Luciferi comes ipse, diem lucemque reportas,
Surge age, rumpe moras, laudesque effunde solutas !
Quis tua, quis solida posuit fundamina terra,

Who sank thy sunless pillars deep in earth?
Who filled thy countenance with rosy light?
Who made thee parent of perpetual streams?
  And you, ye five wild torrents fiercely glad!
Who called you forth from night and utter death,
From dark and icy caverns called you forth,
Down those precipitous, black, jagged Rocks,
For ever shattered and the same for ever?
Who gave you your invulnerable life,
Your strength, your speed, your fury, and your joy,
Unceasing thunder, and eternal foam?
And who commanded—and the silence came—
"Here let the billows stiffen, and have rest?"

  Ye icefalls! ye that from the mountain's brow
Adown enormous ravines slope amain—
Torrents, methinks, that heard a mighty voice,
And stopped at once amid their maddest plunge—
Motionless torrents! silent cataracts!
Who made you glorious as the gates of Heaven
Beneath the keen full moon? Who bade the sun
Clothe you with rainbows? Who with living flowers
Of loveliest blue, spread garlands at your feet?
GOD! let the torrents, like a shout of nations,
Answer! and let the ice plains echo, GOD!
GOD! sing, ye meadow streams, with gladsome voice!
Ye pine-groves, with your soft and soul-like sounds!
And they, too, have a voice, yon piles of snow,
And in their perilous fall shall thunder, GOD!

                                        COLERIDGE.

Sol ubi semper abest? roseo quis lumine tingens
Vultum fluminea fecit te prole parentem?

Vos etiam, quini qui flumina volvitis amnes
Turbida lætitia! quis vos a noctis acerba
Sede, quis exitio, gelidisque excivit ab antris,
Præcipites inter scopulos, et scrupea saxa
Ire jubens, loca perpetua collapsa ruina?
Quis vobis nullo violandam vulnere vitam
Lætitiamque alasque dedit? vis unde, furorque,
Spumæque insomnes, ac fulmina nescia sisti?
Quis pelago dixit—subeuntque silentia dicto—
"Hic tumidi rigeant fluctus; hic unda quiescat?"

Lympha gelu constricta! fero quæ vertice montis
Devolvis rigidos per saxa horrentia fluctus—
Quamque equidem voces credo agnovisse Potentis,
Et fremitum, atque omnem subito frænasse furorem—
O tacitæ decursus aquæ! O sine gurgite torrens!
Quis vobis fulgore dedit splendescere, quali
Sidereæ portæ, plenæ sub frigora lunæ?
Unde, precor, jussus vestras Sol Iride picta
Vestit aquas? qua serta manu funduntur, et una
Cærulei flores, vivum decus? Est Deus, alto
Torrentes clamore fremant, voxque insonet ingens,
Gentis opus! vos arva gelu torrentia, plena
Reddite voce, "Deum!" vos prata recentia rivis,
Et pineta sacrum foliis spirantia murmur;
Hæc quoque, namque licet, nivea quæ mole laborant
Saxa "Deum!" vasto revoluta a monte sonabunt.

September 27th, 1848.

*** *The six following translations were made for "Hymns Ancient and Modern, with some Metrical Translations" etc., published* 1867.

XLIV.—CHRISTMAS

LANIGEROS, acclinis humo, pastoria pubes
    Custodiebat dum greges;
Splendescente polo longe lateque, Jehovæ
    Descendit ales nuntius.
Qui "Quid" ait "tremitis?"—namque anxia pectora terror
    Immanis occupaverat—
"Grata fero: magnum jubeo lætarier et vos
    Et quicquid est mortalium.
Namque in Davidis urbe, satus quoque Davidis idem
    E stirpe, jamjam nascitur
Vestra Salus, Dominus vester, cognomine Christus;
    Signoque vobis hoc erit:
Invenietur ibi cœlestis scilicet Infans,
    Spectabiturque jam viris;
Fascia velarit meritum non talia corpus,
    Condente præsepi caput."
Dixerat ales.   Eo simul apparere videres
    Dicente lucentem chorum
Arce profectorum supera; pæanaque lætum
    His ordiebantur modis:
"Qui colit alta Deo summi tribuantur honores,
    Virisque pax arrideat;
Protenus excipiat cœli indulgentia terras,
    Haud dirimenda sæculis."

cxxx.—PENTECOST

CŒLO profecti vis et ira nuntiæ
   Fuere quondam Numinis:
Nimbos secantis pedibus; instar ignium
   Hac parte, nigros altera.
At prodeunti vis amorque denuo
   Ibant ministri; mollius
Sacer Palumbes dimovebat aera
   Quam mane primo flamina.
Quot occuparant impetu flammæ fero
   Arcem Sinai, suaviter
Tot consecratum nunc in omne defluunt
   Caput, corona nobilis.
Ac vox uti prægrandis arrectas metu,
   Ut clangor aures perculit,
(Cœlestium quo cœtus audito tremunt,)
   E nocte trepidans nubium;
Sic prodeunte Spiritu Dei suos,
   Ut pastor, inventum greges,
Late sonabat vox, profecta cœlitus,
   Tumultuosi turbinis.
Templum Jehovæ quâ, scatetque criminum
   Fecundus orbis undique;
In pervicaci scilicet demum sinu
   Desideratura locum.
Huc, Numen, adsis! Vis, Amor, Prudentia,
   Adsis ut aures audiant;
Bene ominatum quisque captet ut diem
   Amore sospes an metu.

CXXXIX

QUI pretium nostræ vitam dedit, ante "Supremum
    Valete" quam vix edidit,
Solamenque Ducemque viris legarat eundem,
    Quo contubernales forent.
Venit at Ille suæ partem dulcedinis ultro
    Ut hospes efflaret bonus,
Nactus ubi semel esset, amat qua sede morari,
    Casti latebras pectoris.
Hinc illæ auditæ voces, qualemque susurrum
    Nascente captes Vespero;
Quo posuere metus, patitur quo frena libido,
    Spirare viso cœlitus.
Ac virtutis inest si quid tibi, si quid honorum
    Claro triumphis contigit;
Venerit in mentem si quid divinius unquam;
    Hæc muneris sunt Illius.
At candens, at mite veni nunc, Numen, opemque
    Nostræ fer impotentiæ;
Cor nunc omne domus pateat tua; feceris omne
    Cor incola te dignius.
Vosque Patrem, Natum vos tollite; neve recuses
    Tu sancte laudem Spiritus:
Dignus enim tolli, Tria qui Deus audit in Uno,
    Unumve malit in Tribus.

CXCVII

AUXILIUM quondam, nunc spes, Deus, unica nostri ;
    Flante noto portus, præteritoque domus :
Gens habitat secura tuæ tua sedis in umbra ;
    Simus ut incolumes efficit una manus.
Terræ olim neque forma fuit neque collibus ordo :
    Tu, quot eunt anni, numen es unus idem.
Sæcla vides abiisse, fugax ut vesper ; ut actis
    Quæ tenebris reducem prorogat hora diem.
* Stant populi, ceu mane novo juga florea, quorum
    Marcidus ad noctem falce jacebit honos :
* Tu "suboles terrena, redi" nec plura locuto,
    Quippe satæ gentes pulvere pulvis erunt.
Quos genuit, secum rotat usque volubilis ætas ;
    Ut sopor in cassum, luce solutus, eunt.
Tu quondam auxilium, spes nunc, Deus, ultima nostri,
    Sis columen trepidis, emeritisque domus.

* Two stanzas are translated here which do not appear in the received
editions of *Hymns Ancient and Modern*. They are quoted as part of this
hymn by Miss Brontë in *Shirley*, and run as follows :

> Thy word commands our flesh to dust—
>   "Return, ye sons of men ;"
> All nations rose from earth at first,
>   And turn to earth again.

> Like flowery fields the nations stand,
>   Fresh in the morning light ;
> The flowers beneath the mower's hand
>   Lie withering ere 'tis night !

Possibly Miss Brontë quoted from memory, and the true version of the
first stanza may be—

> All nations rose from earth, and must
>   Return to earth again.

CCXX.

QUO chaos ac tenebræ quondam fugere locuto,
  Supplicis, Omnipotens, accipe vota chori :
Quaque jubar nondum micuit quod sole, quod astris
  Clarius est, dicas "Exoriare dies !"
Qui dignatus eras descendere more sequestri
  Alitis ad terram, luxque salusque virûm ;
Ægro mente salus, lux interioris egeno
  Luminis : at toto jam sit in orbe dies !
Unde fides, amor unde venit ; qui Spiritus audis ;
  Carpe, dator vitæ, sancte Palumbes, iter :
Incubet ætherios spargens tua forma nitores
  Fluctubus, ut terræ lustret opaca dies !
Quique, Triplex, splendes tamen integer ; ipse vicissim
  Robur, Amor, Virtus ; usque beate Deus :
Quale superbit aquis indignaturque teneri
  Fine carens pelagus, crescat ubique dies !

CCXLII.—DEDICATION OF A CHURCH

VERBUM superni Numinis
    Qui cuncta comples, hanc domum
  Amore certo consecres
  Et feriatis annuas.
  E fonte pueros hoc fluit
  In criminosos gratia ;
  Beata cogit unctio
  Nitere nuper sordidos.
  Hic Christus animis dat cibo
  Corpus suum fidelibus ;

Cœlestis agnus proprii
Fert ipse calicem sanguinis.
Hinc venia mœstis ac salus
Reis emenda ; dum favet
Judex, et ingens gratia
Scelere sepultos integrat.
Hic, regnat alte qui Deus,
Benignus habitat ; hic pium
Pectus gubernat atria
Desiderantum cœlica
In dedicatam trux domum.
Procella nequidquam furit ;
Atrox eo vis Tartari
Passura fertur dedecus.

 At robur, at laus tibi, Pater,
 Sit comparique Filio ;
 Diique amoris vinculo,
 Dum sæcla currunt, Flamini.

"JOHN ANDERSON, MY JO, JOHN"

JOHN Anderson, my jo, John,
    When we were first acquent
Your locks were like the raven,
    Your bonnie brow was brent:
But now you're grawing auld, John,
    Your locks are like the snow;
Yet blessings on your frosty pow,
    John Anderson, my jo!

John Anderson, my jo, John,
    I wonder what ye mean,
To rise sae early in the morn,
    And sit sae late at e'en.
Ye'll blear out a' your e'e, John;
    And why should ye do so?
Gang sooner to your bed at e'en,
    John Anderson, my jo!

John Anderson, my jo, John,
    When Nature first began
To try her canny hand, John,
    Her masterwork was man.
And you amang them all, John,
    Sae trig frae top to toe,
She proved to be nae journeywork,
    John Anderson, my jo!

IDEM GRÆCÈ REDDITUM.

'ΑΝΔΗΡΙ'ΔΑ, φίλ' ἀνδρῶν,
τὰ πρῶτά μ' εἰσεφοίτας
τρίχ' ἐμφερὴς κορώνῃ
καλὸν δὲ κρᾶτα λεῖος·
γέροντι νῦν ἔοικας,
κάρα δὲ σὸν νιφαργές·
ὄναιο καὶ νιφαργοῦς,
'Ανδηρίδα, φίλ' ἀνδρῶν.

'Ανδηρίδα, φίλ' ἀνδρῶν·
τί δὴ μαθών, ἀναστὰς
ὑπ' ὄρθρον, εἶτα νυκτὸς
ἐς ἀντόλας ἀγρυπνεῖς;
φθερεῖς ἄρ' ὄσσε γ' ἄμφω·
τίς ὧδε δρᾶν σ' ἀνάγκη;
καθ' ὥραν ἔρπ' ἐς εὐνήν,
'Ανδηρίδα, φίλ' ἀνδρῶν.

'Ανδηρίδα, φίλ' ἀνδρῶν·
χειρουργίαν ποτ' οὔπω
Ζεὺς ἐκμαθὼν ἀκμαῖον
ἐκαίνισ' ἔργον ἀνδράς·
σὲ δ' ἐξέχοντα κἀνδρῶν
σὲ πᾶν τὸ σῶμ' ἀμεμφῆ,
οὐκ ἔκτισ' ἐργατής τις
'Ανδηρίδα, φίλ' ἀνδρῶν;

John Anderson, my jo, John,
 Ye were my first conceit;
And ye need na think it strange, John,
 Tho' I ca' ye trim and neat.
Though some folk say ye're auld, John,
 I ne'er can think ye so:
Ye're aye the same kin' mon to me,
 John Anderson, my jo!

John Anderson, my jo, John,
 We've seen our bairnies' bairns,
And yet, my ain John Anderson,
 I'm happy in your airms:
And sae are ye in mine, John,
 I'm sure ye'll ne'er say no;
Though the days are gone that we hae seen,
 John Anderson, my jo!

John Anderson, my jo, John,
 We clamb the hill thegither,
And mony a canty day, John,
 We've had wi' ane anither:
Now we maun totter down, John;
 But hand in hand we'll go,
And sleep thegither at the foot,
 John Anderson, my jo!

        BURNS.

Ἀνδηρίδα, φίλ᾿ ἀνδρῶν·
   νέος νέᾳ γὰρ ᾅδες,
τί θαῦμα κἄν σε κομψὸν
   σὲ δ᾿ εὐπρεπῆ νομίζω;
γέροντά σ᾿ εἶπον ἄλλοι·
   ἐμοὶ δέ γ᾿ αἰὲν ἡβᾷς·
ὡς γὰρ πάλαι μ᾿ ἔτ᾿ εὖ δρᾷς,
   Ἀνδηρίδα, φίλ᾿ ἀνδρῶν.

Ἀνδηρίδα, φίλ᾿ ἀνδρῶν,
   τέκνων με τέκν᾿ ἰδοῦσαν
ἐν ἀγκάλαις ὁμῶς σαῖς
   μάλ᾿ ἀσμένην ἔθ᾿ αἱρεῖς·
μάλ᾿ ἄσμενός συ καὐτός·
   οὐ μὴ τόδ᾿ ἀντιλέξεις·
κεἰ φροῦδ᾿ ἃ δή ποτ᾿ ἴσμεν,
   Ἀνδηρίδα, φίλ᾿ ἀνδρῶν.

Ἀνδηρίδα, φίλ᾿ ἀνδρῶν,
   συνεμποροῦντ᾿ ἐς ἄκραν
εὐδαίμον᾿ ἦματ᾿ ἤδη
   πόλλ᾿ ἔσχομεν συ κἀγώ.
πέδονδε χρὴ καθέρπειν,
   χεροῖν δ᾿ ἔτ᾿ ἐμπλακείσαιν·
ἐκεῖ δὲ συγκαθεύδειν,
   Ἀνδηρίδα, φίλ᾿ ἀνδρῶν.

PROSE ARTICLES

ON METRICAL TRANSLATION [1]

SIR,—A writer in a recent number [2] of this Magazine laid down that there could be no true translation of a Greek or Roman poet which did not reproduce his metre; and that this had been successfully done by the Poet Laureate and others. I venture to think, on the contrary, that what resemblance there is between these modern experiments and their originals, is a *primâ facie* resemblance, and vanishes upon inspection; and that the specimens which the Laureate gave us, whatever may be their value upon other grounds, are, as imitations of metre, worthless.

That the likeness is not so perfect as it has been assumed to be may, perhaps, appear thus. Let us take Mr. Tennyson's alcaic stanzas—the best alcaics, one may well suppose, which our language is capable of producing—and consider a single line:

" Calm as a mariner out in ocean."

This, it will be said, is a perfectly unexceptionable English alcaic line. And such, no doubt, it is; but does it really reproduce Horace? If so, then, supposing we constructed a

---

[1] This and the two following articles afford a clear exposition of Calverley's views upon the subject of which he was so great a master, classical translation.—ED.

[2] The article here commented on will be found in the " London Student," for June, 1868, p. 149. (On Metrical Translation. By Henry Ward Fortescue.)—ED.

Latin line upon its model, we ought to have a *fac simile* of the normal Horatian line.   Take

Sol ut in aëre lucet alto :

Is this a fair sample of Horace? It is a line which any elementary lyric-book would tell us was bad ; a line the like of which could not be found in all Horace's Odes.   The same experiment might be tried on any other metre with the same result. Coleridge's verse—

" In the pentameter aye falling in melody back,"

has been often quoted for its ingenuity and beauty, and I do not presume to question either.   I only say that a *fac simile* of it in Latin would be a pentameter so execrable, that the student of Ovid and Tibullus would hardly recognize it as a pentameter at all.

The truth I take to be this : that we modern experimentalists adopt—and I dare say must adopt, to make metrical composition possible at all in English—not merely a different, but a diametrically opposite, principle to what our predecessors followed. We study to produce such verses as it shall be impossible to read without, at the same time, involuntarily scanning them. They are to " scan themselves," to quote Dr. Whewell's phrase ; or, as Mr. Fortescue puts it, " The words, read as they are spoken, should fall rightly into the metre."   The ancients, I contend, made it a special point that their verses should *not* " scan themselves," and every form of line which did so they held bad on that account.   We select, in other words, for our standard precisely those lines which Horace or Ovid carefully excluded, frame verse after verse upon their model, and call the result a reproduction of Horace's or Ovid's versification.

My first proposition, as to the principle on which the moderns work, I need hardly verify.   As to the second, it may of course be said, that we cannot tell how the Greek and Roman poets read their lines.

K K

We have, however, this evidence as to how they did *not* read them.   There are in every metre certain types of line which the writers in it manifestly avoided.   In an alcaic ode (for instance) such a line as I propounded just now, or a line of the forms, " *Fortia corpora fudit Hector,*" " *Fœda cadavera barbarorum.*" A pentameter, again, ending with a monosyllable, would not be found in all Latin literature.   And so with other metres.   This avoidance is a simple fact, and one for which we are bound to account in some way.

Now if we suppose they meant their verses to be read as they are scanned, there is no apparent reason—I think I may say there is no conceivable reason—why any one of these types of line should have been objected to.   " Aùsa morì mulièr marìto," and "Mòrdet aquà taciùrnus àmnis" (read as accented), are rhythmically identical with *fœda cadavera barbarorum*, and with any other line which scans.   A pentameter ending with a monosyllable is rhythmically identical with any other penta-metre scanned : *e.g.*, there is surely no difference in sound between " Sídera tángit equís," and " Sídera tángite quís."   On that supposition, I say, all these lines, which were as a matter of fact rejected, would be perfectly admissible.   And in English, where the supposition is true, they are all (as one would expect) admitted freely.   I appeal to Mr. Fortescue himself whether

> " Beautiful innocent, unrepining—"
> " Crocus, anemone, tulip, iris—"

(which are identical in construction with two of my model bad Latin lines)—would not be thought rather good than otherwise in English.   As to any objection to pentameters which end with a monosyllable, they do so almost uniformly.

If, on the other hand, we adopt the supposition that the old poets (like the modern) read their verses by an accent which was so far arbitrary that it was wholly independent of the scansion, and was intended partially to conceal the scansion, then one sees at once why all these lines might have been disallowed. " Aúsa móri múlier maríto," and " Mórdet áqua tacitúrnus ámnis "—read as, rightly or wrongly, I was taught to read them at school—are two different lines, and are both good because they do not carry their scansion upon their face ; and " Fortia corpora fudit Ajax " is bad because it does. This hypothesis, and no other that I can think of, would account for the condemnation of all the lines, in what metre soever, which are actually condemned. Why, for instance, would such a verse as

$$\mu\epsilon\lambda\alpha\tilde{\imath}\nu\alpha\ \nu\acute{\nu}\xi,\ \mu\epsilon\lambda\alpha\tilde{\imath}\nu\alpha\ \nu\acute{\nu}\xi,\ \mu\epsilon\lambda\alpha\tilde{\imath}\nu\alpha\ \nu\acute{\nu}\xi,$$

be a bad iambic? The books would of course say that it has no cæsura. But why is a verse bad which has no cæsura? If all verses are to be scanned in reading them, a verse without a cæsura sounds just the same as a verse with any number.

What appears to me to be the almost universal fallacy of metrical writers is the assumption that when you have got the scansion of a line you have got its rhythm. Mr. Fortescue speaks of " metre or rhythm " throughout as convertible terms. I deny that the rhythm of the *Propria quæ maribus* is the same as the rhythm of the " Æneid." Any metre may, no doubt, as he says, be imitated in English : lines, that is, may be made in any metre which scan. Even so intricate a one as *Super alta vectus Atys* is, I am told, copied, and that correctly, in the Laureate's " Boadicea."

" Adiitque opaca silvis redimita loca deæ."
" Yell'd and shriek'd between her daughters o'er a wild confederacy."
" Soldier, sailor, tinker, tailor, gentleman, apothecary."

What the metre of the second and third may be, and how far they correspond with the first, I am not competent to say. The last I had always mistaken for prose. However, the lines in " Andromeda " are (most of them) undeniable hexameters : but what then ?   The lines

> "When little Samuel woke and heard his Maker's voice,
>   At every word He spoke, how much did he rejoice,"

are equally undeniable iambics : and the same claim that Mr. Kingsley has to have reproduced the rhythm of Homer, Dr. Watts has to have reproduced that of Æschylus.   I do not suppose that if Mr. Fortescue had to translate the " Prometheus Vinctus," he would feel obliged to represent the iambic lines by the "Little Samuel" metre, and the anapæstic ones by the metre of Owen Meredith's "Lucile : " but I do not see how, consistently with his principles, he could do otherwise.

Perhaps I may be allowed to make some comments on Mr. Fortescue's own versions, to which indeed he invites criticism— that is to say, on their merits as imitations.   As to the first [1] ode, I should say that he was bound, on his own showing, to translate it not only into sapphics but into Horatian sapphics.   It would be no imitation of Pope's metre, for example, to write it as handled by Keats, or by Mr. Morris.   Now the "dactyl in the middle," on which Mr. Fortescue's sapphic line is made to hinge, is *not*, I submit, a characteristic of Horace's line.   It is there, of course, but it only appears when you take the verse to pieces : and I confess that my despised old friend,

> " Sordid, unfeeling, reprobate, degraded "

seems to me more Horatian than any line in the copy before me. Could Mr. Fortescue read the ode he has translated into the metre into which he has put it ?   Of course he could if he scanned it all through ; and in that case I can only put my former question in a different form.   Why is it that we never find in Horace such a line as

> *Ense nudo terruit Hector arcem ?—*

---

[1] The three odes, the translations of which are here criticised, are Hor. Lib. i. Od. ii. ; Lib. i. Od. xxxiv. ; Lib. i. Od. xiv.—ED.

In an alcaic one naturally looks to the two final lines. Of Mr. Fortescue's third lines, *one* seems to me (for an obvious reason) really to resemble one of Horace's: the remainder to be much less like it than Mr. Jingle's fragment,

> "In hurry poste-haste for a licence."

They are all exactly in the metre

> "My brother Jack was nine in May,"

if we substitute a dissyllable ("April" suppose) for the monosyllable at the end. Can Horace's third lines be read, by scanning them or otherwise, into this metre? Some perhaps could, such as the first in this ode; but that is no more a fair sample of Horace's versification than

> "Cornua velatarum obvertimus antennarum,"

is a fair sample of Virgil's. Of the fourth lines, I can only say that they scan too well; the scansion is (of course intentionally) *pronounced* in all of them: and consequently they are all precisely like each other, and none, to my ear, at all like Horace. As to the remaining ode, I should imagine that to a person unacquainted with Horatian metres (and it is for the benefit, I presume, of such that these translations are made) the first two lines of every stanza would appear to be lax Alexandrines, the third the metre of "When the British warrior-queen" (or of "Over rivers and mountains" occasionally, as in the case of the last stanza but two); and the fourth no recognizable metre whatsoever.

One more criticism I would venture on upon a different point. I submit that "Trembled the"—"Romans be"—"turn the helm" (though the next word did not begin with a consonant) —are not dactyls. Surely "helm" and "realm" are as distinctly long syllables as any can be. I do not mean to say that we are to conform rigorously to the Greek and Latin rules. I should admit that the second syllable of words like "disallowed," "warranted," or "organ-voiced" is short, and I think Mr. Tennyson made a false quantity when he placed "organ-voiced" where he did in the *Milton* alcaics. He might plead that without the aid of some actual Latin adjective such as "atlantean," or some exceptional English compound, such as "un-swan-like," for a central word, it seems impossible to imitate the most frequently recurring form of the Horatian third line. But at least we should remember that these rules were not arbitrary ones : it was from conformity to them, or rather to the theories of musical sound which they embodied, that the Greek verse derived its character, its melody and grace ; and we cannot surely ignore them utterly, as most metrical writers habitually do, without sacrificing what really, much more than the metre, constitutes the essence and the "rhythm" of the verse. A Greek line is, in fact, a succession of vowels, separated by consonants introduced sparingly, and under such restrictions that it flows on uninterruptedly from syllable to syllable. The flow of an English line is generally choked (so to speak) by blocks of consonants thrown in *ad libitum*.

Compare

"Silenced but unconvinced, when the story was ended, the blacksmith,"

or,

"Clasped each other's hand, and interchanged pledges of friendship,"

with the first line of the "Iliad." "Silenc'd but" is a dactyl, *encdb* a short syllable. "Interchang'd pledges" is a reproduction of μῆνιν ἄειδε. Only conceive the havoc that we should make in one of Homer's lines if we inserted here and there such encumbrances as *ncdb*, *ndgpl*, or even Mr. Fortescue's *dth*, *nsb*, etc., between two of the short vowels. Compare again a pentameter by one of the very best of our metrical writers :

"Joyous knight-errant of God, thirsting for labour and strife"—

with

> "Impia quid dubitas Deianira mori."

The Latin pentameter of which the former is really a counterpart, is this :

> *Troius ni terrent ob cor, versat per labor et stryx.*

Does this bear the faintest resemblance to one of Ovid's pentameters? I have a strong belief that any line which obeys the same laws of euphony as the Greeks and Romans observed—such a line as "The moan of doves in immemorial elms," or as many of Mr. Kingsley's own—resembles and reminds one of their poetry far more than these concatenations of so-called dactyls and spondees, which seem to me, even when they scan perfectly, to be not so much verses as skeletons of verses.

Metre (if I may end with a metaphor) is, in my view, a sort of framework whose office it is to support the verse. It is possible to train a rose or a vine upon a trellis so that, while it adheres firmly, it is still left to follow its own devices and form its own pattern over the laths, which are only seen here and there amongst the leaves and tendrils. It would also be possible to force every branch and spray into strict conformity with the lines of the frame, so that the outline of its squares should be the only outline visible. The former method seems to me to be the way in which Homer and Virgil, and all poets ancient or modern, whose works I am linguist enough to read, have dealt with metre ; and the latter the way it is dealt with by metrical translators.

I am, Sir, yours very faithfully,

C. S. CALVERLEY.

THE "ÆNEID" OF VIRGIL[1]

A TRANSLATOR has two main duties to consider—his duty towards his original, and his duty towards his readers. Translators of the old school almost ignored the former consideration; those of the new—amongst whom Professor Conington's "Horace," and in a less degree his "Æneid," justify us in classing him—on the contrary hold it paramount. Specimens of translation on the older principle may be found of course in Pope and Dryden *passim :* in Lord Derby not unfrequently, as when he renders

" Dulces docta modos et citharæ sciens "—
" Skilled with transcendent art
To touch the lyre and breathe harmonious lays."

This is Horace done into Johnsonese : or rather into that smooth commonplace which is nobody's style in particular, and Horace's least of all. Probably Brady and Tate went as far it is possible to go in this direction (though parallel instances might be easily found in Pope) in transmuting the single word " always " into

" Through all the changing scenes of life,
In trouble and in joy."

We may take that as the extreme case of the one school ; and Milton's " storms unwonted shall admire," etc. (procellas emirabitur insolens," κ. τ. λ.), as the extreme case of the other.

Professor Conington has not, as we hinted above, dealt with Virgil quite as he dealt with Horace, for reasons which he explains in his preface. An ode of Horace, he says, is for close scrutiny, an Æneid for rapid reading. Accordingly he has not attempted to represent "the characteristic art of Virgil's lan-

[1] "The Æneid of Virgil translated into English Verse." By John Conington, M.A. (London : Longmans and Co. 1866.)

guage." He has not sought for equivalents of his words or turns of speech—striving rather to be readable, like Scott, than classical, like Milton.

It may be said to this that Virgil's language *is* Virgil. His diction is an essential part of him ; and Milton has taken such pains to show how it may be recast in English, that we cannot help wishing Professor Conington had elected to take more hints from him than he has taken ; without becoming absolutely Miltonic, which would ill accord with Scott's metre. He has followed him at times, though perhaps unconsciously ; wisely at any rate ; as where—

> " Night *invests* the world." (*Nox operit terras.*—Æn. iv. 352.)
> cf. "Night invests the sea."—Par. Lost, i. 208.

At others he has not, when he might have done so with advantage ; as in Æn. v. 113 : "Et tuba commissos medio *canit* aggere ludos : "

> " And from a mound the trump *proclaims*
> The festal onset of the games."

This is good, but conventional compared with Milton's

> " To arms the matin trumpet *sang*."

Again, his

> " Wallowing, unwieldy, enormous—
> She knew not, eating death "—

are happy representations, one of a rhythm, and one of an idiom, so peculiar and characteristic as to be worth preserving. His "hope conceiving from despair " is palpably imitated from Virgil's

> " Una salus victis, nullam sperare salutem,"

and expresses it perhaps more forcibly than Professor Conington's rendering, which is neat enough nevertheless.

But it is hardly fair to criticise Professor Conington for not having represented what he deliberately declines to represent. As a fair specimen of what he has done we will quote these lines (there are plenty as good) from Æn. vii. :

> " With measured pace they march along
> And make their monarch's deeds their song ;
> Like snow-white swans in liquid air,
> When homeward from their food they fare,
> And far and wide melodious notes
> Come rippling from their slender throats,
> While the broad stream and Asia's fen
> Reverberate to the sound again.
> Sure none had thought that countless crowd
>   A mail-clad company :
> It rather seemed a dusky cloud
> Of migrant fowl, that, hoarse and loud,
>   Press landward from the sea."

This passage from Book ii. seems to us very easy, and is most accurate :

> " Meantime Heaven shifts from light to gloom,
> And night ascends from Ocean's womb,
> Involving in her shadow broad
> Earth, sky, and Myrmidonian fraud :
> And through the city, stretched at will,
> Sleep the tired Trojans, and are still."

Here the third and fourth lines are absolutely literal. We will add one ingenious rendering of a line similar in character to the second, which latter, by the way, we thought bore a different meaning to that assigned to it : [1]

> " Now *dews precipitate the night*,
> And setting stars to rest invite."   (p. 35.)

These extracts will bear us out in saying that Professor Conington has produced a version singularly faithful (save in the

---

[1] The line in question is in the original—" Vertitur interea cœlum, et ruit Oceano nox."—Æn. ii. 250.—Ed.

point which he abandons), and pleasant and spirited withal, of a poem, as he remarks, little known to English readers. He apologizes for appearing in the field after Dryden, and, we think, unnecessarily. Dryden was a great poet, but not a translator at all. His "Virgil" is in no sense Virgil, but Dryden simply. We conceive, with all deference to Professor Conington, that there *was* a radical difference between the Roman and the "Caroline" poet; nay, more, that the heroic couplet (though opinions differ as to metres) is of its nature incapable of representing hexameters or any Latin measure except elegiacs, and perhaps Ovid's hexameters, which are elegiacs in disguise. We admit the professor's plea for the occasional use of "mote" (might), "eyne," etc., on the strength of Virgil's archaisms; though we protest against "treen," which appeared in one of "Horace's Odes," and which seemed to us not quite, but almost, as intolerable as "been" for the plural of "bee."

We may notice in conclusion one characteristic of Professor Conington's work which adds greatly to its value—that he never makes the vagueness of poetic phraseology a means of escape from a difficulty. A writer in "Frazer's Magazine" of September, upon recent translations of Horace (who ignores, by the way, Conington's "Horace" altogether), gives us incidentally several model translations of his own, of which the following is a sample:

> "Me the poetic doves in days far-gone
>   Covered with fresh-cropt leaves, when found,
>   A truant child that dared to pass
>   Beyond my own Apulia's bound,
>   Sleeping in Vultur's mountain grass,
> Tired out with lonely play in that long summer noon."

The last two lines, it will be observed, are represented in the Latin by "ludo fatigatumque somno;" except the one word "Vultur's." This we take to be the worst translation possible;

not so much because the text is absurdly spun out, and has a perfectly gratuitous tail appended to it to eke out a needless Alexandrine, as because "fatigatum somno," the only ambiguous expression, is shirked entirely. We would advise the writer, if he intends completing the Odes, to glance meantime at Professor Conington's version of them, and if he is preparing a criticism of recent translations of Virgil, not to leave wholly unnoticed the very able work we have just reviewed.

"HORÆ TENNYSONIANÆ" [1]

TO those who still love occasionally to "brood and live again in memory with those old faces of their infancy" under whose supervision they acquired the art and mystery of Latin versification, and to try upon the *corpus vile poetarum hodiernorum* if their hand retains aught of its ancient cunning, the Laureate's works offer many attractions. Besides being, as Mr. Church proclaims him to be, "*poeta recentioris ætatis maximus*," his muse is pre-eminently classical. He often consciously, often perhaps unconsciously, catches the tone of some ancient bard of Greece or of Rome. He likes now and then to cull a phrase or a line from one of them, and work it into his own poetry, as—

"This way and that dividing the swift mind."

Though he does not of course adopt the actual rules of Latin prosody, his verse is framed always upon the rhythmical principles of which those rules were the embodiment; and in consequence there is the same sort of grace and finish about it which distinguished the verse of Horace and of Virgil. Between Horace especially, and the modern poet, there exist, we

[1] "Horae Tennysonianae ; sive Eclogae e Tennysono Latine Redditae." Cura A. J. Church, A.M. (London : Macmillan and Co. 1869.)

think, in point of style and workmanship, many similarities. A stanza of " In Memoriam " is a thing compact *teres atque rotundum*, as is a stanza in a Horatian ode. Both writers are equally intolerant of any but the right word, and both have the gift of making it fit into its place apparently by a happy accident. The condensed phraseology, the abruptness, the ease (attained probably "*per laborem plurimum*," until art became a second nature) which characterize the odes of Horace characterize also the cantos, so to call them, of " In Memoriam." Even Mr. Tennyson's compound epithets are paralleled, and more than paralleled, in Horace, and indeed in Virgil. " *Zephyris agitata Tempe* " is as much a compound epithet as " wind-swept " in English, and " *Segnesque nodum solvere Gratiæ* " is a three-barrelled compound epithet for which our language can furnish no equivalent. Latin literature is, in fact, far richer in elaborate compounds than English is, or ever could be, since the Latin tongue expressed naturally, by means of its inflections, what ours, barren of inflections, can only indicate in an artificial way by inserting a hyphen ; *e.g.* that " wind " is an ablative governed by " swept," a participle. The contributors to the present volume, however, have chosen to translate the Laureate, when he writes any metre other than blank verse, into Ovidian Elegiacs, rather than Horatian Alcaics or Asclepiads. Two only, the Editor and Professor Seeley, have constructed each an Alcaic Ode out of the pages of " In Memoriam."

Of Mr. Church's Ode, which opens the volume (as in its original English it opened Mr. Tennyson's), we may speak in almost unqualified praise, and the same may be said of his contributions generally. He has constantly succeeded in expressing most difficult English in Latin that is never forced and always forcible, as only a true scholar could. In only one case that we have noted he has made no attempt, and as we think wisely, to find an equivalent for the phrase before him :

> " Nocturna luce coruscans
> Unda tuum molli geminabat murmure nomen,"

does not of course pretend to represent—

> "And rapt in wreaths of glowworm light
> The mellow breaker murmured Ida ; "

but to intimate that it cannot be represented. Should not "rapt" be "lapt," by the way? Elsewhere "football" is printed for "footfall," and "spirited" for "spirted" purple.— How Mr. Church can deal with English which is not absolutely impossible, the following extracts may suffice to show :

> "And doubtless unto thee is given
> A life that bears immortal fruit
> In such great offices that suit
> The full-grown energies of Heaven."

> "Tu quoque jam peragis, credo, felicius ævum,
> Quodque facis nunquam mors abolebit opus ;
> Tu quoque, cælicolum jam viribus auctus adultis,
> Officio fungi nobiliore potes."

> " This garden-rose that I found
> Forgetful of Maud and me,
> And lost in trouble and moving round
> Here at the head of a tinkling fall,
> And trying to pass to the sea."

> "Hanc equidem inveni oblitam dominæque meique,
> Hic ubi fit strepitus desilientis aquæ.
> Flos se perpetuos frustra volvebat in orbes,
> Si jungi æquoreis forte daretur aquis."

What can be prettier? Mr. Church's version of King Cophetua we think inferior to the preceding one by Mr. Hessey, except the last stanza, which is excellent. *Per contra*, we prefer his rendering of "As through the land at eve we went" to the "altera versio" subjoined.

We have devoted some space to the editor and largest contributor. As we have mentioned Professor Seeley's Ode, we may add that we have no possible fault to find, except with the first line, and perhaps with the last, which latter probably could not be put into Latin as simple as the English within the space allotted. The first line *looks*, at any rate, a terrific denunciation of the creature, "the linnet born within the cage," which Mr. Tennyson only says that he "envies not in any mood." The accident of the first word being printed in capitals gives to it a fictitious emphasis and glare.—One of the editor's most able coadjutors is Mr. Kebble, of Lincoln. *Notent tirones* how "sandy bar" and "babble" are skilfully disposed of in the pentameter,

> "Visus arenosas increpuisse moras."

Tesquis reminds one unfortunately of Bland. No. xxxiii. by the same author is a masterly production; and take this extract from "Aylmer's Field:"

> "The heads of chiefs and princes fall so fast,
> They cling together in the ghastly sack—
> The land all shambles."

> "Stricta ducum procerumque ruentia pulvere colla !
> Scilicet in tetris capiti caput hæret acervis.
> Cæde fluit tellus."

There are two good versions of "Come down, O maid," by Messrs. Kebbel and Sotheby. The latter, in an attempt on "Tears, idle tears," has, we should say, like all his predecessors, signally failed. "Vivax" is not "fresh," nor

> "Forma fenestrarum sensim quadratior exstat"

anything like

> "The casement slowly grows a glimmering square."

The thing altogether is untranslatable. And the latter remark may possibly apply to

> "Now sleeps the crimson petal, now the white," etc.

At any rate lines like these give, surely, no idea of the poetry and beauty of their original :

> " Regali in xysto cessat nutare cupressus,
> Et niveus dormit purpureusque calyx ;
> Marmoreo nec pinna, vides ? micat aurea labro ;
> Sed pyralis vigilat : tu mihi, cara, vaca ! " etc.

These and all the succeeding verses appear to us worthless, till we come to the last four, which are graceful and good. Recurring to No. xxv., is *tamen* (on p. 83) used for " but " ? We remember only one precedent, if so ; Ovid's line—

> " Nil mihi rescribas, attamen ipse veni,"

which has been variously emended. The true reading, which has lain hid from the interpreters, is, we have no doubt, "attagen," the *attagen Ionicus* of Horace, a bird whose name, dear to the epicure, would naturally pass into an equivalent for "deliciæ," as our English word "duck" is said to have done. The last syllable of *attagen* (vocative) would be, of course, short, *more Græco*.

Honourable mention ought to be made of Mr. Day, for a most able version of part of the "Lotus-eaters." The beginning of the poem is not done so successfully by another contributor :

> " Eja ! agite, o socii, validis incumbite remis ;
> In manibus terræ—

is no translation whatever of the original ; and the " wandering fields of barren foam " are wholly ignored, unless there is meant to be a glimpse of them in the final verse. Nor do we like "Character " and " The Blackbird " as they appear here, from somewhat similar reasons, viz., that the Latin is vague and spun out. Lines 4-6 of the former are unintelligible without the English ; and what the construction or the meaning is of the three last on the same page we have failed, even by the light of the English, to discover. The opening line does not scan at all, and the tenth from the end scans only by the skin of its teeth.

All this time we have omitted to notice what, considering the difficulty of the translator's task, and the ease with which it has been surmounted, is, perhaps, the gem of the volume—a set of Hendecasyllables, "O Swallow, Swallow," by the late Professor Conington. Every stanza is a feat of scholarship, and the whole makes a charming little poem. We quote one stanza—all are equally good :

> "Procne nostra, volans volans ad Austrum.
> Lautis incide tectulis, ibique
> Quæ dico tibi dic meæ puellæ."

Of two or three other pieces by the same eminent hand we need only say that they are there.

Mr. Brodribb's "Tithonus" abounds in beautiful passages, which we would quote if we had space. Is not "kindly," however (p. 132), used in the sense of the "kindly fruits of the earth," and does not genialis mean something different? "Meus proprius," again, is, we think, only found in prose. Turning back to Mr. Church's poem on p. 17, risu seems to be used for cum risu, "smilingly." Is this legitimate? Surely you could not say, "Lacrymis sic fatur," unless "obortis" followed. "Risu cognoscere," "solvuntur risu," etc., are accountable enough. Then, is "Virgo inventrix" satisfactory for St. Cecily? does not inventrix want a genitive? We demur also to "male saucius," for "badly wounded," and are prepared to distinguish Horace's "male tussiit." Nor do we like "serrata" much more than we should "serrated" in the English. There are several words, such as xystus, trichila, and the prosaic pedetentim, which, it seems to us, unnecessarily mar this volume.

From the foregoing remarks it will be seen that we think

highly of these translations as such. Whether or no it is pure waste of time to translate at all is a question upon which certainly much time has been wasted, and which, after all, concerns nobody except the translators. The title, we confess, puzzled us at first. The title-page hints that *Horæ* means here *Eclogæ Latinè redditæ*, which simplifies things; but then what is *Horæ Paulinæ?* Does "Tennysonian hours" mean hours during which Tennyson was the presiding genius—hours spent (by the contributors) in analyzing Tennyson? Anyhow these pages contain several admirable specimens of an art believed by many to be doomed—doomed, perhaps not even "after many a summer"—to decay and fall and pass away.

CHISWICK PRESS : PRINTED BY CHARLES WHITTINGHAM AND CO.
TOOKS COURT, CHANCERY LANE, LONDON.